8-89

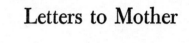

Letters to Mother

Letters

to Mother

An Anthology

Edited by Charles Van Doren

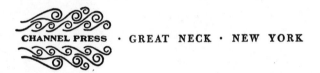
CHANNEL PRESS · GREAT NECK · NEW YORK

Library of Congress
Catalog Card Number: 59-7441

Printed in the United States of America
by The Haddon Craftsmen, Inc., Scranton, Pennsylvania

First Printing: January 1959
Second Printing: February 1959
Third Printing: September 1959

Copyright Acknowledgments

Henry James: from *The Letters of Henry James,* Volume I, selected and edited by Percy Lubbock. By permission of Macmillan & Co., Ltd., London, and the Macmillan Company, New York.

William James: from *The Letters of William James,* edited by Henry James. Copyright 1920 by Henry James; 1948 by William James and Margaret James Porter. Published by The Atlantic Monthly Press. By permission of Paul R. Reynolds & Son, New York.

Samuel Johnson: from *The Letters of Samuel Johnson,* Volume I, collected and edited by R. W. Chapman. By permission of the publisher, The Clarendon Press, Oxford.

Helen Keller: from *The Story of My Life,* by Helen Keller. Copyright 1902, 1903 by Helen Keller; reprinted by permission of Doubleday & Company, Inc.

Joyce Kilmer: from *Memories of My Son, Sergeant Joyce Kilmer,* by Annie Kilburn Kilmer. Published by Brentano's, New York, 1920.

Mary Lamb: from *Blockade,* by Robert Carse, published by Rinehart and Company, Inc., New York. Reprinted by permission of the College of William and Mary.

T. E. Lawrence: from *The Letters of T. E. Lawrence,* edited by David Garnett. Copyright 1938, 1939 by Doubleday & Company, Inc. Published in England by Jonathan Cape, Ltd., Bedford Square, London. By permission.

Nikolai Lenin: from *The Letters of Lenin,* translated and edited by Elizabeth Hill and Doris Mudie. Published by Harcourt, Brace and Company, Inc. Published in England by Chapman & Hall, Ltd., London. By permission.

Meriwether Lewis: from *Original Journals of the Lewis & Clark Expedition, 1804-1806,* Volume VII, edited by Reuben Gold Thwaites.

By permission of the publishers, Dodd Mead & Co., New York.

Henry Wadsworth Longfellow: from *Life of Henry Wadsworth Longfellow,* Volume I, edited by Samuel Longfellow. By permission of the publisher, Houghton Mifflin Company.

Elijah P. Lovejoy (Letter of Elijah P. Lovejoy, Alton, Illinois, August 31, 1836). By permission of The Chicago Historical Society.

Thomas Babington Macaulay: from *The Life and Letters of Lord Macaulay,* by George Otto Trevelyan. By permission of the publishers, Longmans, Green & Co., Inc.

Marie Antoinette: from *Marie Antoinette à Marie Thérèse,* edited and annotated by George Girard. (Translation of letter by Charles Van Doren.) Reprinted by permission of Éditions Bernard Grasset, Paris.

Harriet Martineau: from *Harriet Martineau's Autobiography,* Volume II, edited by Maria Weston Chapman; published in Boston, 1877, by James R. Osgood & Company.

Guy de Maupassant: from *The Portable Maupassant,* translated by Lewis Galantier. Copyright 1947 by The Viking Press, Inc., N.Y., and reprinted with their permission.

Giuseppi Mazzini: from *Mazzini's Letters,* translated by Alice de Rosen Jervis. Published by E. P. Dutton & Co., Inc. Reprinted by permission of the publisher.

Felix Mendelssohn: from *Felix Mendelssohn—Letters,* edited by G. Selden Goth. Copyright 1945 by Pantheon Books, Inc. By permission.

William Morris: from *The Life of William Morris,* Volume I, by J. W. Mackail. By permission of the publishers, Longmans, Green & Co., Inc.

Wolfgang Amadeus Mozart: from *The Letters of Mozart & His Family,* Volume I, edited by Emily Anderson. By permission of Macmil-

A Note of Thanks

A book of this sort is always the result of the care, cooperation, and assistance of many persons. The editor wishes particularly to express his gratitude to the many devoted members of the staff of The New York Public Library who rendered him such generous help and advice during the two years of preparation of the volume. In addition he would like to acknowledge the cooperation of the following individuals and institutions: The Alamo, Mrs. Clyde C. Sierk, Director; The American Antiquarian Society, Mr. Clarence S. Brigham, Director; The Berkshire Athenaeum, Mr. Robert G. Newman, Librarian; The British Museum; The Chicago Historical Society; The Colonial Society of Massachusetts, Mr. Walter Muir Whitehill, Editor; The Columbia University Library; The Connecticut Historical Society, Mr. Thomoson R. Harlow, Director; The Essex Institute, Mr. Paul O. Blanchette, Assistant Librarian; The Foster Hall Collection, University of Pittsburgh, Mr. Fletcher Hodges, Jr., Curator; Freer Gallery of Art, Smithsonian Institution, Mrs. Bertha M. Usilton, Librarian; George Eastman House, Mr. Beaumont Newhall, Curator; Georgia Historical Society, Mrs. Lilla M. Hawes, Director; Historical Society of Delaware, Mrs. Ruthanna Hindes, Librarian; Illinois State Historical Library, Mr. Clyde C. Walton, State Historian; The Library of Congress; The Library of Harvard University; The Maine Historical Society, Mrs. Marian B. Rowe, Librarian; The Maryland Historical Society, Mrs. James W. Foster, Director; The Massachusetts Historical Society, Mr. Stephen T. Riley, Librarian; The New Hampshire Historical Society, Mrs. Mary C. Conner, Assistant Librarian; The New Jersey Historical Society, Mr. Fred Shelley, Librarian; The New York State Historical Association, Miss Dorothy Barck, Librarian; The Pierpont Morgan Library, Mr. Herbert Cahoon, Curator of Manuscripts; The Princeton University Library, Mr. Alexander P. Clark, Curator of Manuscripts; The Society for the Preservation of New England Antiquities, Mr. Abbott Lowell Cummings, Assistant Director; The Vermont Historical Society, Mrs. Clara E. Follette, Librarian; The Virginia State Library, Mr.

John W. Dudley, Assistant Archivist; The Wisconsin State Historical Society, Miss Josephine L. Harper, Manuscripts Librarian; and Dr. E. G. Chuinard of Portland, Oregon. The editor wishes also to thank the many persons who contributed letters after the plan of the book had been described on a nationwide television program.

Finally, the editor must attempt, although without much hope of success, to put into words the debt he feels to his two research assistants, Richard and Elizabeth Barnett. They were capable, enthusiastic, careful, thorough, and—most important of all—indefatigable. Without them the book could never have existed.

TABLE OF CONTENTS

INTRODUCTION 1

ONE: Letters from Belletrists 9

SAMUEL BUTLER, *"In Search of My Own Bread"* 10
JOHN JAY CHAPMAN, *"To the Bottom with the French"* 14
RICHARD HARDING DAVIS, *"Spending Hearst's Money"* 16
WILLIAM RANDOLPH HEARST, *"Song-and-Dance Artists"* 20
WILLIAM DEAN HOWELLS, *"Home! My Heart Leaps ..."* 23
SAMUEL JOHNSON, *"I Shall Endeavour to Obey You ..."* 24
CHARLES ELIOT NORTON, *Report from Abroad* 26
MARGARET FULLER OSSOLI, *"Gay, Impetuous, Ardent"* 28
JOHN RUSKIN, *"It Made Me Think of Somebody Else"* 31

TWO: Letters from Churchmen and
Scientists 35

LOUIS AGASSIZ, *A Student all His Life Long* 36
LUTHER BURBANK, *"I Almost Have to Cry for Joy ..."* 40
ST. CATHERINE OF SIENA, *"Mother of My Soul ..."* 43
WILLIAM ELLERY CHANNING, *"A Mother Trembling"* 44
MICHAEL FARADAY, *"First and Greatest Sweetness"* 46
OLIVER WENDELL HOLMES, *"Read This Sentence Over"* 51
THOMAS HUXLEY, *"I Don't Know Whether She Is Pretty"* 53
JOHN NEWMAN, *"Years Which Never Can Come Again"* 56
JOHN WESLEY, *"Give Me Your Thoughts ..."* 58

THREE: Letters from Explorers and
Travelers 61

GERTRUDE BELL, *"Oh Mother, Mother"* 62
AMELIA EARHART, *"The Adventure Was Worth While"* 64
T. E. LAWRENCE, *"All Out of Aristophanes or Juvenal"* 65

MERIWETHER LEWIS, *"Agreeably Disappointed"*   69
HARRIET MARTINEAU, *". . . Make One Another Happy"*   73
ROBERT EDWIN PEARY, *"Nothing Seems Impossible"*   77
CECIL JOHN RHODES, *"I Average £100 Per Week"*   81
THOMAS SAUNDERS, *"The Heat of Youth Is Past"*   84

FOUR: Letters from Fighting Men   87

CHARLES FRANCIS ADAMS, *"I Do My Best For My Horses"*   88
ANONYMOUS R.A.F. PILOT, *"You Must Not Grieve . . ."*   94
WILLIAM BARKER CUSHING, *"Steady Men, Steady!"*   96
ROBERT HOLMES DUNHAM, *"One of the Unfortunate"*   99
ICHIZO HAYASHI, *"The Day After Tomorrow I Must Die"*   101
FRANCIS SCOTT KEY, *"His Friends Have Urged Me"*   103
JOYCE KILMER, *"Elle Est Jolie et Jeune"*   104
SUSAN LAMB, *"How That Will Worry Ma!"*   106
CARL SCHURZ, *"It Is Hard to Desert"*   109
GEORGE WASHINGTON, *"Really and Truely My Situation"*   111

FIVE: Letters from Historians and
          Philosophers   117

HENRY ADAMS, *"Sauerkraut and Pickled Potatoes"*   119
LOUIS DEMBITZ BRANDEIS, *"Mothers Like You"*   123
JAMES BRYCE, *"The Owner of Blue China . . ."*   124
THOMAS CARLYLE, *The Sage of Chelsea*   125
RALPH WALDO EMERSON, *"The Lyceum Makes Money"*   130
EDWARD GIBBON, *"But Few Have Read"*   132
ELBERT HUBBARD, *"All the Money I Want"*   137
WILLIAM JAMES, *"Empty Purse and Cold Hearth . . ."*   138
THOMAS B. MACAULAY, *"Images of Tenderness"*   143
FRIEDRICH NIETZSCHE, *"A Hugely Famous Animal"*   146
HENRY DAVID THOREAU, *"At the Back-Door in Concord"*   151
CARL VAN DOREN, *"My Whole Ambitions . . ."*   155

SIX: Letters from Painters and Musicians   159

PAUL CÉZANNE, *"The Bourgeois Are Unwilling . . ."*   160
FELIX MENDELSSOHN, *"The Parrot Must Be Removed"*   162

WOLFGANG AMADEUS MOZART, *"Viva Maestro"* 167
GIACOMO PUCCINI: *"I Am Longing to Have Some Beans"* 170
VINCENT VAN GOGH, *"Peasants Are More Useful ..."* 173
RICHARD WAGNER, *"Through All the Jungle"* 175
JAMES WHISTLER, *The Man Who Painted the Portrait* 180

SEVEN: Letters from Poets 183

CHARLES BAUDELAIRE, *"We Shall Kill Each Other"* 185
GEORGE GORDON BYRON, *"A Gipsylike Disposition"* 195
JOHN DONNE, *"Assist Me With Your Blessings"* 204
MARGARET FLEMING, *"Us Two Loving Creatures"* 207
JOHANN WOLFGANG VON GOETHE, *"The Best Fare ..."* 208
THOMAS GRAY, *"Forty Deals Without Intermission"* 211
HENRY WADSWORTH LONGFELLOW, *"Eye of the Stranger"* 215
WILLIAM MORRIS, *"A Useful Trade"* 217
EZRA POUND, *"The Spectacle of Human Imbecility"* 220
WALT WHITMAN, *"That Middling-Sized Ordinary Man"* 223
WILLIAM CARLOS WILLIAMS, *"True Faith Dares All"* 229

EIGHT: Letters from Revolutionaries and Humanitarians 231

ANONYMOUS UNION NURSE, *"This Is Just Like Home"* 232
SUSAN B. ANTHONY, *"An Undercurrent of Joy and Love"* 233
HENRY GEORGE, *"Known Even in Philadelphia"* 234
HELEN ADAMS KELLER, *"Beauty Is a Form of Goodness"* 236
NIKOLAI LENIN, *"Fairly Lonely ... and Pretty Senseless"* 240
ELIJAH PARISH LOVEJOY, *"I May Even Die Its Martyr"* 243
GIUSEPPE MAZZINI, *"We Have to Act Worthily"* 247
FLORENCE NIGHTINGALE, *"I Wish for No Other Earth"* 252
LINCOLN STEFFENS, *"I Ought to Give Her a Ring"* 254

NINE: Letters from Statesmen and Rulers 259

JOHN Q. ADAMS, *"The Suitable Style of An Ambassador"* 262
PRINCE ALBERT, *"Certain Dark Sides"* 270
BENJAMIN DISRAELI, *"An Admirer of the Blonde"* 271
ELIZABETH I, *"To Prove What I Could Do"* 275

BENJAMIN FRANKLIN, *"He Lived Usefully"*   278
JAMES ABRAM GARFIELD, *"Don't Be Disturbed"*   280
MARIE ANTOINETTE, *"Anyone Except Common People"*   281
NAPOLEON BONAPARTE, *"For A Wretched Woman!"*   284
NICHOLAS II, *"C'est à vomir!"*   286
CHARLES STEWART PARNELL, *Uncrowned King of Ireland*   292
WILLIAM PITT, *"Violent Beyond Expectation"*   293
FRANKLIN D. ROOSEVELT, *"What Pain I Caused You"*   294
THEODORE ROOSEVELT, *"A Perfect Dream of Delight"*   297
HARRY S. TRUMAN, *"The President des Etats-Unis"*   301
VICTORIA LOUISE, *"One Must Abandon Dreams"*   307

TEN: Letters from Storytellers   311

LOUISA MAY ALCOTT, *"Grandmothers Are Always Kind"*   313
ANTON CHEKHOV, *"Material for Three Dissertations"*   314
GUSTAVE FLAUBERT, *"The Artist Is a Monster"*   321
NATHANIEL HAWTHORNE, *"Authors Are Always Poor . . ."*   323
HENRY JAMES, *"Vulgar, Vulgar, Vulgar"*   325
GUY DE MAUPASSANT, *"As For Me, I Sneeze"*   330
MARCEL PROUST, *" . . . To Stop My Nervous Laughing . . ."*   332
GEORGE SAND, *"To Walk Out Quite Alone"*   336
MARK TWAIN, *"A Lazy, Idle Vagabond"*   340
THOMAS WOLFE, *"I Have Spoken to You Plainly"*   346

TO MY MOTHER

I owe you life, the most valuable of all gifts. I cannot repay it with a book—yet this one is dedicated to you with love, which makes all gifts equal.

INTRODUCTION

Dear Reader:

THE idea for this book could have come from many things—
a poem, a painting, a letter. But it didn't; my inspiration was
a cartoon. For that I am grateful, because I could never become
pompous or pedantic in a book that germinated while I flipped
through the pages of a magazine, spotted a cartoon, read it, and
laughed.

The cartoon was printed in *The New Yorker* for December 3,
1955, and is the work of Alan Dunn. It shows a classroom in
what looks like an Ivy League college. An intent, bookish professor of history, wearing *pince nez,* is addressing a class of
students. "Now, in amplification and clarification of the international situation facing the United States in July, 1945," he says,
"I refer to the following passage—page 340—which starts, 'Dear
Mama and Mary.'"

Like any other good creative work, a cartoon will stimulate
second thoughts. It was momentarily amusing to consider the way
some scholarly professor might someday stuffily refer his students
to the "Dear Mama" letters in Harry Truman's memoirs, the first
volume of which had then just been published. But it next seemed
certain indeed that historians of the future would frequently turn
to the intimate correspondence in this autobiography for information and for insight.

I took *Year of Decisions* from my shelf, and thumbed through
it, reading the wonderful letters the President wrote to his mother
and sister in those crucial days after President Roosevelt's death.
None was more moving than this one:

> Dear Mama and Mary: Well, I have had the most momentous,
> and the most trying time anyone could possibly have, since
> Thursday, April 12th.

1

Maybe you'd like to know just what happened. . . .

It was the only time in my life, I think, that I ever felt as if I'd had a real shock. I had hurried to the White House to see the President, and when I arrived, I found I was the President. No one in the history of our country ever had it happen to him in just that way. . . .

I remember how excited I became. This *was* a unique view of history. Here were intimate, honest, unself-conscious letters from the man who stood at the center of the great events of those days. I suddenly felt that I understood Mr. Truman better than I ever had before. In these letters he revealed more than the events he undertook to describe; he revealed himself. Most of all, he revealed simplicity and directness—qualities we think of as particularly American.

I realized more than this. It was important that the letters were addressed to his mother. They could scarcely have been written to anyone else. Those pleasing qualities of simplicity and directness are not always characteristic of our relations with friends or strangers. But if there is anyone in the world whom we should not have to deceive, who is most likely to know us for what we are and love us anyway, who will never prefer complexity of thought and expression to simplicity and directness of feeling, who is so interested in us that we do not have to make our letters "interesting" and consequently, perhaps, false—that person is our mother. And so, suddenly, I began to plan a book of letters to mothers.

I very quickly came face to face with some rude facts. There were not many letters like Harry Truman's—in fact, there are no others just like them—and the reason is simple enough, although it took me a while to see it. The distressing truth is that most men's mothers are not around to receive letters by the time their sons get to be Presidents of the United States. Mothers live longer than fathers, on the average, but they do not live long enough. Only one other letter written by a President during his term of office is included in this book: that was a noteworthy letter when it was penned, and it still touches me. It was written by James Garfield on August 11, 1881, less than six weeks before he was to die from the assassin's bullet that wounded him on July 2:

Dear Mother. Don't be disturbed by conflicting reports about my condition. It is true I am still weak and on my back, but I am gaining every day. . . .

This letter in facsimile was spread all over the country, "as showing to the public, not only the President's tender consideration for his mother, but his unshaken courage."

Somewhat disheartened, I turned to the political leaders of other lands. Napoleon I was Emperor of the French at the youthful age of thirty-five; his mother outlived him by fifteen years. Napoleon had family troubles; I suppose everyone does, but his were particularly difficult, for he had made his brothers and sisters kings and queens and princes and princesses and grand dukes and grand duchesses, and so family quarrels were as likely as not to involve all Europe in civil war. Napoleon's youngest brother caused the Emperor especial heartache. Jerome had married a Baltimore girl at the age of nineteen, going A.W.O.L. to do it, and that was hardly correct behavior for a Bonaparte. Napoleon wrote to his mother:

> Mr. Jerome Napoleon has arrived at Lisbon with the woman he is living with. [The Emperor refused to recognize the American marriage.] . . . If he shows himself unworthy of the name he bears, and seems inclined to persist in his *liaison*, I shall show him no mercy. . . . I want you to write to him. Tell him that I have been like a father to him. Tell him that it is his sacred duty to obey me. . . .

Nothing could reveal more clearly the power of Napoleon, but the letter also shows his weakness, which is everybody's weakness. He needs his mother's help just as much as if he were not ruler of all Europe. Incidentally, the upshot was that he did not mercilessly condemn his brother and ruin his career—instead he made him King of Westphalia, and their mother probably had a good deal to do with it.

There are other letters in this book from men and women who have ruled countries and determined the fate of peoples—from John Quincy Adams, for instance, and from Czar Nicholas II, Charles Stewart Parnell, Catherine Parr, and Marie Antoinette— but such letters are in the minority. This should not be surprising; more than that, it should not be a disappointment. For this book is not solely about history seen from an odd and revealing point of view, although at first I thought it would be. It is about human character.

Let me put it this way: Harry Truman's letters are engrossing and important because he was President of the United States, and was writing about events played out in the center of the stage of the world; but they could have been about subjects totally un-historical, and would still have revealed much of the essential character of their writer. This realization opened a broad and rich vista before me. I had only to make a list of all the people in history who interested me, and then see if I could find any of their letters to their mothers. I had a hunch that only occasionally would I be disappointed.

Twice my expectations were not justified. The author of our national anthem was on my list, and one letter to his mother is included in this book. But it is a dull letter. I apologize for it, and for my belief that Francis Scott Key was a colorless man. The other disappointment is more serious. Mark Twain was a great man, yet his letters to his mother are either pedestrian or forced. His daughter Susie once remarked that "the difference between papa and mama is that mama loves morals and papa loves cats." Susie, I am afraid, knew only the public face of her father. He wanted to be more than a teller of hilarious tales; he wanted to find philosophies that would explain the good he sensed and the evil he saw and experienced. But he did not believe that his audience—and this included his wife and daughters —would allow it; even after fourteen years of labor on a biography of Joan of Arc, he feared signing the manuscript with his own name, because then America "wouldn't take it seriously."

I hoped that in his letters to his mother he might reveal more of himself. But they are performances. Not that they're not funny:

> When we visited you a month ago, it seemed to us that your Keokuk weather was pretty hot; Jean and Clara sat up in bed at Mrs. McElroy's and cried about it, and so did I; but I judge by your letter that it has cooled down, now, so that a person is comparatively comfortable, with his skin off. Well it did need cooling; I remember that I burnt a hole in my shirt, there, with some ice cream that fell on it; and Miss Jenkins told me they never used a stove, but cooked their meals on a marble-topped table in the drawing-room, just with the natural heat. If anybody else had told me, I would not have believed it.

The trouble is that Twain is trying too hard to be funny. He knows it's expected of him, apparently even by his mother.

I was surprised by other letters not because they were dull but because they showed an aspect of the character or life of the writer that I could not have predicted. Prince Albert, for example, wrote to his mother before his marriage to Queen Victoria:

Apart from my relations with her [Victoria], my future position will have certain dark sides, and the skies above me will not always be blue and unclouded. Still, life, wherever one is, has its storms, and it is a support to one to feel that one has used all one's endeavours and strength in some great object, decisive for the welfare of so many.

It is significant that what must have seemed the ideal marriage for all the other men of the world, at least from the materialist's point of view, was not so to him.

One of the most charming letters in the collection is from Nathaniel Hawthorne. It was written when he was seventeen, and it is whimsical and amusing; in it he tells his mother that he thinks perhaps he will be an author when he grows up, "because the illegibility of my handwriting is very author-like." I had not known this side of Hawthorne. The brooding moralist is familiar to everyone, but Hawthorne was, I find, much more than that.

In the same vein, I was unprepared to discover William James, who had always struck me as a sobersided individual, writing to his mother about a girls' school that was in the building opposite his own. James spent his afternoons watching the girls through a telescope! All of the girls were ugly, however—or so he assured his mother. No doubt he used the information thus gathered in the working out of his psychology in later years.

I misjudged William's brother Henry, too. I suppose everyone thinks of Henry James as having been a very serious youth, and probably he was, most of the time. But can you guess what he called his mother when he addressed her in a letter? Mater? Mother? Mummy dear? I think it will surprise you as much as it did me. His letters start: Dear Mammy.

Joyce Kilmer had an even odder name for his mother. She was a most distinguished looking lady of good family, but Joyce's letters always begin: Dear Brat.

And yet I am forced to say that the extraordinary thing about these letters is that there are so few surprises in them. Nine tenths are typical of the character, the speech, the ideas, the needs of their authors. That is why they reveal so much, and why, at least to me, they are so fascinating.

What would you expect to find in a letter of Baudelaire's, for example? Interminable, morbid self-accusations? Guilty misery? Despair? They are there, at great length, in the longest and one of the finest letters in this book. What would you expect from Lord Byron? Wit? Energy? Biting sarcasm? They are all there, too, in a few of his many letters; I wish we could print them all, because no one ever wrote better letters. Byron's were penned while he was on a trip, which event is the cause for many of the letters in this book. (You do not write to your mother if you are living in the same house with her; some of the people on my original list are not represented here because they apparently never left home.)

Other letters seem almost exaggeratedly typical. Brandeis's show that at a tender age the future jurist dedicated himself to reform. William Ellery Channing, at eighteen, told his mother:

> I am resolved to prosecute divinity. My highest hopes of happiness are beyond the grave, and I cannot do more good to mankind than by teaching them also to lay up treasures where neither moth nor rust can corrupt them.

Agassiz writes about a scientific expedition. Chekhov's letters overflow with precise description of persons and places. Franklin's are practical and businesslike. Gibbon's are written in the grand style that makes the *Decline and Fall of the Roman Empire* one of the greatest sustained *tours de force* in the history of history:

> Since I have mentioned my Book let me add that it will probably make its appearance about the middle or end of February: and that one of the very first Copies of it shall be carefully transmitted to Charles Street. The Public I know not why except from the happy choice of the subject, have already conceived expectations, which it will not be easy to satisfy: the more especially as lively ignorance is apt to expect much more, than the nature and extent of historical materials can enable an author to produce.

This is an informal, private letter from Gibbon to his mother, and makes it easy to see why the great history is written as it is; he could write no other way.

John Jay Chapman's letter is quick-witted, funny, and angry—just what we would expect. John Donne's letter of comfort is filled with questions about the nature of God and of human suffering, and is an attempt to establish logically the debt he owes his mother. Perhaps his mother would have told him that his logic was not necessary, but the letter is a fine one nevertheless. John Wesley's letter is similarly suggestive of the man. He has been reading Thomas à Kempis:

Another of his tenets, which is indeed a natural consequence of this, is that all mirth is vain and useless, if not sinful. But why then, does the Psalmist so often exhort us to rejoice in the Lord and tell us that it becomes the just to be joyful? I think one could hardly desire a more express text than that in the 68th Psalm. "Let the righteous rejoice and be glad in the Lord. Let them also be merry and joyful."

Wesley, of course, is right about this. We would do well to remember that religion and laughter are not opposites.

Other letters are typical in other ways. The style of Whitman, in verse and prose, is unique. He breaks all the grammatical rules because he wishes to encompass more and more on his page, to enclose greater things in a sentence, even in a word, than any writer before him. Whitman's "lists" are infamous—but he was able to describe certain things superbly. It took a master of words to describe the three-day parade of the Union Army through Washington after the war was over, and Whitman was there, and was such a master. Therefore, his is a great letter. Stylistically, Thoreau's letter is also typical; I almost feel, reading it, that with it he is practicing for *Walden.* So with Thomas Wolfe; you would expect his letters to be voluminous, wouldn't you? Well, they are.

Mazzini, we know, had a passion for liberty. His letters are a continuous and searching discussion of human freedom. Lenin's letter is not—it is about conditions in Siberia, in the prison camps. Marie Antoinette's letter is about the boredom of her life, though she does not seem entirely aware of it. Maupassant's are about the difficulties of *la vie bohème.* What else would we anticipate? Hearst's are not letters, they are telegrams. Again, what would you expect from a newspaperman? "Who," you can imagine Hearst growling, "has time for letters any more?"

The telegram and telephone have now usurped the place of the personal letter; today's letters to mother, when sent at all, are likely to bear such predictable return addresses as an APO number, a college dormitory, or a foreign hotel. Tomorrow's historians will not have many troves from our decades as rich as the famed Paston Letters—that collection of some ninety years of business-minded correspondence between members of the Paston family in fifteenth and early sixteenth century England. (There is, regrettably, no Paston letter here; I was not able to select one that could stand alone, be representative, *and* be interesting.) Many other letters are lacking because they were dull; some I left out with reluctance, just because a book must stop somewhere.

One such letter was sent by John Gunther, the son of the famed foreign correspondent. John was born in Paris, and educated at schools in Vienna, London, New York, and Deerfield, Massachusetts. He died of a brain tumor when he was seventeen; he fought it for fifteen months, and the story of his battle against despair is beautifully told in his father's book, *Death Be Not Proud.* The last letter that John wrote is so cheerful and so moving that I'd like to quote its closing lines:

> O! How wonderful food is again! Bacon and eggs! salt! How I eat! mushrooms! last night I played poker with some fellow patients!—great fun! I've almost finished the English anthology we were reading.
>
> Lots of love and kisses.

There are letters that were never even written that I would like to see in these pages. I wish we could read a letter to his mother from Abel; I wish we could find one written by Cain. I would be willing to trade any possessions for the privilege of reading letters to their mothers from Achilles, Augustine, Mary, and Jacob; or from Aeneas, Cupid, Cesarion, Ishmael, Solomon, and Don Juan. Frightening though they would be, I would like to read letters from Nero, Richard III, Orestes, and Lizzie Borden. And why should we stop there? Why not letters from Romulus and Remus; from Hamlet, Oedipus, and Professor Higgins; and from Ruth, Sir Galahad, Isaac, and John the Baptist. How about letters from Telemachus, Hercules, the Prodigal Son; from Moses, Hamnet, and Helen; from Tarzan, Paul Bunyan, and Tom Thumb? The greatest letter of all, of course—I almost hesitate to suggest it—would be from Jesus.

Those letters that are in these pages are the best I could find. I hope you enjoy reading the book.

Sincerely yours,
CHARLES VAN DOREN

New York, New York
December, 1958

ONE

Letters from

Belletrists

"BELLETRIST" is a hundred-dollar word, and as with many such, it is difficult to say exactly what it means. A belletrist is a man of letters, but not a storyteller; he writes philosophical essays, but he is not a philosopher; he is usually a critic, but not always; he indulges in historicizing, but he is not a historian. He is, in short, a professional writer who can write in any style and on any subject. He is a valuable man to have around.

Dr. Samuel Johnson is ordinarily said to have been the first belletrist in England, and he is included here. His letter is almost a caricature of the man: its tone is an amalgam of piety and command. The Great Cham of Literature was nearly fifty when he wrote it, but it is clear that he is still afraid of his mother. Some of his enemies in London would have been delighted to know this.

Ruskin was nearly fifty when he wrote his letters, too. It appears that his mother is still worried about whether he wears his rubbers when it rains. I doubt that mothers should still be thinking about such things after fifty years, but we must accept the fact that they do as one of the immutable laws of life.

William Randolph Hearst would be astonished to find himself in a company of belletrists, and I am still a little surprised at myself for having placed him here. He was a professional writer, and he did write in many styles and on many subjects, but his editorials and articles never lived beyond the last edition of the day, and their literary quality was not such to deserve longer life. On the other hand, Hearst did have untold influence on the way all of us write today, if not on the way we think. Cézanne fought stuffiness in art because of belief; Hearst hacked away at tradi-

9

tion and limitations and conservative newspaper practice. He was impelled by circulation and revenue and advertising sales, but he did fight and he did win. He pushed over a lot of little icons, set a number of styles, and gave us correspondents like Richard Harding Davis.

There's no need to apologize for placing Davis in this group. Even if he had never written anything but letters, he'd have earned a place here. I've included one long letter he wrote from Cuba; but I'd also like you to read these few lines from another letter addressed to his mother:

> What was best was your wishing to see me. Of course you know that I feel that too . . . But because that cannot be, we are still no further away than we ever were and when the pain to see you comes, I don't let it hurt and I don't kill it either for it is the sweetest pain I feel. If sons will go off and marry, or be war correspondents, or managers, it doesn't mean that Home is any the less Home. You can't wipe out history by changing the name of a boulevard, as somebody once said about the French . . . You will never know how much I love you all and you must never give up trying to comprehend it. God bless you and keep you, and my love to you every minute and always.

Readers who remember *The Way of All Flesh* will recognize its genesis in Samuel Butler's letter; on the other hand, readers who know only Margaret Fuller's florid style will be surprised by the sweet simplicity of her love for her baby. John Jay Chapman is outrageously funny about the Germans, and Howells is touchingly homesick. Norton's letter is included because it is a typical letter from a young man on the Grand Tour, all excitement and wonder at having met a Great Literary Figure—except that Norton was not then eighteen years old, or twenty; he was thirty, and that is revealing about Norton. It would seem, by the way, that belletrists' mothers live to a good old age. If your son is in doubt about what career to follow, maybe this will help you to help him make up his mind.

"In Search of My Own Bread"

SAMUEL BUTLER

Samuel Butler (1835-1902; English novelist, Homeric scholar and translator.) This remarkable letter, written when Butler was twenty-three, shows the difficulties he had in selecting a career: difficulties shared and even embroidered upon by Ernest Pontifex in The Way of All Flesh. Butler ultimately became not only a brilliant writer, but also an accomplished painter, scientist, and musician. His first choice of occupation, however, was farming, and he spent four years (1860-64) raising sheep in New Zealand, and incidentally discovering the locale for Erewhon.

As a Homeric scholar, he is best known for his theory that The Odyssey *was written by a woman,* a theory which has never been disproved.

I hope you won't be thoroughly convinced by Butler's letter that his father always did treat him with "unwise and necessary pressure." Butler's father was a minister, and his father before him a renowned bishop and scholar; when young Sam refused to become a clergyman because of loudly voiced religious doubts, the decision was no light blow to the Reverend Thomas Butler. But he did not cut his son off without a shilling, nor did he cast him out of the family; instead, he staked Sam to a sheep-run in New Zealand, and even edited and published the young man's first book, creating it from letters sent by Samuel from New Zealand.

I regret that I must also caution you not to accept too strongly the deep affection that Butler expresses in this letter for his mother. Just as the clergyman-father of Butler-Pontifex in The Way of All Flesh *is mean and holier-than-thou, the mother is passive, dull, hypocritical . . . and Butler's mother was the model.*

Butler had one affair of the heart by mail, and never married.

Joh. Coll. Camb. May 10, 1859.

Dear Mamma—I was in hopes that my visit to Langar [the family home] had been productive of good effects, but I fear it has not; for on my sending a letter to Langar I have received one in return of purport which has not astonished me though I need not say it has perturbed me.

If I am the pig-headed fool you think me the best school for me is adversity. If, then, it so turns out that my refusal to turn lawyer or farmer brings considerable adversity on my head—it is good for me; when I would fain fill myself with the husks, I shall be brought humble enough back again, and, if rejected, shall feel that I cannot greatly wonder.

Most fathers on hearing my case, even as I should state it,

would say: "Serves him right." Most sons would say that I was unfeelingly treated altogether with unwise and unnecessary pressure.

I would emigrate, learn to farm in England, turn homeopathic doctor, or learn to paint, in which last I have strong reason to believe I should succeed. But "No" from my father. To the other two courses, namely the law or a schoolmaster's life, I say "No" not less decidedly. You would, with the best intentions in the world, make me a bed that I know very well would not fit me. I know that when I am in, escape is impossible; and, knowing that I have duties to myself to perform even more binding on me than those to my parents, with all respect adopt the alternative of rejecting the pounds, shillings, and pence and going in search of my own bread my own way.

No man has any right to undertake any profession, for which he does not honestly believe himself well qualified, to please any other person. I should be preferring the hollow peace that would be patched up by my submission (for you could never forget that this submission had been obtained by money pressure), and the enjoyment of more money, to undergoing the great risk and trial which I see before me. I am old enough by this time to know my own mind and deliberately accede to my father's proposal that I should receive no more from him if I refuse to do what he wishes; it is fair play; I don't question his right to do what he likes with his own—I question his wisdom greatly, but neither his motives nor his determination to stick to them.

One thing I trust—that is that I shall be allowed to correspond with Langar; for, though I am not in the least uneasy about my right to choose my own profession at my age, I know that I have no right to either write insulting letters to you or to cease informing you and hearing from you how we are mutually faring, unless compelled to do so by one or both of you. I should be very sorry to think that any connection other than the money connection should cease. That I regard as ceased already. My father said that after the Michaelmas quarter it should cease. I am not proud enough to say "Let it cease now," though I would I were in a position to say so; but can scarcely expect that he will continue to support me till then as soon as he knows that I have made up my mind to reject either the law or a schoolmaster's life and either to emigrate or turn artist.

I have some £58 in hand, no debts; France has, or rather will have at Midsummer, more than enough money of mine to pay my bill at the end of this term over and above this £58. My pupil pays me £10 at the beginning of June. I have a matter of £200; altogether at the end of this term I stand possessed of £270. If, after a full statement of my affairs to Hayllar, he is of opinion that I may venture on the profession with a probability at the end of four or five years of making my living by it, I shall embark on it; make my £270 (with the aid of a little pupil work for which I must spare an hour a day) (I mean in London—not here) last me three years; and then borrow from two friends up here who have promised to assist me, or if the worst comes to the worst—but this would not be till the wolf was actually at the door—borrow on my reversion of the Whitehall property, which I believe to amount to some £7000.

I shall continue to reside here till October because I shall have to pay for these rooms and attendance anyhow, and cannot afford to pay for others in London at the same time; moreover my scholarship continues to pay me while I am in residence and the long vacation is the best paying time. I shall not try for pupils but devote myself entirely to the profession I intend to embark on —I have no time to lose. I should not either read for the Voluntary for which I see I should get plucked; there were many questions for which I should have been plucked this time if I had answered them as I believe they should be answered, and have not sufficient control over myself to write the received explanation when I do not believe it. If I fail, and at the end of a year I should know whether or not I was going to succeed, I should either then make the best of a bad business and go off to New Zealand with whatever money I could raise, or go in for the civil service examinations, and try for an appointment under government or whatever else might then seem best—but be sure I shall come down for no money from Langar.

One thing in my father's letter struck me as either an additional proof that he is perfectly unaware of my real disposition and character or else as a most undeserved and ungenerous taunt. He said: "Neither am I disposed to sacrifice the other children to you." Either he supposes that I would see one penny taken from them to supply me withal, in which case he betrays great ignorance of my disposition, or else by such remarks as these he is completing the estrangement between us. I never asked him for an allowance. What he gave I took and have employed well; for that capital so laid out I can show good interest—especially during the six months I was in Heddon Street; true, I fear the interest is not such as you like, but it is such as I feel all precious to me, though I see that this storm has been brought about by no other means. But for this I should have been quietly ordained and none of this sad business would ever have come about. But I say deliberately, it is better as it is for you and for my father and for me.

For you, in that you will have peace in me eventually, though not now, which, had I been ordained, you never would, for all these doubts would have come about then, and I should have had my pounds, shillings, and pence, and been a fettered, miserable man.

For me it is better that, at the cost of any present distress, I should have been saved such anguish as I know would then have been my lot.

The like applies to the bar and to the schoolmaster in a less degree; you would never have had any real peace and pleasure in me; but when I have succeeded, and succeed I must and will eventually, you will both be happy enough to receive me back, and have real pleasure and comfort in me then, if not now.

I am not petulantly in a huff, imagining that you will come round when you see I won't give in. I don't expect anything of the kind, don't expect to receive a penny from my father now or at his death, which I heartily desire may be long averted. But I say: Rather than give up my Christian liberty to choose a profession [in] which I honestly believe I can succeed, should be able to speak the truth in and get my living by—rather than give up this I give up the money which my father has allowed me till now.—I remain, dear Mamma, your affectionate son,

S. Butler.

"To the Bottom with the French"

JOHN JAY CHAPMAN

John Jay Chapman (1862-1933; American essayist, poet, and play-wright.) Chapman was graduated from Harvard Law School in 1884 and was admitted to the bar, but he did not practice after 1898, embarking instead on a literary career. His temper was mercurial and he had a highly developed sense of guilt. But his essays were extremely popular as well as respected. Chapman was one of the great letter writers of his time, and I regret having been able to uncover only one letter to his mother. His letters to his friends were easy, witty, and trenchant. This one, so much concerned with Trevelyan's biography of John Bright, an English statesman, is not a shining example of his style—unless you enjoy Chapman's comments, as I did, about the superiority of travel aboard a French vessel. One of my favorite jokes, by the way, comes from Chapman's Memories and Milestones. He says: "I had a classmate at college who had never been far from South Boston, and one evening while dancing he slipped and fell to the ground. He arose at once with great aplomb, remarking, coldly, 'These cursed American floors!'"

The "little-England point of view" to which he refers is the theory, maintained by Chesterton and others, that England would never be happy again until she dispensed with her empire and became as great as she had been under Elizabeth I. It was an unpopular view before World War I, but has many adherents now.

On board the Provence
June 21: 1914

Dear Mama—I never enjoyed a voyage so much; and I think the French are the only people who understand ocean travel. The arrangements, customs, food, and service are infinitely better than on the swinish German steamers or the brutal Britons. I'd rather go to the bottom with the French than float about eternally with the beastly Teutons. Although the ship is or *must be* so full, it doesn't seem crowded. The stewards and stewardesses are polite, and efficient. The sea is calm—that's a great point and much to the credit of the French. Scarcely any one drinks anything. When I consider the cork-popping on the German line— the hours over swilling tables of odious food—the gross salutations and imprecations from unwiped lips—calling a blessing upon the indulgence—I shudder. The boys are extremely happy and do lots of work every day. I have taken the time to read Bright's Life with more care than I should have given on land. It gives me the best glimpse into English politics that I've ever had. Bright himself was so bored with the fictitious character of the English system—the fact that it is all *a game*. But I think he

was the greatest figure of the century in English politics so far
as enduring interest goes. The rest are so mad about ephemeral
details that one forgets and confuses them. Bright has always in
mind something that *remains true*. Just now the Jingoes are on
top and it may be a long time—before the little-England point of
view comes to the front again. One would think from reading
this life of Bright that Disraeli had made a failure. But if you go
to England you find Bright forgotten and Disraeli their *great man*
—their George Washington. I say this to their shame: for I think
Dizzy was a humbug and quite properly stands for *all the humbug* in British life—which under the present Imperialism is particularly rampant. . . .

I shall go so far as to encourage their industries by purchasing
two or three light flannel suits later in the summer and perhaps a
tweed sporting suit. The absurd fondness for sport has this good
in it that it produces wonderful men's clothes. At the sacrifice of
all reason art is produced—as usual. Umbrellas too are good. I
shall call on the Laugels and Ferays of course—and immediately
—as we hope to leave Paris almost at once.

Your affectionate son

Jack

"Spending Willie Hearst's Money"

RICHARD HARDING DAVIS

*Richard Harding Davis (1864-1916; American journalist and
author.) He was one of the leading personalities of the Gilded
Age—an age, like our own, when being a personality was a career
in itself. He wrote slick and popular short stories for* Scribner's
and for other magazines, and collected them in Gallegher *and*
Other Stories *(1891). But his main occupation was covering wars;
he was the first of the great War Correspondents, the father of
his profession, the progenitor of a breed. He covered the Spanish
War in Cuba, the Graeco-Turkish War, the Spanish-American
War, the Russo-Japanese War, and the First World War. (The
letter printed here concerns his experiences in Cuba.) His honeymoon was characteristic; it was spent in South Africa, while he
covered the Boer War.*

Like all war correspondents, he hated war. If everyone in the world had just one chance to cover just one war, maybe we wouldn't have any more wars.

Cardenas—North Coast of Cuba.
January 16th, 1897.

DEAR MOTHER:

It is very funny not knowing what sort of a place you are to sleep in next and taking things out of a grab bag, as it were— In Europe you can always guess what the well known towns will give you for you have a guide book, but here it is all luck. Matanzas was a pretty city but the people were awful, the hotel was Spanish and the proprietor insolent, though I was spending more of Willie Hearst's money than all of the officers spend in a week, the Consul could not talk English or Spanish, he said he hadn't come there "to go to school to no Spaniard" and he gloried in the fact he had been there three years without knowing a word of the language. His vice-Consul was worse and everything went wrong generally. Every one I met was an Alarmist and that is polite for liar. They asked Remington if he was the man who manufactured the rifles and gave us the *Iowa Democrat* to read. To-night I reached here after a six hours ride through blazing fields of sugar cane and stopped on my way to the hotel to ask the Consul when the next boat went to Saqua la Grande— I had no letter of introduction to him as I had to the Matanzas consul, but as soon as he saw my card he got out of his chair and shook hands again and was as hearty and well bred and delightful as Charley himself and unlike Chas he did not ask me 14 francs for looking on him. He is out now chasing around to get me a train for to-morrow. But I won't go to-morrow. My hotel looks on the plaza and the proprietor and the whole suite of attendants are my slaves. It is just as different as can be. My interpreter does it, he calls himself *my valet,* although I point out to him that two shirts and twelve collars do not constitute a wardrobe even with a rubber coat thrown in. But he likes to play at my being a distinguished stranger and I can't say I object. Only when you remember the way I was invited to see Cuba and expected to see it, and now the way I am seeing it from car windows with *a valet.* What would the new school of yellow kid journalists say if they knew that. For the first time on this trip I have wished you were both with me, that was to-night. I never see anything really beautiful but that it instantly makes me feel selfish and wish you could see it too. It has happened again and again and to night I wish you could be here with me on this balcony. The town runs down a slope to the bay and in the middle of it is the Plaza with me on the balcony which lets out of my sleeping room—"the room" so the proprietor tells me, "reserved only for the Capitain General." It is just like the description in that remarkable novel of mine where Clay and Alice sit on the balcony of the restaurant. I have the moonlight and the Cathedral with the open doors and the bronze statue in the middle and the royal palms moving in the breeze straight from the sea and the people walking around the plaza below. If it was in any way as beautiful as this Clay and Alice would have ended the novel that night.

I got a grand lot of letters to-day which Otto, my interpreter brought back from Havana after having conducted Remington there in safety. I must say you are writing very cheerfully now, but I don't wonder you worried at first but now that I am a commercial traveller with an order from Weyler which does everything when I find it necessary, you really must not worry any more but just let me continue on my uneventful journey and then come home. I shall have been gone so long and my friends, judging from Russell and Dana and Irene's letters, will be so glad to see me, that they will have forgotten I went out to do other things than coast around in trains. As a matter of fact this is a terribly big problem and most difficult to get the truth of, I find myself growing to be the opposite of the alarmist, whatever that is, although you would think the picturesque and dramatic and exciting thing would be the one I would rather believe because I want to believe it, but I find that that is not so, I see a great deal on both sides and I do not believe half I am told. As we used to say at college, "It is against history," and it is against history for men to act as I am told they are acting here— They show me the pueblo huddled together around the fortified towns, living in palm huts but I know that they have always lived in palm huts, the yellow kid reporters don't know that or consider it, but send off word that the condition of the people is terrible, that they have only leaves to cover them, and it sounds very badly. That is an instance of what I mean. In a big way there is no doubt that the process going on here is one of extermination and ruin. Two years ago the amount of sugar shipped from the port of Matanzas to the U. S. was valued at 11 millions a year. This last year just over shows that sugar to the amount of $800,000 was sent out. In '94, 154 vessels touched at Matanzas on their way to America. In '95 there were 80 and in '96 there are 16. I always imagined that houses were destroyed during a war because they got in the way of cannon balls or they were burned because they might offer shelter to the enemy, but here they are destroyed, with the purpose of making the war horrible and hurrying up the end. The insurgents began first by destroying the sugar mills, some of which were worth millions of dollars in machinery, and now the Spaniards are burning the homes of the people and herding them in around the towns to starve out the insurgents and to leave them without shelter or places to go for food or to hide the wounded. So all day long where ever you look you see great heavy columns of smoke rising into this beautiful sky above the magnificent palms the most noble of all palms, almost of all trees— It is the most beautiful country I have ever visited. I had no recollection of how beautiful it was or else I had not the knowledge of other places with which to compare it. Nothing out of the imagination can approach it in its great waterfalls and mossy rocks and grand plains and forests of white pillars with plumes waving above them. Only man is vile here and it is cruel to see the walls of the houses with blind eyes, with roofs gone and gardens burned, every church but one that I have seen was a fortress with hammocks swung from the altars and rude barricades thrown up around the doorways— If this is war I am of the opinion that it is a senseless wicked institution made for soldiers, lovers and correspondents for different reasons, and for no one else in the world and it is too expensive for the others to keep it going to entertain these few gentlemen— I have seen very little of it yet and I probably won't see much more, but I have seen all I want. Remington had his mind satisfied even sooner— but then he is an alarmist and exaggerates things— The men who wear the red badge of courage, I don't feel sorry for, they have their reward in their bloody bandages and the little cross on their tunic but those you meet coming back sick and dying with fever are the ones that make fighting contemptible—poor little farmers, poor little children with no interest in Cuba or Spain's right to hold it, who have been sent out to die like ants before they have learned to hold a mauser, and who are going back again with the beards that have grown in the field hospitals on their cheeks and their eyes hollow, and too weak to move or speak. Six of them died while I was in Jaroco, a town as big as Marion and that had been the average for two months, think of that, six people dying in Marion every day through July and August— I didn't stay in that town any longer than the train did— Well I have been writing editorials here instead of cheering you up but I guess I'm about right and when I see a little more I'll tell it over again to *The Journal*— It is not as exciting reading as deeds of daring by our special correspondent and I haven't changed my name or shaved my eyebrows or done anything the other men have done but I believe I am getting near the truth. They have shut off provisions going or coming from the towns, they have huddled hundreds of people who do not know what a bath means around these towns, and this is going to happen— As soon as the rains begin the yellow fever and smallpox will set in and all vessels leaving Cuban ports will be quarantined and the island will be one great plague spot. The insurgents who are in the open fields will live and the soldiers will die for their officers know nothing of sanitation or care nothing. The little Consul has just been here to see me and we have had a long talk and I got back at him. He told me he had seen the Franco-German war as a correspondent of *The Tribune* and I asked him if he had ever met another correspondent of *The Tribune* at that time a German student named Hans who cabled the story of the battle of Gravellote and who Archibald Forbes says was the first correspondent to use the cable. The Consul who looks like William D. Howells wriggled around in his chair and said "I guess you mean me but I was not a German student, I was born and raised in Philadelphia and Forbes got my name wrong, it is Hance." So then I got up and shook hands with him in my turn and told him I had always wanted to meet that correspondent and did not expect to do so in Cardenas, on the coast of Cuba.

Thank you all for your letters. Lots of love.

DICK.

"Two Miniature Song-and-Dance Artists"

WILLIAM RANDOLPH HEARST

William Randolph Hearst (1863-1951; American newspaper publisher.) For political purposes, his father—George Hearst, an American mining magnate—bought the San Francisco Examiner, *then made William responsible for its management. The young*

Harvard graduate's methods worked; the paper made money, and by 1887 William Randolph Hearst controlled it completely. Then he reached across the continent and bought the Morning Journal, *a struggling New York daily, turning it into a fabulously successful tabloid with techniques that gave rise to the phrase "yellow journalism." After the* Journal *came the Chicago* American, *the Chicago* Examiner, *and the Boston* American. *By 1925 he owned newspapers in cities of every section of the United States. But the world changed faster than his journalistic style and his political views. In 1941 he was forced by the depression to consolidate his holdings, and auctioneers and department stores sold a large part of his great collection of furniture, paintings, tapestries, and other treasures, many of them still packed in crates that had never been opened. He did, however, retain San Simeon, his great estate in California. It gave rise to his sobriquet, "Lord of San Simeon."*

In 1915 Hearst was the father of three boys when his wife presented him with twin sons. The series of telegrams sent by the happy father to his mother have been included instead of letters because the telegrams are as good (and as long!) as many letters, and because the telegram seems to have been Mr. Hearst's natural means of communication. We remember Hearst as a man who presided like a feudal lord over an incredibly powerful empire. These telegrams remind you that he was also a man, and could be a witty, tender one at that.

New York, October 22, 1915

Mrs. P. A. Hearst, Care the *Examiner* (Telephone this tonight) San Francisco

We think Phoebe or Elbert, we can't tell which, will arrive about Christmas and we want you surely to be here for the festivities.

Will

December 2, 1915
New York, N. Y. 5:55 AM

Mrs. Phoebe A. Hearst, *Examiner*, San Francisco

We cannot call them Phoebe because they are not of that persuasion, but we could call them Phoebus and Apollo, for just at sunrise two of the loveliest boys you have ever seen were born to Mr. and Mrs. William Randolph Hearst.

[Evening of December 2nd]

MRS. P. A. HEARST

George was full of sentiment. He looked lovingly at the twins but said that what he wanted to know most was how his mama was. William was more matter-of-fact. He said he thought boys would be much better than girls to play with and wouldn't muss up the playroom with dolls and dishes and other useless things. John looked the twins over very critically and didn't seem much encouraged by their personal appearance. Finally he said hopefully that perhaps they would look better when they got their hats on. For my part I can't get used to the little things. They look so funny lying together on their little bed doing almost the same things at the same time in the same jerky little way, for all the world like two miniature song-and-dance artists. We are not going to name them until you come. Then we will have a grand christening party for the twins and William and John. Love from all.

Will

[A few hours later]

Romulus and Remus are getting along wonderfully well. Mother also doing well. Father slowly recovering from shock of surprise and delight. Romulus weighs 6 pounds 7 ounces; Remus 6 pounds 4 ounces; pretty good for eight months. Romulus is a brunet; Remus a blond. Both are handsome, taking after their father. All the family including the new arrivals send love and hope that the great event will add some happiness to your birthday tomorrow and other birthdays for many years to come.

[The next day, December 3rd]

MRS. P. A. HEARST

George, William, John and also Elbert and Edward, or whatever their names will be, hope you had a happy birthday and wish you would come as soon as possible to New York. Millicent and I second these sentiments. The twins must have excellent consciences, judging from the way they sleep. Furthermore, they both have blue eyes, florid complexions and fine tenor voices.

They seem to prefer the night life of New York and are widest awake about two o'clock in the morning, just like Father.

Will

"Home! How My Heart Leaps . . ."

WILLIAM DEAN HOWELLS

William Dean Howells (1837-1920; American editor, novelist, and essayist.) This letter was written while Howells was United States Consul at Venice (1861-65), a post awarded him for having compiled a campaign biography of Lincoln for the 1860 elections. When he returned home he embarked on a remarkably active literary career; he was the author of some twenty novels—the best known of which is the famous Rise of Silas Lapham—*several works of criticism and collections of essays, and thirty-one plays. After 1871 he was for twenty years editor of* The Atlantic Monthly, *and later conducted the department in* Harper's Magazine *called "The Editor's Easy Chair."*

Howells exerted great influence from these important positions, and was able to encourage a number of young exponents of realism, among them Stephen Crane, Hamlin Garland, and Frank Norris. He was generally considered the leading American writer during the latter part of his career; he was the first president of the American Academy of Arts and Letters. His reputation suffered after his death, but in the mid-1950's a reviving interest in Howells made itself felt. The daughter he mentions in this letter—Mildred—edited a book of his letters. "Elinor" is Howells's wife.

Venice, October 28, 1864

Dᴇᴀʀ Mᴏᴛʜᴇʀ:

I will enclose a few lines in Elinor's letter, for though I have hardly time to write, I should feel guilty to let a letter go home without my hand in it.

Father speaks of my taking office for four years more. I doubt if I could manage it, and if I could, I wouldn't. When I go home,

I want to go home to live, "be it ever so humbly." I am sure it will be better than the proudest life here. I only consent to remain here till spring because I think I see very great advantage in doing so; and as soon as I have notes for half a dozen papers on Italian cities I shall be off for home. Home! How my heart leaps at the thought! O mother, you mustn't think that this separation has not been as hard for me as for you. Many a time I've been so homesick I hardly knew what to do—almost as homesick as in the old childish days when it almost broke my heart to be five or ten miles away from you. (Do you remember how one Sunday morning Joe and I came riding back on the same horse from Dayton to Eureka? It was in the fall, and I can hear the hum of a spinning-wheel now, that sounded out of a log cabin door. O me—O me! I am so sorry to be no longer a child, though then I had my troubles, too!) The world isn't so wide now as it was then, and for three years I have borne to be four thousand miles away from you. Well, patience. It will not be much longer now —but O, my dear mother, we can never meet again in the old way. I am wrong to tell you, but every morning I think of some-one lying so lonesomely there under the red autumn leaves, and I reproach myself for each moment's happiness, as if it were for-getfulness of him in a sad captivity.

I long to show you our little girl, who grows so good and fair. You should see how sunnily her hair is coming out of the darker color she was born with; and how sunnily her little life has issued from my gloomier nature. I hope she will be as much like her mother in character as she is like me in looks.

I'm rushing my book forward, and it's nearly done—there are but three chapters more to copy. I have very great hopes of it, as a book calculated to succeed and to do good.

Dear love to all.

Your affectionate son,

WILL.

"I Shall Endeavour to Obey You . . ."

S A M U E L   J O H N S O N

Samuel Johnson (1709-1784; English lexicographer, essayist, poet, and conversationalist.) He was a large, ugly, slovenly, nearsighted man, his face scarred by scrofula. He was also slothful, dilatory, splenetic, and greedy; but he was "a profound moralist and an heroically good man"; in fact, one of the best and most lovable men who ever lived. He was immensely learned. He compiled what was to his time the best English dictionary, wrote The Lives of the Poets, and edited Shakespeare. "London" and "The Vanity of Human Wishes" are his two most famous poems; he also wrote The Rambler and The Idler, long series of essays, as well as numerous ephemera. But it is as a talker that he is best known and will always be remembered—thanks to Boswell's The Life of Samuel Johnson, the greatest biography in the language. It is possible that no author ever exerted greater power than Dr. Johnson; he could make or break a book or a writer with a sentence.

He was subject to melancholy and was deeply religious. He honored his mother and supported her for many years, despite the poverty under which he labored for most of his life. A year after this letter was written his mother died, and to pay the expenses of her funeral Johnson wrote Rasselas in the evenings of one week. It is a philosophical tale expressing the melancholy opinion that "human life is everywhere a state in which much is to be endured and little to be enjoyed." He was a very great but not a happy man.

Sa. 13 Jan. '58

Honoured Madam,

The account which Miss gives me of your health pierces my heart. God comfort and preserve you and save you, for the sake of Jesus Christ.

I would have Miss read to you from time to time the Passion of our Saviour, and sometimes the sentences in the Communion Service, beginning 'Come unto me, all ye that travel and are heavy laden, and I will give you rest'.

I have just now read a physical book, which inclines me to think that a strong infusion of the bark would do you good. Do, dear mother, try it.

Pray, send me your blessing, and forgive all that I have done amiss to you. And whatever you would have done, and what debts you would have paid first, or anything else that you would direct, let Miss put it down; I shall endeavour to obey you.

I have got twelve guineas to send you, but unhappily am at a loss how to send it to-night. If I cannot send it to-night, it will come by the next post.

Pray, do not omit any thing mentioned in this letter: God bless you for ever and ever.

I am your dutiful son
Sam: Johnson

Report from Abroad

CHARLES ELIOT NORTON

Charles Eliot Norton (1827-1908; American author and editor.) Norton was born in Cambridge and died there; he graduated from Harvard in 1846 and was from 1873-1897 Professor of the History of Art at that institution. From 1864 to 1868 he edited The North American Review *with James Russell Lowell; in 1865, with E. L. Godkin and others, he founded* The Nation. *This letter was written on a visit to Europe, and demonstrates Norton's interest in things artistic and literary.*

Oxford, Star Inn, 2 July, 1857.

. . . DURING my short stay in London, I saw but few people. Clough I saw every day, and on Saturday I dined with him and his wife. We had a pleasant little party there at dinner, with nobody of much consequence, but after dinner two or three people came in, among whom were Mr. Coventry Patmore and "the angel in the house." I was glad to see them both. His face and figure answer well to his poems,—slight, delicate, refined, and sensitive. He has the look and bearing of a gentleman, and talks easily and pleasantly. He introduced me to his wife, and with her I had but five or six words of commonplace talk. She is not pretty, but she looks kindly and good, and I dare say is an angel to her husband. I did not see her wings, and perhaps she only wears them at home.

On Sunday I drove to Denmark Hill to see Ruskin, and had a most pleasant visit to him. His father and mother were kind as ever. Mrs. Ruskin showed me her flowers, and talked in her quaint, decided, moral way, so as to remind me more than once of our own dear Aunt Wigglesworth. She takes the greatest pride in "John," but she combats his opinions and lectures him publicly in a way which would be hard to bear, had he not a very sweet disposition and a most dutiful respect for her. She is a good old lady, who has lived in a narrow circle of strong interests all her life, has thought for herself in her narrow circle of thoughts, and does not know how large the world is, or how different other people are from herself. Ruskin is coming to Oxford this week, so that I hope to see him here, for he means to spend some days here preparing the lectures on "The Political Economy of Art" he is to deliver on the 10th and 13th of this month, at Manchester. He is indefatigable. Few men work so much and so satisfactorily, and if in working hastily he commits mistakes, the great mass of what he does is done well, and few men ever work with a sincerer desire to do good by it. He is unspoiled both by praise and by abuse, of both of which he has received enough to ruin a common man, but his heart is still fresh. It is pleasant to hear his friends speak of him,—the Brownings, Rossetti, Mrs. Gaskell: they all speak with warmth of his kindness, his generosity, and his faithfulness. I have known few men who seem to me to have such lovable qualities. One day, as we were travelling in Italy, Mrs. Gaskell and her daughters and I were talking about the books we would choose if we were shut up in prison or on a desolate island. At last we agreed to choose one book by a living author, and when it came to Mrs. Gaskell's turn to tell us what she had chosen, she said "Modern Painters," which was the best choice, by far, that was made.

Ruskin gave me a note of introduction to Dr. Acland* of Oxford, his special friend, and a man very distinguished in his profession. The note was so affectionate in its expression that I should like to have kept it—not for any vanity, but because it would have pleased you to see it. . . .

Last Saturday, in London, I went to see a semi-private exhibition of pictures by some of the Pre-Raphaelites,—Rossetti, Millais, Holman Hunt, Seddon, Hughes, Davis, and others. Many of the pictures are interesting, some of them beautiful, many of them full of thought, and as careful, exact studies from nature, some of them are hardly to be surpassed. Rossetti's are by far the best,

* Sir Henry Wentworth Acland, appointed in 1858 Regius Professor of Medicine at Oxford.

for in force and beauty of colour he stands above the others, and also in depth and delicacy of imaginative power. Among his pictures were those of "Mary, the Mother of Jesus" and the "Mary Magdalene" that we saw at Ruskin's last year, the picture of Dante's vision at the time of the death of Beatrice, and, as a companion-piece to this, the anniversary of the death of Beatrice, representing Dante becoming aware of the presence of the persons who had been watching him as he drew an angel upon certain tablets. The picture of Seddon of Mount Zion was admirable as a portrait of the scene. Altogether the collection represented artists faithfully studying from nature, and depicting her as they found her, not content with conventional modes of painting, sincere, and always bringing before you something worth attentive study, thought perhaps occasionally running into excess in very minuteness, and attempting impossibilities. When, as with Rossetti, these characteristics are combined with real poetic feeling and the exquisite sense of colour, they produce works which no others of our day can be compared with. The whole exhibition of seventy-two pictures is in striking contrast to the Paris exhibition of twenty-seven hundred. In that were cleverness, absence of feeling, and the study of what was effective and sensational, rather than what was true. I believe great good will come out of this school of the Pre-Raphaelites, and that its influence will do much for the art of the next generation.

"Gay, Impetuous, Ardent"

M A R G A R E T   F U L L E R   O S S O L I

Margaret Fuller Ossoli (1810-1850; American writer, critic, and editor.) She was born Sarah Margaret Fuller in Cambridgeport, Massachusetts, and grew up to become a member of the Boston Transcendentalist circle, preceding Emerson as editor of The Dial. *While serving as European correspondent for Horace Greeley's* New York Tribune, *she met and married the Marquis Giovanni Angelo Ossoli, a supporter of Mazzini in the Revolution of 1848 in Italy. She was returning with her husband and child to America when her ship was wrecked off Fire Island, and the entire family was drowned. The second letter here printed was thus her last. If the reader finds in it an extraordinary prescience, I will have to admit that I find it, too.*

The character of Zenobia in Hawthorne's Blithedale Romance *is supposed to have been taken from Margaret Fuller. She was a vigorous feminist and a well-known literary figure. During her lifetime she was not, however, as influential as she was controversial.*

FLORENCE, December 1, 1849.—I do not know what to write about the baby, he changes so much,—has so many characters. He is like me in that, for his father's character is simple and uniform, though not monotonous, any more than are the flowers of spring flowers of the valley. Angelino is now in the most perfect rosy health,—a very gay, impetuous, ardent, but sweet-tempered child. He seems to me to have nothing in common with his first babyhood, with its ecstatic smiles, its exquisite sensitiveness, and a distinction in the gesture and attitudes that struck everybody. His temperament is apparently changed by taking the milk of these robust women. He is now come to quite a knowing age,—fifteen months.

In the morning, as soon as dressed, he signs to come into our room; then draws our curtain with his little dimpled hand, kisses me rather violently, pats my face, laughs, crows, shows his teeth, blows like the bellows, stretches himself, and says *"bravo."* Then, having shown off all his accomplishments, he expects, as a reward, to be tied in his chair, and have his playthings. These engage him busily, but still he calls to us to sing and drum, to enliven the scene. Sometimes he summons me to kiss his hand, and laughs very much at this. Enchanting is that baby-laugh, all dimples and glitter,—so strangely arch and innocent! Then I wash and dress him. That is his great time. He makes it last as long as he can, insisting to dress and wash me the while, kicking, throwing the water about, and full of all manner of tricks, such as, I think, girls never dream of. Then comes his walk;—we have beautiful walks here for him, protected by fine trees, always warm in mid-winter. The bands are playing in the distance, and children of all ages are moving about, and sitting with their nurses. His walk and sleep give me about three hours in the middle of the day.

I feel so refreshed by his young life, and Ossoli diffuses such a power and sweetness over every day, that I cannot endure to think yet of our future. Too much have we suffered already, trying to command it. I do not feel force to make any effort yet. I suppose that very soon now I must do something, and hope I shall feel able when the time comes. My constitution seems making an effort to rally, by dint of much sleep. I had slept so little, for a year and a half, and, after the birth of the child, I had such anxiety and anguish when separated from him, that I was consumed as by nightly fever. The last two months at Rome would have destroyed almost any woman. Then, when I went to him, he was so ill, and I was constantly up with him at night, carrying him about. Now, for two months, we have been tranquil. We have resolved to enjoy being together as much as we can, in this brief interval,—perhaps all we shall ever know of peace. It is very sad we have no money, we could be so quietly happy a while. I rejoice in all Ossoli did; but the results, in this our earthly state, are disastrous, especially as my strength is now so impaired. This much I hope, in life or death, to be no more separated from Angelino.

Last winter, I made the most vehement efforts at least to re-deem the time, hoping thus good for the future. But, of at least two volumes written at that time, no line seems of any worth. I had suffered much constraint,—much that was uncongenial, harassing, even torturing, before; but this kind of pain found me unprepared;—the position of a mother separated from her only child is too frightfully unnatural.

Your loving child,
Margaret

FLORENCE, May 14, 1850.—I will believe, I shall be welcome with my treasures,—my husband and child. For me, I long so much to see you! Should anything hinder our meeting upon earth, think of your daughter, as one who always wished, at least, to do her duty, and who always cherished you, according as her mind opened to discover excellence.

Give dear love, too, to my brothers; and first to my eldest, faithful friend! Eugene; a sister's love to Ellen; love to my kind and good aunts, and to my dear cousin E.,—God bless them!

I hope we shall be able to pass some time together yet, in

this world. But, if God decrees otherwise,—here and HERE-AFTER,—my dearest mother,

Your loving child, Margaret.

"It Made Me Think of Somebody Else"

JOHN RUSKIN

John Ruskin (1819-1900; English author and critic.) Almost wholly self-educated, Ruskin spent his early years alternately studying drawing and music, and accompanying his parents on their extensive travels throughout Europe. His Modern Painters *(1843-60) received lavish praise and established his reputation as England's foremost art critic and historian, an eminence which he held for almost sixty years; it also made the reputation of the painter E.M.W. Turner. In his later years Ruskin took an increasing interest in social and economic questions, while at the same time attempting to improve the taste of his times. He was a supporter of the Pre-Raphaelite movement in art and was strongly opposed to the materialistic tendencies of his age. He was also a distinguished literary critic, and his phrase "the pathetic fallacy," invented to designate the illusion that external objects seem actuated by human feelings, has taken its place in the language of criticism. Among his books are* The Seven Lamps of Architecture *(1849),* Stones of Venice *(1851-53) and* Sesame and Lilies *(1863).*

When these letters were written, Ruskin's mother was eighty-six years old, almost blind, and unable to get along without the assistance of a niece, Joanna, who served as companion and nurse. You can almost visualize her nodding her head in calm acceptance of the honors heaped on her son; she had schooled him in drawing and daily reading of the Bible herself, and gave him regular lessons in music and composition when he was a tot. Then each evening Ruskin's father read to him from Pope, Shakespeare, and Scott. Sad to say, neither of his parents ever allowed him to own or play with a toy.

Cambridge, 23rd May, 1867.

My Dearest Mother,—All went well to-day—and pleasingly, if anybody had been there to please. But it is a great deal, yet, to have one's honour thought of, by Mother—and Mistress—and by a loving little cousin like Joan. Else, what good would there be in it? The form of admission is—first that you put on a scarlet gown, furred with white: then the Latin orator takes you by the hand (right hand by right hand, which you reach across to him), and leads you up the middle of the Senate House, to the front of the Vice-Chancellor's seat. There, putting you to stand by yourself before the Vice-Chancellor, he himself stands aside, turns to the spectators, and delivers a Latin laudatory speech (recommendatory of you for the honour of degree), some ten minutes or fifteen minutes long;　in my case, there being nothing particular to rehearse—except that I had written books "exquisite in language and faultlessly pure in contention with evil principles," with much more to a similar effect, which, having been all said in Latin, I wished that the young ladies present could better understand that learned language than I fear even Cambridge young ladies may be expected to do (N.B.—One a very sweet, though shortcoming, likeness of Rosie, with her *very* smile, so that it made me start). The orator dwelt more on the *Crown of Wild Olive* than on any other of my books, which pleased me, as it was the last.

The Oration finished, he takes your hand again and gives it to the Vice-Chancellor (but it made me think of Somebody else—whom it much more belongs to). The Vice-Chancellor stands up, and after a little bit more of Latin which I didn't understand, because I was looking him full in the face (having kept my eyes on the ground through the Oration, I thought it proper to show that I *could* look straight) and I was wondering if he would think it impudent, instead of minding what he was saying. But presently came "I admit thee doctor of this University —in the name of the Father, and the Son, and the Holy Ghost."

Which I heard, not inattentively, and retired backwards about six steps, and then turned and went down to join the rest of the Masters at the lower part of the Senate House. (The little bit of backing was said by one of the young ladies *here*, to have been very gracefully done.) One can hardly get any directions from anybody, and so I had to do what seemed to me fittest, out of my head.

After that, I had a walk of a mile and a half in the country, and thought over many things. I am to have a quite quiet evening here, with a little music and mineralogy, so I hope to be fresh for my lecture to-morrow. It is rather bright—but terribly cold. I have a very comfortable room, however, and hope that nothing is now likely to interfere with my success.

I will telegraph after lecture to-morrow, and then write to Joanna. Dear love to her. . . .

Ever, my dearest mother, your most affectionate son,

J. RUSKIN, LL.D.

Keswick, 16th August, 1867.

THE LETTER I have sent to Joanna to-day will seem a strange answer to your hope "that I have always some one with me on my mountain rambles"—but that would be quite impossible. If I have a definite point to reach, and common work to do at it —I take people—anybody—with me; but all my best *mental* work is necessarily done alone; whenever I wanted to think, in Savoy, I used to leave Couttet at home. Constantly I have been alone on the Glacier des Bois—and far among the loneliest aiguille recesses. I found the path up the Brezon above Bonneville in a lonely walk one Sunday; I saw the grandest view of the Alps of Savoy I ever gained, on the 2nd of January 1862, alone among the snow wreaths on the summit of the Salève. You need not fear for me on "Langdale Pikes" after that; humanly speaking, I have never the least fear on these lonely walks—I always think them the safest—for as I never do anything foolhardy, nor without careful examination of what I am about, I have always, even in my naughtiest times, felt that I should be taken care of, and that— though if I was to suffer any accident, it might come, of course, at any time—yet it was *more likely* to come when I had people with me, than when I was alone.

And, in mere paltry and arithmetical calculation of danger, I assure you there is more, nowadays, in a walk in and out of London—from possible explosion of all sorts of diabolical machines and compositions, with which its shops and back streets are filled—than in twenty climbings of the craggiest peaks in Cumberland.

I have, however, been very shy of the *bogs*, which are a new acquaintance to me, and of which I had heard awful stories—

usually I have gone a good way round, to avoid them. But that hot day, whether I would or no, I couldn't get from one pike of Langdale to the other without crossing one. I examined it carefully—and I am sure all the bog-stories about these *mountain* bogs are nonsense: it was as sound brown earth under the squashy grass as anybody need wish to walk on—though, of course, in a dark night, one might have tumbled into pools, as one might on Clapham Common into a horsepond.

TWO

Letters from Churchmen and Scientists

I PUT THEM together for several good reasons. A churchman is an interpreter between God and man; a scientist is an interpreter between the Universe and man. (God is not only the Universe—the Universe is *one* of the things He is.) Because both churchmen and scientists are such interpreters, we accord them vast respect; we fear them, too, and sometimes we make fun of them. This is appropriate, I think. For one thing, they do not really care; for another, when they fail us we should let them know about it. Finally, both scientists and churchmen are concerned with miracles. We used to think that churchmen *made* miracles. Now we think that scientists do. And we're probably wrong both times.

Californians will love Luther Burbank's letter; Belgophiles will, perhaps, object to Faraday's happiness at finding that he is to leave the country and come home; Brazilians will be delighted by Agassiz's excitement at the prospect of visiting their beautiful country. Channing was not going anywhere; in any case, his "highest hopes of happiness" lay "beyond the grave." Oliver Wendell Holmes, who was, of course, a doctor—that is why he is here—writes a charming and sensible letter to his mother. Reading it, I'm sure he was a good doctor.

Huxley's first letter is a handsome catalogue of careful observation of flora and fauna; his second describes in much the same terms the girl he is going to marry. His letters are interesting but

35

cold, and I suspect that he was, too. Newman's letter is passionate, although it is also descriptive; the subject under observation is himself, written upon his return to a scene of his childhood. Read it, for it is a great letter. So is John Wesley's, the best of this group. It is about joy. He writes his mother that he sees no wrong in cheerfulness. Indeed, he believes in it, but he is respectful of his mother's wisdom in this matter:

> I hope when you are at leisure you will give me your thoughts on that subject, and set me right if I am mistaken.

I hope she told him that he was not. If there is any difference between churchmen and scientists it lies in this area. Man should fear God, but God can make man happy. The Universe can not.

A Student All His Life Long

JEAN LOUIS RODOLPHE AGASSIZ

Jean Louis Rodolphe Agassiz (1807-1873; Swiss-American naturalist.) Agassiz did not come to the United States until 1846, when he presented a series of lectures at the Lowell Institute in Boston; but he remained here for the rest of his life, and is closely associated with American science in the nineteenth century. "He came in a spirit of adventure and curiosity; he stayed because he loved a land where he could think and act as he pleased; a land where nature is rich but tools and workmen are few, and tradition none." By his establishment of the Museum of Comparative Zoology at Harvard and the Anderson School of Natural History at Buzzards Bay, Massachusetts, he set the pattern for all future marine and natural history museums in his adopted country. He published over 450 books and papers on various subjects; he also found time to help his second wife, Elizabeth Cabot Cary Agassiz, organize the Agassiz School for Girls, predecessor of Radcliffe College.

Before everything, however, he was a great teacher. The two letters printed here reveal how this could be true; so also do these words, written at his death by one of his students, Theodore Lyman: "We buried him from the chapel that stands among the college elms. The students laid a wreath of laurel on his bier and their manly voices sang a requiem. For he had been a student all his life long, and when he died he was younger than any of them."

Cambridge, March 22, 1865.

DEAR MOTHER,—You will shed tears of joy when you read this, but such tears are harmless. Listen, then, to what has happened. A few weeks ago I was thinking how I should employ my summer. I foresaw that in going to Nahant I should not find the rest I need after all the fatigue of the two last years, or, at least, not enough of change and relaxation. I felt that I must have new scenes to give me new life. But where to go and what to do?

Perhaps I wrote you last year of the many marks of kindness I have received from the Emperor of Brazil, and you remember that at the time of my début as an author, my attention was turned to the natural history of that country. Lately, also, in a course of lectures at the Lowell Institute, I have been led to compare the Alps, where I have passed so many happy years, with the Andes, which I have never seen. In short, the idea came to me gradually, that I might spend the summer at Rio de Janeiro, and that, with the present facilities for travel, the journey would not be too fatiguing for my wife. . . . Upon this, then, I had decided, when most unexpectedly, and as the consummation of all my wishes, my pleasure trip was transformed into an important scientific expedition for the benefit of the Museum, by the intervention of one of my friends, Mr. Nathaniel Thayer. By chance I met him a week ago in Boston. He laughed at me a little about my roving disposition, and then asked me what plans I had formed for the Museum, in connection with my journey. I answered that, thinking especially of my health, I had provided only for the needs of myself and my wife during an absence of six or eight months. Then ensued the following conversation.

"But, Agassiz, that is hardly like you; you have never been away from Cambridge without thinking of your Museum."

"True enough; but I am tired,—I need rest. I am going to loaf a little in Brazil."

"When you have had a fortnight of that kind of thing you will be as ready for work as ever, and you will be sorry that you have not made some preparation to utilize the occasion and the localities in the interest of the Museum."

"Yes, I have some such misgiving; but I have no means for anything beyond my personal expenses, and it is no time to ask sacrifices from any one in behalf of science. The country claims all our resources."

"But suppose some one offered you a scientific assistant, all expenses paid, what would you say?"

"Of that I had never thought."

"How many assistants could you employ?"

"Half a dozen."

"And what would be the expense of each one?"

"I suppose about twenty-five hundred dollars; at least, that is what I have counted upon for myself."

After a moment's reflection he resumed:—

"If it suits you then, Agassiz, and interferes in no way with the plans for your health, choose your assistants among the employees of your Museum or elsewhere, and I will be responsible for all the scientific expenses of the expedition." . . .

My preparations are made. I leave probably next week, from New York, with a staff of assistants more numerous, and, I think, as well chosen, as those of any previous undertaking of the kind.*

. . . All those who know me seem to have combined to heighten the attraction of the journey, and facilitate it in every respect. The Pacific Mail Steamship Company has invited me to take passage with my whole party on their fine steamer, the Colorado. They will take us, free of all expense, as far as Rio de Janeiro,— an economy of fifteen thousand francs at the start. Yesterday evening I received a letter from the Secretary of the Navy, at Washington, desiring the officers of all vessels of war stationed along the coasts I am to visit, to give me aid and support in everything concerning my expedition. The letter was written in the kindest terms, and gratified me the more because it was quite unsolicited. I am really touched by the marks of sympathy I receive, not only from near friends, but even from strangers. . . . I seem like the spoiled child of the country, and I hope God will give me strength to repay in devotion to her institutions and to her scientific and intellectual development, all that her citizens have done for me.

I am forgetting that you will be anxious to know what special work I propose to do in the interest of science in Brazil. First, I

---

* Beside the six assistants provided for by Mr. Thayer, there were a number of young volunteer aids who did excellent work on the expedition. William James, the famed philosopher and psychologist, was one of these young men, but he found his duties on the trip annoying, and he became ill while in Brazil.

hope to make large collections of all such objects as properly belong in a Museum of Natural History, and to this end I have chosen from among the employees of our Museum one representative from each department. My only regret is that I must leave Alex. in Cambridge to take care of the Museum itself. He will have an immense amount of work to do, for I leave him only six out of our usual staff of assistants. In the second place, I intend to make a special study of the habits, metamorphoses, anatomy, etc., of the Amazonian fishes. Finally, I dream sometimes of an ascension of the Andes, if I do not find myself too old and too heavy for climbing. I should like to see if there were not also large glaciers in this chain of mountains, at the period when the glaciers of the Alps extended to the Jura. . . . But this latter part of my plan is quite uncertain, and must depend in great degree upon our success on the Amazons. Accompanied as I am with a number of *aides naturalistes,* we ought to be able among us to bring together large collections, and even to add duplicates, which I can then, on my return, distribute to the European Museums, in exchange for valuable specimens.

We leave next week, and I hope to write you from Rio a letter which will reach you about the date of my birthday. A steamer leaves Brazil once a month for England. If my arrival coincides with her departure you shall not be disappointed in this. With all my heart,

Your LOUIS.

At Sea, July 7, 1866.

Dear Mother,—When you receive this letter we shall be, I hope, at Nahant, where our children and grandchildren are waiting for us. Tomorrow we shall stop at Pernambuco, where I shall mail my letter to you by a French steamer.

I leave Brazil with great regret. I have passed nearly sixteen months in the uninterrupted enjoyment of this incomparable tropical nature, and I have learned many things which have enlarged my range of thought, both concerning organized beings and concerning the structure of the earth. I have found traces of glaciers under this burning sky; a proof that our earth has undergone changes of temperature more considerable than even our most advanced glacialists have dared to suggest. Imagine, if you can, floating ice under the equator, such as now exists on the coasts of Greenland, and you will probably have an approximate idea of the aspect of the Atlantic Ocean at that epoch.

It is, however, in the basin of the Amazons especially, that my researches have been crowned with an unexpected success. Spix and Martius, for whose journey I wrote, as you doubtless remember, my first work on fishes, brought back from there some fifty species, and the sum total known now, taking the results of all the travelers who have followed up the inquiry, does not amount to two hundred. I had hoped, in making fishes the special object of my researches, to add perhaps a hundred more. You will understand my surprise when I rapidly obtained five or six hundred, and finally, on leaving Parà, brought away nearly two thousands,—that is to say, ten times more than were known when I began my journey. A great part of this success is due to the unusual facilities granted me by the Brazilian government. . . . To the Emperor of Brazil I owe the warmest gratitude. His kindness to me has been beyond all bounds. . . . He even made for me, while he was with the army last summer, a collection of fishes from the province of Rio Grande du Sud. This collection would do honor to a professional naturalist. . . .

Good-by, dear mother.

With all my heart,
Your LOUIS.

"I Almost Have to Cry for Joy . . ."

LUTHER BURBANK

Luther Burbank (1849-1926; American naturalist and plant-breeder.) He was almost completely self-educated; he gained his early knowledge of the science and art of hybridization from his own garden and from books borrowed from the public library. I do not know of any better argument in favor of public libraries.

The Burbank potato, which he successfully grafted in 1873, was the first of the 618 new varieties of flowers, fruits, grasses, vegetables, and shrubs that he developed. Burbank was born in the East, but in 1875 he took up residence in Santa Rosa, Cali-

fornia, where he lived and worked on his experimental farm until his death. The two letters that follow express his immediate and lasting infatuation with that "chosen spot of all this earth."

[Conclusion of a letter written October 31, 1875]

Santa Rosa, Cal.

. . . I FIRMLY believe from what I have seen that it is the *chosen spot of all this earth* as far as *Nature* is concerned, and the people are far better than the average Californians in other places. The climate is perfect—all must like it. The air is so sweet that it is a pleasure to drink it in. The sunshine is pure and soft; the mountains which gird the valley are lovely. The valley is covered with majestic oaks placed as no human hand could arrange them for beauty. I cannot describe it! I almost have to cry for joy when I look upon the lovely valley from the hillsides. The gardens are filled with tropical plants, palms, figs, oranges, vines, etc.

Great *rose trees* climb over the houses, loaded with every color of blossoms. English ivy fills large trees and flowers are everywhere even now, which is the driest of the dry season. (By the way, it has just begun to rain.) Do you suppose I am not pleased to see fuchsias in the ground in front yards twelve feet high, the trunk ten inches in circumference, and loaded with various colors of blossoms?

Mallows, which there is a little herb, here has a trunk six inches in diameter, eight feet high, as large as a quince bush; chrysanthemums with bushels of great blossoms, rose trees thirty feet high, of all kinds and colors; veronica *trees,* geranium *trees,* the birds singing and everything like a beautiful spring day all the time. I can see them all. The sweet gum tree of Australia grows here to be *seventy-five feet* high in five years. It is a beautiful tree. Honeysuckles, snowberries, etc., grow wild on the mountains. There are so many plants more beautiful that they are neglected.

A *family* can live here, I am quite sure, for about one-half what they can there and far more comfortably. Meat costs but little, flour is better and cheaper, fruit is nothing, almost, very little fire is needed, and such warm expensive houses are not necessary.

I have written eight big pages and I think I have given you as fair an idea of the place as I can unless I write a book

Everything is changing all the time here. Have given you a truthful description of my experience so far.

Love to all,
LUTHER.

P.S.—A fog is hardly ever seen here—the wind never blows hard. I wish you could see California fruit. I bought a pear at San Francisco, when I thought I was *hungry,* for five cents. It was so large that I could only eat two-thirds of it. I threw the rest away. Grapes are so abundant that all are allowed to help themselves to the nicest kinds at the vineyards. There is no skin to them and very small seeds; the pulp is the whole grape. If you try to squeeze one out it will split like a plum. They are very sweet and nice and are so plentiful that they are often used as hog feed.   LUTHER.

Sunday Afternoon.

IT IS RAINING hard. I have nothing special to do, so I write some more and run the risk of having you throw the whole letter away rather than read so much, but you said nobody ever wrote when they got out here, so I will show you that it is not so in every case. The rains come down here very steadily, quietly but fast, with no wind. I am told that is the case always. There is no such disgusting *blue feeling* when it rains, as there is East. All appear to feel as contented and happy as can be. There is a rosebush in town the trunk of which is *twenty-four inches* in circumference, *twenty-seven feet* high, covers nearly a whole house and at some times has several thousand blossoms open at one time.

I send you one of the Santa Rosa papers, which, with my letter, will keep you in reading a week or so. I mean to get a piece of land (hire or buy) and plant some, then I can do other work just the same. There is a petrified forest near here. Mean to see it before I go to work.

There is one thing about the climate which is very peculiar, which is this: anyone can study or write or think with a connected clearness which is delightful. Mental effort is no effort at all. I should rather write a week here than five minutes there. Everybody is agreed to that.

I came across a directory of this county just now. I take a few ideas from it: The cause of the great growth and prosperity of this place *just now* is the new railroad, which has given it a start.

It is the county seat and is called the prettiest town in the state. Is noted for its polite and obliging people and beautiful gardens and lovely surroundings. It is situated in a marvelously fertile valley containing a hundred square *miles.* The educational advantages are ahead of any California city of its size. (The above is from the directory.) I saw a ten-acre lot of squashes yesterday. The ground seemed almost *covered* with them, nearly all of which were as large, yes, larger than *any that I ever saw before.* They are for cattle feed.

Alfred is a little blue. He is out of work, while all the rest are busy. He just bought twenty dollars worth of tools. He runs a little too much on cheek perhaps, but is liked very much, I guess. I want you should all write. Am in a hurry to hear how Emma is. Suppose I shall hear about Wednesday. Good-bye.

LUTHER.

"Mother of My Soul . . ."

ST. CATHERINE OF SIENA

St. Catherine of Siena (1347-1380; Roman Catholic religious.) She was the youngest of a family of twenty-five children; an "ordinary" child, at the age of six she had a vision of Our Lord. She became a Dominican tertiary at eighteen, and for three years spoke only to her confessor. Thirteen years later her sanctity was so renowned that she was called upon to mediate a peace between the Florentines and Pope Urban VI. The year before that, in 1377, she journeyed to Avignon, where for seventy years the Pope and the Papal State had resided under the control of the King of France, and succeeded in helping the Pope return to Rome, thus ending the "Babylonian Captivity." On her way home from France she stopped to succor some of her followers who had fallen ill in Genoa, and on the receipt of an anxious letter from her mother, wrote the letter below. St. Catherine was sanctified in 1461.

DEAREST MOTHER IN CHRIST SWEET JESUS. Your unworthy, miserable daughter Catherine strengthens and comforts you in the precious blood of the Son of God. Ardently have I desired to see you as my mother, not only of my body, but also of my soul, for I thought, that when you had attained to loving the soul more than the body, all inordinate affection would die in you, for then you would not suffer so much in not having me about you, but rather would it console you, in being to the glory of God . . .

It is true, dearest Mother, that if you loved the soul more than the body, you would be comforted and not comfortless. I will, that you learn of our dear Mother Mary, who to the glory of God and our salvation gave us her Son and surrendered Him to the death on the Cross. And when He had ascended into heaven she remained behind with the disciples. But she gave up that comfort also of being with the disciples and let them go forth into the world to the praise and glory of her Son. I will, dearest Mother, that you shall learn of her. You know that I must fulfil the will of God, and I know that you will that I should so live. It was the will of God that I departed, and my departure was not without His secret counsel [*mistero*], and it has not been without fruit.

It was His will that I remained here; it was not the will of men; whosoever says so does not speak truth . . . And as a good and dear mother you must be content and not comfortless . . . Remember that when your sons went forth into the world for the sake of worldly gain you did not gainsay them, and now it is so hard for you, now when it is for the sake of eternal life, so that you even speak of dying if I do not write to you soon. All that comes of your loving that part of myself which I have from you, more than that which I have from God—you love the flesh with which you have clothed me. Lift up your heart a little and your mind to that most holy Cross which assuages all pain . . . and do not believe yourself forsaken, either by God or by me . . . We shall come soon, with the help of God, as soon as Neri, who has been ill, is well enough to travel. Master Giovanni and Brother Bartolommeo have also been ill . . . I say no more . . . Remain in the holy, sweet love of God. Sweet Jesus, Jesus love.

"A Mother Trembling With Anxiety . . ."

WILLIAM ELLERY CHANNING

William Ellery Channing (1780-1842; American Unitarian clergyman.) Channing was born and bred in New England, but the first job he obtained after graduating from Harvard in 1798 had nothing to do with the church or with Boston. He accepted an invitation to become a tutor in the private home of a distinguished Virginia family, and the letter below is the first written to his mother after his arrival in the South. Four years later he returned to Boston and was installed as minister of the Federal Street Church, a post he held until his death. He was at first a Liberal Congregationalist, but it was the Berry Street Conference of Ministers that put him in the forefront of the "Unitarian Controversy," and that resulted in the formation of the American Unitarian Association (1819), which he helped found. His most famous sermon, "The Moral Argument Against Calvinism," was both an attack on New England orthodoxy and a statement of a more liberal Christian doctrine. Channing was one of the most prominent leaders in the anti-slavery campaigns of the years before the Civil War.

November, 1798.

My dear Mother,—A favourable opportunity has just offered, by which I can write to all my friends without subjecting them to the expense of postage. I begin with you. To you I owe the highest obligations. The anxiety and tenderness which you discovered at my departure from Newport will never be forgotten. I wish that my friends were not so deeply interested in my welfare. It makes both them and me unhappy. Every misfortune I experience is aggravated by thinking on the pain which it will occasion them. I often wish that I had been thrown loose on the wide ocean of life, without one eye to watch with friendly care my various successes, or shed a tear over my follies and miseries. When I was dashing over the billows, on my passage, I felt no fear for myself; but I was distressed when I remembered that I had left a mother behind me who was trembling with anxiety lest her son might be buried in the merciless waves. I understand from Francis's letter, that you had many high winds after I left you; and did not every gale come to me loaded with the sighs of a mother? I mention this because I wish you not to make yourself unhappy by your concern for me. I know that I am far from home, where nothing but your good wishes can reach me. I am far from your social fireside. I am neither a sharer in your joys, nor the object of your fond attentions. But still the same sun shines upon us, the same providence is extended to both of us, and the same God who protects and blesses you, will watch over me, and mete me out a portion of happiness. Our distance from each other cannot remove either of us from our common Parent. It is this truth which consoles me in my absence from home, and I wish that it might banish from your bosom those corroding fears for my safety, which, added to the load of your domestic cares, must make life wearisome to you. I feel every day more and more attached to my new abode. I am treated with every attention which hospitality can bestow. My duties are neither numerous nor irksome, and I can find time enough for study. I am resolved to prosecute divinity. My highest hopes of happiness are beyond the grave, and I cannot do more good to mankind than by teaching them also to lay up treasures where neither moth nor rust can corrupt them. My dear mother, though I have so lately left you, I begin already to anticipate the moment when I shall see you again. Time has swifter wings than the eagle. Months and years will fly away,—and with what rapture shall I press you all to my bosom! Hope is the anchor of the soul. I lean upon it perpetually. I paint more blissful scenes in prospect than I have ever yet experienced; and should they prove as baseless as the fabric of a vision, I can still boast of the happiness which they give in anticipation. I dare not ask, but I should like to receive, a few lines from you.

Your affectionate son.

"The First and Greatest Sweetness . . ."

MICHAEL FARADAY

Michael Faraday (1791-1867; English chemist and physicist.) A good journeyman bookbinder was lost to the English publishing world when Michael Faraday happened to hear a lecture by Sir Humphrey Davy on the wonders of chemistry. He immediately began to study the subject, and shortly after became Davy's assistant at the Royal Institution. Within a year the younger man had so impressed the older that Faraday was asked to join Sir Humphrey on a leisurely tour of the Continent.

In 1825 Faraday was made director of the laboratory, and from 1833 he was professor of chemistry at the Royal Institution. He discovered benzene, and two chlorides of carbon; he lique-

fied several gases; he produced new kinds of optical glass; but
his most significant achievement was his demonstration, in 1831,
of electromagnetic induction. In an experiment that is now
familiar to every high school student, he passed magnets through
a coil of wire, then passed a current through another coil (which
had been insulated from and spirally arranged to still another
coil) and thereby was able to establish the momentary existence
of an induced current of electricity. From this simple mechanism
stems the modern dynamo.

Rome: April 14, 1814.

MY DEAR MOTHER,—It is with singular pleasure I commence
writing after so long a silence, and the pleasure is greatly increased by the almost certainty that you will get my letter. We
are at present in a land of friends, and where every means is
used to render the communication with England open and un-
obstructed. Nevertheless, this letter will not come by the ordinary
route, but by a high favour Sir H. Davy will put it with his own,
and it will be conveyed by a particular person.

I trust that you are well in health and spirits, and that all things
have gone right since I left you. . . . Mr. Riebau and fifty other
friends would be inquired after could I but have an answer. You
must consider this letter as a kind of general one, addressed to
that knot of friends who are twined round my heart; and I trust
that you will let them all know that, though distant, I do not
forget them, and that it is not from want of regard that I do not
write to each singly, but from want of convenience and propriety;
indeed, it appears to me that there is more danger of my being
forgot than of my forgetting. The first and last thing in my mind
is England, home, and friends. It is the point to which my
thoughts still ultimately tend, and the goal to which, looking over
intermediate things, my eyes are still directed. But, on the contrary, in London you are all together, your circle being little or
nothing diminished by my absence; the small void which was
formed on my departure would soon be worn out, and, pleased
and happy with one another, you will seldom think of me. Such
are sometimes my thoughts, but such do not rest with me; an
innate feeling tells me that I shall not be forgot, and that I still
possess the hearts and love of my mother, my brother, my sisters,
and my friends. When Sir H. Davy first had the goodness to ask

me whether I would go with him, I mentally said, "No; I have a mother, I have relations here." And I almost wished that I had been insulated and alone in London; but now I am glad that I have left some behind me on whom I can think, and whose actions and occupations I can picture in my mind. Whenever a vacant hour occurs, I employ it by thinking on those at home. Whenever present circumstances are disagreeable, I amuse myself by thinking on those at home. In short, when sick, when cold, when tired, the thoughts of those at home are a warm and refreshing balm to my heart. Let those who think such thoughts useless, vain, and paltry, think so still; I envy them not their more refined and more estranged feelings: let them look about the world unencumbered by such ties and heart-strings, and let them laugh at those who, guided more by nature, cherish such feelings. For me, I still will cherish them, in opposition to the dictates of modern refinement, as the first and greatest sweetness in the life of man.

I have said nothing as yet to you, dear mother, about our past journey, which has been as pleasant and agreeable (a few things excepted, in reality nothing) as it was possible to be. Sir H. Davy's high name at Paris gave us free admission into all parts of the French dominions, and our passports were granted with the utmost readiness. We first went to Paris, and stopped there two months; afterwards we passed, in a southerly direction, through France to Montpellier, on the borders of the Mediterranean. From thence we went to Nice, stopping a day or two at Aix on our way; and from Nice we crossed the Alps to Turin, in Piedmont. From Turin we proceeded to Genoa, which place we left afterwards in an open boat, and proceeded by sea towards Lerici. This place we reached after a very disagreeable passage, and not without apprehensions of being overset by the way. As there was nothing there very enticing, we continued our route to Florence; and, after a stay of three weeks or a month, left that fine city, and in four days arrived here at Rome. Being now in the midst of things curious and interesting, something arises every day which calls for attention and observations. The relics of ancient Roman magnificence, the grandeur of the churches, and their richness also—the difference of habits and customs, each in turn engages the mind and keeps it continually employed. Florence, too, was not destitute of its attractions for me, and in the Academy del Cimento and the museum attached to it is contained an inexhaustible fund of entertainment and improvement;

indeed, during the whole journey, new and instructive things have been continually presented to me. Tell B. I have crossed the Alps and the Apennines; I have been at the Jardin des Plantes; at the museum arranged by Buffon; at the Louvre, among the *chefs-d'oeuvre* of sculpture and the masterpieces of painting; at the Luxembourg palace, amongst Rubens' works; that I have seen a GLOWWORM!!! water-spouts, torpedo, the museum at the Academy del Cimento, as well as St. Peter's, and some of the antiquities here, and a vast variety of things far too numerous to enumerate.

At present I am in very good health, and so far is travelling from disagreeing with me that I am become somewhat heavier and thicker than when I left England. I should have written to you long ago, but I had no hopes of getting a letter conveyed; but at present I conclude that you will surely have this. I have a thousand things more to say, but do not know how to select one from the other, so shall defer them all to a more convenient opportunity. When you write into the country, remember me, if you please, to all friends there, and more particularly to those to whom I have written. At present, I bid farewell for a time to all friends, wishing them much happiness.

I am, dear Mother, with earnest wishes for your health and welfare, your dutiful son,

M. FARADAY.

P.S. There is no certain road open at present by which you can write to me, so that, much as I wish it, it must be deferred a little longer. We have heard this morning that Paris was taken by the Allied troops on March 31, and, as things are, we may soon hope for peace, but at present all things are uncertain. Englishmen are here respected almost to adoration, and I proudly own myself as belonging to that nation which holds so high a place in the scale of European Powers.

Adieu, dear Mother, at present. Your dutiful son,

M. FARADAY.

Bruxelles: April 16, 1815.

My very dear Mother,—It is with no small pleasure I write you my last letter from a foreign country, and I hope it will be with as much pleasure you will hear I am within three days of England. Nay more, before you read this letter I hope to tread on British ground, but I will not make too sure, lest I should be disappointed; and the sudden change and apparently termination of our travels is sufficient to remind me that it may change again. But, however, that is not at all probable, and I trust will not happen.

I am not acquainted with the reason of our sudden return; it is, however, sufficient for me that it has taken place. We left Naples very hastily, perhaps because of the motion of the Neapolitan troops, and perhaps for private reasons. We came rapidly to Rome, we as rapidly left it. We ran up Italy, we crossed the Tyrol, we stepped over Germany, we entered Holland, and we are now at Brussels, and talk of leaving it tomorrow for Ostend; at Ostend we embark, and at Deal we land on a spot of earth which I will never leave again. You may be sure we shall not creep from Deal to London, and I am sure I shall not creep to 18 Weymouth Street; and then—but it is of no use. I have a thousand times endeavoured to fancy a meeting with you and my relations and friends, and I am sure I have as often failed: the reality must be a pleasure not to be imagined nor to be described. It is uncertain what day we shall get to London, and it is also uncertain where we shall put up at. I shall be thankful if you will make no inquiries after me anywhere, and especially in Portland Place, or of Mr. Brande. I do not wish to give occasion for any kind of comments whatever on me and mine. You may be sure that my first moments will be in your company. If you have opportunities, tell some of my dearest friends, but do not tell everybody—that is, do not trouble yourself to do it. I am of no consequence except to a few, and there are but a few that are of consequence to me, and there are some whom I should like to be the first to tell myself—Mr. Riebau for one. However, let A. know if you can.

I come home almost like the prodigal, for I shall want everything.

· · · · · ·

I cannot find in my heart to say much here to B. and R., because I want to say it myself, and I feel that I am too glad to write it. My thoughts wander from one to another, my pen runs on by fits and starts, and I should put all in confusion. I do not know what to say, and yet cannot put an end to my letter. I would fain be talking to you, but I must cease.

Adieu till I see you, dearest Mother; and believe me ever your affectionate and dutiful son,

M. FARADAY.

'Tis the shortest and (to me) the sweetest letter I ever wrote you.

"Please Read This Sentence Over Twice..."

OLIVER WENDELL HOLMES

Oliver Wendell Holmes (1809-1894; American essayist and physician.) He was not a medical dilettante. He was Professor of Anatomy at Dartmouth (1838-40), and Professor of Anatomy and Physiology at the Harvard Medical School from 1847-82; and in 1842 he published The Contagiousness of Puerperal Fever. *But fifteen years later, Holmes turned his hand to a more popular form of literary effort, contributing to the first issues of* The Atlantic Monthly *a series of light, witty causeries, published in 1858 as* The Autocrat of the Breakfast-Table. *In this volume appeared "The Chambered Nautilus," "Old Ironsides," and "The Deacon's Masterpiece, or The Wonderful One Horse Shay," poems as famous as any ever written in America, though perhaps not as good as some. Holmes wrote many other poems, three novels, and memoirs of Ralph Waldo Emerson and John Lothrop Motley.*

He was a Bostonian through and through, and he loved his city as only a true Bostonian of the nineteenth century could: "Boston State-House is the hub of the solar system," he wrote in The Autocrat. *"You couldn't pry that out of a Boston man if you had the tire of all creation straightened out for a crowbar." It was this tone of amused affection that endeared him to his readers. Looking back, we might be inclined to say nowadays that the greatest thing he left behind him was none of his literary or medical works, but his son, the great Supreme Court Justice, Oliver Wendell Holmes.*

The "Amelia" of this letter is Amelia Lee Jackson, a remarkable woman whom Holmes married in 1840. At the time the letter was written, Holmes was a few years away from leaving his career as a physician and medical professor for the world of literature. But it was just about this time, I think, that he made a remark which all of us who teach in college have borrowed at one time or another. "I have so much to do at Harvard," he said, "that I occupy a settee, not a chair."

Pittsfield, June 11, 1854.

My DEAR MOTHER,—I received Ann's letter a few days ago, and would answer it direct to her but for two reasons—first, that writing to you is the same thing; second, that Amelia is actually writing at this moment to Ann herself. Two letters, from husband and wife, would be too much for a person confined to her bed.— And first, I hope you will stay at Salem as long as Ann can keep you; that is, until you feel ready to come to Pittsfield, if, as is likely, you make up your mind to give us that delight. At any rate, I hope you will make a good long stay in Salem; it must be one of the curative means that can be most relied upon to keep the mind cheerful and bright. I would give more for your being with Ann than for all the salves and 'intments that were ever stirred up.— Please read this sentence over twice, and believe it. Healing is a living process, greatly under the influence of mental conditions. It has often been found that the same wound received in battle will do well in the soldiers that have beaten, that would prove fatal in those that have just been defeated.

We are going on as pleasantly as ever. I did not tell you that I had been at work with electricity as a part of my summer plan of instructive amusements. The old machine is mounted on its ancient footing, or rather, with new splendor, and gives sparks an inch long. I have been making various kinds of apparatus, and really reminded myself of my young days more than by anything I have done for a long time. I find that many of my old tastes return upon me whenever they get a chance; chemistry will have its turn by and by, perhaps mineralogy, and the rest of them. I learn something new, and often learn things I can make useful in instruction. But perhaps the pleasantest thing about it is that I can do so easily what I used to find so difficult,—realize my ideas with my hands with so much comfort and satisfaction.

But in the meantime the garden has been growing into beauty in the most magical way under the hands principally of great A and little a. I am fairly astonished at the way in which they work.

Would you believe it,—I was stopping to rest with a tolerably heavy wheelbarrow of gravel yesterday, when Amelia took hold of it and trundled it along as if she had been a Paddy.

Went to meet'n to-day—or rather to church—heard Mr. P———. Saw Mr. and Mrs. Newton, Judge Curtis, and others whom we have not met. Very glad to see the Newtons always—gentlemen and ladies—scarce articles in republican America. We always keep dark and lie low for the first week or two, before beginning to visit and be visited. When we begin that series of operations you shall hear of the result. Infinitely pleased and delighted with Ann's letter—don't let her tire herself—John must write. I enclose a kiss to be fairly divided.

Your aff. son & bro.

"I Don't Know Whether She Is Pretty . . ."

THOMAS HENRY HUXLEY

Thomas Henry Huxley (1825-1895; English biologist and educator.) The grandfather of Julian and Aldous Huxley was educated at Ealing School and Charing Cross Hospital, whence he entered the Royal Navy medical service; the letters below were written while he was assistant surgeon on H.M.S. Rattlesnake, *collecting biological specimens in the South Pacific. He became a lecturer at the Royal School of Mines in 1854, and taught there for thirty-one years; he was Hunterian professor in the Royal College of Surgeons (1863-69), and Fullerian professor in the Royal Institution (1863-67); and he was president of the Royal Society from 1881-85.*

Thomas Huxley was the foremost advocate in England of the Darwinian theory, though he never accepted it without qualifications. He thought "transmutation may take place without transition," thereby anticipating the findings of modern research, and he thought that in highly civilized societies the "struggle for existence" had come to an end and been replaced by the "struggle for enjoyment," an attractive theory. From 1863, when he published Man's Place in Nature—*a work purporting to show that there was no qualitative difference between the morphology of man and that of the animals—he was, with Darwin, the subject*

*of attacks from many quarters. He left his mark on English public
education when he served on the London School Board (1870-72),
insisting that, among other reasons, the Bible be read in schools
because it was "the most democratic book in the world." He was
a sufficiently great man to be amused rather than distressed at
the discovery that the heaviest brain that had ever been weighed
up to his time was that of a congenital idiot. The second heaviest,
by the way, was Goethe's.*

May 15, 1847

AFTER A LONG and somewhat rough passage from the Cape, we
made the highland of the Isle of France on the afternoon of the
3rd of this month, and passing round the northern extremity of
the island, were towed into Port Louis by the handsomest of tugs
about noon on the 4th. In my former letter I have spoken to you
of the beauty of the places we have visited, of the picturesque
ruggedness of Madeira, the fine luxuriance of Rio, and the rude
and simple grandeur of South Africa. Much of my admiration has
doubtless arisen from the novelty of these tropical or semi-tropical
scenes, and would be less vividly revived by a second visit. I have
become in a manner *blasé* with fine sights and something of a
critic. All this is to lead you to believe that I have really some
grounds for the raptures I am going into presently about Mauri-
tius. In truth it is a complete paradise, and if I had nothing better
to do, I should pick up some pretty French Eve (and there are
plenty) and turn Adam. *N.B.* There are *no* serpents in the island.
    This island is, you know, the scene of St. Pierre's beautiful
story of Paul and Virginia, over which I suppose most people have
sentimentalised at one time or another of their lives. Until we
reached here I did not know that the tale was like the lady's
improver—a fiction founded on fact, and that Paul and Virginia
were at one time flesh and blood, and that their veritable dust
was buried at Pamplemousses in a spot considered as one of the
lions of the place, and visited as classic ground. Now, though I
never was greatly given to the tender and sentimental, and have
not had any tendencies that way greatly increased by the elegan-
cies and courtesies of a midshipman's berth,—not to say that, as
far as I recollect, Mdlle. Virginia was a bit of a prude, and M.
Paul a pump,—yet were it but for old acquaintance sake, I
determined on making a pilgrimage. Pamplemousses is a small

village about seven miles from Port Louis, and the road to it is lined by rows of tamarind trees, of cocoanut trees, and sugar-canes. I started early in the morning in order to avoid the great heat of the middle of the day, and having breakfasted at Port Louis, made an early couple of hours' walk of it, meeting on my way numbers of the coloured population hastening to market in all the varieties of their curious Hindoo costume. After some trouble I found my way to the "Tombeaux" as they call them. They are situated in a garden at the back of a house now in the possession of one Mr. Geary, an English mechanist, who puts up half the steam engines for the sugar mills in the island. The garden is now an utter wilderness, but still very beautiful; round it runs a grassy path, and in the middle of the path on each side towards the further extremity of the garden is a funeral urn supported on a pedestal, and as dilapidated as the rest of the affair. These dilapidations, as usual, are the work of English visitors, relic-hunters, who are as shameless here as elsewhere. I was exceedingly pleased on the whole with my excursion, and when I returned I made a drawing of the place, which I will send some day or other.

Since this I have made, in company with our purser and a passenger, Mr. King, a regular pedestrian trip to see some very beautiful falls up the country.

["Nettie" is Henrietta Anne Heathorn, whom young Thomas Huxley met in Sydney, Australia, fell in love with, and married in 1855. Here he answers his mother's questions about the girl to whom he is engaged.]

Sydney, Feb. 1, 1849.

[After describing how he had just come back from a nine months' cruise]—First and foremost, my dear mother, I must thank you for your very kind letter of September 1848. I read the greater part of it to Nettie, who was as much pleased as I with your kindly wishes towards both of us. Now I suppose I must do my best to answer your questions. First, as to age, Nettie is about three months younger than myself—that is the difference in *our years*, but she is *in fact* as much younger than her years as I am older than mine. Next, as to complexion she is exceedingly fair, with the Saxon yellow hair and blue eyes. Then as to face, I really don't know whether she is pretty or not. I have never been able to decide the matter in my own mind. Sometimes I think she is, and sometimes I wonder how the idea ever came into my head. Whether or not, her personal appearance has nothing whatever to do with the hold she has upon my mind, for I have seen hundreds of prettier women. But I never met with so sweet a temper, so self-sacrificing and affectionate a disposition, or so pure and womanly a mind, and from the perfectly intimate footing on which I stand with her family I have plenty of opportunities of judging. As I tell her, the only great folly I am aware of her being guilty of was the leaving her happiness in the hands of a man like myself, struggling upwards and certain of nothing.

As to my future intentions I can say very little about them. With my present income, of course, marriage is rather a bad look out, but I do not think it would be at all fair towards N. herself to leave this country without giving her a wife's claim upon me. . . . It is very unlikely I shall ever remain in the colony. Nothing but a very favourable chance could induce me to do so.

Much must depend upon how things go in England. If my various papers meet with any success, I may perhaps be able to leave the service. At present, however, I have not heard a word of anything I have sent. Professor Forbes has, I believe, published some of MacGillivray's letters to him, but he has apparently forgotten to write to MacGillivray himself, or to me. So I shall certainly send him nothing more; especially as Mr. MacLeay (of this place, and a great man in the naturalist world) has offered to get anything of mine sent to the Zoological Society.

"Years Which Never Can Come Again ..."

JOHN HENRY NEWMAN

John Henry Newman (1801-1890; English Roman Catholic churchman and cardinal.) Cardinal Newman was educated at Oxford and was ordained a priest in the Anglican Church, but by the year this letter to his mother was written he was already the acknowledged leader of the Oxford Movement, a campaign to restore to the English church the doctrine of apostolic succession.

His Tracts for the Times *gave the Oxford Movement its strongest intellectual expression. Resigning from the Anglican Church, Newman was ordained a priest in the Roman Catholic Church in 1847, and he was soon the most influential Catholic in England. He was rector of Dublin Catholic University (1854-58), and there delivered lectures later collected and published as* The Idea of a University, *which maintained the duty of a university to be the training of the mind rather than the dissemination of useful knowledge. His* Apologia pro sua Vita, or, History of My Religious Opinions, *was written in 1864 in answer to animadversions cast by Kingsley upon Newman and the English Catholics. The book is not only a moving and effective exposition of the author's spiritual life, but it is also one of the classics of English prose style.*

In 1879 Pope Leo XIII created him Cardinal of St. George in Valebro and, by special dispensation, allowed him to live in England. Cardinal Newman was the author of other books and many poems, but the work which will perhaps outlast all others is the beautiful hymn, "Lead Kindly Light." It was written when he was thirty-one, the year before he wrote the following letter to his mother.

Alton: September 20, 1834.

I LEFT STEVENS this morning and got here about two o'clock. As I got near the place I many times wished I had not come. I found it so very trying. So many strong feelings, distinct from each other, were awakened. The very length of time since I was here was a serious thought, almost half my life: and I so different from what a boy, as I then was, could be: not indeed, in my having any strong stimulus of worldly hope then which I have not now—for, strange though it may seem, never, even as a boy, had I any vision of success, fortune, or worldly comfort, to bound my prospect of the future—but because, after fifteen years, I felt, after all, that I was hardly the same person as to all external relations, and as regards the particular tempering and colouring of my mind.

And then the number of painful events, and pleasant too, which have gone between my past and my present self. And, further, the particular season at which we lived here, when I was just entered at Oxford, so that this place is, as it were, the record, as it was the scene, of my undergraduate studies and opinions. The Oxford reminiscences of that time have been effaced by my constant residence there since, but here I am thrown back upon those years which never can come again.

There are many little incidents stored in my memory which now waken into life. Especially, I remember that first evening of my return from Oxford in 1818, after gaining the scholarship at Trinity, and my Father saying 'What a happy meeting this!' Often and often such sayings of his come into my mind, and almost overpower me; for I consider he did do very much for me at a painful sacrifice to himself, and was so generous and kind. . . .

All these various thoughts so troubled me as I came along, and the prospect opened clearer and clearer, that I felt quite sick at heart. There was something so mysterious, too, in seeing old sights, half recollecting them and doubting. It is like seeing the ghosts of friends. Perhaps it is the impression it makes upon one of God's *upholding* power which is so awful—but it seemed to me so very strange that everything was in its place, after so long a time. As we came near, and I saw Monk's Wood, the church and the hollow on the other side of the town, it was as fearful as if I was standing on the grave of some one I knew, and saw him gradually recover life, and rise again. Quite a lifetime seems to divide me from the time I was here. I wished myself away from the pain of it, and then the excitement caused a reaction, and I got quite insensible and callous, and then again got disgusted with myself and thought I had made a great fool of myself in coming here at all, and wondered what I should do with myself now I was here. Meanwhile the coach went on and I found myself at the Swan.

"Give Me Your Thoughts On That Subject"

JOHN WESLEY

John Wesley (1703-1791; English theologian, evangelist, and founder of Methodism.) John was the fifteenth child of Samuel Wesley, a well-known nonconformist clergyman. He went to Oxford, and was there the irregular leader of that group of young men (including his brother Charles, author of 6,500 hymns) who, being conspicuous for the regularity and earnestness of their religious life and study, came to be called, somewhat derisively, "methodists." He was ordained priest in the Anglican Church in

1728, and accompanied Governor Oglethorpe to Georgia as a missionary among the colonists and Indians (1835-38). Shortly after his return to England he embarked wholeheartedly on his life work, the foundation and establishment of the Methodist Church. He preached in the open fields and to improvised congregations, inveighing against High Church practices on the one hand, and against the Deistic faithlessness of the age on the other. He avoided most of the excessive doctrinaire piety of the Evangelicals, while remaining himself an exceptionally pious man. He was cheerful and also charitable, a combination rarer than one would like. In short, he was—if the simplicity of the phrase may be forgiven—one of the nicest men who ever lived in England.

Wesley was the author of many works of theology, twenty-three collections of hymns, and the editor of a number of books. His most famous work is probably his Journal, *a fascinating account (1735-90) of an extraordinary eighteenth century life.*

Oxon, May 28, 1725.

DEAR MOTHER,—My brother Charles, I remember, about a month or two since, was bemoaning himself, because my brother and I were to go into the country, and he was to be left behind. But now I hope he has no reason to complain, since he had the good fortune to go down in my stead. It was indeed very reasonable that he should, since he had never been at Wrott before, and I have; besides that, my father might probably think it would be an hindrance to my taking Orders, which he designed I should do on Trinity Sunday. But I believe that would have been no impediment to my journey, since I might have taken Bugden in Huntingdonshire, where Bishop Reynolds ordained, in my way; and by that means I might have saved the two guineas which I am told will be the charge of Letters Dimissory.

I was lately advised to read Thomas à Kempis over, which I had frequently seen, but never much looked into before. I think he must have been a person of great piety and devotion, but it is my misfortune to differ from him in some of his main points. I can't think that when God sent us into the world He had irreversibly decreed that we should be perpetually miserable in it. If it be so, the very endeavour after happiness in this life is a sin; as it is acting in direct contradiction to the very design of our creation. What are become of all the innocent comforts and pleasures of life, if it is the intent of our Creator that we should never taste them? If our taking up the cross implies our bidding adieu to all joy and satisfaction, how is it reconcilable with what Solomon so expressly affirms of religion—that her ways are ways of pleasantness and all her paths peace? A fair patrimony, indeed, which Adam has left his sons, if they are destined to be continually wretched! And though heaven is undoubtedly a sufficient recompense for all the afflictions we may or can suffer here, yet I am afraid that argument would make few converts to Christianity, if the yoke were not easy even in this life, and such an one as gives rest, at least as much as trouble.

Another of his tenets, which is indeed a natural consequence of this, is that all mirth is vain and useless, if not sinful. But why then, does the Psalmist so often exhort us to rejoice in the Lord and tell us that it becomes the just to be joyful? I think one could hardly desire a more express text than that in the 68th Psalm, 'Let the righteous rejoice and be glad in the Lord. Let them also be merry and joyful.' And he seems to carry the matter as much too far on the other side afterwards, where he asserts that nothing is an affliction to a good man, and that he ought to thank God even for sending him misery. This, in my opinion, is contrary to God's design in afflicting us; for though He chasteneth those whom He loveth, yet it is in order to humble them: and surely the method Job took in his adversity was very different from this, and yet in all that he sinned not.

I hope when you are at leisure you will give me your thoughts on that subject, and set me right if I am mistaken. Pray give my service to any that ask after me, and my love to my sisters, especially my sister Emly. I suppose my brothers are gone.—I am

Your dutiful Son.

THREE

Letters from Explorers and Travelers

A LL EXPLORERS ARE travelers, but not all travelers are explorers. So we use the words, but perhaps we use them wrongly. Perhaps we should reserve explorer for those who seek out geographical novelty, and let traveler, surely a more general word, stand for those who make safaris through the human heart—which is different, travelers find soon enough, in different places. The greatest travelers never left home—Defoe, Swift, Burton—but all the letter writers in this category did. Some of them went very far away, but all wrote home to mother.

Perhaps Amelia Earhart was more an adventurer (not an adventuress, which is a different thing altogether) than anything else. She loved danger, and lived with it. I shall not quote her letter here because it is so short—it is the shortest in the book, and with a line or two I would give it all away. Knowing something about her, though, I am moved by her letter; it typifies the attitude of explorers, travelers, and adventurers. They are all willing to take whatever risk is necessary.

The letters come from far-flung places. Gertrude Bell's is from Persia, when women didn't go there. T. E. Lawrence's second letter is from Athens, and is one of the greatest pieces of writing about that city I have ever read. Meriwether Lewis writes from a point 1,609 miles above the entrance of the Missouri. It is a trait of explorers rather than travelers, this exactness. Harriet Martineau's is from England—she has not yet become the traveler she will be. She is, however, a professional, and perhaps that is why her letter is the least exciting of the lot. Peary's is not from anywhere; that is to say, it is about his longing to go everywhere. It is a beautiful letter. Cecil Rhodes's is from Africa, and it is the kind of letter you never forget, because it describes in simple, clear language something you have always wanted to know about: in this case, how they mine diamonds at Kimberley. Thomas Saunders' letter is from Maryland, and was written in 1756. It is very businesslike and serious, but we may laugh:

> i have 160 Acrer of good land wich i bougt before i was married my wife is but young about 22 years old now and seems pregnant Enough soe you need not fear Grand Children.

What would it mean to be not pregnant enough?

"Oh Mother, Mother"

GERTRUDE MARGARET LOWTHIAN BELL

Gertrude Margaret Lowthian Bell (1868-1926; English traveler, archaeologist, and government official.) Gertrude Bell was one of the most remarkable women of her time. She was educated at Oxford, when most women did not go to college, and then joined her father, Sir Hugh Bell, in Teheran, when most women did not go to Persia. She spent much of her life in the Near East, the last fifteen years of it in various important positions as a link between the Colonial government and the Arabs—at a time when no women were involved in such activities. She is most famous as an explorer; in 1913 she traveled to Haïl, in the interior of Arabia, when she was only the second Western woman to explore that part of the world.

I do not know the name of the man who is the subject of the following letter, but I am not sorry not to know it. It is a beautiful letter, and explains itself in all important respects; it is possible that too complete a knowledge of the circumstances lying behind it would lessen its effect.

After reading this letter, you ought to look into Gertrude Bell's translation of the poems of Hafiz. They are fragile songs and odes of love, of passion, of exotic singing birds and lush, perfumed flowers; and when you read them, remembering that Miss Bell was no stranger to love, both the letter and the poems will mean more.

By the way, this letter was written to Florence Bell, Gertrude's stepmother. I mention that only because many of us have been exposed to fairy tales and folk-tales in which the stepmother is a monster. It is good to be reminded how beloved a stepmother may be.

Gulahek, Sunday, 18 Sep., 1892.

I CAN'T TELL you how I long for these days to be over when I feel the least sensible, or how I cling to them when I don't. It's only the bitter pleasure of being within reach, for we have not seen much of each other since we came back from Lar, and especially since my father's letter we don't feel that we have any right to meet.

Yesterday afternoon we sat in the Movara garden and discussed it in all its bearings, we felt we could not go on pretending to each other any more when things looked so black for us. . . . We talked much of you; I had given him several of your letters to read for I wanted him so much to know you, and he does know a little from them and from me how dear and how beloved you are. "Perhaps when you go home she will write once to me," he said, which sounded so pathetic and made my own unhappiness seem so endlessly selfish, for I have you for help and for consolation when I go home and he has nobody and nothing in front of him but more years of this weary place. He was devoted to his own mother who died a few years ago—if only she had been alive she would have known how to help, as you will know. The thing I can bear least is that you or Papa should ever think anything of him which is not noble and gentle and good. That is all of him that I have ever known, I wish I could pass on my impression to you untouched and unspoiled, the side of him he has shown a woman when he loved her— do you remember Browning. He quoted that to me once long ago and I wondered vaguely if it were more than a form of words. Everything I think and write brings us back to things we have spoken of together, sentences of his that come flashing like sharp swords; you see for the last three months nothing I have done or thought has not had him in it, the essence of it all.

It's very horrid of me to write like this, it will only make you sorry quite uselessly and needlessly. You must not think for a moment that if I could choose I would not have it all over again, impatience and pain and the going which is yet to come. It is worth it all, more than worth it. Some people live all their lives and never have this wonderful thing; at least I have known it and have seen life's possibilities suddenly open in front of me— only one may cry just a little when one has to turn away and take up the old narrow life again; I am so foolishly hopeful, not because I see any good way through our difficulties, but only because it is so impossible to believe that one cannot have the one big thing one wants more than life when one has had all the little things one didn't really care much about. But I know that's a bad argument! I wish I could go on and on writing to you, it's so consoling and I hate coming away from you and back to this place which is full of memories and things which are past, past. But you must have had enough of me—no not that, I can't call for more of your sympathy than you will give, can I? Oh Mother, Mother.

GERTRUDE.

"The Adventure Was Worth While"

AMELIA EARHART

Amelia Earhart Putnam (1897-1937; American aviatrix.) This, the shortest letter in this collection, was never mailed, but was found among Mrs. Putnam's papers by her husband and biographer after she did not return from her projected New Guinea-to-Hawaii Trans-Pacific flight in July, 1937. It was not written in that year; it dates from 1928, and was written before she took off from Newfoundland on the successful flight to Burry Port, Wales, that made her the first woman to fly the Atlantic. The letter was addressed to her mother, but with the safe arrival of its author, it was put away and presumably forgotten. Between 1928 and 1936 Amelia Earhart made many significant flights, most notably, perhaps, her solo over the Atlantic in 1932 and her 1935 leap from Hawaii to California, both firsts for a woman. She was the author of Last Flight (edited by her husband, 1938).

May 20, 1928

Even though I have lost, the adventure was worth while. Our family tends to be too secure. My life has really been very happy, and I didn't mind contemplating its end in the midst of it.

"All Out of Aristophanes or Juvenal"

THOMAS EDWARD LAWRENCE

Thomas Edward Lawrence (1888-1935; English archaeologist, soldier, and author.) The young archaeological student on the way to his first "dig" in Syria thought it "extraordinary good fortune" that his boat kept breaking down in such marvelous places as Naples and Athens. I think we may agree. It gave him an opportunity to see these places, and gives us an opportunity to read what he said about them. The legendary Lawrence of Arabia who rode with the Arabs, won brilliant desert victories, and organized governments during the First World War was only twenty-two when he wrote these letters, but he had already demonstrated certain gifts that foreshadowed his future achievements. For instance, he took first class honors in history at Oxford (so, by the way, did Gertrude Bell). And though some of the facts in Seven Pillars of Wisdom *have been doubted in recent years, no one has ever doubted its author's command of the English language. After the war T. E. Lawrence refused a peerage and other honors, and joined the RAF as an aircraft-man (the equivalent of private) under the name of T. E. Shaw. His death in 1935 resulted from a motorcycle accident.*

These letters are exquisitely written. The first of the two is a quite conscious little literary essay, perfect of its kind, although somewhat cold; the second is an essay upon what is almost a "set" subject, the first visit to Athens of a classical scholar. And yet it is remarkable just the same, albeit the difficulty of the task is admitted: "There will never be a great book on Athens unless it is one by an enemy." Only such a person, Lawrence says, can resist the city's spell.

August 1910   Le Petit Andelys

THE BOOK I had was *Petit Jehan de Saintré*, a XV Cent. novel of knightly manners—very good:—I have wanted to read it for a long time, but the Union copy was so badly printed that I had not the heart for it. Now I have found (for 1 f. 25) a series quite nicely typed on fairly good paper. So far I have only got 4 volumes, because they are rather much to carry: it is altogether glorious to have found good French books at last. I can read Molière and Racine and Corneille and Voltaire now:—a whole new world. You know, I think, the joy of getting into a strange country in a book: at home when I have shut my door and the town is in bed—and I know that nothing, not even the dawn—can disturb me in my curtains: only the slow crumbling of the coals in the fire: they get so red and throw such splendid glimmerings on the Hypnos and the brasswork. And it is lovely too, after you have been wandering for hours in the forest with Percivale or Sagramors le desirous, to open the door, and from over the Cherwell to look at the sun glowering through the valley-mists. Why does one not like things if there are other people about? Why cannot one make one's books live except in the night, after hours of straining? and you know they have to be your own books too, and you have to read them more than once. I think they take in something of your personality, and your environment also—you know a second hand book sometimes is so much more flesh and blood than a new one—and it is almost terrible to think that your ideas, yourself in your books, may be giving life to generations of readers after you are forgotten. It is that specially which makes one need good books: books that will be worthy of what you are going to put into them. What would you think of a great sculptor who flung away his gifts on modeling clay or sand? Imagination should be put into the most precious caskets, and that is why one can only live in the future or the past, in Utopia or the Wood beyond the World. Father won't know all this—but if you can get the right book at the right time you taste joys—not only bodily, physical, but spiritual also, which pass one out above and beyond one's miserable self, as it were through a huge air, following the light of another man's thought. And you can never be quite the old self again. You have forgotten a little bit: or rather pushed it out with a little of the inspiration of what is immortal in someone who has gone before you. NED

December 1910   Messageries Maritimes

Before you reach Athens you pass through green fields and over small streams, that effectually wash away the taste and smell of the sea. The rail lands you in the midst of a very modern looking town of squares and gardens, with a character partly French but not wholly European or Asiatic; too bright for the one and too clean for the other. It was above all things quiet, the quietest town imaginable, with few trams, and those slow ones, no motors or bicycles and very few carts. The streets are usually asphalt-paved, and there seemed hardly any dogs to bark and fight. Even the vegetable-hawkers shouted like men, not like jackals or fog horns. Everywhere were palm trees and mimosa, with green lawns. I had to go back through the town to reach the Acropolis, and chose therefore to wander into by-streets, that I might come out at the Theseion; and the further I went the stronger became a curious sense of unreality, almost of night-mare. Here was a town full of people speaking the same tongue and writing the same character as the old inhabitants of 3000 years before. Some of them looked like what we know and hope the old Greeks were, others of them are visibly of the class of metics or βαναυσοι or freedmen, whom Aristotle so loudly scorned. The Athenians to whom he appealed were never more than a handful, a little party who held by themselves walking in the gardens, and looking out dispassionately upon the world around them: they had heard (as I did) tousled black-haired women calling loudly for their children Gorgo or Aristomenes, and they had seen (as I saw) the two women up the street hurrying breathlessly along, tiring their hair, to meet the procession of priests in vestments this time, but still the same under-current of back-biting and slander, and ill-natured comment of the neighbours. A cabbage-seller past me, before just such a sausage-stall as one had looked for in the street of Victory that leads to the Temple of Theseus, driving his ass, and chaffering with Demosthenes, a fisherman. It was all out of Aristophanes or Juvenal, all in keeping, so that it seemed quite natural when I walked up a little hill, and passed under the pillars of the temple. It stands today as perfect as ever it was, with the added beauty of the stains and hollows with which Time has endowed its stones. When you have passed around one of the angles of its cellar wall, you see framed between two pillars the sunlight on the steps of the Propylea and the pediment of the Erectheum. The rock of the Acropolis is very large and high and steep. The quiet was really almost uncanny, as I walked up the shallow valley below Mars Hill, and along the processional way to the gateway of the citadel. There were no boys to bother one, no loud bellows'd leather sellers, only a misty sunlight in which all Attica, Phaleron, Salamis, Eleusis, and the distant Peloponnese lay motionless, 'drowned in deep peace', below the rock platform of the Wingless Victory. To get there I had to climb up the white marble staircase of the Propylea within the entrance gate. There were no porters, no guides, no visitors, and I walked through the doorway of the Parthenon, and on into the inner part of it, without really remembering who or where I was. A heaviness in the air made my eyes swim, and wrapped up my senses: I only knew that I, a stranger, was walking on the floor of the place I had most desired to see, the greatest temple of Athene, the palace of art, and that I was counting her columns, and finding them what I already knew. The building was familiar, not cold as in the drawings, but complex, irregular, alive with curve and subtlety, and perfectly preserved. Every line of the mouldings, every minutest refinement in the sculptures were evident in that light, and inevitable in their place. The Parthenon is the proto-cathedral of the Hellenes. I believe I saw the Erectheum, and I remember coming back to look again at the Propylea, and to stand again beside the Niké Apteros: but then I came down again into the town, and found it modern and a little different. It was as though one had turned from the shades of the ancestors, to mix in the daily vocations of their sons: and so only this about Athens, that there is an intoxication, a power of possession in its ruins, and the memories that inhabit them, which entirely prevents anyone attempting to describe or to estimate them. There will never be a great book on Athens unless it is one by an enemy: no one who knew it could resist its spell, except by a violent attack upon its spirit, and who can attack it now of artists, when Tolstoy is dead? He, and he alone, could have uprooted Greek culture in the world. I am coming back by Athens I think next year to stay a little time. For the present

I am only confused with it: I do not know how much was Athens, and how much the colouring of my imagination upon it.

N.

"I Have Been Agreeably Disappointed"

MERIWETHER LEWIS

Meriwether Lewis (1774-1809; American explorer.) Of the two young army captains who led the great expedition to the Pacific in 1805, Lewis is the better known; and this is fair enough, because the idea for the trip was his in the first place. He cherished a plan to search for a land route to the West from the time he was eighteen, retaining his enthusiasm and keeping up his agitation for the scheme through long years in the army. He served on many fronts between 1795 and 1801. He was a member of the militia that suppressed the Whiskey Rebellion, and he fought with Anthony Wayne in the Indian Wars along the Northwest Frontier. During the latter campaign he met William Clark, under whom, in fact, he served. In 1801 Lewis's great chance came at last. Thomas Jefferson, newly elected President, offered him the job of private secretary. Lewis accepted with alacrity. For two years he had the relaxed ear of the President and pressed his proposal at every conceivable opportunity. Jefferson, at last convinced himself, convinced Congress of the feasibility and worth of the expedition, and funds were appropriated in 1803. Lewis collected Clark and set off up the Missouri, followed it to its source, crossed the Great Divide, and descended the Columbia River to the Pacific. Upon his return Lewis resigned his commission and was appointed governor of the new province of Louisiana. In 1809 he died at an inn in Tennessee, while traveling to Washington. Although Jefferson believed that he had committed suicide, it is now generally held that he was robbed and murdered.

FORT MANDAN, 1609 MILES ABOVE THE
ENTRANCE OF THE MISSOURI—
March 31st., 1805.

DEAR MOTHER:—I arrived at this place on the 27th. of Oct. last, with party under my command destined to the Pacific Ocean,

by way of the Missouri and Columbia rivers. The near approach
of winter, the low state of the water and the known scarcity of
timber which exists on the Missouri for many hundred miles
above the Mandans, together with many other considerations
equally important, determined my friend and companion Capt.
Clark and myself to fortify ourselves and remain for the winter
in the neighborhood of the Mandans, Minetares and Ahwahar-
ways, who are the most friendly and well disposed savages that
we have yet met with. Accordingly we sought and found a
convenient situation for our purposes a few miles below the
villages of these people on the north side of the river in an extensive and well timbered bottom, where we commenced the
erection of our houses on the 2d. of Nov. and completed them so
far as to put ourselves under shelter on the 21st. of the same
month, by which time the season wore the aspect of winter.
Having completed our fortify[cation] early in Dec. we called it
Fort Mandan, in honor of our friendly neighbors. So far we have
experienced more difficulties from the navigation of the Missouri
than danger from the savages. The difficulties which oppose
themselves to the navigation of this immense river arise from the
rapidity of its currents, its falling banks, sand bars and timber
which remains wholly or partially concealed in its bed, usually
called by the navigators of the Missouri, and the Mississippi
"sawyer" or "planter," one of these difficulties the navigator never
ceases to contend with from the entrance of the Missouri to this
place; and in innumerable instances most of these obstructions
are at the same instant combined to oppose his progress or
threaten his destruction. To these we may also add a fifth, and
not much less inconsiderable difficulty—the turbid quality of the
water—which renders it impracticable to discover any obstruction, even to the depth of a single inch. Such is the velocity of
the current at all seasons of the year, from the entrance of the
Missouri to the mouth of the great river Platte, that it is impossible to resist its force by means of oars or poles in the main
channel of the river; the eddies which therefore generally exist
on one side or the other of the river, are sought by the navigators,
but these are almost universally encumbered with concealed
timber, or within reach of the falling banks, but notwithstanding, are usually preferable to that of passing along the edges of
the sand bars, over which the water, tho' shallow, runs with
such violence that if your vessel happens to touch the sand, or is
by any accident turned sidewise to the current, it is driven on

the bar and overset in an instant, generally destroyed, and always attented with the loss of the cargo. The base of the river banks being composed of a fine light sand, is easily removed by the water. It happens when this capricious and violent currents set against its banks, which are usually covered with heavy timber, it quickly undermines them, sometimes to the depth of 40 or 50 paces, and several miles in length. The banks being unable to support themselves longer tumble into the river with tremendous force, destroying everything within their reach. The timber thus precipitated into the water with large masses of earth about their roots are seen drifting with the stream, their points above the water, while the roots, more heavy, are dragged along the bottom until they become firmly fixed in the quick sand, which forms the bed of the river, where they remain for many years, forming an irregular tho' dangerous chevaux-de-frise to oppose the navigator. This immense river, so far as we have yet ascended, waters one of the fairest portions of the globe, nor do I believe there is in the universe a similar extent of country equally fertile, well watered, and intersected by such a number of navigable streams. The country as high up the river as the mouth of the river Platte, a distance of 630 miles, is generally well timbered. At some little distance above this river the open or prairie country commences. With respect to this open country, I have been agreeably disappointed. From previous information I had been led to believe that it was barren, sterile and sandy; but, on the contrary, I found it fertile in the extreme, the soil being from one to twenty feet in depth, consisting of a fine black loam, intermixed with a sufficient quantity of sand only to induce a luxuriant growth of grass and other vegetable productions, particularly such as are not liable to be much injured, or wholly destroyed by the ravages of the fire. It is also generally level, yet well watered, in short, there can exist no other objection to it, except that of the want of timber, which is truly a very serious one. This want of timber is by no means attributable to a deficiency in the soil to produce it, but owes its origin to the ravages of the fires, which the natives kindle in these plains at all seasons of the year. The country on both sides of the river, except some of its bottom lands, for an immense distance is one continued open plain, in which no timber is to be seen except a few detached and scattered copse, and clumps of trees, which, from their moist situation, or the steep declivities of hills, are sheltered from the effects of fire. The general aspect of the

country is level so far as the perception of the spectator will
enable him to determine, but from the rapidity of the Missouri, it
must be considerably elevated, as it passes to the N. West; it is
broken only on the borders of the water courses. Game is very
abundant, and seems to increase as we progress—our prospect
of starving is therefore consequently small. On the lower portion
of the Missouri, from its junction with the Mississippi to the
entrance of the Osage river we met with some deer, bear and
turkeys. From thence to the Kancez river the deer were more
abundant. A great number of black bear, some turkeys, geese,
swan and ducks. From thence to the mouth of the great river
Platte an immense quantity of deer, some bear, elk, turkeys, geese,
swan and ducks. From thence to the river S[ioux] some bear,
a great number of elks, the bear disappeared almost entirely,
some turkeys, geese, swan and ducks. From thence to the mouth
of the White river vast herds of buffalo, elk and some deer, and
a greater quantity of turkeys than we had before seen, a circumstance which I did not much expect in a country so destitute of
timber. Hence to Fort Mandan the buffalo, elk and deer increase
in quantity, with the addition of the cabie [cabra], as they are
generally called by the French engages, which is a creature
about the size of a small deer. Its flesh is deliciously flavored.
The ice in the Missouri has now nearly disappeared. I shall set
out on my voyage in the course of a few days. I can foresee no
material obstruction to our progress and feel the most perfect
confidence that we shall reach the Pacific ocean this summer.
For myself, individually, I enjoy better health than I have since
I commenced my voyage. The party are now in fine health and
excellent spirits, are attached to the enterprise and anxious to
proceed. Not a whisper of discontent or murmur is to be heard
among them. With such men I feel every confidence necessary
to insure success. The party, with Capt. Clark and myself, consists of thirty-one white persons, one negro man, and two
Indians. The Indians in this neighborhood [assert] that the Missouri is navigable nearly to its source, and that from a navigable
part of the river, at a distance not exceeding a half a days march,
there is a large river running from south to north along the
western base of the Rocky Mountains, but as their war excursions
have not extended far beyond this point, they can give no account
of the discharge or source of this river. We believe this stream
to be the principal South Fork of the Columbia river, and if so,
we shall probably find but little difficulty in passing to the ocean.

We have subsisted this winter on meat principally, with which our guns have furnished us an ample supply, and have, by that means, reserved a sufficient stock of the provisions we brought with us from the Illinois to guard us against accidental want during the voyage of the present year. You may expect me in Albemarle about the last of next Sept.—twelve months. I request that you will give yourself no uneasiness with respect to my fate, for I assure you that I feel myself perfectly as safe as I should do in Albemarle, and the only difference between three or four thousand miles and 130 is that I can not have the pleasure of seeing you as often as I did while at Washington.

I must request of you before I conclude this letter, to send John Marks* to the college of Williamsburgh as soon as it shall be thought that his education has been sufficiently advanced to fit him for that seminary; for you may rest assured that as you regard his future prosperity you had better make any sacrifice of his property than suffer his education to remain neglected or incomplete. Give my love to my brothers and sisters and all my neighbors and friends, and rest assured yourself of the most devoted filial affection of yours,

MERIWETHER LEWIS.

* Lewis's young stepbrother.

"No Doubt We Shall Make One Another Happy"

HARRIET MARTINEAU

Harriet Martineau (1802-1876; English traveler and author.) At the age of sixteen, Harriet Martineau became deaf; and as she had been born without the senses of taste and smell, it would have been understandable had she retired to the leisurely life of an English gentlewoman. She did not, of course, for she still had eyes. They served her more than well, and she became one of the most traveled and best educated women of her age. She was a student of philosophy and politics, and an early popularizer of the theories of Malthus and John Stuart Mill; she was at times even consulted by cabinet ministers. From 1834 to 1836 she made her famous journey to America, the subject of the second of these letters, and also the subject of her book, Society in America *(1837), which annoyed many Americans.*

July 8, 1833.

Dearest Mother,—I have rather put off writing, feeling that I have much to say, and now I must write after all more briefly than usual. Mrs. Ker has told you that I am well, and so I go on to what you most want to know next. About our future. I know of no risks that you are not at present aware of, and I have no fresh doubts. You are aware that I must travel, after 1834, for a year or little short of it; and we all know that my resources depend on health, and in some degree on popularity. I say "in some degree," because I am pretty sure that I can now never be without employment unless I choose. I wish to put the pension out of the question because, though it is as fully designed for me as ever, I am just as likely to refuse as to accept it; and besides, it is intended for purposes of *improvement*, unless sickness should oblige me to live upon it. But I incline more and and more to refuse it, though I need not make up my mind till I see how I am circumstanced with respect to the people when it is offered. I have every hope of being able to supply my annual £150, and you are as well aware of the chances against it as myself. I shall be very happy to invest £200 in furniture, in addition to that of my own two rooms, and you can take it out, if that plan will make you easy, at your convenience. If not, we shall not differ about these matters, I am sure. My advice is that we begin modestly,—with a house which we may keep *after a time*, when our income may be reduced. With prudence I think we may hope to live comfortably on our means, while I may be laying by something against a time of rest, if it should please God to preserve my health. I see no other plan which promises equal comfort for the three parties concerned, and if you are willing to trust to our industry and care, so am I; and I have no doubt we shall make one another happy, if we at once begin with the change of habits which our change of position renders necessary. I fully expect that both you and I shall occasionally feel as if I did not discharge a daughter's duty, but we shall both remind ourselves that I am now as much a citizen of the world as any professional *son* of yours could be. You shall be most welcome to my confidence, as ever, and to any comfort that may be derived from living in the same house, and meeting at the same table, and taking frequent walks, and having many mutual friends. My hours of solitary work and of visiting will leave you much to yourself; this you know and do not fear; so now the whole case is before you, and you know exactly under what feelings I say "Come." I may just mention that I see no sign of disapprobation on any hand, though there are naturally doubts here and there as to how a removal from a place where you have lived so many years may affect you. *We,* however, know that removal to be necessary, whether you come to London or fix your abode elsewhere; there is another chance, dear mother, and that is, of my marrying. I have no thoughts of it. I see a thousand reasons against it. But I could not positively answer for always continuing in the same mind. It would be presumptuous to do so; and I especially feel this when I find myself touched by the devoted interest with which some few of my friends regard my labours. I did not know till lately any thing of the enthusiasm with which such services as I attempt can be regarded, nor with what tender respect it could be testified. I mean no more than I say, I assure you; but, strong as my convictions are against marrying, I will not positively promise. As for my money prospects, the sale *cannot* now fall below the point of profit, and large profit; and there is the cheaper edition to look to, which every body says will yield an income for years to come. . . .

Do not trouble yourselves about the vagabond who took my name at the police-office the other day. Nobody but "The Age" will take her to be me.

I have been *doing* again about the factory business. What a sweet letter from Ellen! I am much obliged by Aunt Rankin's bag. Dear love to you two from

Yours most affectionately,
H. MARTINEAU.

It seems right, dear mother, to tell you that they are not at all shy of me. In all the letters we carry from one place to another the sentiment is amusingly uniform, namely: 'The authoress and instructress of statesmen is forgotten in the,' &c., &c. This looks as

if pedantry was the common consequence of acquirement among
the women. Miss J———'s cheerful intelligence makes her friends
every where. We have begun a regular plan of Bible-reading and
discussion together, and are quite disposed to rest invariably on
the Sundays. When I told the General what is thought among us
(and especially by Lord Durham) of the American Report on
Sunday travelling, he was highly delighted, the author being
his most intimate friend. He will introduce him to us at Washington, and thinks he has a good chance for the presidency next
time; but every man thinks so of his particular friend.

We have been exquisitely happy at Stockbridge, with the
Sedgwicks. Miss Sedgwick is all I heard of her, which is saying
every thing. All these Mr. Sedgwicks, her brothers, with their
wives and blooming families, are an ornament to their State.
They are among the first people in it, gracing its literature and
its legislation, and spreading their accomplishments through the
fair country in which they dwell. Such a country, of mountain
and lake and towering wood! I was 'Lafayetted,' as they say, to
great advantage. All business was suspended, and almost the
whole population was busy in giving me pleasure and information. I never before was the cause of such a jubilee. If Ellen
thought much of my mode of leaving Liverpool, what would she
think here? We were carried to Pittsfield, to an annual agricultural assemblage, where I learned much of the people, and
was made to drink the first out of a prize cup. O, the bliss of
seeing not a single beggar,—not a man, woman, or child otherwise than well dressed! Captain Hall says no women appear
at these public meetings, and that they are dreadfully solemn.
We saw as many women as men, and few but smiling faces;
but Captain Hall went to *one* meeting, on a wet, cold day, and
drew a general conclusion, as is his wont. I am told he was
asked if he would take a *piece* of something at dinner, and
answered that he would have a *bit*,—*that* was the proper word;
piece sounded very improper to English ears! What a traveller!

I have learned more than I well know how to stow, at Stockbridge, the unrivalled village, where the best refinements of the
town are mingled with the wildest pleasures of the country.
We are to go again and again if they say true; and this morning
at six we departed from amid a throng of tearful friends, feeling
that we shall never meet with kinder. I never saw so beautiful a
company of children as were always offering me roses, or lying
in wait for a smile or an autograph, or to bring me lamp or

water, or whatever I might want. Miss Sedgwick is the beloved
and gentle queen of the little community. They gave me letters
to Van Buren (the Vice-President, and centre of all the political
agitation here), expecting that I should meet him at Washington;
but on arriving here I found that he has just returned from the
Falls, and had been inquiring for me, and after dinner he called
with his son. He is simple in his manners, and does not *look* the
wily politician he is said to be, nor as if he had the cares of
this great Republic on his shoulders. He hopes to welcome me
to Washington.

"Nothing Seems Impossible"

ROBERT EDWIN PEARY

*Robert Edwin Peary (1856-1920; American arctic explorer.) The
acrimonious debate over who had discovered the North Pole
almost overshadowed the accomplishment itself during the early
years of the twentieth century. Dr. Frederick S. Cook, who
claimed to have arrived there on April 8, 1908, had many partisans. But when his proofs were checked and doubled-checked
they were found to be spurious, and the honor of being the first
man to stand at Latitude 90°00'00" N devolved on Commander
Peary, U.S.N. With one companion, he reached the Pole on April 6,
1909. He had tried and failed many times before this final success.
He had made assaults in 1886, 1893, 1895, 1898, 1901, 1905, and
1908. These letters show Peary's determination; they also reveal
that he had long dreamed of accomplishing a feat of "lasting
fame."*

*Peary and his mother were particularly close. His father died
when he was three, and it was due entirely to his mother's
efforts and thrift that the future explorer received an education.*

*In the first of these two letters, Peary wonders where he will be
in ten years: Maine, Patagonia, Sweden, or perhaps Australia?
The answer is that he was in Greenland, investigating its value as
a base for polar explorations; but the point is that Peary knew
he'd be in some far-off place. And he shows himself equally able
to manage the uncertain future in his second letter; he explains*

why it would be wise to visit the Isthmus, and become an expert. Just seven years later, Robert Edwin Peary was director of ship canal surveys in Nicaragua.

[On His Twentieth Birthday]
May 6, 1876

THE ONLY WAY in which I have celebrated is by indulging in vague wonderings, whether the contest with the world will be harder than the contest with the college? Will it prove too much for me? Whether in ten years I shall be in Maine, in Patagonia, in Sweden or in Australia, or whether it will all be blank to me then. It seems almost an impossibility to me how anyone, as some of our farmers do, can look forward to living their life out in the same place and doing the same things that their fathers and grandfathers did before them. Today as I think of what the world is and that I have my life before me, nothing seems impossible. I wish that as in the story books, some fairy might place the mirror of life before me and tell me to look at whatever scene I wished. Yet if it could be so, I can hardly say but I should close my eyes and refuse to look. How many have wished and wondered about the mysterious future as I do, and yet if the curtain were permitted to be drawn aside, would shrink from doing it for fear of gazing upon rugged rocks and yawning graves, in place of the velvety paths they wish for.

August 16, 1880

I WANT to have a good long talk with you on a subject I have been thinking of for a long time, and that is in regard to going to the Isthmus. I want to discuss the pros and cons with you. I don't want to live and die without accomplishing anything or without being known beyond a narrow circle of friends. I would like to acquire a name which would be an open sesame to circles of culture and refinement anywhere, a name which would make my mother proud, and which would make me feel that I was the peer of anyone I might meet.

This and questions of similar nature I have been thinking of a great deal the past year and it is this which has made you think I was sober and perhaps sad. I have got to the point where the years do not have leaden feet and I feel as if I must do something before too many of them slip by. What good will fame or a name do me if it comes when I am an old man? I want to have some years to enjoy it in and then, my Mother, I want you to have some pleasure from it. Here I am, twenty-four years old and what have I done, what I am doing, or what am I in the way of doing? Nothing. It will not be long before I am thirty and if I remain here I may be earning two thousand a year as a draftsman, a machine, working so many hours a day and known only on the pay roll of the department. When I think of these things it makes me so restless that I can hardly keep quiet. I feel myself already thirty or forty years old and nothing accomplished, and I feel a feverish desire to do something at once. What think you, Mother? Is it the restlessness of ambition which spurs men on to the front of their fellows or is it an ineffective uneasiness productive only of unrest to its unfortunate possessor?

Thinking of all these things and wondering what I could do it has seemed to me that there is more opportunity for a lasting fame to be obtained on the little strip of land called the Isthmus —an area about half as large as the state of Maine—than anywhere else on the globe.

Many men have made themselves world known by looking forward, seeing something sure to be of importance in the future, making the subject thoroughly their own and then when the right moment comes, stepping forward as the chief authority on the subject.

In regard to the Isthmus, though so much has been written, but little is known about it. Leaving out of the question the possibility that a thorough geographical knowledge of the country might show a route for the great canal, there are many other things, as the mineralogy, flora, fauna, etc. of the country of which really nothing is known, and when, as is certain to be the case, the Isthmus takes its place as a great center, he who is authority on these subjects can no longer be obscure.

I have thought that I would be that. Now of the importance of the goal you can have but one idea as to my being able to reach it. What think you? Can I do it? If nothing more I could write a book for my Mother to read.

The short time I have been here has widened my horizon vastly and among the many striving for fame or fortune or both I feel myself overmastered by a resistless desire to do something.

I am having my travelling fever later than many but it is none the less genuine for that.

You may call this only a whim of mine but it is a whim which has been present almost every waking and many sleeping moments for nearly a year now and is tightening its hold on me every day. The fact that I have been successful in whatever I have really striven for thus far, may, like the straw, show the tendency of the wind, though I know as well as you, Mother, that like the straw my successes have been the veriest trifles as compared with the difficult problem of life itself.

I have been studying myself and comparing myself with those about me, and though I have not by any means learned my lesson completely, yet I know more of it than ever before. I have all my Mother's sensitiveness to surroundings with perhaps my father's inability to overcome their effects if depressing or distasteful. I am not of that phlegmatic temperament which permits one to become a machine, of high intelligence it may be, yet none the less a machine, and why should I enter a useless struggle with nature to change my very constitution? The engineer does not attempt to change the course of nature, he simply conforms to her and by his skill enables her at the same time she is following her own laws, to aid him. There are men who are capable of becoming machines and there are men who can do nothing unless permitted to do it in their own way, and the world has need of both. If it was a case of daily bread with me, it would be different, but I do not strive for money but for fame though money as a secondary consideration would be no objection. . . .

Next summer I shall spend with you working up my notes, etc. and preparing future work. In the Fall I may return to Washington for a few months to obtain the benefit of certain advantages which I could not elsewhere. Then when the dry season begins, in December or January, I would return to the Isthmus, and so on, spending my winters there and my summers with you.

The objections are the greater danger and possible chances of death, though these are greatly exaggerated and more fanciful than real. But even if they were not, would it not be just as well to meet the gray old mower in full harness, struggling for a grand object, as on a lingering bed of sickness? 'To all men young and old death cometh soon or late,' and a nameless grave on the Isthmus is no worse than a marble surmounted one in sight of homes and cultivated fields. And would it not sound

just as well to say that he died on the Isthmus working out a
great idea as any way it could be put? And would not my
Mother feel a touch of pride in the midst of her sorrow? But
these are merely possibilities and I mention them simply to show
that I have thought of all these things.

"I Average £100 Per Week"

CECIL JOHN RHODES

*Cecil John Rhodes (1853-1902; English administrator and finan-
cier.) South Africa in 1870 was reputed to be good for one's
health, and that was the reason Cecil Rhodes went there in the
first place. He was a sickly boy of seventeen, and his mother
despaired of his ever having the strength to amount to anything.
A year later there was a diamond rush at the Vaal River in the
Orange Free State, and the frail young man took a few digging
tools and a Greek dictionary and brought out the beginnings of
what was to become the greatest fortune in the world. After the
consolidation of the Kimberley Mines and the formation of the
De Beers Company in 1888, Rhodes had a monopoly of all South
African diamond production, and could therefore set prices and
control the world market.*

*From 1881 on he gave his time increasingly to politics. His
dream was the establishment of a united British Africa, with a
string of possessions from Cape to Cairo. To this end he acquired
Bechuanaland, Rhodesia and the Transvaal for the Empire, and
played a key role in bringing about the Boer War. He died before
the war came to a conclusion. He left £6,000,000 to public service, and endowed 170 scholarships at Oxford for youths of the
United States, Germany, and British Possessions.*

*I do not approve of the form in which this letter is printed,
intersticed as it is with comments and interpolations and explanations. But I was unable to find the original letter in its
entirety, and so offer this version by Basil Williams, a biographer
of Rhodes; within quotation marks it presents extracts from
Rhodes's original letter, interspersing helpful background material.
The letter itself, with its description of the kopje full of diamonds,
and of men, like ants, digging furiously in it, is so interesting that*

I hope the reader will forgive me. The "Herbert" to whom Rhodes refers is his eldest brother.

" . . . Fancy an immense plain with right in its centre a great mass of white tents and iron stores, and on one side of it, all mixed up with the camp, mounds of lime like ant-hills; the country round is all flat with just thorn trees here and there: and you have some idea of Dutoitspan, the first spot where dry diggings for Diamonds was begun." Here were the principal hotels of the place, all in the Market Square: Benning and Martin's, which floated the Union Jack, Parker's opposite with the Stars and Stripes, and next door a hotel with the Prussian Eagle. Martin, the friendly host of the Union Jack hotel, generally managed to find a bed for the English new-comer, even if it were only a shakedown on the table, where a noisy party was playing loo till dawn. Staying here, no doubt, on the night of his arrival, Cecil went on next day to Colesberg Kopje or New Rush, where Herbert had already secured three claims "in the richest diamond mine the world ever produced." . . . "Imagine," he continues to his mother, "a small round hill at its very highest part only 30 feet above the level of the surrounding country, about 180 yards broad and 220 long; all round it a mass of white tents, and then beyond them a flat level country for miles and miles, with here and there a gentle rise. . . . I should like you," he says, "to have a peep at the kopje from my tent door at the present moment. It is like an immense number of ant-heaps covered with black ants, as thick as can be, the latter represented by human beings; when you understand there are about 600 claims on the kopje and each claim is generally split into 4, and on each bit there are about 6 blacks and whites working, it gives a total of about ten thousand working every day on a piece of ground 180 yards by 220." He then describes how the kopje is divided off into claims. "Take your garden, for instance," he tells his mother, "and peg the whole off into squares or claims 31 ft. by 31 ft., and then the question is how to take all the earth out and sort and sieve it. All through the kopje roads have been left to carry the stuff off in carts like the following [here comes a rough diagram]; that is of every claim of 31 ft., 7 ft. 6 inches are not allowed to be worked, but is left for a road . . . the roads are the only ground that remain of the original level. . . . The carting on the kopje is done chiefly by mules, as they are so very hardy, and have so few diseases. There are constantly mules, carts and all going head over heels into the mines below as there are no rails or anything on either side of the roads, nothing but one great broad chasm below. Here and there where the roads have fallen in, bridges have been put, and they are now the safest part of the kopje. . . . On each side of every road there is now a continuous chasm from top to bottom of the kopje varying in depth from 30 to 60 ft."

He then explains the rough system of digging and sifting then used on the Fields, and some of the difficulties to be overcome. "To begin with the ground is first picked, then the lumps mashed up and you put the stuff through a very coarse wire sieving, this lets the fine stuff pass through and keeps all the stones, which are thrown on one side; it is then hoisted out of the claim, and either carried or carted to the sorting table, where it is first put through fine wire sieving, which sieves all the lime dust away; what remains is put on the sorting table, and then one sorts away with a small scraper, spreading the stuff out on the table with one scoop and then off with the next. The diamonds are found in all ways; the big ones generally in the hole by the caffre, or else in the sieving; and the small ones on the table. . . . They are only found on these kopjes, and along the river, where they very likely have been carried by water. There are reefs all round these diamond mines, inside which the diamonds are found. The reef is the usual soil of the country round, red sand just at the top and then a black and white stony shale below. Inside the reef is the diamondiferous soil. It works just like Stilton cheese, and is as like the composition of Stilton cheese as anything I can compare it to. . . . They have been able to find no bottom yet, and keep on finding steadily at 70 ft. You will understand how enormously rich it is, when I say that a good claim would certainly average a diamond to every load of stuff that was sorted—a load being about 50 buckets. . . . The question now of course is, how are the roads to be worked? Every claim-holder has an interest in them, as a portion of every man's claim is the road, and one has no idea of leaving ground, every load of which stands a fair chance of holding a diamond. . . . Some day I expect to see the kopje one big basin where once there was a large hill." In this prediction Rhodes showed himself a true prophet; for in the place of Colesberg Kopje now stands a huge crater, from the edge of which men working at the bottom look no bigger than ants.

He concludes the letter with a business-like statement of his

own and his brother's prospect. "Have you ever read those tales," he asks his mother, "where they find some wonderfully big diamonds? Well! on this kopje I should think nearly every day they find a diamond over 50 carats. The only misfortune is, that they almost all have a slightly yellow tinge, and are getting quite unsaleable. Diamond buyers now give only £4 per carat for yellow stones of any size or shape, that is a 70 carat would not fetch more than £280. I found a 17⅞ carat on Saturday, it was very slightly off, and I hope to get £100 for it; does it not seem an absurd price? Yesterday I found a 3½ perfect stone, but glassy, which I sold for £30 as they are rather dangerous stones to keep, having a nasty habit of suddenly splitting all over. . . . You must not however think that every diamond one finds is a beauty, the great proportion are nothing but splints— but still even of these you very seldom find one that is not worth 5s. Rough diamonds are of all shapes, sizes and colour under the sun, some are flat, some round, some like two pyramids with their bases joined, some have black spots in the centre, others are yellow, and in fact they take every form you can think of. . . . I find on an average 30 carats a week and am working one of the few whole claims in the kopje: a claim in fact that will take me 4 years to work out at the present rate. Diamonds have only to continue a fair price and I think Herbert's fortune is made. When I tell you at the present moment he owns in all 3 whole claims on this kopje: the one I am working, 1 whole claim, Beecher's 1 quarter, Chadwick a half, another whole claim at the top of the kopje and another ¼ I bought. Mine and Beecher's however yield far the most. I average about £100 per week.
—Yrs., C. RHODES."

"The Heat of Youth Is Past"

THOMAS SAUNDERS

Thomas Saunders (eighteenth century American colonial farmer.) Little is known about the Saunders family. In 1776, the names of Thomas, Joseph, William, and Elizabeth Saunders occur in a list of the inhabitants of Bush River Lower Hundred, Maryland. In 1778, Thomas Saunders, farmer, and William Saunders took the oath of fidelity in Harford County, Maryland. Other than that we can say only that the written word is not his ordinary means of communication—and yet there is a queer eloquence about this letter. At any rate, Thomas's affection for his mother is stated as well as anyone could state it: "Consider that your Growing older daly and not to hurt y'r self for me that has been like the prodigall son."

Octob'r the 9 1756.

Hon'rd Mother

These with my kind love and duty to you hoepeing these fue lines will find you in good health as i and my family is at present thanck god for it my wife and son gives their kind loves and duty to you your Grandson is goeing on of four years old since the soeventh day of last august we have lost one. dear mother i rec'd the Cask of Brases and pewter Books and sundrys wich you sent me by Wm Dallam Junior and i humbly thanck you for them But it is not in my power at present for to make you a return for i have like a great many other prodigall sons gone thorugh a great deal of trouble but by the assistance of god through his all mighty grace it apeiares to be all most over for now the heat of youth is past all my Care is in Virtue and honesty and for my ofspring thats Come and to Come i thanck god he inpires me with a spirit of industry and ever has done so since i left you i bought an irich Convict servant Named Owen desmond from Cork Just as i was married he soon after Rob'd me of the Chief of my Cloaths and also my Wifes and run a way and i never heard of him since his first Cost was twenty pounds and at the same time lost a mare Cost me Eight pounds thes losses seem to hurt me at first but thanck god i rubd through them and saved my land wich was of more value than all but was obliged to mortgage it But it is Just Cleer i have 160 Acrer of good land wich i bougt before i was married my wife is but young about 22 years old now and seems pregnant Enough soe you need not fear Grand Chilldren Enough from that one branch you seem'd to mention some thinge about Religion i beg you give your self noe trouble about that for my Chief Care is that also i desire youl Consider that your Growing older daly and not to hurt y'r self for me that has been like the prodigall son but i thanck god it has not hurt me much since it Enlivens my mind to devine grace it is very troublesome times or Else you might Expect to see me soon for i am afraid of being prest aboard of a kings ship and then maybe i might not giet a shoar redyly pray give my kind love and service to all friends and relations in generall my son is named after my father John so no more at present from your most loving and affectionate son till death

THO'S SAUNDERS

PS pray derect for Thos Saunders Joyner at the head of Bush river Maryland. i had not oppertunity to write by Wm. Dallam for they gott loaded in pertuexent river above 100 miles of but you may send by him an answer if you please or by Capt Meleglin or any Capt thats Coming to patapesco river and i shall recvie it safe home ever you intrusted to pack those goods they did not pack them safe Considering what rouges sailors is

FOUR

Letters from

Fighting Men

M OST MEN FIGHT at one time or another during their lives, and lots of women do, too. These men (and one woman) did their fighting in wars, and wrote well—in some cases, beautifully—about the wars they were in. Some of them were professionals, some were not. The letters from the nonprofessionals are better. This is not surprising: soldiers accept war, and even like it, because they no longer can really see it. Civilians hate it, but retain the ability to be fascinated by it. And that is necessary for all good writing.

I shall never forget Charles Francis Adams's letter about the horses. I do not think anyone could forget it. We tend to be sentimental about horses nowadays, since they are no longer a necessary part of our culture, but Adams is not sentimental. One of the many shocking things about modern war is the waste of fine machinery, machinery made lovingly and to last. Adams is shocked by the waste of horses, in much the same way. The difference is that horses scream when they are hurt. Perhaps this is one of the reasons machines have replaced horses in warfare— machines do not scream.

There are two letters from "ordinary" soldiers here; one of the soldiers is an anonymous R.A.F. pilot, the other an American— Robert Holmes Dunham, a victim of the "Black Bean" episode during the conflict between Mexico and the Republic of Texas. There is something special about these two letters. The anonymous letter,

87

we might say, is "so English." We shed tears for England, and
sometimes, now, they seem like foolish tears—but we shed them
because she makes men who write letters like this one. The
letter written by Dunham is terrifying. I almost wish that I had
never read it; but having read it, I understand our history better.

Cushing's letter I have included because it is full of the wild
bravery of its writer, but also because it is difficult to see why he
wrote it to his mother; it might well have frightened her to death.
George Washington's are here because he is George Washington.
They are also extremely interesting, especially the second one,
written when he was fifty-five.

Mrs. Lamb must represent all the brave women who have stood
by their husbands and lovers, in spirit or in body, in the fire and
chaos of war. She was not quite a combatant; her letter shows
that she was some distance from the battle she describes; yet she
was closer than many women get. Her letter is bloodcurdling,
perhaps because of its restrained tone. Even more bloodcurdling
is the letter from the Japanese kamikaze pilot. Some American
soldier shot this man down not long after the letter was written.
It was right that this should be so, insofar as there is anything
right about war. Yet how much harder it would have been to
pull the trigger had the unknown gunner understood the kind of
man he was going to kill.

There is one thing to be said for war. Sergeant Joyce Kilmer
reminds us of it in his last letter to his "Dear Brat":

> I want you to meet all the Regimental Intelligence Section—a
> fine bunch of men and good comrades. We have taken big
> chances together, and it has made us the best of friends.

But surely there is a better way of making friends.

"I Do My Best For My Horses"

CHARLES FRANCIS ADAMS

*Charles Francis Adams (1835-1915; American lawyer, historian,
and railroad authority.) He was the second son of Charles Francis
Adams, American ambassador to England during the Civil War;*

he was the grandson and greatgrandson of Presidents of the United States, and was the brother of Henry and Brooks Adams. He left the Union army a brevet brigadier general. From 1869 to 1879 he was a member of the Massachusetts Board of Railroad Commissioners; through the influence of Carl Schurz he was appointed chairman of the government board for the Union Pacific Railroad in 1874, and later (1884) its president, but he lost the post sixteen years later because of pressure exerted by Jay Gould, who found it uncomfortable to work with so honest a man. Adams had been given enough time to put the railroad on a solid footing, however. He spent most of the rest of his life dabbling in history and scholarship: he co-authored Chapters of Erie and Other Essays *with his brother Henry, wrote a biography of R. H. Dana and one of his father, and lectured at Oxford University. He was an "ordinary" member of an extraordinary family, and thus an extraordinary man.*

Camp of 1st Mass. Cav'y
Potomac Creek, May 12, 1863

. . . . . .

It is by no means a pleasant thought to reflect how little people at home know of the *non*-fighting details of waste and suffering of war. We were in the field four weeks, and only once did I see the enemy, even at a distance. You read of Stoneman's and Grierson's cavalry raids, and of the dashing celerity of their movements and their long, rapid marches. Do you know how cavalry moves? It never goes out of a walk, and four miles an hour is *very* rapid marching—"killing to horses" as we always describe it. To cover forty miles is nearly fifteen hours march. The suffering is trifling for the men and they are always well in the field in spite of wet and cold and heat, loss of sleep and sleeping on the ground. In the field we have no sickness; when we get into camp it begins to appear at once.

But with the horses it is otherwise and you have no idea of their sufferings. An officer of cavalry needs to be more horse-doctor than soldier, and no one who has not tried it can realize the discouragement to Company commanders in these long and continuous marches. You are a slave to your horses, you work like a dog yourself, and you exact the most extreme care from your Sergeants, and you see diseases creeping on you day by day and your horses breaking down under your eyes, and you have two resources, one to send them to the reserve camps at the rear and so strip yourself of your command, and the other to force them on until they drop and then run for luck that you will be able to steal horses to remount your men, and keep up the strength of your command. The last course is the one I adopt. I do my best for my horses and am sorry for them; but all war is cruel and it is my business to bring every man I can into the presence of the enemy, and so make war short. So I have but one rule, a horse must go until he can't be spurred any further, and then the rider must get another horse as soon as he can seize on one. To estimate the wear and tear on horseflesh you must bear in mind that, in the service in this country, a cavalry horse when loaded carries an average of 225 lbs. on his back. His saddle, when packed and without a rider in it, weighs not less than fifty pounds. The horse is, in active campaign, saddled on an average about fifteen hours out of the twenty four. His feed is nominally ten pounds of grain a day and, in reality, he averages about eight pounds. He has no hay and only such other feed as he can pick up during halts. The usual water he drinks is brook water, so muddy by the passage of the column as to be of the color of chocolate. Of course, sore backs are our greatest trouble. Backs soon get feverish under the saddle and the first day's march swells them; after that day by day the trouble grows. No care can stop it. Every night after a march, no matter how late it may be, or tired or hungry I am, if permission is given to unsaddle, I examine all the horses' backs myself and see that everything is done for them that can be done, and yet with every care the marching of the last four weeks disabled ten of my horses, and put ten more on the high road to disability, and this out of sixty—one horse in three. Imagine a horse with his withers swollen to three times the natural size, and with a volcanic, running sore pouring matter down each side, and you have a case with which every cavalry officer is daily called upon to deal, and you imagine a horse which has still to be ridden until he lays down in sheer suffering under the saddle. Then we seize the first horse we come to and put the dismounted man on his back. The air of Virginia is literally burdened today with the stench of dead horses, federal and confederate. You pass them on every road and find them in every field, while from their carrions you can follow the march of every army that moves.

On this last raid dying horses lined the road on which Stoneman's divisions had passed, and we marched over a road made pestilent by the dead horses of the vanished rebels. Poor brutes! How it would astonish and terrify you and all others at home with your sleek, well-fed animals, to see the weak, gaunt, rough animals, with each rib visible and the hip-bones starting through the flesh, on which these "dashing cavalry raids" were executed. It would knock the romance out of you. So much for my cares as a horse-master, and they are the cares of all. For, I can safely assure you, my horses are not the worst in the regiment and that I am reputed no unsuccessful chief-groom. I put seventy horses in the field on the 13th of April, and not many other Captains in the service did as much. . . .

The present great difficulty is to account for our failure to win a great victory and to destroy the rebel army in the recent battle. They do say that Hooker got frightened and, after Sedgwick's disaster, seemed utterly to lose the capacity for command—he was panic stricken. Two thirds of his army had not been engaged at all, and he had not heard from Stoneman, but he was haunted with a vague phantom of danger on his right flank and base, a danger purely of his own imagining, and he had no peace until he found himself on this side of the river. Had he fought his army as he might have fought it, the rebel army would have been destroyed and Richmond today in our possession. We want no more changes, however, in our commanders, and the voice of the Army, I am sure, is to keep Hooker; but I am confident that he is the least respectable and reliable and I fear the least able commander we have had. I never saw him to speak to, but I think him a noisy, low-toned intriguer, conceited, intellectually "smart," physically brave. Morally, I fear, he is weak; his habits are bad and, as a general in high command, I have lost all confidence in him. But the army is large, brave and experienced. We have many good generals and good troops, and, in spite of Hooker, I think much can be done if we are left alone. Give us no more changes and no new generals!

As for the cavalry, its future is just opening and great names will be won in the cavalry from this day forward. How strangely stupid our generals and Government have been! How slow to learn even from the enemy! Here the war is two years old and throughout it we have heard but one story—that in Virginia cavalry was useless, that the arm was the poorest in the service. Men whom we called generals saw the enemy's cavalry go through and round their armies, cutting their lines of supply and exposing their weakness; and yet not one of these generals could sit down and argue thus: "The enemy's cavalry almost ruin me, and I have only a few miles of base and front, all of which I can guard; but the enemy has here in Virginia thousands of miles of communication; they cannot guard it without so weakening their front that I can crush them; if they do not guard it, every bridge is a weak point and I can starve them by cutting off supplies. My cavalry cannot travel in any direction without crossing a railroad, which the enemy cannot guard and which is an artery of their existence. A rail pulled up is a supply train captured. Give me 25,000 cavalry and I will worry the enemy out of Virginia." None of our generals seem to have had the intelligence to argue thus and so they quietly and as a fixed fact said: "Cavalry cannot be used in Virginia," and this too while Stuart and Lee were playing around them. And so they paralyzed their right arm. Two years have taught them a simple lesson and today it is a recognized fact that 25,000 well appointed cavalry could force the enemy out of Virginia. How slow we are as a people to learn the art of war! Still, we do learn.

But the troubles of the cavalry are by no means over. Hooker, it is said, angrily casting about for some one to blame for his repulse, has, of all men, hit upon Stoneman. Why was not Stoneman earlier? Why did not he take Richmond? and they do say Hooker would deprive him of his command if he dared. Meanwhile, if you follow the newspapers, you must often have read of one Pleasonton and his cavalry. Now Pleasonton is the *bête noire* of all cavalry officers. Stoneman we believe in. We believe in his judgment, his courage and determination. We know he is ready to shoulder responsibility, that he will take good care of us and won't get us into places from which he can't get us out. Pleasonton also we have served under. He is pure and simple a newspaper humbug. You always see his name in the papers, but to us who have served under him and seen him under fire he is notorious as a bully and toady. He does nothing save with a view to a newspaper paragraph. At Antietam he sent his cavalry into a hell of artillery fire and himself got behind a bank and read a newspaper, and there, when we came back, we all saw him and laughed among ourselves. Yet mean and contemptible as Pleasonton is, he is always *in* at Head Quarters and now they do say that Hooker wishes to depose Stoneman and hand the command over to Pleasonton. You may imagine our sensations in prospect of the change. Hooker is powerful, but Stoneman is successful. . . .

Potomac Run, near Falmouth, Va.
December 9, 1862

. . . . . .

AFTER a day or night of duty, it is strange what a sense of home and home comfort one attaches to the bivouac fire. You come in cold, hungry and tired and I assure you all the luxuries of home scarcely seem desirable beside its bright blaze, as you polish off a hot supper. And such suppers! You've no idea how well we live, now we've added experience to hunger. This evening, I remember, I had army-bread fried in pork—and some day I'll let you know what can be made of that dish—hot coffee, delicate young roast pig, beefsteak and an arrangement of cabbage, from the tenement of a neighboring mud-sill. This, with a pipe of tobacco, a bunk of fir branches well lined with blankets and a crackling fire before it left little to be desired. There is a wild luxury about it, very fascinating to me, though I never realise the presence of danger and that excitement which some men derive from that; to me camp always seems perfectly secure and my horses kick and champ on the other side of my fire, and my arms hang on the ridge of my bunk, practically as little thought of by me as though the one were in the stable at Quincy, and the other hanging over my mantelpiece in Boston. My enjoyment springs from the open air sense of freedom and strength. It's a lawless sort of feeling, making me feel as if I depended only on nature and myself for enjoyment.

This is all very well when the weather is fine, even in December; but next morning a change came o'er me, for early in the morning it began to rain and snow and, by the time we were relieved, at noon it snowed most heartily, so that I sincerely pitied the miserable creatures who relieved us. Home we rode, wet and cold, and as I walked sulkily along, I tried to think of one crumb of comfort awaiting me when I got back into camp. I couldn't think of one, unless indeed the commissary might have procured some whiskey. Wrong again! I got into camp and found Colonel Sargent there with three companies from Hooker's head-quarters and things looked lively enough, though far from cheerful, and as luck would have it Henry Davis was there, established in the midst of discomfort in his usual comfort. So I passed the evening with him, cursing Col.———— (in which chorus we all unanimously concur), smoking the best of tobacco, drinking hot whiskey punch and eating plum-cake fresh from Washington. . . .

The next time Henry passes a bookstore let him stop and buy for her [Mary] a little volume called "Ten Years of Soldiers' Life in India." It contains the life of Major Hodson taken from his own letters and is one of the most touching and charming books of these later days, to say nothing of the character of Hodson himself —my ideal of a Christian gentleman and soldier. I wonder none of you ever heard of him.

"You Must Not Grieve For Me"

ANONYMOUS R.A.F. PILOT

This letter was found among the personal belongings of a Royal Air Force bomber squadron pilot, reported missing and presumed to be killed in World War II. The letter was addressed to his mother, and was to be sent to her in the event of his death.

DEAREST MOTHER,

Though I feel no premonition at all, events are moving rapidly, and I have instructed that this letter be forwarded to you should I fail to return from one of the raids which we shall shortly be called upon to undertake. You must hope on for a month, but at the end of that time you must accept the fact that I have handed my task over to the extremely capable hands of my comrades of the Royal Air Force, as so many splendid fellows have already done.

First, it will comfort you to know that my role in this war has been of the greatest importance. Our patrols far out over the North Sea have helped to keep the trade routes clear for our convoys and supply ships, and on one occasion our information was instrumental in saving the lives of the men in a crippled lighthouse relief ship. Though it will be difficult for you, you will disappoint me if you do not at least try to accept the facts dispassionately, for I shall have done my duty to the utmost of my ability. No man can do more, and no one calling himself a man could do less.

I have always admired your amazing courage in the face of continual setbacks; in the way you have given me as good an education and background as anyone in the country; and always kept up appearances without ever losing faith in the future. My death would not mean that your struggle has been in vain. Far from it. It means that your sacrifice is as great as mine. Those who serve England must expect nothing from her; we debase ourselves if we regard our country as merely a place in which to eat and sleep.

History resounds with illustrious names who have given all, yet their sacrifice has resulted in the British Empire, where there is a measure of peace, justice, and freedom for all, and where a higher standard of civilization has evolved, and is still evolving, than anywhere else. But this is not only concerning our own land. To-day we are faced with the greatest organized challenge to Christianity and civilization that the world has even seen, and I count myself lucky and honoured to be the right age and fully trained to throw my full weight into the scale. For this I have to thank you. Yet there is more work for you to do. The home front will still have to stand united for years after the war is won. For all that can be said against it, I still maintain that this war is a very good thing; every individual is having the chance to give and dare all for his principle like the martyrs of old. However long the time may be, one thing can never be altered—I shall have lived and died an Englishman. Nothing else matters one jot nor can anything ever change it.

You must not grieve for me, for if you really believe in religion and all that it entails that would be hypocrisy. I have no fear of death; only a queer elation. . . . I would have it no other way. The universe is so vast and so ageless that the life of one man can only be justified by the measure of his sacrifice. We are sent to this world to acquire a personality and a character to take with us that can never be taken from us. Those who just eat and sleep, prosper and procreate, are no better than animals if all their lives they are at peace.

I firmly and absolutely believe that evil things are sent into the world to try us; they are sent deliberately by our Creator to test our metal because He knows what is good for us. The Bible is full of cases where the easy way out has been discarded for moral principles.

I count myself fortunate in that I have seen the whole country and known men of every calling. But with the final test of war I consider my character fully developed. Thus at my early age my earthly mission is already fulfilled and I am prepared to die with just one regret, and one only—that I could not devote myself to making your declining years more happy by being with you; but you will live in peace and freedom and I shall have directly contributed to that, so here again my life will not have been in vain.

Your loving Son.

"Steady Men, Steady!"

WILLIAM BARKER CUSHING

William Barker Cushing (1842-1874; American naval officer.) He graduated from the U.S. Naval Academy in 1861, and immediately entered active service. He was a lieutenant and commanded a gunboat before he was twenty. His reconnaissance expeditions in the Cape Fear River in the early spring of 1864, and his sinking of the Confederate ironclad ram Albemarle at Plymouth, North Carolina, on the night of October 27, 1864—the latter feat winning him the thanks of Congress and a promotion, an award equivalent to a modern Congressional Medal of Honor—exhibited such extraordinary bravery, such coolness in extreme emergency, and such total disregard for his own safety that Gideon Welles, Secretary of the Navy, was led to judge Cushing "the hero of the war." He was a consummate hero, but he was otherwise more a pathetic than an interesting man. The war over, Cushing found nothing to do. He served in the navy until his death, brought about by frustration of his natural talents—he should ideally have been a seventeenth century pirate—and by disabilities resulting from war experiences. Two of his brothers died heroic deaths, one at Gettysburg, the other in Arizona fighting the Apaches.

The letter included here describes a battle in the Nansemond River, in Virginia, on April 14, 1863. Cushing and Lamson were in command of a flotilla of vessels which attempted to steam up the

*river and was repulsed by Confederate fire from the shore.
Returning downstream they tried to cross the bar into the Lower
Nansemond, but one of their vessels ran aground and was caught
in a cross fire. Cushing in the* Commodore Barney *then began to
attack the batteries on the shore.*

*This letter was addressed to his mother, but the fact is that
Cushing had one eye on her and one eye on his hometown newspaper, which printed the letter on the front page. It was written
the day after the battle, when the writer was still under the
influence of the excitement of the fighting, and it contains some
exaggerations of fact if not of tone.*

April 15, 1863

DEAR MOTHER:

Another fight and another victory! Again I have passed through
the ordeal of fire and blood, and again I thank God for being safe
in life and limb. Suffolk is besieged by the enemy, thirty thousand
strong, and contains an army of fifteen thousand to defend it. The
town is situated on this river (the Nansemond) and its water
communication must remain open or our force will be in desperate
position. Who do you suppose was selected to perform the dangerous task of guarding the rear, and preventing the crossing of ten
thousand of the flower of the southern army? Who but your son,
that ex-midshipman, ex-master's mate, hair-brained, scapegrace,
Will Cushing! Yes, it is even so. I am senior officer commanding in
the Nansemond river. I have my vessel and two others now. I had
two more, but they were disabled in action, and have been towed
to Hampton Roads. I am six miles from the city, at a place called
Western Branch, the point most desired by the enemy. I draw too
much water to go up further, but sent my light boats up above.

Yesterday morning, as they were on their way down, they en-
countered a battery at a distance of three hundred yards, and
swarms of riflemen in the bushes on the banks. A sharp action
ensued, in which two of the boats were disabled, and but one
left uninjured, but the captain of her, like the brave fellow he is,
got them around the point out of range, and we managed to get
them as far as the bar here when one, the Mount Washington,
got aground. The rebels soon appeared in force, bent upon driving
us and crossing the river. They opened with artillery from two
positions, a cross-fire, and their seven pieces sent a hail of shot

and shell around us. . . . I had but two vessels afloat, but I silenced their fire in an hour. In a short time they again went into action; this time unmasking a regularly constructed battery not five hundred yards from us, and so situated as to rake the narrow channel completely. It was impossible to get our disabled steamer off from the bar until high water, five hours ahead, and I determined to fight on the spot as long as the *Barney* was above water. I sent the light steamer down to guard another coveted point, and was soon exchanging death calls with the enemy.

Well, it was a hard fight, and at close quarters most of the time; so close that their infantry riddled the two vessels with bullets. *Crash!* go the bulkheads—a rifle shell was exploded on our deck, tearing flesh and woodwork. A crash like thunder is our reply— and our heavy shell makes music in the air, and explodes among our traitor neighbors with a dull sullen roar of defiance. Up goes the battle flag, and at once the air is filled with the smoke of furious battle, and the ear thrills with the unceasing shriek and whistle of all the shell and rifled bolts that sinful man has devised to murder his fellow-creatures. *Crash! Crash!* Splinters are flying in the air; great pools of blood are on the deck, and the first sharp cry of wounded men in agony rises upon the soft spring air. The *dead* cannot speak—but there they lie motionless, lifeless, and mangled, who a moment ago smiled on the old flag that floated over them, and fought for its glory and honor. Sprinkle ashes over the slippery deck—the work must still go on. The rifled gun—my best, is disabled, for three shots have struck it— the muzzle is gone, the elevator is carried away, and the carriage is broken. Steady men, steady! Fill up the places of the killed and wounded—don't throw a shot away. The wheel of the howitzer is torn off by the shell, and the gun rendered useless—never mind! Work the remaining guns *with a will*—for we can and *must* be victorious. And so the time wore away, until the rising river promised to release the imprisoned steamer, when I signaled to the (*Stepping Stones*) to move up and take her in tow. This duty was gallantly performed, and the old *Barney* remained alone under the rebel cannon.

And here let me pause to give credit to one who will never earn more glory than he grasped in our desperate combat then. Lieutenant Lamson is one of the class next below me, and commanded the disabled steamer . . . I fought within a hundred yards of him and we are sworn friends for life. Well, I silenced the battery, and anchored at night where I had fought all day.

My vessel is riddled with cannon balls and bullets, and I have lost three killed and nine wounded—four of them mortally—men who lost arms and legs. The loss on the other vessels is proportionately severe. I am no braggart, but I challenge the world to furnish a more determined fight, or a victory more richly earned. The enemy *shall* not *cross* here. I will not give way one inch. Even now the thickets on the banks are alive with their sharpshooters; and as I write the quick whirr of the rifle bullet is often heard, sent from the bank five hundred yards ahead, in the vain hope of injuring the hated Yankee. A good providence seems to watch over my fortunes, though I do not deserve its protection. I may go into action again at any moment, probably to-morrow. I have every confidence in my gallant crew and officers, and do not doubt the result if my life is spared. Love to all. In haste, Your affectionate son.

"I Was One of the Unfortunate"

ROBERT HOLMES DUNHAM

Robert Holmes Dunham (....-1843). Death was no more than thirty minutes away when Robert Dunham wrote this letter. It is only by accident—by a series of incredible accidents—that we have it. Dunham is one of the most revered heroes in Texas history; yet what you will read in his letter is almost all that we know about its author.

In 1842, an expedition set out from the Republic of Texas to avenge a Mexican raid on San Antonio. The little Mexican town of Mier was its goal; but by the time the army reached its destination, two mass and acrimonious defections had dwindled its numbers to no more than three hundred men. Nevertheless, the attack began, and for a while it appeared that the onslaught would be successful. Then a large Mexican force appeared; the Texans were taken as prisoners, the battle was lost.

The president of Mexico in 1842 was Antonio López de Santa Anna. His had been the brutal order that led to the massacre at Goliad; he was responsible for the savagery at the Alamo. He was to be only a little less bloodthirsty in his treatment of the men of the Miers Expedition.

Robert Holmes Dunham was one of the men captured at Mier. Along with his fellow-Texans, he was force-marched toward Mexico City. In desperation, some two hundred of the prisoners attempted to escape. They were successful in that they broke away from their captors; but they escaped not into freedom, but into the vastness of parched, hostile Mexico.

For weeks Dunham and the others in this ragged band wandered in a hopeless search: first for an escape route, then in a desperate quest for food and water. Some of the men died of thirst; some of starvation; some of diseased wounds.

When only one hundred and seventy six men were left, they surrendered to the Mexicans again.

Santa Anna ordered that a basket of beans be prepared. Into the basket went seventeen black beans and one hundred and fifty-nine white beans. Each man in the group was forced to draw a bean; the ones who blindly selected a black bean were killed immediately.

Someone permitted Robert Holmes Dunham to scribble out this letter before he was shot.

Dunham entrusted the letter to Abraham Hadenburg, a friend who was one of those who had picked a white bean from the basket. Hadenburg kept the letter with him, and carried it back to Texas when he obtained his freedom in September, 1844. But he was unable to locate Dunham's mother or even any distant relatives. Eventually he turned the letter over to the officials of the Waco Post Office, who carried on the search for a while; in time the letter was forgotten, and then it was lost. When the Waco Post Office was demolished, a laborer found it. Dunham's farewell message was forwarded to Governor Sam Houston. Today, the fragments that remain can be seen at the State Museum of the Alamo in San Antonio.

Mexico

Dear Mother

I write to you under the most awful feelings that a son ever addressed a mother for in half an hour my doom will be finished here on earth for I am doomed to die by the hands of the Mexicans for our late attempt to escape the * * * by Santa Anna that every tenth man should be shot we draw lots I was one of the unfortunate I can not say anything more I die I hope with firmness farewell may god bless you and may he in this my last hour for-

give and pardon all my sins A D Hadenburge will * * * should
he be * * * all to inform you farewell

"your affectionate sone
R. H. Dunham."

March 25th 1843

"The Day After Tomorrow I Must Die"

ICHIZO HAYASHI

*Ichizo Hayashi (1921-1945; Japanese kamikaze.) He was a student
of political economy at Tokio University before the war. He was
killed at Okinawa, a pilot in a "specialized attack" squadron (i.e.,
in a suicide attack), at the age of twenty-three. This is the last
letter he wrote to his mother from Wonsan in Korea. Hayashi was
a Christian.*

MOTHER,

The time has come when I must give you sad news.

You love me more than I will ever be able to love you. What
will you think of this letter? I am desperately sorry.

I have been really happy; perhaps I was too spoilt. But it is
not my fault. I loved you, and it was so nice to be petted by you.

I am glad that I was selected as a pilot of a "specialized attack"
group, but I can hardly restrain my tears when I think of you.

You did all you could to educate me, to help me to face the
future. I am very sad that I must die without having given you
anything in exchange—neither happiness nor serenity. I can
hardly ask you to make the sacrifice of my life as well, nor to
take pride in my death, however glorious it may be. It is better
that I should not speak of all that to you.

I never dared to refuse the young girl you intended me to
marry. I did not want to lose your affection, and I was so happy to
receive your letters.

I would have loved to see you once again and to go to sleep
in your arms. But the only place where I could have met you is
Moji. For the day after tomorrow I must leave, the day after
tomorrow I must die.

It is possible that I shall fly over Hakata. I will bid you farewell in silence from above the clouds. Mother, you used to dream of a splendid future for me, and I am going to disappoint you. I shall never forget your anxiety when I had to pass examinations. I joined this group in spite of your disapproval, but I can see now that I would have done better to follow your advice.

Try to comfort yourself by remembering that I am a very good pilot, and that it is very rare that a member of the air force with so few hours in the air to his credit is chosen for such a mission.

When I am dead, you will still have Makio. You preferred me because I was the elder, but believe me, Makio is worth far more than I. He is very good at looking after all the family interests. You will also have my sisters Chiyoko and Hiroko, and your grandchildren.

Cheer up. My soul will always be near you. Your joys will be mine, but if you are sad, I shall be sorrowful too.

Sometimes I feel tempted to come back to you, but that would be a cowardly action.

When I was baptized the priest said these words over me: "Renounce your own self." I can remember that very well. I will commit my soul to our Saviour before I die, pierced by American bullets. For everything is in God's hands. There is neither life nor death for those who live in God. Jesus Himself has said: "Thy will be done."

I read the Bible every day. Then I feel very close to you. When I crash to my death, I shall have the Bible and the Book of Psalms in my aircraft. I will also take along the mission badge which the director of the college gave me, and your medal.

Perhaps I did not take that marriage business as seriously as I should have done. I would not like to give the impression that I lacked respect for my betrothed and her family. Could you make her understand that it is better to make an end. I would really have liked to marry her: I would gladly have given you that happiness. I did not have time.

I ask only one thing of you: that you should forgive me. But I can go in peace, for I know that you always forgive me. Mother, how I admire you! You have always been so much braver than I. You are capable of forcing yourself to do painful things, and I find it impossible. Your only fault is that you spoilt me too much. But I myself wanted you to do so and I do not reproach you for that.

When I crash on to the enemy I will pray for you that all your prayers may be granted. I have asked Ueno to bring you this letter, but you must never show it to anybody. I am ashamed of it. I have the impression that it is not I whom death is waiting for. When I think that I shall never see you again, I am overcome with grief.

"Some of His Friends Have Urged Me..."

FRANCIS SCOTT KEY

Francis Scott Key (1779-1843; American lawyer and poet.) Fort McHenry, now a national historic site, overlooks Baltimore where the Patapsco River empties into Chesapeake Bay. On September 14, 1814, it had a distinctly unpromising future. A British fleet, flush with the achievement of having burned Washington, was maneuvering into position to accord the same treatment to Baltimore. Key was not a combatant; as he hurriedly informed his mother in this letter, he hoped to intercede for an old friend who was being held prisoner by the British. The British admiral agreed to release the friend; but since he intended to destroy Fort McHenry during the night, he decided to keep Key prisoner during the bombardment. The young lawyer spent the night on H.M.S. Maiden, watching the storm break over Baltimore. When "by dawn's early light" he saw "the flag was still there," he wrote a poem about it on the back of an envelope he found in his pocket. The poem was published a week later in the Baltimore American. Set to the music of an old song, "Anacron in Heaven," by John Stafford Smith, "The Star-Spangled Banner" was officially adopted as the National Anthem by Congress in 1931.

Key was the author of Poems *(posthumously published, 1857). They are not read, but it does not matter. His fame is secure, and will last as long as we do.*

Geo Town
2 Sep 1814.

My dr Mother,

You have made allowances, I hope, for our confusion & anxiety here, & have therefore excused my not writing sooner. Indeed for two or three days after our disgrace I had neither time or mind to do anything, and since then I have been much engaged. I had however a promise from Mr. Munro that he would write to Taney often & soon, so that you might know I was well. You have since no doubt heard how mercifully we have all been spared here. The enemy not even entering our Town, which I am sure they would have done, had they not gone off with such unnecessary precipitation. They have today left Alexandria & I trust we shall see no more of them. I hope we shall be grateful to God for this deliverance & remember how much more light our chastisement has been than we expected or deserved.

I am going in the morning to Balto. to proceed in a flag-vessel to Genl Ross. Old Dr. Beans of Marlbro' is taken prisoner by the Enemy, who threaten to carry him off. Some of his friends have urged me to apply for a flag & go to try to procure his release.

I hope to return in about 8 or 10 days, though it is uncertain, as I do not know where to find the fleet. As soon as I get back I hope I shall be able to get out to Fredk.

The children will be delighted to see their mother. Give my love to them & to Papa.

> God bless you my dr. mother
> Ever yr most affect. son
> F. S. KEY

"Elle Est Jolie et Jeune"

JOYCE KILMER

Joyce Kilmer (1886-1918; American poet.) This is the last letter he wrote to his mother before being killed in action somewhere near Seringes, France, on July 30, 1918. Although Kilmer's life was short, he did do more than write "Trees." He was on the editorial staff of The New York Times Magazine, *and published three volumes of poems and two of criticism.*

Heywood Broun, in It Seems to Me *(1933), complained that "Trees (if I have the name right) is one of the most annoying pieces of verse within my knowledge. . . . Trees maddens me, because it contains the most insincere line ever written by mortal man. Surely the Kilmer tongue must have been not far from the*

Kilmer cheek when he wrote, 'Poems are made by fools like me.' "

Annie K. Kilmer, to whom this letter is addressed, wrote a biography of Joyce in 1920, titled Memories of My Son.

Headquarters Co., 165th Inf.,
A. E. F., France, June 28, 1918

Dear Brat—I received three letters from you yesterday and today, the first I have had for a long time. Your letters always come in bunches like that, and this morning I received two admirable boxes of Mirror candy, in perfect condition. I certainly was delighted to get it, as it is a long time since I have had any candy. My gratitude is so great that I even will refer to it as "Sweets." I was also glad to get your picture taken on shipboard. You must send to Larchmont another copy of the picture of yourself looking at my photograph, you sent me some weeks ago, as I had to remove it from its mount and cut it down to make it fit into my wallet.

All the rest of the fellows in the Intelligence Section (there are nine of us, nearly all college graduates and men of some standing —editors, brokers, etc.) have pictures of their mothers, but none of them so good looking as mine. You would be amused at some of the scenes when your picture is exhibited. Tired from a long hike from a stay in the trenches, I am having an omelet and some fried potatoes and some vin rouge beaucoup in a French peasant's little kitchen. It is a cottage such as you and I often visited in Derbyshire and Cambridgeshire—a low grey stone building with rose trees against the wall; a tiny garden and a geometrically neat path. The kitchen floor is of stone; the table is without a cloth, but shining from much polishing. The only thing to distinguish it from the typical English rural cottage is the crucifix on the wall and the wooden shoes at the door. (People wear sabots out-of-doors, cloth slippers in the house, leather shoes on Sunday.) After such a repast as I have described I take out my wallet to pay my bill, and the sharp eyes of little Marie or Pierre intently watching this strange soldat Americain, spy the picture. At once an inquisitive but delighted infant is on my knee demanding a closer inspection of the picture. Then mama must see it, and grandpere, and veuve vatre from across the street (the man of the house can't see it; he is away from home on the errand that brought me across the sea). Well, they all say "elle est jolie ma foi et jeune aussi." These comments have been made on your picture many times, in many towns, which I will one day show you on a map of France.

I have not much anxiety for my father, for I look on his condition as a state of rest really necessary to a mind so constantly busy, but I am glad that from you I have inherited the power of readily escaping from worry and work and entering with enthusiasm into whatever mirth I find around me—in finding good and true and merry friends everywhere. I think that some of this quality would have helped my father very much and increased his bodily and mental health. I worried grievously about you for a while, and wished that I could have been with you when my father was taken ill, but I don't worry now; you are too spirited and courageous for anybody to worry about. I certainly admire you more than ever, and look forward eagerly to regular banquets at Henri's and Rector's with you.

I want you to meet all the Regimental Intelligence Section—a fine bunch of men and good comrades. We have taken big chances together, and it has made us the best of friends. You will like them and they will like you.

Yours affectionately, JOYCE.

"How That Will Worry Ma!"

SUSAN ANNE CHAFFEE LAMB

Susan Anne Chaffee Lamb (1839-1892; American housewife.) She was born in Providence, Rhode Island, but she married a Virginian, William Lamb. He was called to active service when war came, made a major, and sent to take over the defense of the Cape Fear River approaches. Mrs. Lamb remained in Norfolk with her two children; when Union troops seized the city and her third child was born, her husband made plans for her to join him. By the fall of 1862, Major (now Colonel) Lamb had made Fort Fisher "sufficiently impregnable," and he sent for his wife. She wrote letters to the War Department and to the White House, and was finally given permission to cross through the lines. With her children, she moved into a house the colonel built for her a mile up the beach from the fort; they called it The Cottage. They were comfortable enough there, though the house was lonely and exposed to the weather, and though at night they could hear firing from the fort—the great guns protecting Confederate blockade runners as they made their run through the Union fleet.

By the end of 1864, Wilmington was the only open port in the Confederacy, and it was obvious that a great battle would have to be fought for Fort Fisher, one that might decide the war. The attack came on Christmas Day, and it was unsuccessful. Mrs. Lamb describes it in this letter, written in early January, but never finished; it was found many years later in a writing desk, and was given to Colonel Lamb. However, the fort, weakened by thousands of shells thrown into it, by casualties, and by lack of support from ground troops further inland, was attacked again on January 15, 1865, and taken by a combined sea and land operation in which Lieutenant Commander W.B. Cushing, among many others, played an heroic part. Mr. and Mrs. Lamb lived through the Reconstruction period and on into a better peace. She died in 1892; her husband survived her by seventeen years.

Her letter can remind us that war is the most terrible and the most unnecessary of human actions.

"The Cottage"
January 9th, 1865

I KNOW YOU have been anxious enough about us all, knowing what a terrible bombardment we have had, but I am glad that I can relieve your mind on our behalf and tell you that we are all safe and well, through a most merciful and kind Providence. God was with us from the first, and our trust was so firm in him that I can truly say that both Will and I "feared no evil."

I staid in my comfortable little home until the fleet appeared, when I packed up and went across the river to a large but empty house, of which I took possession; a terrible gale came on which delayed the attack for several days, but Saturday it came at last in all its fury; I could see it plainly from where I was; I had very powerful glasses, and sat on a stile outdoors all day watching it— an awful but magnificent sight.

I kept up very bravely (*for you know I am brave*, and *would if I thought I could*, whip Porter and Butler myself), until the last gun had ceased and it began to get dark and still. I was overcome at last and laid my head on the fence and cried for the first and last time during it all. I then got my carriage and rode to a fort nearby to learn the news, but my heart failed as I approached it, and I returned to the house and waited a dispatch which I received about 11 o'clock, saying all was well. I was quite touched with a little incident which occurred during the day; the little ones looked very grave and thoughtful; at last Dick came to me in the midst of the roaring and awful thundering and said: "Mama, I want to pray to God for my papa." He knelt down and said his little earnest prayer; then jumped up, exclaiming and dancing about: "Oh, sister, I am so glad! I am so glad! Now God will keep care of my papa."

The shelling was even more terrific on Sunday, and I, not knowing how long it might continue, concluded to go to Fayetteville, and started Sunday noon in a small steamer, with the sick and wounded, to Wilmington, where I was obliged to stay for several days in great suspense, not able to get away and not able to hear directly from Will, as the enemy had cut the wires—and then a martyr to all kinds of rumors—one day heard that Will had lost a leg, etc., etc.; but I steadfastly made up my mind to give no credit to anything bad. At last I heard again that we had driven our persecutors off, and I returned again to the place where I went first, and the next day Will came over for me and took me to the fort, which I rode all over on horseback, but we did not move for nearly a week. The fort was strewn with missiles of all kinds—it seemed a perfect miracle how any excaped—the immense works were literally skinned of their turf, but not injured in the slightest; not a bomb-proof or a magazine—*and there are more than one*—touched; the magazine the enemy thought they had destroyed was only a caisson; the men had very comfortable quarters in the fort—pretty little white-washed houses—but the shells soon set fire to them, making a large fire and dense smoke, but the works are good for dozen of sieges—plenty of everything; particularly plenty of the greatest essential—brave hearts. Our beloved General Whiting was present, but give up the whole command to Will, to whom he now gives, as is due, the whole credit of building and defending his post, and has urged his promotion to Brigadier-General, which will doubtless be received soon, though neither of us really care for it.

We expect the Armada again, and will give him a *warmer* reception next time. The fort, expecting a longer time of it, was reserving their heaviest fire for nearer quarters. Butler's "gallant troops" came right under one side of the fort, but our grape and canister soon drove them off, and *not* Porter's shell, which did not happen to be falling that way at that time; they left their traces sufficiently next morning.

The "gallant fellow" who stole the horse from the inside of

the fort was doubtless so scared he didn't know where he was. The *true* statement of the thing is, that an officer, unauthorized by Will or the General, sent a courier outside the fort with a message to some troops outside, and soon after he left the fort, was attacked and killed by a Yankee sharp-shooter hidden under a bridge. The poor body fell and the *horse* was taken, and the flag spoken of, in the same way, was shot from the parapet and blew outside, when it was taken. When any of them see the inside of the fort, they will never live to tell the tale.

Ah, mother! you all, at home peacefully, do not know the misery of being driven from home by a miserable, cruel enemy! 'Tis a sad sight to see the sick and aged turned out in the cold to seek a shelter. I cannot speak feelingly because of any feeling myself, as God is good to us, and has so favored us with life, health and means, and my dear, good husband has provided me a comfortable home in the interior, where I can be safe.

Will had worried so much about you, dear mother, thinking you would be so anxious about us. He often exclaims, when reading some of the lying accounts; "How that will worry Ma."

How is my darling Willie? We do so want to see our boy. I think Will will have to send for him in the Spring. Kiss the dear one dozens of times for his father and mother.

Though it was a very unpleasant Christmas to me, still the little ones enjoyed theirs. Will had imported a crowd of toys for them, and they are as happy as possible with them.

I have not heard from my dear home since last August, and you can imagine how very anxious I am to hear, particularly of dear Sister Ria. Is she with George? Do write me of all the dear ones I love so much. How I would love to see you all, so much, and home!

"It Is Hard to Desert"

CARL SCHURZ

Carl Schurz (1829-1906; American journalist, statesman, and general.) He first came to the United States in 1852, and lived to be a hero and an example to a generation of Americans. He was born and educated in Germany, took part in the insurrection in Baden and the Palatinate in 1849, was arrested, but escaped to

Switzerland and then to America. He became a leading member of the Republican Party, a more radical organization then than now, and was appointed minister to Spain in 1861. But he resigned to enter the Union army as soon as the war broke out.

Schurz served at the second battle of Bull Run, at Chancellorsville, Gettysburg, and Chattanooga, and was discharged as a major general of volunteers. After the war he was editor of the New York Evening Post, *and was a senator from Missouri (1869-75), after which he served as Secretary of the Interior. His* Reminiscences of a Long Life *(1905-06) was an especially popular account of an immigrant's life in America.*

In at least one respect he was a prophet. In a letter to Theodore Petrasch on October 12, 1864, he said:

I will make a prophecy, that may sound peculiar. In fifty years Lincoln's name will be inscribed close to Washington's on this Republic's roll of honor.

Philadelphia, May 5, 1862

I AM very thankful to S. for not giving you the first newspaper report of my illness. You would have worried unnecessarily. I was actually quite sick for a couple of weeks so that I had to keep to my bed for about eight days. But the disease was not typhus fever. I suffered from a very severe and continuous headache and such great exhaustion that I could hardly stir. Now I have had some perfectly quiet days here in Philadelphia and am again quite well. In a few days I shall be as strong as ever.

We hope to be relieved of our uncertainty within a short time. The President has not yet accepted my resignation nor declared himself concerning my future. Still, I shall hear something definite in two or three days. This condition of uncertainty about the immediate future is decidedly unpleasant, but one must become accustomed to slowness of decision in our government.

I well know, dear Mama, that you could not rejoice in the thought of seeing me in the army instead of in a foreign country; but when a man has fought as I have, for a good cause to which he is bound with all the force of conviction, it is hard to desert it just at the moment a final decision is pending. It is hard to sit inactive and lazy abroad when the result of years of labor, nay, the fate of the republic to which one has dedicated himself,

hangs by a thread. I confidently believe that it will not be necessary to secure much more help in a military way. We know now
that we are strong enough to overthrow the rebels, and while I
do not believe that despite all of our victories the matter will end
in a few weeks, it does seem certain that two principal battles
will end the major operations, unless a great reverse happens to
us. But then will begin the most serious of all undertakings;
namely, so to dispose the results of victory as to insure to the
country a great, free, and peaceful future. And in this business I
shall be in no sense superfluous. In order fully to solve the problem
that will fall to me in this connection I must have secured a footing in the army. The spirit of the army will be of the greatest
importance in the solution of the great questions, and unfortunately (so far as the principal leaders are concerned) it has not
thus far been what it ought to be.

When you examine the entire situation of affairs the thought
will come to you of itself that the cause is worthy of a sacrifice. It
is true I should often think more of the question of personal advantage, but you must pardon me if I cannot always do so. When
one has done all he can for a good and great cause, the consciousness of fulfilling one's duty in great measure is also not without
value. If the President shall now refuse to accept my resignation,
I shall have done my part and we will go back, but in no case
without seeing you all again.

So, dearest Mama, write me quite fully how you are; and whatever wishes you may have I shall be happy to fulfill them. We are
now all well. The children have both had the measles but are
now well again. Margarethe is on the whole also well.

"Really and Truely My Situation"

GEORGE WASHINGTON

George Washington (1732-1799; American statesman and soldier.)
Pater patriae had already made several irrevocable commitments
to the American cause by the time the first of these letters was
written. He had been among the Virginia Burgesses who as-
sembled at the Raleigh Tavern in 1774 following the Colonial
Governor's dissolution of the Virginia Assembly. He had been

chairman of the committee which adopted the Fairfax Resolutions, and he had been a Virginia delegate to both the first and second Continental Congresses.

By 1787, the date of the second letter, General Washington had won the War of Independence and had retired to Mount Vernon. The newborn country was still trying to govern itself by Articles of Confederation, but soon would incorporate itself as the United States, and would need George Washington again. The tone of this second letter is extremely businesslike. I suspect that old Mrs. Washington was being just a trifle difficult.

In a recent article, Dumas Malone conceded that when you come right down to it, George Washington is the greatest American. It is hard to dispute this opinion.

Mount Vernon, 14 August, 1775.

Honored Madam,

If it is in my power to avoid going to the Ohio again, I shall; but if the command is pressed upon me, by the general *voice* of the country, and offered upon such terms as cannot be objected against, it would reflect dishonor upon me to refuse; and *that,* I am sure, must or *ought* to give you greater uneasiness, than my going in an honorable command, for upon no other terms I will accept of it. At present I have no proposals made to me, nor have I any advice of such an intention, except from private hands.

Mount Vernon, 15 February, 1787.

Hond. Madam,

In consequence of your communication to George Washington, of your want of money, I take the (first safe) conveyance by Mr. John Dandridge to send you 15 guineas, which believe me is all I have, and which indeed ought to have been paid many days ago to another, agreeable to my own assurances. I have now demands upon me for more than 500£, three hundred and forty odd of which is due for the tax of 1786; and I know not where or when, I shall receive one shilling with which to pay it. In the last two years I made no crops. In the first I was obliged to buy corn and this year have none to sell, and my wheat is so bad, I cannot neither eat it myself nor sell it to others, and Tobacco I make none. Those who owe me money cannot or will not pay it without suits, and to sue is to do nothing; whilst my expences, not from any extravagance, or an inclination on my part to live splendidly, but for the absolute support of my family and the visitors who are constantly here, are exceedingly high; higher indeed than I can support without selling part of my estate, which I am disposed to do, rather than run in debt, or continue to be so; but this I cannot do, without taking much less than the lands I have offered for sale are worth. This is really and truely my situation. I do not however offer it as any excuse for not paying you what may really be due; for let this be little or much, I am willing, however unable, to pay to the utmost farthing; but it is really hard upon me when you have taken every thing you wanted from the Plantation by which money could be raised, when I have not received one farthing, directly nor indirectly from the place for more than twelve years, if ever, and when, in that time I have paid, as appears by Mr. Lund Washington's accounts against me (during my absence) Two hundred and sixty odd pounds, and by my own account Fifty odd pounds out of my own Pocket to you, besides (if I am rightly informed) every thing that has been raised by the Crops on the Plantation. Who to blame, or whether any body is to blame for these things I know not, but these are facts; and as the purposes for which I took the Estate are not answered, nor likely to be so, but dissatisfaction on all sides have taken place, I do not mean to have any thing more to say to your Plantation or negros since the first of January, except the fellow who is here, and who will not, as he has formed connections in this neighborhood, leave it. As experience has proved him, I will hire. Of this my intention, I informed my brother John sometime ago, whose death I sincerely lament on many accounts, and on this painful event condole with you most sincerely. I do not mean by this declaration to withhold any aid or support I can give from you; for whilst I have a shilling left, you shall have part, if it is wanted, whatever my own distresses may be. What I shall then give, I shall have credit for; now I have not, for tho' I have received nothing from your Quarter, and am told that every farthing goes to you, and have moreover paid between 3 and 4 hundred pounds besides out of my own pocket, I am viewed as a delinquent, and considered perhaps by the world as [an] unjust and undutiful son. My advice to you, therefore, is to do one of two things with the Plantation. Either let your grandson Bushrod Washington, to whom the land is given by his Father, have the whole interest there, that is, lands and negros, at a reasonable rent; or, next year (for I presume it is too late this, as the overseer may be engaged) to let him have the land at a certain yearly rent during your life; and hire out the negros. This would ease you of all care and trouble, make your income certain, and your support ample. Further, my sincere and pressing advice to you is, to break up housekeeping, hire out all the rest of your servants except a man and a maid, and live with one of your children. This would relieve you entirely from the cares of this world, and leave your mind at ease to reflect undisturbedly on that which ought to come. On this subject I have been full with my Brother John, and it was determined he should endeavor to get you to live with him. He alas is no more, and three, only of us remain. My house is at your service, and [I] would press you most sincerely and most devoutly to accept it, but I am sure, and candor requires me to say, it will never answer your purposes in any shape whatsoever. For in truth it may be compared to a well resorted tavern, as scarcely any strangers who are going from north to south, or from south to north, do not spend a day or two at it. This would, were you to be an inhabitant of it, oblige you to do one of 3 things: 1st, to be always dressing to appear in company; 2d, to come into [the room] in a dishabille, or 3d, to be as it were a prisoner in your own chamber. The first you'ld not like; indeed, for a person at your time of life it would be too fatiguing. The 2d, I should not like, because those who resort here are, as I observed before, strangers and people of the first distinction. And the 3d, more than probably, would not be pleasing to either of us. Nor indeed could you be retired in any room in my house; for what with the sitting up of company, the noise and bustle of servants, and many other things, you would not be able to enjoy that calmness and serenity of mind, which in my opinion you ought now to prefer to every other consideration in life. If you incline to follow this advice, the House and lots on which you now live you may rent, and enjoy the benefit of the money arising therefrom as long as you live. This with the rent of the land at the Little Falls, and the hire of your negros, would bring you in an income which would be much more than sufficient to answer all your wants and make ample amends to the child you live with; for myself I should desire nothing; if it did not, I would most cheerfully contribute more. A man, a maid, the phaeton and two horses, are all you would want. To lay in a sufficiency for the support of these would not require ¼ of your income, the rest would purchase every necessary you could possibly want, and place it in your power to be serviceable to those with whom you may live, which no doubt would be agreeable to all parties.

There are such powerful reasons in my mind for giving this advice that I cannot help urging it with a degree of earnestness which is uncommon for me to do. It is, I am convinced, the only means by which you can be happy. The cares of a family, without any body to assist you; the charge of an estate the profits of which depend upon wind, weather, a good overseer, an honest man, and a thousand other circumstances, cannot be right or proper at your advanced age, and for me, who am absolutely prevented from attending to my own plantations, which are almost within call of me, to attempt the care of yours, would be folly in the extreme; but [by] the mode I have pointed out, you may reduce your income to a certainty, be eased of all trouble, and if you are so disposed, may be perfectly happy; for happiness depends more upon the internal frame of a person's own mind, than on the externals in the world. Of the last, if you will pursue the plan here recommended, I am sure you can want nothing that is essential. The other depends wholly upon yourself, for the riches of the Indies cannot purchase it.

Mrs. Washington, George and Fanny join me in every good wish for you, and I am, honored madame, your most dutiful and aff. son.

FIVE

Letters from Historians and Philosophers

HISTORIANS AND PHILOSOPHERS, like bridgebuilders, work from opposite sides of a chasm and—ideally—meet in the middle. The philosopher is concerned with what men should do if they were good enough, and with what men might do if they were wise enough. He makes a pattern for human action; a template, as it were, for all of us to follow. But he cannot do this until he knows what men are doing and have done. And that is what the historian knows. He examines the past; he thus helps to explain the present; and he suggests what must be done in the future in order to avoid failure and repeat success (if any).

Philosophers and historians are therefore handy people to have around. But mankind is notoriously unwilling to take advantage of their talents. We do not listen to them; instead, we tend to think of them as solemn, humorless men working in remote solitude, and we make them even more forbidding by giving them labels: Existentionalist, Positivist, Subjectivist. Emerson was amused at one such label a hundred years ago, and remarked to his mother:

> You must know I am reckoned here a Transcendentalist, and what that beast is, all persons in Providence have a great appetite to know.

Sometimes we not only label philosophers, but ridicule them. We consider them dreamers of impossible dreams (not realizing that this is sadder for us than for them); we call them impractical, our favorite word of contempt. But the best historians and philoso-

117

phers live in this world; when they do not, we call them something else—fanatics, perhaps, or saints. Louis D. Brandeis was a philosopher as well as a jurist, and you'll find this almost too practical statement in a letter to his mother:

> You often said, dearest mother, that I find fault—but I always told you candidly that I felt and sought to change only that little which appeared to me to be possible of improvement.

In many ways, these letters from historians and philosophers reveal as much or more about their authors than some of their works. An extraordinary change in Nietzsche is made apparent by two of his letters, written twenty years apart. The first says:

> I have been very wicked and do not know whether you will or can forgive me. . . . Write to me soon and write severely, for I deserve it; and no one knows better than I do how much I deserve it.

This from school; but after he grew up and became the philosopher of the superman, he wrote thus:

> Really, these dissertations on Christianity and the opinions of this man and that as to what I should do and ought to think on the subject should no longer be directed to my address. My patience won't stand it! . . . I know that if people of this kind, even including my mother and sister, had an inkling of what I was aiming at, they would have no alternative but to become my natural enemies.

Carlyle, on the other hand, sets no limitations on his discussions with his mother. He is moved on his birthday to write to her in sweet, gentle little words:

> This time Nine-and-forty years, I was a small infant few hours old, lying unconscious in your kind bosom; you piously rejoicing over me,—appointed to love me while life lasted to us both.

And Gibbon discloses a suspicion to his mother that he would never have admitted to critics or booksellers. Talking about his massive history, he says:

> Almost every body that reads has purchased, but few persons (comparatively) have read them; and I find that the greater number, satisfied that they have acquired a valuable fund of entertainment, differ [defer] the perusal to the summer, the country, and a more quiet period.

More than one hundred and seventy years later, how true this perception remains; *The Decline and Fall of the Roman Empire* is still packed in many suitcases, along with bathing suits and tennis rackets, to be read *this* summer, at last.

If you enjoy reading a writer's own reaction to his success, James Bryce's letters will amuse you as much as Gibbon's. His Lordship expresses surprise at

> the compliments paid me by the newspapers and by friends or acquaintances on the "impartiality" as they call it of my U.S. book. . . . But in fact this detachment never cost me any trouble or even thought at all: it came of itself without any exertion: whereas the (other) difficulties . . . were serious, and made me more than doubtful of any merit for the book beyond that of a careful collection of facts.

All the letters in this section are fine. But if you were to ask me to choose the sentence that I think the finest, it is one written by Thoreau. "It is still a cardinal virtue with me to keep awake," he says. And he means *really* awake—awake to the whole world, to land and sky and people and things and sorrow and joy. What a virtue that is, and how difficult.

"Sauerkraut and Pickled Potatoes"

HENRY BROOKS ADAMS

Henry Brooks Adams (1838-1918; American historian and philosopher.) Adams, the grandson of one American President and the greatgrandson of another, was the profoundest pessimist America has yet produced. He graduated from Harvard and then spent two years studying and traveling in Europe; the two letters I've included were written during this first of his protracted stays abroad. When the Civil War began he became private secretary to his father, who was then minister to England (1861-68); at war's end he returned to America to seek a career in journalism. He taught history at Harvard, introducing the seminar method of advanced study, and edited the North American Review. *In*

1877 he left Harvard and spent the rest of his life writing and contemplating the relationship of man and the universe.

The major fruit of this endeavor was the two companion volumes, Mont-Saint Michel and Chartres, *"a study of 12th Century Unity," and* The Education of Henry Adams, *"a study of 20th Century Multiplicity." He wrote a number of other works, the most famous of which is his nine-volume* History of the United States During the Administrations of Jefferson and Madison, *which claims the honor of being the greatest American work of history. As a result of this study and reflection he concluded that the second law of thermodynamics, or "entropy," applies to human history as much as to mechanical energy; i.e., human institutions, like individuals, must follow the law of senescence and decay, and both man and the "celestial universe" are doomed.*

Despite his vast learning and the fame which he attained, Adams professed to believe that his education was wholly inadequate and his life a failure. If this were true we should forget him and his work, which perhaps would serve Henry Adams right. It is not true, however, and we will not and can not forget him.

Dresden, November 8, 1859.

AT No. 4, Kleine Schiessgasse we're getting on as well as could be expected. Frightful kindness overwhelms me from all sides, and I am put to my trumps to be polite. I daren't even joke except in my letters, and ever have a benign smile on my face. Certainly if I don't become as stiff as a German it's not because I don't try. You would scream to see me contest with the Herr Hofrath which of us shall enter a room first. I open the door and stand back with a bow; he says with a gesture towards the room: "bitte recht sehr; après vous;" to which I smile deprecatingly and remark: "bitte, Herr Hofrath, wollen Sie so gut sein;" if he still insists, I yield and precede; if not, he enters and I close the door after him with the highest respect. He is frightfully learned and buried in science, so that he seldom comes out, but is a good old soul and very kind. This afternoon he has been showing me all over the royal natural history collection, of which he has the care. He wants a stuffed swordfish and a lot of American sea-weeds. I should like to help him, but hardly know who to apply to.

The Frau Mutter is benign as ever. Yesterday afternoon we all went to a concert; that is the Professor, the Mother, the Augusta and I. There *we* met two of *our* friends, a Countess Rodolorowowski or something that sounds like that, and her mother. Goodness gracious, the formalities, the bowing and scraping and hopping up and down, the air of majesty with which those corpulent ladies swelled about and visited their acquaintances at the other tables. My eye, wasn't it rum. Meanwhile I sat next the amiable Fräulein (who looked deuced pretty and all the Lieutenants envied me) and I think, take the four hours through, I may have spoken about ten words an hour; in the interval sitting still and looking at my kid gloves. The Countess, too, was particularly gracious and addressed several remarks to me. Only think!

As for the Fräulein, ain't she a one-er, that's all. She reminds me all the time of Nelly Lowe; in fact I call her "Miss Nelly" now. She's a will of her own and gives me the most immense delight. A perfect little Tartar, and smooth as a cat. I'll do her the justice to say however, she doesn't seem to have any designs on my person, and it's only within a few days that she has begun to recognize my presence at all, for I don't talk a great deal and haven't paid her any profuse attention, seein' as the German girls never know what to make of it when a person takes any notice of them. So I laugh at her nonsense and avoid personal contact.

With the brother, Theodor, about twenty-four or five years old, I'm better acquainted. He has a large collection of coins and is passionately fond of all sorts of antiquarian rubbish. If papa wants any particular German coins I might perhaps be able to get them through young Reichenbach. The other day we went off on a foot-excursion and from nine o'clock till nearly four we hardly stopped. Visited a lot of villages, old churches, graveyards, and pretty walks and views. The neighborhood of Dresden is, as you know, remarkably pretty, and as the Theodor knows every foot of it and its history, and the local legends in which Saxony abounds, it is very pleasant to wander about, though I was pretty tired when I returned. Just now I am in hopes of getting up a still more interesting excursion. You must know Saxony has lots of ghosts, ruined castles, haunted churchyards and the like. Madame Reichenbach is superstitious and in her heart, if she only dared say it, believes them all. Indeed I believe every man in Germany, high or low, has more or less of this, and they gravely assert that the White Lady who is said to haunt half the royal places in

Germany and announce by her appearance the death of the King or the birth of an heir to the throne, has been seen so often and the fact so clearly authenticated that it is impossible to doubt it, and they tell a lot of ordinary ghost stories to prove it.

When sensible people talk this way, I can only make a face, shrug my shoulders and politely smile. Of course I believe that it's all stuff and nonsense, and wish I could see one of their white ladies. But as this is impossible, I have set to work to see if we couldn't hunt up a ghost, and just as sure as I can find a promising one, I am going after him; and we propose (to Madame's horror) to select some haunted ruin and sleep there a night to see if the spectre will be hospitable. Of course it must be really romantic; otherwise it will only be a bore.

I'm pretty well settled now for the winter. Three mornings in the week at nine o'clock I go down and take riding lessons; three others my fencing master comes and teaches me how to use a rapier. This secures a tolerable amount of exercise and regularity. At eight o'clock in the evening I am summoned to tea and we talk till past nine, but then usually to bed. At one we dine. Madame is horrified that I don't eat anything. She's accustomed to German appetites and seems to think that a man must starve if he doesn't swill sauerkraut and pickled potatoes. Still I will say she does spare me the sauerkraut as much as possible, and her table is the best I have yet seen. . . .

Paris, 1, July, 1860.

I'M WAITING patiently for papa's speech to arrive. The sketch I've seen of it and the papers which Charles sent me, gave me the general idea, which was precisely what we would expect. It's all right. This session has gone off admirably for him, and couldn't be better. As for you, I know that in many ways you must feel homesick; but have there never been times at home when you felt homesick and unhappy too? For my own part, I'm getting dreadfully old and cautious. I find that people are unhappy everywhere and happy everywhere. Charles writes me a plan according to which I should study law in Washington and stay with you always. I never knew before this how I liked Quincy and Boston, and how sorry I should be to cut loose of them altogether; but this course, which certainly is the one I should choose and follow, if it will go, finishes setting me afloat. I shall make up my bed in Washington, and no doubt it will be just as pleasant as anywhere else. At all events, whether it is or not, it's the place that my education has fitted me best for, and where I could be of most use. So if papa and you approve this course and it's found easy to carry out, you can have at least one of your sons always with you. For my own part, it's the only idea I've met with as to my own course that satisfies me entirely. . . .

"When Mothers Like You Are Increased"

LOUIS DEMBITZ BRANDEIS

Louis Dembitz Brandeis (1856-1941; American jurist.) He was described by Chief Justice Charles Evans Hughes as "master of microscope and telescope," because he combined technical proficiency in the law with powerful social vision. Brandeis was still a young attorney in Boston when he wrote this short letter to his mother, but he was already known as "the people's counsel" because of his many activities in the public interest. "The Brandeis brief" became a model for advocating the validity of social legislation. In 1916 he was appointed to the Supreme Court by Woodrow Wilson, and he retired in 1939. Brandeis's opinions while a member of the high court were distinguished for their hospitality to economic experimentation and for close scrutiny of anything that might put restraints on freedom of expression. Brandeis University is named after him.

November 12, 1888

I MUST send you another birthday greeting and tell you how much I love you; that with each day I learn to extol your love and your worth more—and that when I look back over my life, I can find nothing in your treatment of me that I would alter. You often said, dearest mother, that I find fault—but I always told you candidly that I felt and sought to change only that little which appeared to me to be possible of improvement. I believe, most beloved mother, that the improvement of the world, reform, can only arise when mothers like you are increased thousands of times and have more children.

"The Owner of Blue China..."

JAMES BRYCE

James Bryce, Viscount Bryce of Dechmont (1838-1922; English statesman and historian.) The very model of a distinguished British public servant, Lord Bryce deftly managed a life of law, diplomacy, and the making and writing of history. He was a Liberal M.P. for twenty-seven years; from 1907 to 1913, ambassador to the United States; a founder of the League of Nations; and, at various times, he was also Chief Secretary for Ireland, professor of civil law at Oxford, and president of the Board of Trade. Bryce wrote a large number of books, the best known of which are The Holy Roman Empire *(1862, originally an essay) and* The American Commonwealth, *the classic short study of nineteenth century America.*

This letter I cherish for two thoughts: first, his reminder that "one would like to draw from success more than the mere pleasure of succeeding"; and second, his perplexity—and how much keener it would be today!—that there is so little curiosity in the world except over personal matters.

Oxford.
February 24, (1889)

Among English voices, sights and occupation, India is already fading away like as a dream when one waketh; yet perhaps it is rather as when one puts away a subject into a dark corner of one's mind, not to be bewildered by thinking longer over it, yet knowing one can draw it out again. People ask me but few questions touching it: how little curiosity except over the personal matters of the moment there is in the world!

I have been set to thinking how little love of enquiry for its own sake there seems to be in the world by the compliments paid me by the newspapers and by friends or acquaintances on the "impartiality" as they call it of my U.S. book. Trevelyan for instance said, "How difficult you must have found it to avoid indicating your own feelings on questions and to maintain the same tone, with nothing sensational from the beginning to the end." As people say this, I suppose they express the usual tendency: but in fact this detachment never cost me any trouble or even thought at all: it came of itself without any exertion: whereas the difficulties of arranging topics, of varying manner of treatment, of settling what to say about such matters as Public Opinion and the Merits of Democracy, of avoiding (which I haven't quite done) that lapsing into platitudes which you and Papa used to make merry over thirty-five years ago—all these were serious, and made me more than doubtful of any merit for the book beyond that of a careful collection of relevant facts.

The reception given it, now that I realise it from the reviews and what friends tell me, is far beyond what I could have expected. What most surprised me is to be told by so many people, not all of whom can be flatterers, and many of whom have no special interest in history or politics, that they find it so interesting, and can read all of it with enjoyment. I tell Minnie to keep my head from being turned with these compliments: yet though the praise is more than is good for one, there comes also a sense of humility in thinking how far one comes short of keeping in actual life and political action on the sort of level which people seem to find in the book, and which indeed I have wished to place it on. Like the owner of the blue china, I feel called on to try to live up to it: and even, though conscious of so many deficiencies, in a way encouraged to try to use to better purpose and with more constancy such knowledge as I have gathered, and such influence as the acceptance of the book may give me. One would like to draw from success something better than the mere pleasure of succeeding. Of that, the best part by far is your gratification, and that of the girls and Annan. I am indeed more glad than I can tell you to have been permitted to procure this enjoyment for you—to whom with Papa I owe most of whatever taste or turn for literature I have.

The Sage of Chelsea

THOMAS CARLYLE

Thomas Carlyle (1795-1881; Scottish essayist and historian.) All Scotsmen may not be dour and dyspeptic, but at the age of thirty, Thomas Carlyle had little reason to feel anything but his countrymen's legendary despair. The son of a stonemason, he had successively tried and given up the law, teaching, and encyclopedia writing, all with equal disgust. Then his translations of some of the works of Goethe gained him his first reputation and his first "hero," and started him on his life's work.

In 1824 and 1825 he visited Paris and London, where he met Coleridge, Lamb, Hazlitt, and other literary men. In 1826 he married talented Jane Welsh; and before long they moved to Craigenputtock, a solitary farmstead in Dumfriesshire, where he wrote essays on Burns, Voltaire, Goethe, and completed a somewhat autobiographical satire, Sartor Resartus, *or "The Tailor Re-Tailored," according to which all material things and all conventions, creeds, and customs of mankind are considered as* clothes, *i.e., as symbols of an immaterial, eternal reality beyond the reach of sense perception. In 1834, still seeking "bread and work," he settled at Cheyne Row, Chelsea, London, where he remained for the rest of his life: thus his sobriquet, "The Sage of Chelsea."*

Carlyle wrote a number of books, the best known of which is History of the French Revolution; *its thesis is that history is much less a chain of events (though it is that) than a revelation, through great leaders, of the operation of eternal justice in human society. He was a crusty, difficult, lovable and great man; a more solicitous son than a considerate husband.*

Chelsea, 12th September, 1840.

... I HAVE had wearisome Americans here: they are sent by kind friends, and I study to receive them as well as I can. They claim nothing of me but a little of my company, poor fellows! We had certain American *women* in the summertime; they had come over here as "delegates," to discourse and speculate in a grand assemblage gathered in London from all the world to *civilize* Africa, and look after the black slaves. *Female* delegates were a class of persons the Assemblage did not understand, but rather scunner'd* at, and finally had to reject. The good women were very angry; and determined to preach for their own behoof still; they themselves, in a meeting-house they borrowed. The audience met accordingly; the main female delegate got up to discourse, and sad enough,—could find nothing to say, but sat

* Viewed with great disapproval or disgust.

down again in a very broken manner! People thought *her* also "gey idle o' Wark." Yet I think she was a good kind of woman. She had been here with us before that, she and three others, her bottle-holders; rigid-looking elderly Quakeresses;—terribly disappointed that I would not crusade with them in favour of the black slaves, as the one thing needful; I told them, as usual, that the *green* and *yellow* slaves, grown green with sheer hunger in my own neighbourhood, were far more interesting to me! I added moreover that I myself had been a slave all the days of my life; and still had a hard battle to fight, at all moments, to get any portion of my own just will made good. In fine, I did not hide from them that I considered their black-slave concern a business lying in *their* parish, not mine.

We have great work with *Temperance* here: ballad-singers satirizing it on the streets; on the other hand, rough earnest men, reformed drunkards as they profess themselves, speaking to great crowds about it on the Sundays, who listen very considerately. I understand it is making real progress. The very Irish, poor wretches, are abjuring drink by the million. I say, it is the *first beginning of emancipation* to them. I could almost weep to hear these poor rude workmen zealously calling on their fellow-creatures, in such way as they can, to awake into manhood, and abjure the slavery of Gin! They speak evidently from the heart: *this* is something practical and true they are talking of,—while nothing but *organ* psalmody and vague *jinner-janner** is going on all round them from those *hired* to speak. A Scotch Bricklayer in this quarter is said to be one of the most zealous: a head man among the Teetotallers from the North Country was telling us this Bricklayer's history, a while ago. He had sunk into tippling habits, saw his affairs gradually crumbling to ruin; his Wife made no complaint in words, but her silent sorrow maddened the man, as he thought of himself and it; coming home one night from the Tavern, mazed, mad, given up to the Devil, he determined to kill her: she was asleep with the child beside her; he took the carving knife; had his hand raised to strike her,—when by God's great mercy, she awoke; the look she gave him cut his heart asunder; he burst into tears, into prayer; and considers himself now (for his worldly affairs are all prospering again) as consecrated by Heaven to warn his

* Twiddle-twaddle.

fellow-creatures as to the matter, by all means, in all places and times.—Surely we will wish these poor people prosperity more and more.— . . .

Chelsea, 24 March, 1843.

M Y DEAR MOTHER—Having a few minutes to myself to-day I will again scribble you a line. The Doctor sent me down Alick's Letter; the best news in which was that you were in your usual tolerable state of health; that you had walked out with him "to the top of Potter Knowe." I am very glad to hear so much authentically particularized.—Since yesterday, in order to be farther from the fire in these warmer days, and have my *side* to the light, which I like better, I have shifted my writing-table; and now every time I look up, *your* affectionate sorrowing face looks down on me from the Picture Frame above the mantel-piece*: my dear good Mother! It has a sorrow in it, that face, which goes into my very heart. But it is not to be called a mere "sorrow" either; it is a noble *weariness* rather, as of much work *done*. I will wish all men and all women such a "sorrow."

Chelsea, 5 December, 1844.

M Y DEAR MOTHER— . . . Yesterday which was my birthday, I meant to have written to you: I said to myself, "It is the least thou canst do on *her* behalf for bringing thee into the world!" I rightfully purposed and meant: but just at the time intended for that pious object, an impertinent visitor was pleased to drop in, and my hands were tied! I reflected that you could not have *got* the Letter any sooner at anyrate; and so decided to write to-day.

Dear Mother, many thoughts, sure enough were in my head all yesterday! This time Nine-and-forty years, I was a small infant a few hours old, lying unconscious in your kind bosom; you piously rejoicing over me,—appointed to love me while life lasted to us both. What a time to look back, thro' so many days, marked all with faithful labour by you, with joy and sorrow! I too could weep over them: but we will not weep, dear Mother;—surely we

* The painting by Maxwell, hung at this time over the drawing-room or study mantel-piece. In later years Carlyle had it hung over the fireplace in his bedroom.

may say withal as the Old Hebrew devoutly did, "Hitherto hath the Lord helped us!" Yes; for all our sorrows and difficulties, we have not been without help;—neither shall we be. Your poor "long sprawl of an ill-put-together thing," as you once defined me, has grown up to be a distinct somewhat in this world; and his good Mother's toil and travail with him was not entirely in vain. Much is come and gone; and we are still left here:—and ought not our true effort, and endeavour more than ever, for the days that yet remain, to be even this, That we may serve the Eternal Maker of us; struggle to serve Him faithfully, Him and not the Enemies of Him! Even so.—My ever-loved Mother, I salute you with my affection once more, and thank you for bringing me into this world, and for all your unwearied care over me there. May God reward you for it,—as assuredly He will and does: I never can reward you!—

Alas, here comes in another Visitor; who falls to my lot, Jane being out: so I have to break off abruptly while my tale is but half told! I will write again before long.— . . .

Chelsea, 29 June, 1853.

My dear good Mother—. . . This morning we had again a Note from John: he is very punctual about writing; which, as well as his being near you and always within reach, is a great comfort to us. In the Note before last he told us of a *ham* you were about sending; good kind Mother! It was very wise and right that he advised you not to send it at present; but the thought of its being intended to be sent is, and will remain, a thing of real value to me. It is one of a thousand such things with which my poor life, ever since it began, has been made rich by you. Whatever other things have gone wrong with me, the love of my true Mother never went wrong; but followed me ever inseparable, in good and evil fortune, and I should be harder of heart than is suitable for man if I could ever forget that fact. And, alas, what can I do in return for you, dear Mother? Nothing, nothing! I will try to *live* by the noble example you showed; and to hold fast for myself, and speak abroad as I can for others, the precious simple *wisdom* I learned from my Mother: let that be a comfort to her in her old age, in looking back upon a long life that has many sorrows in it. And let us all take Courage, courage; and look, with humble trust, for a good issue to *all* that was really *good* in us; and thro' Time and thro' Eternity, never quit that sacred hope. Oh thank you, thank you, dear pious-hearted Mother for the precious breeding you gave me: things that I feel to be *wise,* to be God's *truth,* and fit to be spoken aloud before all mortals, and even thundered in their ears in these sad days,—how often do I find with an unspeakable tenderness of recollection, "*That is thy Mother's,* now; that thou got from thy poor Mother, long ago! May God reward her for it,—as of a surety He will and does!"—I think, the older I grow, the more entirely I feel myself my Father's and my Mother's Son; and have more and more reason to be thankful, and piously proud, that I had such Parents. Courage, dear Mother, we will not fear anything, but hope till death and thro' death! The soul that has been devoutly loyal to the Highest, that soul has the eternal privilege to *hope.* For GOOD is appointed it, and not evil, as God liveth!

. . . Jane is going off towards you, she decides, on Saturday first, . . . Poor little Jeannie, she is greatly failed, and I think even failed since last year; but she has a wonderful spirit in her still, and fights along never yielding.—. . .

I am ever my good old Mother's affectionate Son,—with blessings and prayers,—

T. CARLYLE

"The Lyceum Makes Money by Me . . ."

RALPH WALDO EMERSON

Ralph Waldo Emerson (1803-1882; American philosopher, poet lecturer, and essayist.) Transcendentalism, as Emerson noted to his mother in this letter, seemed in 1840 to mean all things to all men. It still does; and that may be because a philosophy that insists on the supremacy of the unseen, the spiritual, over the felt and experienced, is as pliable as a soft piece of taffy.

But there is no doubt that there was an American Renaissance centering around Concord, Massachusetts, in the 1840's; that Emerson was its chief light; and that Emerson, Thoreau, Margaret Fuller, Hawthorne, and William Henry Channing, among others, comprised the Transcendental Club. Emerson's renunciation of formal Christianity in favor of a transcendent spiritual philosophy was expressed in Address at Divinity College *in 1838; he had earlier resigned his ministry of the Second Church, Boston, on a matter of principle. He became the most popular lecturer in the history of America, and his addresses were revised and published as* Essays *(1841-1844). Among other well known works are* English Traits *and* Representative Men. *He is one of the chief American poets, and above all one of the most quotable, and most widely quoted, men who ever lived. Indeed, it has been suggested that he was capable only of apothegms and not of sustained philosophical thought. Those who love him do not think it matters.*

Emerson's mother raised Waldo and five other children solely by her own efforts after the early death of her husband.

Providence 28 March 1840

MY DEAR MOTHER

Only last evening I received your little note & the accompanying pacquet. Certainly I ought to have written before,—but since I have been in this town, I have been the most dissipated villager. You must know I am reckoned here a Transcendentalist, and what that beast is, all persons in Providence have a great appetite to know: So I am carried duly about from house to house, and all the young persons ask me, when the Lecture is coming upon the Great Subject? In vain I disclaim all knowledge of that sect of Lidian's,—it is still expected I shall break out with the New Light in the next discourse. I have read here my essay on the Age, the one on Home, one on Love, & one on Politics,—These seem all to be regarded as mere screens & subterfuges while this dread Transcendentalism is still kept back. They have various definitions of the word current here. One man, of whom I have been told, in good earnest defined it as 'Operations on the Teeth'; A young man named Rodman answered an inquiry by saying "it was a nickname which those who stayed behind, gave to those who went ahead." Meantime, all the people come to lecture, and I am told the Lyceum makes money by me. Tell William I find Mr Farley & his wife as usual very frank & friendly. He is very popular here, and with his honest social common sense everywhere welcome. Somebody said of him, "he strikes twelve the first time." I dined with Dr Wayland, the other day, who was very frolicsome & good-natured in his mood. Mrs W., you know, is a sister of Mrs Bartol. I found Mr & Mrs Eben. Francis in this Hotel on my arrival here, with *William's old friend* Miss

Babson. Of that last incarnation I had forgot the existence, but Time who keeps the pyramids had kept her almost as unchanged. Mr & Mrs F. had their old friendliness & inquired with interest after William. Mr F tho't he shd. stop in at his office in Wall St, on his return. They were going to Richmond, Va. I had yesterday a letter from Carlyle, chiefly about books. He tells me that, that same R. M. Milne, the poet has actually written a review of my pieces, & sent it to the Westminster, though it was not certain that it would be accepted by the editors. I have very good accounts of Waldo & Ellen duly sent by Lidian who also gives an excellent account of Alexander. She says "his face is a blessing." Waldo's lessons are duly read, but he refuses to read to Sophia. I am requested here, to remain another week & read more lectures. I *may* read three more. And now I think I have gossipped long enough about myself. How is it with you & Susan & William & Willie? the same serene diligent affectionate day, I doubt not, that I saw dawn & decline nine or ten times. It makes one calm to think of Staten Island. I wish every joy may there abide.—Elizabeth, it seems, was getting quite well & was going down to Salem, but Edward has gone away again seeking his fortunes, & that has distressed her & made her ill. but L. thinks she will recover herself presently. Mrs Brown has good news from her husband. Ellen can stand alone.

With my love to Susan I beg you to acknowledge her pursuing kindness which brings this pacquet of the boy's clothes safe to my hand. I did not breathe a word of it in my letter home but kept that & the cane for a surprise but Alexander has certainly blabbed for Lidian writes very gaily about the suit. Do not let William forget to get all the items from Susan for my April account. Your affectionate son Waldo—

"Everybody Has Purchased, But Few Have Read..."

EDWARD GIBBON

Edward Gibbon (1737-1794; English historian.) His health in childhood was poor, and his education thus notably irregular; a fact, considering his vast learning, to give hope to all those with similar youthful difficulties. He became a Roman Catholic when he was fifteen; his father considered this insufferable, and so placed him under the care of Pavilliard, a Calvinist minister, at Lausanne. Gibbon remained for five years, long enough to become a staunch Protestant again and to fall in love with Susanne Curchod, afterward Madame Necker and mother of Madame de Staël. But his father disapproved of this interest, also; the affair was broken off on Gibbon's return to England in 1758. He served in the militia, attaining the rank of colonel; in 1774 he was elected to Parliament. In September, 1783, he settled permanently in Lausanne, where he wrote the last volumes of his great history.

He tells in his Autobiography, *a singularly passionless work, of how he had cast about for years for a subject on which to write, and of how, while sitting on the steps of the Capitol in Rome, he had heard the barefoot friars singing in the Temple of Jupiter. Thereupon he decided that he would write the story of the* Decline and Fall of the Roman Empire, *that empire representing, at its height, the height of human organization, while its destruction was the "triumph," as he put it, "of barbarism and religion." The first volume of this work appeared in 1776 and received an acclaim unequalled by any other historical work before or since.*

When Gibbon wrote this letter, which includes a few words lamenting the state of public affairs in America, the first winter of the Revolution was ending; in just a fortnight, Howe would evacuate 8,000 troops from Boston to Halifax. Fortunately for us, perhaps, Gibbon paid only passing attention to such contemporary problems; his record in Parliament was barren of achievement or opinion; it neither interrupted his writing of books nor of letters.

Wed. 3/1/76

D<small>EAR</small> M<small>ADAM</small>.

Had I not been engaged in hastening and finishing the Impression, I would with great pleasure have made you a Christmas visit. I may truly say to you and not to Bath, for I have never much relished the style and amusements of that seat of idleness which so many people are fond of; and I am much inclined to think that if you fixed your residence in any other part of the

Kingdom, I might pass the remainder of my life without ever seeing Bath again.—Since I have mentioned my Book let me add that it will probably make its appearance about the middle or end of February: and that one of the very first Copies of it shall be carefully transmitted to Charles Street. The Public I know not why except from the happy choice of the subject, have already conceived expectations, which it will not be easy to satisfy: the more especially as lively ignorance is apt to expect much more, than the nature and extent of historical materials can enable an author to produce. However if the first volume is decently received in the World, I shall be encourged to proceed; and shall find before me a stock of labour and of amusement sufficient to engage my attention for many years. The prosecution of some scheme is in my opinion the circumstance the most conducive to the happiness of life, and of all schemes the best is surely that the success of which chiefly depends on ourselves. Parliamentary business, and agreable society fill up the intervals of my time; and my situation would in every respect be a comfortable one, if I could only put an end to my Buckinghamshire sale, which is still attended with difficulties, and will hardly be decided without the interposition of Chancery. You will not wonder that I lose time and catch at every hope, rather than involve myself in that Labyrinth of Chicane and expence.—I say nothing of public affairs. Never did they wear a more melancholy aspect. We much fear that Quebec will not hold out the winter. The Provincials have everywhere displayed courage and abilities worthy of a better Cause; and those of my Ministerial friends who are the best acquainted with the state of America, are the least sanguine in their hopes of success for next year.—An odd discovery is just now made. At a sale in the Country an old cabinet was going to be knocked down for twenty shillings, when the curiosity of some people present urged them to examine it more closely. Two private drawers were found; one of which contained bank notes to a very large amount: the other held an older and more valuable curiosity; the individual ring of Queen Elizabeth, the Earl of Essex Lady Nottingham &c: you remember the story. It was in a very fine purse embroidered with pearls; and is authenticated by a writing found in the same purse of an old Lady Cook who attended the Queen in her visit to the Countess and picked up the ring when her Majesty threw it from her with horror and indignation. I have seen the purse and ring (a yellow kind of Diamond) at Barlow's a silk Mercer in King Street Covent Garden, who affirms that he has read the paper; but the Mystery which is made about the place of the sale, and the name of the present proprietor, leaves room for suspicion. Horace Walpole is determined if possible to get to the bottom of the affair.*

I hope dear Madam that not only your health but your beauty likewise are perfectly restored; but I must desire an explicit and *satisfactory* answer about your promised visit to London. The air will, I am sure, be of the greatest service to you; and as the spring will soon advance upon us, you may easily connect London with Essex, Sussex or any other part of the Kingdom, where you have any visits to make or promises to fullfill.

I am Dear Madam most truly Yours

E Gibbon

Bentinck Street January 3d of the new year 1776. May you find it an agreable introduction to many happy ones.

PS. Mess. Gosling and Clive will honour your order whenever you chuse to draw for the last half year: and on every future occasion I will take care that it shall be ready for your draught: which I think, once for all, will be the best way of settling it.

Fri. 13/4/81

Dᴇᴀʀ Mᴀᴅᴀᴍ.

I am always obliged to you for waking me by a friendly pinch from my silent lethargy, and I think it most prudent to write before I fall asleep again.

An author must always begin on the subject of his own work, the subject always most interesting to himself: but on this

---

* The Essex ring now preserved in Westminster Abbey is believed on very good evidence to have descended to the Thynnes of Longleat from Essex's daughter, Lady Frances Devereux. It was sold by the family in 1911 and its latest purchaser, the late Mr. Ernest Makower, bought and presented it to the Abbey in 1937. G's story, to which there is no reference in Horace Walpole's works, seems to have been a *canard*.

occasion he may assume the privilege of friendship and justly believe that it is not less interesting to you. Your praise has afforded me real satisfaction, not only because I wish to please you, but as I do not know any person (where questions of pure learning are not concerned) from whose approbation I should derive more pride. To speak frankly I am of your opinion with regard to the improvement of the style, nor is it very surprizing that long practise should make a workman more expert and ready at his trade. I am curious to learn what passage in Prior you have in your eye: but as the works of that agreable poet are not extremely familiar to me, the resemblance is more probably the effect of chance than of design. The reception of these two volumes has been very unlike that of the first and yet my vanity is so very dextrous, that I am not displeased with the difference. The effects of novelty could no longer operate, and the public was not surprized by the unexpected appearance of a new and unknown Author. The progress of these two Volumes has hitherto been quiet and silent. Almost every body that reads has purchased, but few persons (comparatively) have read them; and I find that the greater number, satisfied that they have acquired a valuable fund of entertainment, differ the perusal to the summer, the country, and a more quiet period. Yet I have reason to think, from the opinion of some judges that my reputation has not suffered by this publication. The Clergy (such is the advantage of total loss of character) commend my decency and moderation: but the patriots wish to damn the work and the Author. . . .

My health this winter has been perfect without the slightest attack of the gout, and I rejoyce to hear that you revive with the Spring. A friend like Mrs. P was a real loss and I think with you that in such an intimate connection the heart is of much more importance than the head. Embrace in my name Sara and the tame Cat. I hope the former is not offended with, and I am persuaded that the latter adores, me but am much disappointed that her Bath residence has not produced any shining adventures: a pair of small neat horns might peep very gracefully out of a laurel crown, which her husband well deserves, though I think with you that his effusions are too frequent and precipitate. Adieu Dear Madam. I am still ignorant and indeed indifferent about the precise moment of my parliamentary beatification. Lord S is chaired next Monday at Coventry; but it is needless to mention that family as you hear the earliest and most copious accounts of them. Once more Adieu.

I am Dear Madam most truly Yours
Bentinck Street. April 13th 1781.   **E. Gibbon**

"Dear Mother, I Have All the Money I Want ..."

ELBERT HUBBARD

Elbert Hubbard (1856-1915; American businessman, author, and lecturer.) At the age of thirty-five, Hubbard abandoned a successful career in soap to begin a life of travel, study, and philosophizing; the letter below is his first announcement, to his mother, of that decision. He stayed at Harvard less than a year of the four he had planned to devote to studies; apparently he already knew everything necessary for a successful "literary" career. He wrote books, articles, and stories, printing them himself on his presses at East Aurora, New York, and sold more copies of them than he ever had of bars of soap. He edited and largely wrote himself a periodical, The Philistine, *for many years. His most famous work is* A Message to Garcia *(1899), which was purchased a thousand copies at a time by businessmen, whose philosopher Hubbard is. Indeed, they bought upwards of forty million copies to inspire their employees to greater effort. Hubbard would still do very well today.*

My dear Mother:

Next to the selection of my parents, I have completed the most important move of my life. In fact, my death can not be a matter of as much importance—or fraught with greater moment. So, to you, above all others, I write it first—I have sloughed my commercial skin. That is to say, I have sold out my entire financial interest in the Soap Business. My last share was transferred today and the money is in the bank to my credit. Why have I gone and done this thing? Because, dear Mother, I have all the money I want and there is a better use I can make of my time.

That excellent man, S. Hubbard, M.D., and myself are probably the only men in the whole U. S. who have all the money they desire.

The next question is: What do I propose to do? I am going to Harvard College, and it is my intention to take a full four years' course. I also hope to spend a year in some university in Germany as well.

John and Frank look upon my plans as a mild form of insanity, but I am at peace with them and all the world besides. I have not paddled away from a sinking ship; the business here was never more prosperous.

I have concluded that he who would excel in the realm of thought must not tarry in the domain of dollars. Another thing, I believe that he who would live long and well must live like a poor man, no matter what his income is. We must be warmed and fed, of course, but we must wait on ourselves and work with our hands a certain number of hours each day.

Many men want to lay up enough money to give their children a start. Money will do it all right, but it is on the down grade. If my boys can not get along without my financial aid, they can't with it.

I wish you and father would both write giving me your blessing to my new arrangement.

With much love, as ever

E.H.

"Empty Purse and Cold Hearth ..."

WILLIAM JAMES

William James (1842-1910; American psychologist and philosopher.) The family of Henry James the Elder, a distinguished American theologian and philosopher in his own right, spent as much time abroad as at home during young William's youth, and so he was educated mainly in England and on the Continent. At eighteen he began to study painting, but concluded that his talent was mediocre; the first letter below concerns the decision he had consequently to make.

Of the two other possibilities James could then envision— science or business—he of course chose the former, and graduated from Harvard Medical School in 1869, having interrupted his stay at Cambridge to accompany Agassiz on an expedition to the Amazon.

After years of study of physiology, anatomy, and hygiene,

James began lecturing on the relation between physiology and psychology, and in 1876 brought about the establishment of the first laboratory of psychological research in the U.S. His impatience and curiosity led him into still other fields; he embraced biology, evolutionary theory, and ultimately philosophy; and in his later years he came to be regarded as the most considerable American philosopher of his time.

James rejected philosophical systems requiring a priori assumptions, and became a thorough empiricist. It was not he, however, but Charles Sanders Peirce who took the next logical step past James's thinking and formulated the theory of pragmatism. Giving full credit to Peirce, James then developed and popularized pragmatism, the view of knowledge and existence that is always associated with his name. He was the brother of Henry James.

Although James expressed concern in this letter for the woman he might someday marry—concern that his choice of a career would consign her to a life of "cold hearth and empty purse"— he had no one in mind at the time. He didn't wed, in fact, for another fifteen years, by which time he was thirty-six years old.

Cambridge, [circa Sept. 1863].

My DEAREST MOTHER,— . . . To answer the weighty questions which you propound: I am glad to leave Newport because I am tired of the place itself, and because of the reason which you have very well expressed in your letter, the necessity of the whole family being near the arena of the future activity of us young men. I recommend Cambridge on account of its own pleasantness (though I don't wish to be invidious towards Brookline, Longwood, and other places) and because of its economy if I or Harry continue to study here much longer. . . .

I feel very much the importance of making soon a final choice of my business in life. I stand now at the place where the road forks. One branch leads to material comfort, the flesh-pots; but it seems a kind of selling of one's soul. The other to mental dignity and independence; combined, however, with physical penury. If I myself were the only one concerned I should not hesitate an instant in my choice. But it seems hard on Mrs. W. J., "that not impossible she," to ask her to share an empty purse and a cold hearth. On one side is *science*, upon the other *business* (the honorable, honored and productive business of printing seems most attractive), with *medicine*, which partakes of [the] advantages of both, between them, but which has drawbacks of its own. I confess I hesitate. I fancy there is a fond maternal cowardice which would make you and every other mother contemplate with complacency the worldly fatness of a son, even if obtained by some sacrifice of his "higher nature." But I fear there might be some anguish in looking back from the pinnacle of prosperity (*necessarily* reached, if not by eating dirt, at least by renouncing some divine ambrosia) over the life you might have led in the pure pursuit of truth. It seems as if one *could* not afford to give that up for any bribe, however great. Still, I am undecided. The medical term opens tomorrow and between this and the end of the term here, I shall have an opportunity of seeing a little into medical business. I shall confer with Wyman* about the prospects of a naturalist and finally decide. I want you to become familiar with the notion that I *may* stick to science, however, and drain away at your property for a few years more. If I can get into Agassiz's museum I think it not improbable I may receive a salary of $400 to $500 in a couple of years. I know some stupider than I who have done so. You see in that case how desirable it would be to have a home in Cambridge. Anyhow, I am convinced that somewhere in this neighborhood is the place for us to rest. These matters have been a good deal on my mind lately, and I am very glad to get this chance of pouring them into yours. As for the other boys, I don't know. And that idle and useless young female, Alice, too, whom we shall have to feed and clothe! . . . Cambridge is all right for business in Boston. Living in Boston or Brookline, etc., would be as expensive as Newport if Harry or I stayed here, for we could not easily go home every day.

Give my warmest love to Aunt Kate, Father, who I hope will not tumble again, and all of them over the way. Recess in three weeks; till then, my dearest and best of old mothers, good-bye! Your loving son,   W.J.

[P.S.] Give my best love to Kitty and give *cette petite* humbug of a Minny a hint about writing to me. I hope you liked your shawl.

Dresden, June 12, 1867.

DEAREST MOTHER,—I have been reading a considerable deal of German, and in a very desultory way, as I want to get accus-

* Jeffries Wyman was a professor at Harvard and a distinguished scientist.

tomed to a variety of styles, so as to be able to read any book
at sight, skipping the useless; and I may say that I now begin
to have that power whenever the book is writ in a style at all
adapted to the requirements of the human, as distinguished from
the German, mind. The profounder and more philosophical
German requires, however, that you should bring all the resources
of your nature, of every kind, to a focus, and hurl them again
and again on the sentence, till at last you feel something give
way, as it were, and the Idea begins to unravel itself. As for
speaking, that is a very different matter and advances much more
slowly. . . .

Life is so monotonous in this place that unless I make some
philosophical discoveries, or unless *something* happens, my letters
will have to be both few and short. I get up and have breakfast,
which means a big cup of cocoa and some bread and butter with
an egg, if I want it, at eight. I read till halfpast one, when dinner,
which is generally quite a decent meal; after dinner a nap, more
Germanorum and more read till the sun gets low enough to go
out, when out I go—generally to the Grosser Garten, a lovely
park outside the town where the sun slants over the greenest
meadows and sends his shafts between the great trees in a most
wholesome manner. There are some spots where the trees are
close together, and in their classic gloom you find mossy statues,
so that you feel as if you belonged to the last century. Often I
go and sit on a terrace which overlooks the Elbe and, with my
eyes bent upon the lordly cliffs far down the river on the other
side, with strains of the sweetest music in my ear, and with pint
after pint of beer successively finding their way into the fast-
nesses of my interior, I enjoy most delightful reveries, *au nombre
desquels* those concerning my home and my sister are not the
least frequent.

In the house (which stands on a corner) my great resource
when time hangs heavy on my hands is to sit in the window
and examine my neighbors. The houses are all four stories high
and composed of separate flats, as in Paris. I live in the 3me.
Diagonally opposite is a young ladies' boarding-school where the
young ladies, very young they are, are wont to relax from their
studies by kissing their hands, etc., etc., etc., to a young English
lout, who has been here in the house, and myself. Said lout left
for England yesterday, for which I heartily thank him, and I shall
now monopolize the attention of the school. We rather *had*
them, for we had a telescope to observe them by. Not one was

good-looking. There has, however, lately arisen in the Christian Strasse, just under my window, a most ravishing apparition, and I begin to think my heart will not wither wholly away. About eighteen, hair like night, and *such eyes!* Their mute-appealing, love-lorn look goes through and through me. Every day for the last week, after dinner, have I sat in my window and she in hers. I with the telescope! she with those eyes! and we communing with each other! ! I will try to make a likeness of her and send with this letter, but I may not succeed. She has only one defect, which is the length of her nose. If that were only an inch and a half shorter, I should propose at once to her Mother for it; but religious difference might intervene, so it is better as it is.

I am expecting T.S. Perry any day now, you may imagine how impatiently. . . . Tell Harry I have been reading some essays by Fr. Theod. Vischer, the *bedeutende Esthetiker,* on Strauss, on Goethe's "Faust" and its critics, etc., etc., which have much interested me. He is a splendid writer for style and matter—as brilliant as any of the non-absolutely-harlequin Frenchmen. The foundation of the thought is, or at least appears to be to my untutored mind, Hegelian; but they were published in 1844 and he may have changed. His "Aesthetik" henceforward appears in the list of "books which I must some day read." Some of the commentaries there quoted on "Faust" are incredibly monstrous for ponderous imbecility and seeing everything in the universe and out of it, except the point. I read this morning an Essay of Kuno Fischer's on Lessing's "Nathan"—one of the parasitic and analytic sort on the whole, but still very readable. The way these cusses slip so fluently off into the "Ideal," the "Jenseitige," the "Inner," etc., etc., and undertake to give a *logical* explanation of everything which is so palpably trumped up *after* the facts, and the reasoning of which is so grotesquely incapable of going an inch into the future, is both disgusting and disheartening. You never saw such a mania for going deep into the bowels of truth, with such an absolute lack of intuition and perception of the skin thereof. To hear the grass grow from morn till night is their happy occupation. There is something that strikes me as corrupt, immodest in this incessant taste for explaining things in this mechanical way; but the era of it may be past now—I don't know. I speak only of aesthetic matters, of course. The political moment both here and in Austria is extremely interesting to one who has a political sense, and even I am beginning to have an opinion— and one all in favor of Prussia's victory and supremacy as a great practical stride towards civilization. I think the French tone in the last quarrel deserved a degrading and stinging humiliation as much as anything in history ever did, and I'm very sorry they did not get it. Of course there's no end of bunkum and inflation here, too, but it is practically a healthy thing. . . .

"Images of Tenderness and Affection"

THOMAS BABINGTON MACAULAY

Thomas Babington Macaulay, Baron Macaulay of Rothley (1800-1859; English historian, essayist, poet, and statesman.) The first of the letters below was written when Macaulay was twelve; lest this cause parents of modern American youngsters to despair, it should be noted that the young man was precocious in everything. He had written a historical compendium and a poem in three cantos before he was eight, and he achieved astonishing literary and social success with an essay on Milton for the Edinburgh Review *when he was twenty-four. He was a Whig M.P. for seventeen years and was twice a cabinet member; his Whig prejudices are discernible in all his writings. His great historical work is* The History of England from the Accession of James the Second, *an unfinished opus in five volumes, but he is most famous for his literary essays, whose prejudiced and, in some cases, wrong opinions, bolstered by extreme confidence and a magnificent style, have influenced four generations of students of English literature. His most popular book of poetry is* Lays of Ancient Rome, *which includes the celebrated "Horatius at the Bridge." Macaulay never married; the close family relationship you will perceive in his letters to his mother encompassed his sister Hannah as well, and he spent much time with her, her children, and her husband, Lord Trevelyan, who wrote the first major biography of Macaulay.*

Shelford: August 14, 1813.

MY DEAR MAMA,—I must confess that I have been a little disappointed at not receiving a letter from home to-day. I hope, however, for one to-morrow. My spirits are far more depressed by leaving home than they were last half-year. Everything brings home to my recollection. Everything I read, or see, or hear, brings it to my mind. You told me I should be happy when I once came here, but not an hour passes in which I do not shed tears at thinking of home. Every hope, however unlikely to be realised, affords me some small consolation. The morning on which I went, you told me that possibly I might come home before the holidays. If you can confirm this hope, believe me when I assure you that there is nothing which I would not give for one instant's sight of home. Tell me in your next, expressly, if you can, whether or no there is any likelihood of my coming home before the holidays. If I could gain Papa's leave, I should select my birthday on October 25 as the time which I should wish to spend at that home which absence renders still dearer to me. I think I see you sitting by Papa just after his dinner, reading my letter, and turning to him, with an inquisitive glance, at the end of the paragraph. I think too that I see his expressive shake of the head at it. O, may I be mistaken! You cannot conceive what an alteration a favourable answer would produce in me. If your approbation of my request depends upon my advancing in study, I will work like a cart-horse. If you should refuse it you will deprive me of the most pleasing illusion which I ever experienced in my life. Pray do not fail to write speedily.

Your dutiful and affectionate son
T. B. MACAULAY

Cambridge: Wednesday.
(Post-mark 1818.)

M<small>Y</small> DEAR M<small>OTHER</small>,—King, I am absolutely certain, would take no more pupils on any account. And, even if he would, he has numerous applicants with prior claims. He has already six, who occupy him six hours in the day, and is likewise lecturer to the college. It would, however, be very easy to obtain an excellent tutor. Lefevre and Malkin are men of first-rate mathematical abilities, and both of our college. I can scarcely bear to write on Mathematics or Mathematicians. Oh for words to express my abomination of that science, if a name sacred to the useful and embellishing arts may be applied to the perception and recollection of certain properties in numbers and figures! Oh that I had to learn astrology, or demonology, or school divinity! Oh that I were to pore over Thomas Aquinas, and to adjust the relation of Entity with the two Predicaments, so that I were exempted from this miserable study! "Discipline" of the mind! Say rather starvation, confinement, torture, annihilation! But it must be. I feel myself becoming a personification of Algebra, a living trigonometrical canon, a walking table of Logarithms. All my perceptions of elegance and beauty gone, or at least going. By the end of the term my brain will be "as dry as the remainder biscuit after a voyage." Oh to change Cam for Isis! But such is my destiny, and since it is so, be the pursuit contemptible, below contempt, or disgusting beyond abhorrence, I shall aim at no second place. But three years! I cannot endure the thought. I cannot bear to contemplate what I must have to undergo. Farewell then Homer and Sophocles and Cicero.

> Farewell happy fields,
> Where joy for ever reigns! Hail, horrors, hail,
> Infernal world!

How does it proceed? Milton's descriptions have been driven out of my head by such elegant expressions as the following:

$$\text{Cos } x = 1 - \frac{x^2}{1\cdot 2} + \frac{x^4}{1\cdot 2\cdot 3\cdot 4} - \frac{x^6}{1\cdot 2\cdot 3\cdot 4\cdot 5\cdot 6}$$

$$\text{Tan } \overline{a+b} = \frac{\text{Tan } a + \text{Tan } b}{1 - \text{Tan } a + \text{Tan } b}$$

My classics must be Woodhouse, and my amusements summing an infinite series. Farewell, and tell Selina and Jane to be thankful that it is not a necessary part of female education to get a headache daily without acquiring one practical truth or beautiful image in return. Again, and with affectionate love to my Father, farewell wishes your most miserable and mathematical son.

T. B. MACAULAY

Trin. Coll.: March 25, 1821.

MY DEAR MOTHER,—I entreat you to entertain no apprehensions about my health. My fever, cough, and sore-throat have all disappeared for the last four days. Many thanks for your intelligence about poor dear John's recovery, which has much exhilarated me. Yet I do not know whether illness to him is not rather a prerogative than an evil. I am sure that it is well worth while being sick to be nursed by a mother. There is nothing which I remember with such pleasure as the time when you nursed me at Aspenden. The other night, when I lay on my sofa very ill and hypochondriac, I was thinking over that time. How sick, and sleepless, and weak I was, lying in bed, when I was told that you were come! How well I remember with what an ecstasy of joy I saw that face approaching me, in the middle of people that did not care if I died that night except for the trouble of burying me! The sound of your voice, the touch of your hand, are present to me now, and will be, I trust in God, to my last hour. The very thought of these things invigorated me the other day; and I almost blessed the sickness and low spirits which brought before me associated images of a tenderness and an affection, which, however imperfectly repaid, are deeply remembered. Such scenes and such recollections are the bright half of human nature and human destiny. All objects of ambition, all rewards of talent, sink into nothing compared with that affection which is independent of good or adverse circumstances, excepting that it is never so ardent, so delicate, or so tender as in the hour of languor or distress. But I must stop. I had no intention of pouring out on paper what I am much more used to think than to express. Farewell, my dear Mother.

Ever yours affectionately
T. B. MACAULAY.

"A Hugely Famous Animal"

FRIEDRICH WILHELM NIETZSCHE

Friedrich Wilhelm Nietzsche (1844-1900; German philologist, poet, and philosopher.) It is a fact of biographical significance that the great, gloomy German philosopher was brought up by his widowed mother in an atmosphere of extreme piety and poverty. After 1889, when loneliness, ill health, instability, and weakening eyesight combined to drive him hopelessly insane, his mother nursed him until she died.

Nietzsche's most productive and least melancholy years were from 1869 to 1880, when he was professor of classical philology at the University of Basel. After that he wandered over Europe looking for a climate that would restore his health.

Nietzsche continued to write despite terrible headaches, and it was during these last painful years that his bitter criticism of Western civilization took final shape. The years he certainly deemed his greatest were 1883 to 1885, which saw the publication of Also Sprach Zarathustra.

Some evidence lately discovered seems to indicate that much of Nietzsche's work was distorted in editions prepared by his sister. In any case, his concept of "superman," his attacks on Christianity, and his hatred of "mob rule" had a profound effect on a generation of writers and thinkers, and the use to which his dicta were put by the Nazis in Germany provides a striking example of applied philosophy.

Thursday Morning, Pforta, April, 1863.

Dear Mother:

If I write to you to-day it is certainly about the saddest and most unpleasant business that it has ever been my lot to relate. For I have been very wicked and do not know whether you will or can forgive me. It is with a heavy heart and most unwillingly that I take up my pen to write to you, more particularly when I think of our pleasant and absolutely unruffled time together during the Easter holidays. Well, last Sunday I got drunk and have no excuse but this, that I did not know how much I could stand and that I happened to be somewhat excited that afternoon. When I returned, Herr Kern, one of the masters, came across me in that condition. He had me called before the Synod on Tuesday, when I was degraded to third of my division and one hour of my Sunday walk was cancelled. You can imagine how depressed and miserable I feel about it, and especially at having to cause you so much sorrow over such a disgraceful affair, the like of which has never occurred in my life before. It also makes me feel very sorry on the Rev. Kletschke's account, who had only just shown me such unexpected confidence.* Through this

* He had just made Nietzsche his assistant.

one lapse I have completely spoilt the fairly good position I succeeded in winning for myself last term. I am so much annoyed with myself that I can't even get on with my work or settle down at all. Write to me soon and write severely, for I deserve it; and no one knows better than I do how much I deserve it.

There is no need for me to give you any further assurances as to how seriously I shall pull myself together, for now a great deal depends upon it. I had once again grown too cocksure of myself, and this self-confidence has now, at all events, been completely shaken, and in a very unpleasant manner.

I shall go and see the Rev. Kletschke to-day and have a talk with him. By-the-bye, do not tell anyone anything about it if it is not already known. Also, please send me my muffler as soon as possible, for I am constantly suffering from hoarseness and pains in my chest. Send me the comb too that I have spoken about. Now, good-bye and write to me very soon, and do not be too cross with me, mother dear.

Your very sorrowful

FRITZ.

Pforta, November 10, 1862.

DEAR MAMMA:

I am very sorry that I was not able to meet you at Almrich yesterday, but I was prevented from coming by being kept in. And thereby hangs a tale which I will tell you.

Every week one of the newest Sixth Form boys has to undertake the duties of schoolhouse prefect—that is to say, he has to make a note of everything in the rooms, cupboards, and lecture rooms that requires repair, and to send up a list of his observations to the inspection office. Last week I had to perform this duty, and it occurred to me that its somewhat tedious nature might be slightly relieved by the exercise of a little humour, and I wrote out a list in which all my observations were couched in the form of jokes.* The stern masters, who were very much sur-

---

* The remarks were very harmless, for instance: "In such and such a lecture room the lamps burn so dimly that the boys are tempted to let their own brilliance shine." "The forms of the Fifth Form Room have recently been painted and manifest an undesirable attachment for those who sit upon them."

prised that anyone should introduce humour into so solemn an undertaking, summoned me to attend the Synod on Saturday and pronounced the following extraordinary sentence: Three hours' detention and the loss of one or two walks. If I could accuse myself of any other fault than that of thoughtlessness, I should be angry about it; but as it is I have not troubled myself for one moment about the matter, and have only drawn this moral from it: To be more careful in future what I joke about.

To-day is Martinmas Day, and we have had the usual Martinmas goose for dinner (in twelve parts, of course). St. Nicholas Day, too, will soon be here. This period of transition from autumn to winter is a pleasant time; it is the preparation for Christmas which I enjoy so much. Let us thoroughly enjoy it together. Write to me soon. My love to dear uncle and Lizzie.

FRITZ.

Sils-Maria, August, 1883.

My dear Mother:

I have received everything in the way of food and the necessaries of life—unfortunately, too, your letter, which made me feel very wretched. Really, these dissertations on Christianity and on the opinions of this man and that as to what I should do and ought to think on the subject should no longer be directed to my address. My patience won't stand it! The atmosphere in which you live, among these "good Christians," with their one-sided and often presumptuous judgments, is as opposed as it possibly can be to my own feelings and most remote aims. I do not say anything about it, but I know that if people of this kind, even including my mother and sister, had an inkling of what I am aiming at, they would have no alternative but to become my natural enemies. This cannot be helped; the reasons for it lie in the nature of things. It spoils my love of life to live among such people, and I have to exercise considerable self-control in order not to react constantly against this sanctimonious atmosphere of Naumburg (in which I include many uncles and aunts who do not live in Naumburg).

Let us, my dear mother, do as we have done hitherto, and avoid all these serious questions in our letters. Moreover, I doubt whether our Lizzie could have read your letter.

My spirits and health have once more been very much impaired by the fact that the ghastly affair of last year is once more abroad and adding woe to woe. As to the *ultimate* outcome of it all, as far as I am concerned, ever since last August I have had the most gloomy forebodings. I am now working like a man who is "putting his house in order before departing." Don't say any more about it. I shall not either, and forgive me if this letter has turned out to be such a melancholy effusion.

Your son,
FRITZ.

Torino, via Carlo Alberto. 6. III.
December 21, 1888.

MY DEAR OLD MOTHER:

. . . The weather is somewhat misty here too, but not so bad as to make me light any fires yet. After a few days of mist the sun and the clear sky always recover the upper hand. There has been a grand funeral here, that of one of our princes, a cousin of the King; a very deserving man in Italy, and also in the Navy, for he was Admiral of the Fleet.

. . . The best news I have comes from my friend Gast, whose whole experience has changed wonderfully. Not only are the leading artists in Berlin—Joachim, de Ahna, those most exacting and spoilt of German artists—most deeply interested in his works, but what will surprise you most is that he moves in the richest and most distinguished circles in Berlin. Perhaps his opera will be produced for the first time in Berlin. Count Hochberg is closely connected with the circles frequented by Gast.

On the whole, your old thing is now a hugely famous animal, not exactly in Germany, for the Germans are too stupid and too vulgar for the loftiness of my spirit, and have always put their foot in it where I am concerned—but I mean everywhere else. My admirers consist of none but the most exceptional natures, nothing but highly placed and influential people in St. Petersburg, Paris, Stockholm, Vienna, and New York. Oh if you only knew on what terms the foremost personages of the world express their loyalty to me—the most charming women, a *Madame la Princesse Tenicheff* not by any means excepted. I have genuine geniuses among my admirers—to-day there is no name that is treated with as much distinction and respect as my own. You see that is the feat—sans name, sans rank, and sans riches, I am nevertheless treated like a little prince here, by everybody, even down to my fruit-stall woman, who is never satisfied till she has picked me out the sweetest bunch from among her grapes.

Fortunately I am equal to all that my task demands of me. My health is really excellent. The most difficult tasks for which no man has yet been strong enough, come lightly to me.

My dear old mother, at the close of the year, I send you my heartiest wishes, and ask you to wish me a year which will in every respect be in keeping with the great things that must happen in it.

YOUR OLD THING.

"Content to Sit at the Back-Door in Concord . . ."

HENRY DAVID THOREAU

Henry David Thoreau (1817-1862; American essayist, naturalist, and philosopher.) The year of these letters, 1843, was an eventful one for their writer. Besides visting New York and Staten Island, which he describes, he had been jailed at Concord for refusing, on principle, to pay his poll-tax. He was released the next morning, but the experience and its meaning became the basis of his essays, On the Duty of Civil Disobedience *(1849), the thesis of which is that that government is best which governs least.*

On July 4, 1845, Thoreau moved into the small house—a hut, really—which he built on the northwest shore of Walden Pond, near Concord; he lived there until September 6, 1847. Walden, or Life in the Woods *was published seven years later, and is one of the great American books. Although Thoreau was not interested in society—"Society is commonly too cheap," he said. "We meet at very short intervals, not having had time to acquire any new value for each other"—he was immersed in social questions, and was one of the most active speakers and writers in the anti-slavery movement in Massachusetts, harboring several runaway slaves and becoming a passionate defender of John Brown. In his* Plea *for the fanatical abolitionist, Thoreau admitted that Brown was unlettered. But, he said, Brown "would have left a Greek accent slanting the wrong way, and righted up a fallen man."*

Staten Island, August 6, 1843.

Dᴇᴀʀ Mᴏᴛʜᴇʀ,—As Mr. William Emerson is going to Concord on Tuesday, I must not omit sending a line by him,—though I wish I had something more weighty for so direct a post. I believe I directed my last letter to you by mistake; but it must have appeared that it was addressed to Helen. At any rate, this is to you without mistake.

I am chiefly indebted to your letters for what I have learned of Concord and family news, and am very glad when I get one. I should have liked to be in Walden woods with you, but not with the railroad. I think of you all very often, and wonder if you are still separated from me only by so many miles of earth, or so many miles of memory. This life we live is a strange dream, and I don't believe at all any account men give of it. Methinks I should be content to sit at the back-door in Concord, under the poplar-tree, henceforth forever. Not that I am homesick at all,— for places are strangely indifferent to me,—but Concord is still a cynosure to my eyes, and I find it hard to attach it, even in imagination, to the rest of the globe, and tell where the seam is.

I fancy that this Sunday evening you are poring over some select book, almost transcendental perchance, or else "Burgh's Dignity," or Massillon, or the "Christian Examiner." Father has just taken one more look at the garden, and is now absorbed in Chaptelle, or reading the newspaper quite abstractedly, only looking up occasionally over his spectacles to see how the rest are engaged, and not to miss any newer news that may not be in the paper. Helen has slipped in for the fourth time to learn the very latest item. Sophia, I suppose, is at Bangor; but Aunt Louisa, without doubt, is just flitting away to some good meeting, to save the credit of you all.

It is still a cardinal virtue with me to keep awake. I find it impossible to write or read except at rare intervals, but am, generally speaking, tougher than formerly. I could make a pedestrian tour round the world, and sometimes think it would perhaps be better to do at once the things I *can*, rather than be trying to do what at present I cannot do well. However, I shall awake sooner or later.

I have been translating some Greek, and reading English poetry, and a month ago sent a paper to the "Democratic Review," which, at length, they were sorry they could not accept; but they could not adopt the sentiments. However, they were very polite, and earnest that I should send them something else, or reform that.

I go moping about the fields and woods here as I did in Concord, and, it seems, am thought to be a surveyor,—an Eastern man inquiring narrowly into the condition and value of land, etc., here, preparatory to an extensive speculation. One neighbor observed to me, in a mysterious and half inquisitive way, that he supposed I must be pretty well acquainted with the state of things; that I kept pretty close; he didn't see any surveying instruments, but perhaps I had them in my pocket.

Love to all from your affectionate son.

Staten Island, October 1, 1843.

Dear Mother,—I hold together remarkably well as yet,—speaking of my outward linen and woolen man; no holes more than I brought away, and no stitches needed yet. It is marvelous. I think the Fates must be on my side, for there is less than a plank between me and—Time, to say the least. As for Eldorado, that is far off yet. My bait will not tempt the rats,—they are too well fed. The "Democratic Review" is poor, and can only afford half or quarter pay, which it *will* do; and they say there is a "Lady's Companion" that pays,—but I could not write anything companionable. However, speculate as we will, it is quite gratuitous; for life, nevertheless and never the more, goes steadily on, well or ill-fed, and clothed somehow, and "honor bright" withal. It is very gratifying to live in the prospect of great successes always; and for that purpose we must leave a sufficient foreground to see them through. All the painters prefer distant prospects for the greater breadth of view, and delicacy of tint. But this is no news, and describes no new conditions.

Meanwhile I am somnambulic at least,—stirring in my sleep; indeed, quite awake. I read a good deal, and am pretty well known in the libraries of New York. Am in with the librarian (one Dr. Forbes) of the Society Library, who has lately been to Cambridge to learn liberality, and has come back to let me take out some un-take-out-able books, which I was threatening to read on the spot. And Mr. McKean, of the Mercantile Library, is a true gentleman (a former tutor of mine), and offers me every privilege there. I have from him a perpetual stranger's ticket, and a citizen's rights besides,—all which privileges I pay handsomely for by improving.

A canoe race "came off" on the Hudson the other day, between Chippeways and New Yorkers, which must have been as moving a sight as the buffalo hunt which I witnessed. But canoes and buffaloes are all lost, as is everything here, in the mob. It is only the people have come to see one another. Let them advertise that there will be a gathering at Hoboken,—having bargained with the ferryboats,—and there will be, and they need not throw in the buffaloes.

I have crossed the bay twenty or thirty times, and have seen a great many immigrants going up to the city for the first time: Norwegians, who carry their old-fashioned farming-tools to the West with them, and will buy nothing here for fear of being cheated; English operatives, known by their pale faces and stained hands, who will recover their birthright in a little cheap sun and wind; English travelers on their way to the Astor House, to whom I have done the honors of the city; whole families of emigrants cooking their dinner upon the pavement,—all sun-burnt, so that you are in doubt where the foreigner's face of flesh begins; their tidy clothes laid on, and then tied to their swathed bodies, which move about like a bandaged finger,—caps set on the head as if woven of the hair, which is still growing at the roots,—each and all busily cooking, stooping from time to time over the pot, and having something to drop in it, that so they may be entitled to take something out, forsooth. They look like respectable but straitened people, who may turn out to be Counts when they get to Wisconsin, and will have this experience to relate to their children.

Seeing so many people from day to day, one comes to have less respect for flesh and bones, and thinks they must be more loosely joined, of less firm fibre, than the few he had known. It must have a very bad influence on children to see so many human beings at once,—mere herds of men . . .

I don't know when I shall come home; I like to keep that feast in store. Tell Helen that I do not see any advertisement for her, and I am looking for myself. If I could find a rare opening, I might be tempted to try with her for a year, till I had paid my debts, but for such I am sure it is not well to go out of New

England. Teachers are but poorly recompensed, even here. Tell her and Sophia (if she is not gone) to write to me. Father will know that this letter is to him as well as to you. I send him a paper which usually contains the news,—if not all that is stirring, all that has stirred,—and even draws a little on the future. I wish he would send me, by and by, the paper which contains the results of the Cattle Show. You must get Helen's eyes to read this, though she is a scoffer at honest penmanship.

"My Whole Ambitions Are for Original Work"

CARL VAN DOREN

Carl Van Doren (1885-1950; American author and historian.) This letter was written while he was studying for a Ph.D. at Columbia University; he taught at that institution for a number of years after 1911, but he was finally able to resolve the conflict discussed in the letter between "creation" and "scholarship" to his satisfaction. He left Columbia and became a literary man, writing novels, stories, critical works, essays, editing The Cambridge History of American Literature, *serving as literary editor of* The Nation *(1919-22) and* The Century Magazine *(1922-25), as editor for* The Literary Guild *(1926-34) and* The Living Library *(1946-1950), and ended his life a highly esteemed creative scholar. His best known works are* The Biography of Benjamin Franklin, *for which he received a Pulitzer prize in 1939, and* The Great Rehearsal *(1948), a work which described the making of the Constitution of the United States out of the Articles of Confederation; the title showed that the author considered this great act of unification, which made possible America as we know it, to be a lesson for the world of today. In order to exist tomorrow, he believed, the world must perform a similar act of unification. Carl Van Doren died at the outbreak of the Korean War. He was a man with a great capacity for friendship, and his large apartment in New York City was for many years a center of good conversation, both creative and scholarly. He gave assistance to a number of struggling young authors, and had great compassion for failure, knowing that it is the most likely thing in the world. His relationship with his mother, a powerful woman and a descendant of pioneers, was always affectionate; yet there is a remarkable stiffness in the style of this letter. It may have been due to youth; or it may have been due to his love of experimentation, for like all good writers he practiced writing in others' styles while he was still an apprentice author; in any case his mature style is extremely easy.*

1 April 1909

MY LOVELY MOTHER,

I have caught a miserable cold in some way and have been sitting about my room all morning and a part of the afternoon studying and half seduced from attention by the warm day outside. My indisposition is nothing, just enough to put me in a melancholic mood—of the kind that will come now and then, no matter how little there is really to bring it on, or how hard I fight against its coming. It seems to me that I have wasted and still waste so much time and get so little done. They tell me here my learning is perhaps the largest among the graduate students in English (altho that is by no means sure) and yet I am the youngest of them all. Next year too I am to have the fellowship. I have the best parents in the world and everything that their kindness can get me. Is it not strange then that I should have sat all these past few hours kicking my heels in sullenness? I can see the folly, well enough, but I cannot forget how much of a dissipation of energy is obligatory upon me. My roommate is wholly bent upon the study of the law. He has a good head and great industry, and what he is doing is a preparation for the thing he most wants. He can grudge every minute stolen from his work, while I am divided. My whole ambitions are for original work, but here I must plod dully on in scholarly pursuits, filling my head with a vast deal of dusty lumber that seems very far from a prospect of ever being useful, and letting my imagination rust in its sheath. I wonder whether it is fair that professors of literature should be obliged in the corrupted currents of this world to do something outside of literature to earn their bread and butter and give only the fagged out hours of their leisure to the only thing they live for. Some days I grow a despicable coward, and am nearly tempted to turn my back upon all the bright ideal to which

I have been true now for nearly a third of my life, and drop my energies to a slighter task where there is a chance of wealth and ease after a time. I know I could be rich—but I don't care to be —and I suppose I could attain some kind of worldly preferment. What is the good of all this feverish distracted effort, and all this silent sacrifice? I ask myself, and then I grow ashamed and vow that I will use the wretched talents that have been given me, and tho I may curse with all my hate the cruelty that gave me a giant's ambition and a child's powers, I will not be downed, but hold my head erect, tho it reach no further than the waist of most of my companions.

On such a day I wish I could be in Urbana again to greet all my beloved ones, and to walk about the kind, quiet old streets until a little calm could find its way into my angry peevish heart. But for your sake it is just as well I am here.

I send you all as much love as you can hold and all I have. There is no one in this world so dear to me.

Your loving son, Carl

SIX

Letters from Painters and Musicians

IT WOULD APPEAR that when painters write letters, they write
about their art. Writers and poets *use* their art in their letters,
and rarely write about writing; instead, they write about themselves. You can argue that this is, after all, one and the same thing,
and I will agree. All artists are preoccupied with themselves and
their work, and must be, for there is no other way to achieve
excellence.

But painters have a special problem. Their art is not of words,
and yet they need words to describe it; they are forced to describe
it because they think of nothing else; because they think of nothing
else, they are the loneliest of all people; because they are lonely,
they try to explain themselves to people who love them. Thus
Paul Cézanne:

> I have still got to work, not so as to be able to add the final polish,
> which is for the admiration of imbeciles . . . I must strive after
> perfection only for the pleasure of giving added truth and learn-
> ing.

If truth were easily come by, the artist would not stop to question what he was doing. But before he can achieve even wisps
of satisfaction, he must face failures and inadequacy. In anguish
he questions himself: How can I justify the attempt to create
beautiful things, when people cannot eat or burn these things
for fuel, or use them to keep the rain from their heads? Says
Vincent Van Gogh:

> When you look at the portrait which I'm sending you you'll see
> that even though I have lived for years in Paris, London and other
> great cities, I still resemble, more or less, a Zundert peasant—
> Toon or Piet Prins, for example. It seems to me sometimes that
> I think and feel like a peasant; only, peasants are more useful in

159

this world than I am. It's only when they have the necessities that people begin to be interested in and to need paintings and books, etc. According to my own evaluation, I am obviously inferior to peasants.

However, I work on my paintings as hard as they work in their fields!

We wish we could assure Van Gogh that peasants are not more useful than he is. Man needs beauty, we insist. But, he wonders, does man need beauty even when he is hungry?

Artists—it is their compelling faith—really do believe that even hungry men need beauty. Not all of us know that.

The musicians included here are a more worldly lot; we tend to reward performers while they are alive, creators after they are dead. When Mozart, at the age of thirteen, wrote out the complete score of Allegri's *Miserere* after having heard it only twice, he was made Knight of the Golden Spur by the Pope —but Mozart the composer died in poverty. The letters of his that are included here were written during his triumphant visits to Milan, Munich, and Worms. Mendelssohn writes a charming letter about a visit to the Queen of England. Wagner writes two letters about his mother, rather than to her—although the letters *are* to her. They are classics of their kind. Puccini writes about poverty, and this at least is a typical complaint of most young artists:

> The season ticket for the Scala is 130 lire during Carnival and Lent. Frightful, isn't it? . . . Curse poverty! Yesterday I sneaked in for nothing to hear *Carmen*. It really is a beautiful work. What a crowd! Tonight I am going to eat beans at Marchi's.

Incidentally, that is the sort of fare Rodolfo and his friends were eating when Mimi came in and lost her key.

"The Bourgeois Are Unwilling to Spend Their Sous . . ."

PAUL CÉZANNE

Paul Cézanne (1839-1906; French landscape, portrait and still-life painter, and water colorist.) The only son of a wealthy banker, he was educated at the College Bourbon, Aix, where he received rudimentary instruction in drawing and painting, and where his closest friend was Émile Zola. After a brief and unsuccessful attempt to study law, he went to Paris and met Manet and the group of young rebels against "official" art who later formed the nucleus of the Impressionist school: Pissarro, Monet, Sisley, Renoir, and Guillaumin. For many years he shuttled between Paris and Provence, painting assiduously but without achieving public recognition. Then in 1886 three important events occurred: he married Hortense Fiquet, who had borne him a son in 1872; his father died, leaving him a substantial fortune; and his forty-year friendship with Zola ended abruptly, chiefly because of Cézanne's abnormally sensitive, suspicious, moody temperament. He spent his last seven years in virtual retirement at Aix, suffering from diabetes but painting diligently until a few days before he died.

By abandoning the literal imitation of nature in favor of a subjective approach which he called painting his "sensations in the presence of nature," Cézanne paved the way for all modern, non-representational schools of painting. Although he predicted that he would become "the primitive of a new art," his pictures were so rarely displayed prior to the last decade of his life that his enormous influence was not apparent until after his death.

Paris, 26th September, 1874

MY DEAR MOTHER,

In the first place let me thank you very much for thinking of me. For some days the weather has been beastly and very cold, but I am not ailing in any way and I make a good fire.

I shall be very pleased to get the promised case, you can always send it rue de Vaugirard 120, I am staying there until the month of January.

Pissarro has not been in Paris for about a month and a half; he is in Britainy, but I know that he has a good opinion of me who have a very good opinion of myself. I am beginning to consider myself stronger than all those around me, and you know that the good opinion I have of myself has only been reached after mature consideration. I have still got to work, not so as to be able to add the final polish, which is for the admiration of imbeciles. And the thing that is commonly so much appreciated is merely the reality of the handwork and renders all work resulting from it inartistic and common. I must strive after perfection only for the pleasure of giving added truth and learning. And believe me, the hour always comes when one makes an impression and one has admirers far more fervent and convinced than those who are only flattered by the empty appearances.*

It is a very bad time for selling, all the bourgeois are unwilling to spend their sous, but this will end. . . .

My dear Mother, remember me to my sisters.

Kind regards to Monsieur and Madame Girard and my thanks. Ever your son,

Paul Cézanne.

"The Parrot Must Be Removed"

JAKOB LUDWIG FELIX MENDELSSOHN-BARTHOLDY

Jakob Ludwig Felix Mendelssohn-Bartholdy (1809-1847; German composer and musician.) His first music teacher was his mother, but by the age of seven young Mendelssohn was musically so advanced that his instruction was then undertaken by a professional. As these letters attest, his mother continued to follow his development with strict attention. Felix began to compose symphonies, concertos, and quartets in his twelfth year, performing them at the musicales his parents held on alternate Sunday mornings; the young composer always conducted and generally played the piano parts, while his brother and two sisters assisted him. His audiences soon grew in size and importance; during the next two decades, he performed in most of the major cities of Europe, always triumphantly.

In 1846, Mendelssohn was abroad, on tour, when he heard of the death of his sister Fanny. This, together with a severe schedule that was beginning to tell on him, produced illness and depression from which he did not recover. He left between one and two hundred works; many, in manuscript form even now, have not yet been published.

Let me assure you, by the way, that Mendelssohn's mother

---

* This passage seems to refer to the Impressionist exhibition in which Cézanne had exhibited his works for the first time. He does not appear to be discouraged by the marked failure.

quickly replied to the first of the letters below, approving her son's betrothal to Cécile Jeanrenaud. The young couple were married eight months later.

The Hague, August 9, 1836.

. . . I RECEIVED your kind letter the day before yesterday and thank you for it from my heart. But you really see more in my last letter than I intended to say, and when you speak of my betrothal, my happiness, and the coming change in my prospects, I can only say that as yet all is very uncertain. But I thank you for the dear, kind words you wrote about the mere possibility, and feel inclined to consider them as your permission to take this step, so necessary for my happiness. In any case I should like to have your consent, that I may no longer be tormented by doubts, on this head at any rate. Indeed, my special object in writing is to ask you for it. If you tell me that you are ready once more to trust me entirely and offer me again the full liberty I have enjoyed in former years, you will make me very happy. You may rest assured that I will not abuse your confidence, and perhaps I have done something to deserve it. Please, tell me so, dear mother.

With all this, however, bear in mind what I wrote in the beginning. All I ask is that you will give me your consent; for, though I suppose my age makes it no longer legally necessary, I will not act without it. But whether I shall be able to avail myself of it on my return to Frankfort, that, as I said before, is a perfect mystery. All depends on the state in which I find matters there, for I really feel completely ignorant now. On one point, however, I am quite clear, and that is that I would gladly send Holland, its Dutchmen, seabaths, bathing cars, Kursaal and visitors to the devil, and wish I were back in Frankfort. When I have seen this charming girl again, I hope the suspense will soon be over, and I shall know whether we are to be anything—or rather everything —to each other, or not; at present I really know very little of her, and she of me, so I cannot answer all your questions about her. This much I can tell you, that she made my stay at Frankfort very happy, just when I needed a little happiness and did not expect to get it; also that her father, Pastor Jeanrenaud, is dead, and that she has been educated at home with the utmost care and tenderness by her mother (a Souchay), that her Christian name is Cécile, and that I love her very much.

Dear mother, there is one thing more I wish to ask, and that is, that you will not allow yourself to be agitated about me. I perceive from your letter that you are very anxious, and that will make me anxious too, whereas I wish to be calm and collected, and go through this affair with the coolness I have always managed to preserve hitherto when taking an important step in life. I beg you also not to speak about the matter to any one, especially not to any one in Frankfort, as it may destroy my whole chance. Dear mother, please answer this immediately.

Frankfort, July 19, 1842.

My dear little Mother,

Here we are back again,* jolly and happy after a jolly, happy trip, and we found the dear children well and blooming, and your sweet letter tells us the same of all of you. A blue sky and warm, clear air are brought by one unforgettably beautiful day after the other—if one only knew how to prove himself sufficiently thankful for such great happiness.

Moreover, I especially enjoy being in Frankfort, among so many good friends and relations in this beautiful part of the world . . .

I owe you further particulars of our time in London, after our trip to Manchester . . . All this I can describe better when I see you, but the details of my last visit to Buckingham Palace I must write you at once because they will amuse you so much, and me, too. As Grahl says—and it is true—the only friendly English house, one that is really comfortable and where one feels at ease, is Buckingham Palace—as a matter of fact, I know several others, but on the whole, I agree with him. Joking apart, Prince Albert had asked me to go to him on Saturday at two o'clock, so that I might try his organ before I left England. I found him all alone; and as we were talking away, the Queen came in, also quite alone, in a house dress. She said she was obliged to leave for Claremont in an hour; "But, goodness! how it looks here," she added, when she saw that the wind had littered the whole room, and even the pedals of the organ (which, by the way, made a very pretty feature in the room), with leaves of music from a large portfolio that lay open. As she spoke,

* Mendelssohn and his wife had just returned from one of his most successful trips to England.

she knelt down and began picking up the music; Prince Albert helped, and I too was not idle. Then Prince Albert proceeded to explain the stops to me, and while he was doing it, she said that she would put things straight alone.

But I begged that the Prince would first play me something, so that, as I said, I might boast about it in Germany; and thereupon he played me a chorale by heart, with pedals, so charmingly and clearly and correctly that many an organist could have learned something; and the Queen, having finished her work, sat beside him and listened, very pleased. Then I had to play, and I began my chorus from "St. Paul": "How lovely are the Messengers!" Before I got to the end of the first verse, they both began to sing the chorus very well, and all the time Prince Albert managed the stops for me so expertly—first a flute, then full at the forte, the whole register at the D major part, then he made such an excellent diminuendo with the stops, and so on to the end of the piece, and all by heart—that I was heartily pleased. Then the Crown Prince of Gotha came in, and there was more conversation, and among other things the Queen asked if I had composed any new songs, and said that she was very fond of singing the published ones. "You should sing one to him", said Prince Albert; and after a little begging she said she would try the "Fruehlingslied" in B-flat. "Yes, if it were still here, for all my music is packed up for Claremont." Prince Albert went to look for it, but came back saying it was already packed. "Oh, perhaps it could be unpacked", said I. "We must send for Lady N. N.", she said. (I did not catch the name.) So the bell was rung, and the servants were sent after it, but came back embarrassed; and then the Queen went herself, and whilst she was gone Prince Albert said to me: "She begs you will accept this present as a remembrance"—and gave me a case with a beautiful ring, on which is engraved "V.R., 1842".

Then the Queen came back and said: "Lady N.N. has left and has taken all my things with her. It really is most unseemly." (You can't think how that amused me.) I then begged that I might not be made to suffer for the accident, and hoped she would sing another song. After some consultation with her husband he said: "She will sing you something of Gluck's". Meantime the Prince of Gotha had come in, and we five proceeded through the corridors and rooms to the Queen's sitting-room, where, next to the piano, stood an enormous, thick rocking-horse, and two great bird-cages and pictures on the walls and beautifully bound books lay on the tables, and music on the piano. The Duchess of Kent came in, too, and while they were all talking I rummaged about a little amongst the music and found my first set of songs. So, naturally I begged her to choose one of those rather than the Gluck, to which she very kindly consented; and which did she choose? "Schöner und schöner"; sang it beautifully in tune, in strict time, and with very nice expression. Only where, following "Der Prosa Last und Mueh'", where it goes down to D and then comes up again by semitones, she sang D-sharp each time; and because the first two times I gave her the note, the last time, sure enough, she sang D—where it ought to have been D-sharp. But except for this little mistake it was really charming, and the last long G I have never heard better or purer or more natural from any amateur. Then I was obliged to confess that Fanny had written the song (which I found very hard, but pride must have a fall), and to beg her to sing one of my own, too. "If I would give her plenty of help she would gladly try," she said, and sang "Lass dich nur nichts dauern" really without a mistake, and with charming feeling and expression. I thought to myself that one must not pay too many compliments on such an occasion, so I merely thanked her very much; but she said, "Oh, if only I had not been so nervous; otherwise I really have a long breath". Then I praised her heartily, and with the best conscience in the world; for just that part with the long C at the close she had done so well, taking it and the three notes next to it all in the same breath, as one seldom hears it done, and therefore it amused me doubly that she herself should have begun about it.

After this Prince Albert sang the Erntelied, "Es ist ein Schmitter", and then he said I must play him something before I went, and gave me as themes the chorale which he had played on the organ and the song he had just sung. If everything had gone as usual, I ought to have improvised dreadfully badly; for that is what nearly always happens to me when I want it to go well, and then I should have gone away vexed with the whole morning. But just as if I were to keep the nicest, most charming recollection of it, without any unpleasantness at all, I have rarely improvised as well. I was in the mood for it, and played a long time, and enjoyed it myself; of course, besides the two themes, I also brought in the songs the Queen had sung; but it all worked in so naturally that I would have been glad not to stop. And they followed me with so much intelligence and attention that I felt more at my ease than I ever have in improvising before an audience. Well, and then she said, "I hope you will come and visit us soon again in England", and then I took my leave; and down below I saw the beautiful carriages waiting, with their scarlet outriders, and in a quarter of an hour the flag was lowered, and the papers said: "Her Majesty left the Palace at 30 minutes past 3". I walked back through the rain to Klingemann's, and enjoyed more than everything giving a piping-hot account of it all to him and Cécile. It was a delightful morning! I must add that I asked permission to dedicate my A minor symphony to the Queen, that having really been the reason for my visit to England, and because the English name would be doubly suited to the Scottish piece; and that, just as the Queen was going to sing, she said: "But the parrot must be removed first, or he will scream louder than I sing"; upon which Prince Albert rang the bell and the Prince of Gotha said, "I will carry him out", upon which I replied, "Allow me to do that", (like cousin Wolf with his "allow me, me, me!") and lifted up the big cage and carried it out to the astonished servants, etc. There is much more to tell when we meet, but if this long description makes Dirichlet set me down as an aristocrat, tell him that I swear that I am a greater radical than ever . . .

"Viva Maestro"

WOLFGANG AMADEUS MOZART

Wolfgang Amadeus Mozart (1756-1791; Austrian composer.) It has been suggested that Mozart's father, an Austrian musician, regarded his son's magnificent talent as a gift of God, a gift it was his duty to put to good use. For whatever reason—duty, or Papa's business acumen—the precocious youngster's extraordinary abilities were not allowed to go undeveloped or unnoticed; Wolfgang first performed in public when he was five, and when he was six his father took him and his older sister on a concert tour to Munich, Vienna, and other cities. They appeared in Paris the next year; in England the next; and by 1768 Mozart had been presented at the court in Vienna, a trail of successes behind him. He was now twelve years old, and working on his first opera; it was produced in Salzburg the next year.

Mozart found it more difficult to achieve recognition as a mature composer than as a precocious child; although his productivity was tremendous, he reaped but little profit from it, and by the time he was thirty he was in poor health. Nevertheless, his greatest works—the last three symphonies, and Figaro, Don Giovanni, The Magic Flute, *along with half a dozen other pieces— were written during the last five years of his life. He died at Vienna in December, 1791, of malignant typhus; there were no ceremonies at his grave, and even his friends followed him no farther than the city gates, deterred by a storm. He was buried in the common ground of St. Marx, and the exact position of his grave is not known.*

Mozart's genius is comic, and is the greatest in that mode that the world has ever known. But the ending of Don Giovanni *and the G Minor Symphony are tragic, and it may have been that he was entering upon a tragic phase when he died. It is irresponsible to wish that men who died young had lived longer, and yet the temptation in Mozart's case is irresistible. There was no diminution in his powers; he was only thirty-five; Shakespeare lived fifteen years longer; and it is possible that Mozart's Lear was still to come. And yet despite the fact that his life was cut off in his prime, the world has never known, I think, a more perfect artist.*

Milan, October 20th, 1770

M<small>Y DEAR MAMMA</small>,

I cannot write much, for my fingers are aching from composing so many recitatives. Mamma, I beg you to pray for me, that my opera* may go well and that we may be happy together again. I kiss Mamma's hand a thousand times and I have many things to say to my sister, but what? God and I alone know. If it is God's will, I shall soon, I hope, be able to tell them to her myself. Meanwhile I kiss her 1000 times. My greetings to all my good friends. We have lost our good little Martha, but with God's help we shall meet her in a better place.

Milan, November 7th, 1772

D<small>O NOT</small> be alarmed at seeing my handwriting instead of Papa's. The reasons are as follows: (1) We are at Signor D'Aste's and

* *Mitridate*

Baron Cristani is here and they all have so much to talk about that Papa simply cannot get time to write; and (2) He is too lazy. We arrived here on the 4th at noon and we are well. All our good friends are in the country or at Mantua except Signor D'Aste and his wife, who have asked me to send their greetings to you and to my sister. Mysliwecek is still here. There is no truth in the report which is being so earnestly discussed in Germany of an Italian war or of the fortifying of the castle at Milan. Excuse my wretched handwriting. When you write to us, do so direct, for it is not the custom here as it is in Germany for people to carry letters about, but they have to be fetched at the post and so we go there every post-day to get them. There is no news here, but we are waiting for some from Salzburg. We hope that you received our letter from Bozen. Well, I cannot think of anything else, so I shall close. Our greetings to all our good friends. We kiss Mamma 100,000 times (I did not bring any more noughts with me) and I kiss Mamma's hands and prefer to embrace my sister in person rather than in imagination.

Munich, January 11th, 1775

THANK GOD, all three of us are quite well. It is impossible for me to write a long letter, as I am off this very . . . moment to a rehearsal of my opera.* To-morrow we are having the dress rehearsal and the performance takes place on Friday, the 13th. Mamma must not worry; it will go off quite well. I am very much distressed that Mamma should suspect [Count Seeau] for he is certainly a charming and courteous gentleman and has more savoir vivre than many of his class in Salzburg. We were at the masked concert yesterday. Herr von Mölk was so astounded and crossed himself so often as he listened to the opera seria, that we were absolutely ashamed of him, for everyone could see quite clearly that he had never been anywhere but to Salzburg and Innsbruck. Addio. I kiss Mamma's hands.

Wolfgang

Munich, January 14th, 1775

Thank God! My opera was performed yesterday, the 13th, for the first time and was such a success that it is impossible for me

* *La Fiesta Giardiniere.*

to describe the applause to Mamma. In the first place, the whole theatre was so packed that a great many people were turned away. Then after each aria there was a terrific noise, clapping of hands and cries of "Viva Maestro". Her Highness the Electress and the Dowager Electress (who were sitting opposite me) also called out "Bravo" to me. After the opera was over and during the pause when there is usually silence until the ballet begins, people kept on clapping all the time and shouting "Bravo"; now stopping, now beginning again and so on. Afterwards I went off with Papa to a certain room through which the Elector and the whole court had to pass and I kissed the hands of the Elector and Electress and Their Highnesses, who were all very gracious. Early this morning His Grace the Bishop of Chiemsee sent me a message, congratulating me on the extraordinary success of my opera. I fear that we cannot return to Salzburg very soon and Mamma must not wish it, for she knows how much good it is doing me to be able to breathe freely.* We shall come home soon enough. One very urgent and necessary reason for our absence is that next Friday my opera is being performed again and it is most essential that I should be present. Otherwise my work would be quite unrecognisable—for very strange things happen here. I kiss Mamma's hands 1,000 times. My greetings to all my good friends. My compliments to M. Andretter and I beg him to forgive me for not yet replying, but it has been impossible for me to find the time. However, I shall do so very soon. Adieu. 1000 smacks to Bimberl.

"I Am Longing To Have Some Beans."

GIACOMO PUCCINI

Giacomo Puccini (1858-1924; Italian operatic composer.) He was a pupil of Ponchielli at the Milan Conservatory, and received a good classical musical education. He was only twenty-five when Manon Lescaut *was triumphantly produced, and he henceforth gave up eating "beans at Marchi's." His next great success was* La Bohème *(1896) followed by* Tosca *in 1900 and* Madame

* Mozart is alluding to the tyrannical attitude of the Archbishop.

Butterfly *in 1904. His music is lovely and constantly melodic, but most of it does not bear a great number of hearings. There are scenes, however—the flower duet in* Madame Butterfly, *for instance—which capture the essence of love and loss, Puccini's two great themes, and are unforgettable. Spring—the Italian word "primavera"—particularly inspired him, and whenever a lover sings the word in one of his operas the music soars to heights that few composers have ever reached.*

In the first line of the Milan letter, Puccini reports on his second lesson with Bazzini. This was Antonio Bazzini, a famed violinist, composer, and director of the Milan Conservatory. Such details were of more than minor interest to his mother; it was her bold action (with some financial assistance from an uncle) that won Puccini a scholarship at Milan. She did it with a letter to the Queen:

Majesty!
You are the Queen, the mother of the poor, the patroness of artists. I am a widow with two children. My children are students of music; Giacomo, the elder, shows great promise. For five generations the Puccinis have been musicians. Giacomo desires to study at the Conservatorio in Milan, but I cannot myself pay his expenses. In your immense generosity, will you come to the help of a mother and her ambitious boy?

Some weeks later a small scholarship was granted. The rest of the story we know.

[Milan]
Thursday, 11 A.M. [1881]

DEAREST MOTHER,
Yesterday I had my second lesson from Bazzini. It is going very well. That is the only lesson I have so far, but on Friday I am beginning Aesthetics. I have made myself this timetable: In the morning I get up at half-past eight, and when I have a lesson I go to it. If I have no lesson I practise the piano a little. I don't need to do much, but I have to practise a bit. I am going to buy a very good "Method" by Angeleri, the sort of method from which one can learn a lot by oneself. I go on till half-past ten; then I have lunch and go out. At one I come home and work for

a couple of hours preparing for Bazzini, then from three to five at the piano again for some reading of classical music. I'd like to take out a subscription for music, but I haven't enough money. At the moment I am reading the *Mefistofele* of Boito, which a friend of mine, Favara, from Palermo, has lent me. At five I go to my frugal meal (special emphasis on the frugal!), and I have Milanese broth, which, to tell the truth, is very good. I have three plates of that, then some other mess, a bit of Gorgonzola cheese, and half a litre of wine. Then I light a cigar and go off to my usual walk up and down in the Galleria. I am there till nine o'clock and come home dead tired. I do a little counterpoint, but no playing; I am not allowed to play at night. Then I get into bed and read seven or eight pages of a novel. And that's my life! . . .

There is one thing that I should like, but I am afraid to tell you, because I know that you have not money to spend. But listen, it isn't much. I am longing to have some beans—and they did cook me some one day, but I couldn't eat them because of the oil, which is sesame or linseed here!—and, well . . . I should like a little oil, but fresh. . . . Do you think you could send me a "wee pickle"? A little is enough. I have promised to let the others in the house taste it too. And so, if my jeremiads bear fruit, will you be so very kind (how I am oiling you, talking of oil!) as to send me a little tin of it, which costs four lire, from Eugenio Ottolini, who has sent one to the tenor Papeschi. Here they are all writing operas as fast as they are able, but I do nothing. I am gnawing my hands with rage.

The other evening I went to hear the *Redemption* (an oratorio by Gounod), and found it very boring. Last night I went to Catalani's new opera. For the most part, people are not going mad about it, but I think that from an artistic point of view it is very good, and if they do it again I shall go back to hear it. I am writing to you in the Dramatic Theory lesson, which I find very dull. I am dying to get home, because I have to compose a *Quartet* for strings for Bazzini. Tonight they are doing *Mignon* and Verdi's *Simon Boccanegra* (revised!). The reserved seats cost fifty lire, and they are all gone already. What a rich city Milan is! Yesterday I went to Monza in the tram. . . .

The season ticket for the Scala is 130 lire during Carnival and Lent. Frightful, isn't it? To get a reserved seat it is 200 lire besides admission, which brings it up to 330. Isn't it appalling?

Curse poverty! Yesterday I sneaked in for nothing to hear *Carmen*. It really is a beautiful work. What a crowd! Tonight I am going to eat beans at Marchi's.

"Peasants Are More Useful . . ."

VINCENT VAN GOGH

Vincent Van Gogh (1853-1890; Dutch postimpressionist painter.) The tragic life of this great painter is almost too well known to need repeating, and yet his painful, sincere friendship with his mother is perhaps less understood than his relationship with his younger brother, Theo. But he wrote a notable series of letters to her as well as to him; one of the most interesting follows.

It is not generally realized that Van Gogh only started to draw seriously when he had but ten years to live. The famous trip to Arles with Gauguin took place in 1888, two years before his death. He wrote this letter from the St. Rémy Asylum, where he was confined in 1889.

DEAR MOTHER:

I wanted to write you again before you left the old house to thank you for your last letter and for the news about the trip from Cor.

I think he [Theo] will be able to do good work there and that life will allow him a little happiness from time to time. What he wrote you reminds me of what my friend Gauguin told me about Panama and Brazil. I didn't know that Isaacson was leaving for the Transvaal. You know that I've never met him, but I have been writing to him lately; he wanted to write an article on my work for a Dutch periodical but I asked him not to do it, thanking him for his loyal interest. From the beginning we were interested in each other's work, and we felt the same way about the Dutch painters, both the early and the modern ones.

I also like the work of De Haan very much.

I want to tell you again that what I promised you is now ready: some landscapes, a little portrait of me, and the study of an interior. But I fear they will disappoint you, and that you will find some portions uninteresting or even ugly. You and Wil* may do what seems right with them; if you like you can give some of them to my other sisters. This is the reason I am sending several more pictures.

That's not important. I would have preferred to have these pictures remain together; I think they would have had more importance some day as a group. But, of course, I know that you don't have room to keep all of them and therefore do what seems right to you with them; however, I recommend that you keep them all for a while, at least. You will be better able to judge which you like after you've had them for a time.

Yes, I agree with you, Theo's new situation is much better, and I hope that Jo's delivery will go well; they will be on top of the world again for a while. It's always good to learn by experience how a human being comes into this world; it teaches many a man more about truth and tranquillity.

The country side is very beautiful here in Autumn, with the leaves all yellow. I only regret that there aren't more vineyards. I went to paint an hour or two away—a big field had turned purple and gold, like the virginia creeper around us, and you could see to the side a square of yellow and farther away a patch which had stayed green.

All under a superb blue sky and on the horizon cliffs the color of lilacs.

Last year I had more chance to paint this sort of scene than now. I would have liked to add some pictures to the ones I am sending you, but I will have to owe them to you until next year.

When you look at the portrait which I'm sending you you'll see that even though I have lived for years in Paris, London and other great cities, I still resemble, more or less, a Zundert† peasant—Toon or Piet Prins, for example. It seems to me sometimes that I think and feel like a peasant; only, peasants are more useful in this world than I am. It's only when they have the necessities that people begin to be interested in and need paintings and books, etc. According to my own evaluation, I am obviously inferior to peasants.

However, I work on my paintings as hard as they work in their fields!

In any case, things aren't going so well in this business of mine. To tell you the truth, it's always been that way, but particularly

---

* Van Gogh's sister.
† The town in Brabant where he was born.

now. However, pictures have never sold for so much as they do these days.

Moreover, when you consider the trouble of learning to handle a brush, nothing more is necessary to keep a man from painting. Compared to others, I can even regard myself as being one of the lucky ones, but think of the fate of those who try this profession and then have to abandon it without having had any success— and there are lots like that.

Let's say that it takes ten years to learn the technique. If you knew how heart-rending it is to have to abandon it after having worked and tried to make ends meet for six years, for example— and how many there are in that situation!

You hear it said that large sums are paid for the pictures of painters who are dead while the paintings of living painters bring much less. The picture business is like the tulip craze— living painters are at a disadvantage. And it is as perilous as the tulip craze.

But it could be said that there are still horticulturists even though the tulip craze is dead and long since forgotten, and that there will always be horticulturists. I think of painting in the same way: it will be kept alive like the culture of flowers. In fact, I consider myself very fortunate to be a painter. But the others!

All this to show you that one should not have illusions. I must mail this letter; I am working now on a portrait of one of the inmates of the asylum. It's strange, but when you live with them for a while you get used to it and you no longer think of them as crazy. Consider yourself kissed by

Your affectionate Vincent

"Through All the Jungle"

RICHARD WAGNER

Richard Wagner (1813-1883; German composer and poet.) Considerable speculation has always surrounded the life and art of Wagner. In part this is due to the iconoclastic nature of his music and his musical theories, but it is also a result of deliberate obfuscation of his chronology and even of his motives.

His father died six months after his birth, and Wagner was therefore particularly dependent on his mother. At the time he wrote the first letter included here he was living a precarious existence as conductor of one small opera company after another; by 1846 (the date of the second letter), he was still having trouble making ends meet, and was ricocheting around Europe in search of a permanent musical address. But he had written Tannhaüser *and started work on* Lohengrin *(1848), his most popular, if not his greatest work, and thus was well on his way.*

Wagner devoted the years after Lohengrin *to a detailed theoretical exposition of the new art form which had been crystallizing in his mind, the word-tone-drama, an organic synthesis of poetry, music, and stage action, in which all the set patterns of opera were discarded. Die* Walküre *(1856) was the most complete musical exposition of this theory. Probably most people nowadays would prefer the Liebestod from* Tristan, *however. It is too long and it is too lugubrious, but those are characteristics of Wagner that must be taken along with his greatness.*

Carlsbad, the 25th July: 35.

ONLY of yourself, dearest Mother, can I think with the sincerest love and profoundest emotion. Brothers and sisters, I know it, must go their own way,—each has an eye to himself, to his future, and the surroundings connected with both. So it is, and I feel it myself: there comes a time when roads part of themselves, —when our mutual relations are governed solely from the standpoint of external life; we become mere nodding diplomats to one another, keeping silence where silence seems politic, and speaking where our view of an affair demands; and when we're at a distance from each other, we speak the most. But ah, how high a mother's love is poised above all that!

No doubt I, too, belong to those who cannot always speak out at the moment as their heart dictates,—or you might often have come to know me from a much more melting side. But my sentiments remain the same,—and see, Mother—now I have left you, the feeling of thanks for that grand love of yours towards your child, which you displayed to him so warmly and so tenderly again the other day, so overpowers me that I fain would write, nay, tell you of it in accents soft as of a lover to his sweetheart.

Yes, and still softer,—for is not a mother's love far more—far more untainted than all other?

Nay, here I won't philosophise,—I simply want to thank you, and again, to thank you,—and how gladly would I count up all the separate proofs of love for which I thank,—were there not too many of them. O yes, I know full well that no heart yearns after me now with so great an inner sympathy or such solicitude, as yours; yes, that perhaps it is the only one that watches o'er my every step,—and not, forsooth, coldly to criticise it,—no, to include it in your prayers. Have you not ever been the only one to stay unalterably true to me when others, judging by mere outward results, turned philosophically away? It would indeed be exacting beyond measure, were I to ask a like affection from them all; I even know it is not possible,—I know it from myself: but with *you* all issues from the heart, that dear good heart I pray God e'er to keep inclined to me,—for I know that, should all else forsake me, 'twould still remain my last, my fondest refuge. O Mother, what if you should prematurely die, ere I had fully proved to you that it was to a worthy son, of boundless gratitude, you shewed so great a love! But no, that cannot be; you still must taste abundant fruits. Ah, the remembrance of that latest week with you; it is a perfect feast to me, a cordial, to call before my soul each several token of your loving care! My dear, dear Mother,—what a wretch were I, if I could ever cool towards thee!

For the future I shall tell the family but little of my doings,— they judge by the outward results, and will learn those without my assistance. In whatever fashion it has come about, I'm independent now, and mean to stay so. O that humbling before Brockhaus is graven deep into my heart, and the bitterest self-reproaches torture me, that I should have given into his hands a right to humble me. I shall get even with him in time, but never, never at one with him; and should that be wrong of me, I prefer to bear that wrong into the grave with me: I withdraw from them entirely. Each side cannot be right, and I was wrong; —yet I will never admit it—*to them*, but place myself in such a situation that I've nothing to admit to them,—whereas my recent great fault was having played into their hands, given them the very smallest right against me. For that matter, we stand so far from one another, that it would be absurd of me to want to be at one with him. Yet, how I do rejoice at this catastrophe, which has brought me full recognition that I have nothing to expect from anybody in this world, but must stand on my own pair of feet! I feel independent at last. It was this feeling I lacked, and that lack which made me negligent and easy-going;—I had a certain vague reliance on some backer, which foolishly did not restrict itself to Apel, but also took other fantastic directions that almost make me laugh at my stupidity. Now I'm undeceived about all that, and very glad to be. My softness needed these experiences,—which will profit me in every way. Only, I straight-way beg them to deny me any sympathy,—'twould irk me;—yourself, your heart, your love shall be my only stand-by, my refuge and hope in every trouble of my coming life. Maternal love requires no reasons,—all other seeks to fathom why it loves, and therefore turns to nothing but regard.

I have been to Teplitz and Prague and found nothing there be-yond the confirmation of my plan not to go to Vienna, and advice to pursue the direction I already have struck. Moritz was in Prague, and gave me many a hint in this respect. From Prague I wrote to all the individuals I have my eye on, so as to know be-forehand where I stand with them, and take no road in vain. I am expecting their answers at Nuremberg, whither I go to-morrow or the next day, as I'm only waiting for a letter from Magdeburg to conclude my business here. I shall make a halt at Nuremberg; when a company is being disbanded, one easily picks something up;—moreover, the Wolframs can give me a deal of information, so that their opinion, perhaps, will save me a journey or two.

My dear, dear Mother,—my good angel,—fare heartily well, and don't fret;—you have a grateful son who never, never will forget what you are to him.—With the tenderest remembrances,
Thy   RICHARD.

My DEAR MOTHER—It is so long since I congratulated you upon your birthday, that it does me real good to be able to observe the proper day at last—so often overlooked by me, alas, in the hurry of business—to tell you how profoundly it rejoices me to know you're near us yet in soul and body, be able still to squeeze your hand from time to time, and recall together with and through yourself my youth you once cherished and shielded. Only in the realisation that you abide with us yet, can your children still dis-tinctly feel themselves one family. Whom life has blown hither and thither, to knit fresh bonds of kindred here and there,—

when they think of you, their dear old Mother who has formed no other ties upon this earth than those which knit her to her children, they all are one again, thy bairns!—God grant this boon may be vouchsafed us long, long yet; and may God preserve you long in full possession of your faculties, that to your life's end you may reap the only joy you can upon this earth,—the joy of a sympathetic onlooker at your children's prospering!

When I feel so driven or withheld, continually struggling, seldom gaining full success, often the prey of dejection at my failures,—nearly always quivering from rough contact with the outer world, which alas so seldom, hardly ever, answers to one's inner wish,—then nothing save a draught of *Nature* can revive me. Often as I have cast myself with tears and bitter cries into her arms, she always has consoled and raised me up by shewing how imaginary are all the sorrows that torment us. If we aim too high, then Nature lovingly reminds us we are really only bits of her, her outgrowths like these trees, these plants, that unfurl from the bud, shoot up and sun themselves, drink in the strengthening air, and neither wither nor decay till they have shed the seed to put forth buds and plants anew, and so the once-created lives its ceaseless links of renovated youth. When I feel my single self so integral a part of Nature, how utterly all idle egoism melts; and if I then would fain extend my hand to all good men, how much the rather must I long for that dear Mother from whose womb I sprang, and who is withering while I—bloom! How it makes one smile at those curious errors and perversities of our human Society, racking its brains for new-fangled devices, whereby these lovely ties of Nature so often get entangled, rent and torn!

Dear Motherkin, whatever strange occurrences have stepped between us, how swiftly all that is effaced! Just as when I steal from out the city's fumes into a leafy dale, stretch my full length on the turf, feast my eyes on the tapering tree-trunks, and list to some sweet woodbird's song until a tear rolls down my cheek unchecked for very happiness,—so do I feel when out through all the jungle of cross-purposes I reach my hand toward thee and cry: May God preserve thee, dear old Mother,—and when at last He takes thee from me, may he do it right gently and softly! Of Death 'twill be no question: *we* shall continue thy life for thee, and an ampler, manyer-sided life than thine could e'er have been. Thank God, then, who so richly blessed thy body!—

Minna, to whose memory I owe my recollection of your birthday this time, sends greetings and congratulations with all her heart. Farewell, good little Mother mine! Thy son

RICHARD.

Dresden, 19. Sept. 1846.

The Man Who Painted the Portrait

JAMES ABBOTT MCNEILL WHISTLER

James Abbott McNeill Whistler (1834-1903; American painter and etcher.) It is ironic that the man who was known during his lifetime as the most scathing wit in London is remembered today as the painter of a gentle portrait of his mother. The fame of the celebrated painting has tended to obscure almost everything else about the painter's life. Born in Lowell, Massachusetts, he was educated at the Imperial Academy in St. Petersburg; his father was building the Moscow-St. Petersburg Railroad at the time. Whistler then transferred to West Point, but he soon gave up the idea of an Army career and went to England, where he spent most of the rest of his life. He was elected president of the Society of British Artists in 1886. "The Portrait of My Mother," originally titled "Arrangement in Grey and Black," was painted in 1872. He painted other famous portraits and wrote The Gentle Art of Making Enemies. *Poor man—he has so many friends!*

The Peacock Room described in the letter is now in a museum in Washington, D. C.

MY OWN DARLING MOTHER,

I must not wait any longer that I may tell you what I have longed to do, the completion of this famous dining room. How I have worked. There must still be another week of it, or even two, before I can leave it, and say *I am content.* It is a *noble* work, though, Mother, and one we may be proud of, so very beautiful! and so entirely new, and original, as you can well fancy it would be, for at least *that* quality is recognized in your son.

Willie has told you of the visit of the Princess Louise to the "Peacock Palace," in Princes Gate, and her delight in the "gorgeous loveliness" of the work. Also the Marquis of Westminster and Prince . . . and all, and everybody else. I know you will be pleased that this testimony of worth should be offered after so much labor, therefore I tell you. The mere visits of Princes, and Dukes, we well know is no *voucher* for the *quality* of a work of art, for they are simply curious people, generally better *mannered* than others about them, but able to look with the same satisfaction upon a *bad* thing, as a good one. Still they are *charming* people, and show *real* delight in this beautiful room, keep up the buzz of publicity most pleasantly in London society, and this is well, and I hope good may result.

I am tired, but well, I am happy to say. Good night, dearest Mother, it is late, and I must get to my work again tomorrow. Tell "Sis" she may come with Annie, at half past four or five, P.M. any day to 49 Princes Gate, to see the room.

Your loving son,
Jamie

London/76

SEVEN

Letters from

Poets

POETS WRITE LOTS of letters. And their letters are usually saved, because all of us, whether for a few brief months during childhood or for all of the months of our lives, honor the poet and know the magic of his art—that he is at once a storyteller, a musician, a historian and a philosopher, and so is able to let us glimpse "first things" in a very special way. One defect of our civilization is that we sometimes forget this when we become matter-of-fact people in a matter-of-fact world.

What is more of a first thing, what is more primordial, than the relationship of mother and child? The psychiatrists tell us that much of our future is ordained during our first twelve months, even during the earliest of those infant months. The poets, let us remember, told us this long ago.

All is not sweetness and love in the letters written by poets to their mothers, because all is not sweetness and love in their understanding of each other or in their day-to-day living with each other, and could never be. Baudelaire's great letter goes deeply into that relationship, and it says some very terrifying things. This, for instance:

> We are evidently destined to love each other, to live for each other, to end our lives as honestly and peacefully as possible. And yet, in the terrible situation in which I am placed, I am convinced that one of us will kill the other, and that finally we shall kill each other. After my death, you shall cease to live; that

is clear. I am the one object for which you live. After your death, above all if you die of some shock I have caused you, I should undoubtedly kill myself.

Baudelaire recognized that his life and that of his mother's were helplessly intertwined. But so it is with all of us, sometimes helplessly, sometimes helpfully. We need the love of our mother more desperately than we need any other love; indeed, unless our parents loved us and we them, we never really learn how to love others or ourselves. John Donne intimated this in one way:

Because I cannot doubt in you, I will forbear more lines at this time, and most humbly deliver myself over to your devotions and good opinion of me, which I desire no longer to live than I may have.

A little girl of eight said it another way:

I long for you with the longings of a child to embrace you—to hold you in my arms. I respect you with all the respect due a mother.

Margaret Fleming wrote those poignant words in a letter to her mother just a few months before she died. Despite her youth, Margaret was a poet; that is why she is here. Indeed, her whole life was a brief, fragile poem, and the saddest line in my book tells the dates of that life: 1803-1811.

But do not for a moment think that poets are always poignant. Imagine yourself to be Lord Byron's mother when you receive this letter:

Dear Madam,—I have no beds for the Hansons or any body else at present. The Hansons sleep at Mansfield. I do not know that I resemble Jean Jacques Rousseau. I have no ambition to be like so illustrious a madman—but this I know, that I shall live in my own manner, and as much alone as possible. When my rooms are ready I shall be glad to see you: at present it would be improper, and uncomfortable to both parties.

Or this one, from Smyrna:

Dear Mother,—I know you will be glad to hear from me: I wish I could say I am equally delighted to write.

In one haughty letter, Byron tells his mother that he is about to return home. His instructions follow:

You will be good enough to get my apartments ready . . . I expect a powerful stock of potatoes, greens and biscuit . . . I don't suppose I shall be much pestered with visitors; but if I am, you must receive them . . . I trust to find my library in tolerable order . . .

And so on. Now read Goethe's letter, telling *his* mother that he will soon arrive for a short visit with some friends:

Put up a bed for the Duke in the small bedroom . . . Have mattresses placed into the little chimney room for his valets . . . We'll eat at 4 o'clock in the afternoon. I say—we'll eat. No banquets. The best of your habitual fare, that's all. Get all the good fruit you can for breakfast. Let the Duke have your silver washbowl.

More and more instructions—and then these lines:

. . . avoid the appearance of having gone to any special trouble. Let it be as though we had been living with you for ten years.

The practical aspects of being a mother are difficult enough under any circumstances. How do you think you'd like being the mother of a poet?

"We Shall Kill Each Other"

CHARLES PIERRE BAUDELAIRE

Charles Pierre Baudelaire (1821-1867; French poet and critic.) The "conseil judiciaire" to which Baudelaire refers in this long letter to his mother was a desperate device she and the poet's stepfather had adopted in a vain attempt to save for him what little was left of his inheritance. For though Baudelaire is well known as the chronicler of abject poverty and debt-ridden despair, the truth is that his father had left him a sizable fortune. Over half of it was gone in two years, and much of the rest was seized by creditors. Baudelaire lived in pursuit of his own concept of the "dandy"—that is, a man who passes in society as one without visible means of support. His mother managed to have him declared financially incompetent before the money was utterly spent or attached, and for the rest of his life funds were doled out to the poet by the "conseil judiciaire," or trustee.

Considering the enormous influence that Baudelaire has had on the poets of the last hundred years, particularly on the French

Symbolists and such modern writers as T.S. Eliot and Paul Valéry, it is astounding that he published only one volume of verse, Les Fleurs du Mal *(1857). But that frequently-suppressed collection of lyrics is a crown incrusted with jewels, and jewels shine far. He wrote several volumes of criticism which were also influential; he was the first to champion Wagner's music in France; and his translations of Edgar Allan Poe first brought the American writer to the attention of European readers.*

The Jeanne mentioned in the letter several times was Baudelaire's notorious mistress.

[February or March, 1861.]

Aᴎ, ᴅᴇᴀʀ Mᴏᴛʜᴇʀ, is any *time* left *us* in which to be happy? I dare not hope so. To be forty, under a conseil judiciaire, with immense debts, and, finally, worse than all, my will gone; ruined! Who can say if the intelligence itself be not dried up? I know nothing. I cannot know anything, since I have lost even the ability to make an effort.

Before all, I want to say something which I do not say often enough to you, and which you no doubt do not know, most of all if you judge me by appearances; it is that my love for you grows without ceasing. I am ashamed to confess that that love does not give me strength enough to raise myself. I look at the past years, the awful years, and spend my time reflecting on the brevity of life; nothing more! and my will rusts more and more. If ever a man knew, in youth, bile and hypochondria, that man is myself. Yet I long to live, and would fain taste a little security, glory, and contentment with myself. Some terrible thing says to me: *Never*, and again something else says, *try*.

With so many plans and projects, accumulated in the two or three portfolios I dare no longer open, what am I likely to achieve? Perhaps nothing, it may be.

April 1st, 1861.

Tʜɪꜱ last page was written a month, six weeks, two months ago, I no longer know when. I have fallen into a sort of perpetual nervous terror; my sleep is frightful, my awakening terrible; impossible to do anything. The copies of my own book remained for a month on my table before I could find courage to address them. I have not written to Jeanne, I have not seen her for nearly three months; and, naturally, since it was impossible, I did not send her one penny. (She came to see me yesterday; she had been in hospital, and her brother, on whom I thought she could rely, sold part of her furniture in her absence. She means to sell the rest to pay some debts.) In this horrible state of mind, impotence and hypochondria, the idea of suicide returned to me; I can say now that it has passed away; but every moment of the day that idea obsessed me. I saw in it complete deliverance, deliverance from everything. At the same time, *and for three months,* by a strange contradiction, but only in seeming, I was *praying all the time* (to whom? to what definite being? Indeed, I know not) for two things: for myself, strength to live; for you, long long years. Let me say in passing, your desire to die is absurd and most unkind, since your death for me would be the last blow, it would mean the eternal loss of my happiness.

In the end, my obsession disappeared, driven away by the violent and inevitable occupation of my article on Wagner, which I wrote in three days in a printing office; without the urge of the printer I could never have done it. Since, I have again become ill with languor, with horror and fear. And physically, too, I have been pretty ill two or three times; but one of the things which I find particularly unbearable is that when I fall asleep and even during sleep, I hear voices very distinctly, whole phrases even, very commonplace and quite trivial, and having no relation to my affairs.

Your letters came; they were not of a nature to comfort me. You are always armed to stone me with the crowd. It all dates from my childhood, as you know. How do you always manage to be to your son the very contrary of a *friend,* except in regard to money, provided again—and it is then your character shows itself at once absurd and generous—that it is not to your hurt? I took care to note all the new poems for you, in the list of contents. It was easy for you to verify that they were all made to fit the book. A book I worked on over twenty years, *and which I can not even control the reprinting of.**

As for M. Cardinne, that is a serious matter, but in a sense

---

* Evidently a question of the second edition of *Les Fleurs du Mal.* His mother had doubtless yet again protested against certain poems which shocked her Catholicism.

opposed, quite opposed, to that in which you take it. In the midst
of all my anguish, I will not have a priest fight against me in
my old mother's mind, and I shall see that is so, if I am able and
have the strength. The man's conduct is monstrous and inex-
plicable. As to burning books, that is never done, except in mad-
houses where they want to see a flare. And I stupidly deprived
myself of a precious copy, to please him, and give him something
he had longed for, for three years! and not a copy is left for my
friends! You always had to fall on your knees before someone.
First, to M. Emon, you remember. Now to a priest, who has not
even the delicacy to hide one wounding thought from you. And
finally he does not even understand that the book starts from a
Catholic idea; but that is a consideration of another kind.

What more than anything saved me from suicide was two ideas
which must seem very childish to you. Firstly, that my duty was to
furnish you with exact details as to the payment of all my debts,
and so *I should first have to go to Honfleur,* where the documents
are put away, intelligible to me alone. The second, shall I confess
it, was that I could not bear to die before having, at least, published my critical works, even if I renounce the plays (a second is
projected), the novels, and finally the large book I have had in
mind for two years, *My Naked Heart,* in which will be heaped up
all my rage.

Ah! if ever that is printed, the *Confessions of J. J.* will seem
pale. You see I am still dreaming.

Unluckily for the achievement of this singular book, I ought
to have kept the heaps of letters from everybody which I have,
for twenty years now, given away or burnt.

Finally, as I told you, an urgent occupation drew me from my
lethargy and sickness for thrice twenty-four hours. The malady
will return.

Relative to the "conseil judiciaire," what you tell me has again
preoccupied me; I believe I have finally found a *compromise,*
which will only *half* ruin me, which will give me immense leisure,
and which will consequently permit me to *enrich* your income,
since, however little I shall then earn, I shall need, at most, *but
the half. I must explain.* This accursed invention! the maternal
invention of a mind too much occupied with money, dishonoured
me, drove me into ever-increasing debt, which killed all friendliness in me, and even fettered my education as artist and man
of letters, which remains still unfinished. Blindness creates worse

scourges than malice. What is certain is that my present situation cannot continue much longer. I do not think I can go mad, but I can become so unsociable that I should pass as mad. . . .

6th May, 1861.

MY DEAR MOTHER, if you are really utterly motherly, and if you are not yet tired out, come to Paris, come and see me, seek me out even. For me, there are a thousand terrible reasons why I cannot go to Honfleur to seek for what I so much want, courage and your tenderness. At the end of March I wrote: *Shall we ever meet again?* I was in one of those states in which the terrible truth grows manifest. I would give I know not what to spend some days with you, you, the only being on whom my life hangs, eight days, three days, some hours.

You do not read my letters attentively enough; you imagine I am lying, or at least exaggerating, when I speak of my despair, my health, my horror of living. I tell you I want to see you and that I cannot come to Honfleur. Your letters are full of errors and false ideas which conversation could put right, but which whole volumes of writing will not suffice to destroy.

Every time I take up the pen to tell you how I am placed, I am afraid. I am afraid of killing you, destroying your feeble body. And I, ceaselessly, and unsuspected by you, am on the verge of suicide! I believe you love me passionately, blindly; your nature is so large! And I loved you passionately in childhood; later, as a result of your injustice, I was lacking in respect, as if maternal injustice could authorise a lack of filial respect. Often I have repented, though, as is my wont, I said nothing to you. I am no longer that violent or ungrateful child. Long meditation on my fate and on your character has led me to understand all my faults and all your generosity. But now, the evil is done, partly by your imprudence and partly by my fault.

We are evidently destined to love each other, to live for each other, to end our lives as honestly and peacefully as possible. And yet, in the terrible situation in which I am placed, I am convinced that one of us will kill the other, and that finally we shall kill each other. After my death, you will cease to live; that is clear. I am the one object for which you live. After your death, above all if you die of some shock I have caused you, I should undoubtedly kill myself. Your death, of which you often speak with too much resignation, would in no way ameliorate my situation; the conseil judiciaire would go on (why should it not?), nothing would be paid, and, to add to my sorrows, I should have *the horrible sensation of complete isolation.* For me to kill myself would be absurd, would it not? "You want to leave your old mother all alone?" you say. Truly, even if I have not strictly the right to do so, yet I think the amount of sorrow endured by me for *nearly thirty years* would justify it. "And God?" you will say. I desire, with all my heart (and with what sincerity no one but myself can know), to believe that an exterior and invisible Being is in charge of my fate; but how am I to believe it?

(The idea of God makes me think of that accursed Curé. In the painful feelings my letter will no doubt arouse in you, I wish you not to consult him. That Curé is my enemy, through sheer stupidity, maybe.)

To return to the idea of suicide, not an obsession, but an idea which returns periodically, there is one thing should reassure you. I cannot kill myself until I have put my affairs in order. All my documents are at Honfleur, in great confusion. Therefore a great deal must be done at Honfleur, and once I am there, I shall not be able again to tear myself from your side. For you may presume that I could not desecrate your house with so detestable an action. Besides, you would go mad. Why then suicide? Is it because of debts? Yes, and yet debts can be overcome. It is above all because of my frightful tiredness, the result of an impossible situation, *too much prolonged.* Every moment shows me I have no more desire to live. A great imprudence was committed by you in my youth. Your imprudence and my *former faults* weigh upon and envelope me. My situation is atrocious. There are people who salute me, there are people who make up to me. There may be some who envy me. My literary situation is more than good, I can do what I will and everything will be printed. As I have a non-popular sort of mind, I shall not gain much, but I shall leave a great reputation behind me, I know, if only I have the courage to live. But my spiritual health is detestable, perhaps lost. I have still many projects: *My Naked Heart, novels, two plays,* one for the Théâtre-Français, will all ever be accomplished? *I think not.* My situation as regards decency is fearful, there is the chief evil. Never any rest; insults, jibes, humiliations, of which you can have no idea, which corrupt the imagination and paralyse it. I make a little money, it is true; if I had no debts, and *if I had no more money of my own,* I should be rich. Meditate that phrase. I could even give you money, I could, without danger, be charitable to Jeanne. I shall refer to her again, but you have provoked me into these explanations. All my money vanishes in a prodigal and unhealthy existence (for I live wretchedly) and in paying or rather inadequately paying off old debts, bailiffs' costs, stamped documents, etc.

In a moment I shall come to real things, I mean present ones, for truly I must be saved, and you alone can save me. I must say everything to you, now. I am alone, without friends or mistress or dog or cat to whom to complain. There is only my father's portrait, and that is always silent.

I am in that horrible state I was in the autumn of 1844. A resignation worse than fury.

And my physical health, which I need for you, for myself, my obligations, is another problem. I must speak of it to you, even though you care so little.

I do not mean those nervous affections which destroy me day by day and which kill my courage, or the vomitings, the insomnias, nightmares, fits of exhaustion. I have spoken of them too often. But there is no point in being ashamed with you. You know that when I was young I had a venereal disease, which later I thought entirely cured. At Dijon, after 1848, it appeared again, and was again suppressed. Now it returns and in a new form, spots on the skin, and an extraordinary lassitude in all the articulations. Believe me, I *know what it is.* Perhaps as a result of the misery in which I am plunged, my terror exaggerates the evil. But what I need is a severe regimen, and certainly, not in the life I am leading, can I give myself up to one.

I leave all on one side and go back to my dreams again, with real pleasure, before coming to the project I want to speak about. Who knows if I shall ever again be able to open to you all my soul, *that you never knew or appreciated!* I write unhesitatingly, so true I know it to be.

There was in my youth a period of passionate love for you, listen and read without fear. I have never said as much to you before. I remember being with you in a carriage, you had come out of a nursing-home to which you had been sent, and you showed me, to prove that you had thought of your son, some pen and ink drawings you had made for me. Do you see how terrible my memory is? Later, the square Saint-André-des-Arts and Neuilly. Long walks, perpetual tenderness! I remember the embankment, so sad at evening. Ah! that was the best time of

mother-love for me. I ask your pardon for calling *best time* what
was doubtless worst for you. But all the time I was living in you
and you were uniquely mine. You were at once my idol and my
friend. Perhaps you will be astonished to see me speak with such
passion of a time so distant; it astonishes me, too. It is perhaps
because I have, once again, conceived a desire to die, that these
ancient things present themselves so vividly to my mind.

Later, you know the frightful education your husband wanted
to impose on me; I am forty, but I cannot think of colleges without anguish, or of the fear my step-father inspired in me. And
yet I loved him, and I am wise enough to-day to do him justice.
Always he was so obstinately clumsy. I pass on rapidly, for I
see tears in your eyes.

Finally, I got away, and then I was completely abandoned. I
became intoxicated with pleasure, with perpetual excitement,
with travelling, fine furniture, pictures, women, etc. To-day I
bear their cruel weight. As to the conseil judiciaire, I have only
one word to say: I know now the immense value of money and
understand the gravity of all things concerned with it; I understand that you could have thought yourself wise and working for
my welfare, but there is still one question, one question which
has always obsessed me. How can this idea never have presented
itself to your mind? "It is possible that my son may never, to the
same degree as myself, know how to behave; but it is also possible
that he may become a remarkable man in other ways. In that
case, what shall I do? Shall I condemn him to a double existence,
contradictory, honourable on one side, odious and scorned on
the other? Shall I condemn him to drag on to old age a deplorable
stigma, an injurious stigma, a cause of impotence and misery?"
It is obvious that if the conseil judiciaire had not been appointed,
my fortune would have vanished, and I should have had to
acquire a taste for work. The conseil was appointed, *all is eaten
up and I am old and wretched.*

Can I rejuvenate myself? That is the whole question. All this
turning back to the past has no other object but to show you that
I have valid excuses, if not a complete justification. If you feel
reproach in what I write, know at least that it in no way changes
my admiration for your large heart, or my gratitude for your
devotion. You always sacrificed yourself; that is your one genius.
Less reason than charity. I ask more, I ask at the same time your
advice, your help, entire understanding between us, so as to
extricate me. I supplicate you, come, come; I am at the end of my

nervous powers, at the end of my courage, at the end of hope. I foresee only a continuation of horror. I foresee my literary existence for ever crippled. I foresee catastrophe. You could easily, for a week, ask hospitality from your friends, Ancelle, for example. I would give I know not what to see you, to embrace you. I foresee catastrophe, yet I cannot go to you now. Paris is horrible. Twice already I have committed a grave imprudence which you will find more severe terms for; I shall end by losing my head.

I demand your happiness, and mine also, in so far as we can still experience *happiness.*

You allowed me to describe my project; here it is. I ask for a half-measure. The alienation of a large sum limited to 10,000 francs for example; 2,000 for my immediate deliverance, 2,000 in your hands to guard against foreseen or unforeseen necessities, of life, of clothes, etc., during one year. (Jeanne will go into a nursing-home, where only what is strictly necessary will be paid.) But I shall talk of her again in a moment. And it is again you who have induced me to do so. Then, 6,000 in the hands of Ancelle or Marin, which will be spent slowly, prudently, in such a way as to pay out perhaps more than 10,000 and so prevent all noise and scandal at Honfleur.

There would be a year of peace. I should be the worst fool and most utter rascal if I did not become young again through it. All the money I shall gain during that time (10,000; 5,000 only perhaps) *will be given into your hands.* I shall not hide from you any one of my affairs, any of my gains. Instead of filling up the deficit this money could be applied to the debts, and so on for subsequent years. Thus I could *perhaps,* by rejuvenating under your very eyes, *pay everything,* without my capital being diminished by more than 10,000, without reckoning, it is true, the 4,600 of preceding years. And the house would be saved, for that is one of the considerations always present to me.

If you agree to this marvellous plan, I should like to reinstal myself at the end of the month, or at once, maybe. I authorise you to come for me. You understand that there is a mass of details which cannot go into a letter. I want, in one word, that no sum be paid without your consent, and after mature discussion between us; in a word, that you should become my real *"conseil judiciaire."* How can one have to associate so horrible an idea with the sweet idea of a mother?

In that case, unfortunately, farewell must be said to the small sums, the small gains, 100, 200, here, there, which the ordinary

life of Paris brings in day by day. Then there will be large specula-
tions and large books, for the payment of which we shall have to
wait longer. Consult yourself only, your conscience and your
God, since you are happy enough to believe in him. Be measured
in what you say to Ancelle. He is kind, but narrow-minded. He
cannot believe that an obstinate and wilful person whom he has
had to reprimand can be an important one. He would let me
starve through sheer obstinacy. Instead of thinking only of money,
think a little of glory, calm and *my life*.

Then, I say, I shall not pay visits of a fortnight, a month or
two months. I shall stay with you always, except when we both
came to Paris.

Proofs can always be sent by post.

I have still another of those false ideas which continually
recur in your letter, to rectify. I am *never bored in solitude*, and
I am *never bored with you*. I only know that your friends will
make me unhappy, but I consent.

Sometimes I have had the idea of convoking a family council
or of applying to a magistrate. Do you know, I should have some
good things to say, even if I said only this. *I have produced eight
volumes in wretched conditions. I can earn my living. I am being
destroyed by my youthful debts.*

I did not do so out of respect for you, out of regard for your
terrible sensitiveness. Deign to be grateful. I repeat, I am determined to have recourse only to you.

From the beginning of next year, I shall consecrate to Jeanne
the income of what capital remains. She will retire somewhere
so as not to be completely alone. This is what happened to her;
her brother pushed her into a hospital to get rid of her, and when
she came out she discovered he had sold some of her furniture
and clothes. In four months, since my flight from Neuilly, I have
given her seven francs.

I implore you, calm, give me calm, work, and a little love.

It is obvious that at this very moment there are horribly urgent
things; thus I have again committed the fault, in this inevitable
meddling with banks, of turning aside for my personal debts
some hundreds of francs which did not belong to me. *I was
absolutely forced to do so*. It goes without saying that I thought
I could immediately put things right. A person in London refuses
me the 400 francs which she owes me. Another who should have
paid me 300 francs is abroad. Always the unexpected. To-day I
had the *terrible courage* to write the person in question a con-

fession of my fault. What scene will take place? I cannot tell. But I wanted to clear my conscience. I hope that, in respect of my name and my talent, there will be no scandal, and that he will not mind waiting.

Goodbye. I am worn out. To go back to my health, I have not slept, nor eaten for nearly three days; my throat is constricted, yet I have to work.

No, I do not say goodbye; for I hope to see you soon.

Oh, read my letter attentively, and try to understand it.

I know that this letter will affect you painfully, but you will certainly find in it some accent of sweetness, of love, and even of hope, so rarely heard by you.

And I love you.

Charles.

7th May [1861].

My dear mother, I may have alarmed you too much this morning; without knowing how, the fever, suffocation and trembling disappeared, and I could eat.

But all the difficulties and disquietudes remain. What insupportable crises!

You did not notice that at the end of the *Wagner* there was a part so far unpublished; I marked it for you, on the first page.

As for the critical articles, you must all the same get used to them. You have had several years in which to do so and anyhow it will go on for ever.

I have seen the person whose visit I feared. How humiliating!

No postage stamps.

I thought it was best to write to you at once.

Charles.

"A Gipsylike Wandering Disposition"

GEORGE GORDON NOEL BYRON, LORD BYRON

George Gordon Noel Byron, Lord Byron (1788-1824; English poet.) These letters illustrate an amusing and "Byronically" different mother-son relationship. Most sons are dependent on their

parents, but Byron's mother was dependent for her entire main-
tenance on him. As the heir of his great-uncle, he became 6th
Baron Byron of Rochdale in 1798. His profligate father, Captain
John "Mad Jack" Byron, had died several years before, so mother
and son were left to each other's mercies from the time the poet
was three. He was educated at Harrow and at Trinity College,
Cambridge, where he started writing. Fugitive Pieces, *a collection*
of poems, was published when he was eighteen; the book was
banned, and Byron's pattern of life was established.

He had no sooner assumed his seat in the House of Lords than
he departed on the celebrated Mediterranean tour, about which
most of these letters were written. He left England on the wings
of a characteristically satiric blast, English Bards and Scotch
Reviewers, *an attack upon the* Edinburgh Review, *which had pil-*
loried his first work. It was on this tour that the Byronic legend
began, partly brought about by fate and genius, partly by a flair
for the melodramatic that no other poet had ever had. Inspired by
the example of Leander (and despite a foot crippled by infantile
paralysis), Byron swam the Hellespont in an hour and twenty
minutes, and then proclaimed to the world that he was the second
man to do so. He returned to England in 1811 and published
Childe Harold, Cantos i and ii (1812), The Giaour and The Bride
of Abydos (1813) and The Corsair and Lara (1814). He also
achieved the most brilliant social success of any English poet
before or since. Young men emulated him; women adored him.
But this last was not an unmixed blessing; within five years of
his triumphant return a series of scandals and consequent un-
friendly public opinion drove Byron, notably unrepentant, from
England for good.

He joined the Shelleys at Lake Geneva; then he went to Italy
and for six years was a leading, if erratic, champion of that nation's
fight for independence and unity. He neglected neither women
nor poetry. The former are too numerous to mention, but the
latter include Childe Harold, Canto iii *and* The Prisoner of
Chillon (1816), Manfred (1817) Childe Harold, Canto iv (1819)
and Don Juan, *his masterpiece, written between 1819 and his*
death (it is unfinished).

In the summer of 1823 he embarked on his last wonderful, mad
adventure. The London Greek Committee persuaded the poet to
transfer his fight for liberty from Italy to Greece. He outfitted a
120-ton brig, said a final farewell to his friends, and sailed from
Genoa. He got near enough to the scene of action for his presence
to encourage the Greek leaders (independence from **Turkish rule**

was won in 1829), but his health had been failing for some time;
he was stricken with fever at Missolonghi and died there in
January, 1824.

When the first of the letters that follow was written, Byron had
been sent by his mother to Nottingham, where he was in the care
of a truss-maker who claimed that he would cure the boy's disability. The man was a charlatan and sadist; Byron's nurse was no
less bestial. You get no hint of the youngster's misery from this
letter, however.

The "Mr. Hobhouse" referred to in Byron's letter of June, 1810,
was John Cam Hobhouse, later Lord Broughton; you can read
of at least one of the revels of these two dashing bachelors in
Canto v of Childe Harolde.

Nottingham, 13 March, 1799

Dear Mama,—I am very glad to hear you are well. I am so
myself, thank God; upon my word I did not expect so long a
Letter from you; however I will answer it as well as I can. Mrs.
Parkyns and the rest are well and are much obliged to you for
the present. Mr. Rogers could attend me every night at a separate
hour from the Miss Parkynses, and I am astonished you do not
acquiesce in this Scheme which would keep me in Mind of what
I have almost entirely forgot. I recommend this to you because,
if some plan of this kind is not adopted, I shall be called, or rather
branded with the name of a dunce, which you know I could
never bear. I beg you will consider this plan seriously and I will
lend it all the assistance in my power. I shall be very glad to see
the Letter you talk of, and I have time just to say I hope every
body is well at Newstead,

And remain, your affectionate Son,
BYRON.

P.S.—Pray let me know when you are to send in the Horses
to go to Newstead. May desires her Duty and I also expect an
answer by the miller.

16, Piccadilly, Febry. 26, 1806.

Dear Mother,—Notwithstanding your sage and oeconomical advice I have paid my *Harrow* Debts, as I can better afford to wait
for the Money than the poor Devils who were my creditors. I have

also discharged my college Bills amounting to £231,—£75 of
which I shall trouble Hanson to repay, being for Furniture, and as
my allowance is £500 per annum, I do not chuse to lose the over-
plus as it makes only £125 per Quarter. I happen to have a few
hundreds in ready Cash by me, so I have paid the accounts; but
I find it inconvenient to remain at College, not for the expence,
as I could live on my allowance (only I am naturally extravagant);
however the mode of going on does not suit my constitution. Improvement at an English University to a Man of Rank is, you
know, impossible, and the very Idea *ridiculous*. Now I sincerely
desire to finish my Education and, having been sometime at
Cambridge, the Credit of the University is as much attached to
my Name, as if I had pursued my Studies *there* for a Century; but,
believe me, it is nothing more than a Name, which is already
acquired. I can now leave it with Honour, as I have paid everything, & wish to pass a couple of years abroad, where I am certain
of employing my time to far more advantage and at much less
expence, than at our English Seminaries. 'Tis true I cannot enter
France; but Germany and the Courts of Berlin, Vienna & Petersburg are still open, I shall lay the Plan before Hanson & Lord C.
I presume you will all agree, and if you do not, I will, if possible,
get away without your Consent, though I should admire it more
in the regular manner & with a Tutor of your furnishing. This
is my project, at present I wish *you* to be silent to Hanson about
it. Let me have your Answer. I intend remaining in Town a Month
longer, when perhaps I shall bring my Horses and myself down
to your residence in that *execrable* Kennel. I hope you have engaged a Man Servant, else it will be impossible for me to visit
you, since my Servant must attend chiefly to his horses; at the
same Time you must cut an indifferent Figure with only maids
in your habitation.

I remain, your's,
BYRON.

Newstead Abbey, Notts, October 7, 1808.

DEAR MADAM,—I have no beds for the Hansons or any body
else at present. The Hansons sleep at Mansfield. I do not know that
I resemble Jean Jacques Rousseau. I have no ambition to be like
so illustrious a madman—but this I know, that I shall live in my
own manner, and as much alone as possible. When my rooms are
ready I shall be glad to see you: at present it would be improper,

and uncomfortable to both parties. You can hardly object to my rendering my mansion habitable, notwithstanding my departure for Persia in March (or May at farthest), since *you* will be *tenant* till my return; and in case of any accident (for I have already arranged my will to be drawn up the moment I am twenty-one), I have taken care you shall have the house and manor for *life*, besides a sufficient income. So you see my improvements are not entirely selfish. As I have a friend here, we will go to the Infirmary Ball on the 12th; we will drink tea with Mrs. Byron at eight o'clock, and expect to see you at the ball. If that lady will allow us a couple of rooms to dress in, we shall be highly obliged: —if we are at the ball by ten or eleven, it will be time enough, and we shall return to Newstead about three or four. Adieu.

Believe me, yours very truly,
BYRON.

Smyrna, April 9, 1810.

Dear Mother,—I know you will be glad to hear from me: I wish I could say I am equally delighted to write. However, there is no great loss in my scribbles, except to the portmanteau-makers, who, I suppose, will get all by and by.

Nobody but yourself asks me about my creed,—what I am, am not, etc., etc. If I were to begin *explaining*, God knows where I should leave off; so we will say no more about that, if you please.

I am no "good soul," and not an atheist, but an English gentleman, I hope, who loves his mother, mankind, and his country. I have not time to write more at present, and beg you to believe me,

Ever yours, etc.
BYRON.

P.S.—Are the Miss—— anxiously expecting my arrival and contributions to their gossip and *rhymes*, which are about as bad as they can be?

B.

Constantinople, June 28, 1810.

My dear Mother,—I regret to perceive by your last letter that several of mine have not arrived, particularly a very long one written in November last from Albania, where I was on a visit to the Pacha of that province. Fletcher has also written to his spouse perpetually.

Mr. Hobhouse, who will forward or deliver this, and is on his return to England, can inform you of our different movements, but I am very uncertain as to my own return. He will probably be down in Notts. some time or other; but Fletcher, whom I send back as an incumbrance (English servants are sad travellers), will supply his place in the interim, and describe our travels, which have been tolerably extensive.

I have written twice briefly from this capital, from Smyrna, from Athens and other parts of Greece; from Albania, the Pacha of which province desired his respects to my mother, and said he was sure I was a man of high birth because I had small ears, curling hair, and white hands!!! He was very kind to me, begged me to consider him as a father, and gave me a guard of forty soldiers through the forests of Acarnania. But of this and other circumstances I have written to you at large, and yet hope you will receive my letters.

I remember Mahmout Pacha, the grandson of Ali Pacha, at Yanina, (a little fellow of ten years of age, with large black eyes, which our ladies would purchase at any price, and those regular features which distinguish the Turks,) asked me how I came to travel so young, without anybody to take care of me. This question was put by the little man with all the gravity of threescore. I cannot now write copiously; I have only time to tell you that I have passed many a fatiguing, but never a tedious moment; and all that I am afraid of is that I shall contract a gipsylike wandering disposition, which will make home tiresome to me: this, I am told, is very common with men in the habit of peregrination, and, indeed, I feel it so. On the 3d of May I swam from *Sestos* to *Abydos*. You know the story of Leander, but I had no *Hero* to receive me at landing.

I also passed a fortnight on the Troad. The tombs of Achilles and Æsyetes still exist in large barrows, similar to those you have doubtless seen in the North. The other day I was at Belgrade (a village in these environs), to see the house built on the same site as Lady Mary Wortley's. By-the-by, her ladyship, as far as I can judge, has lied, but not half so much as any other woman would have done in the same situation.

I have been in all the principal mosques by the virtue of a firman: this is a favour rarely permitted to Infidels, but the am-

bassador's departure obtained it for us. I have been up the
Bosphorus into the Black Sea, round the walls of the city, and,
indeed, I know more of it by sight than I do of London. I hope to
amuse you some winter's evening with the details, but at present
you must excuse me;—I am not able to write long letters in June.
I return to spend my summer in Greece. I write often, but you
must not be alarmed when you do not receive my letters; consider we have no regular post farther than Malta, where I beg you
will in future send your letters, and not to this city.

Fletcher is a poor creature, and requires comforts that I can
dispense with. He is very sick of his travels, but you must not
believe his account of the country. He sighs for ale, and idleness,
and a wife, and the devil knows what besides. I have not been
disappointed or disgusted. I have lived with the highest and the
lowest. I have been for days in a Pacha's palace, and have passed
many a night in a cowhouse, and I find the people inoffensive
and kind. I have also passed some time with the principal Greeks
in the Morea and Livadia, and, though inferior to the Turks,
they are better than the Spaniards, who, in their turn, excel the
Portuguese. Of Constantinople you will find many descriptions in
different travels; but Lady Mary Wortley errs strangely when she
says, "St. Paul's would cut a strange figure by St. Sophia's." I
have been in both, surveyed them inside and out attentively. St.
Sophia's is undoubtedly the most interesting from its immense
antiquity, and the circumstance of all the Greek emperors, from
Justinian, having been crowned there, and several murdered at the
altar, besides the Turkish Sultans who attend it regularly. But it is
inferior in beauty and size to some of the mosques, particularly
"Soleyman," etc., and not to be mentioned in the same page with
St. Paul's (I speak like a *Cockney*). However, I prefer the Gothic
cathedral of Seville to St. Paul's, St. Sophia's, and any religious
building I have ever seen.

The walls of the Seraglio are like the walls of Newstead gardens, only higher, and much in the same *order;* but the ride by the
walls of the city, on the land side, is beautiful. Imagine four miles
of immense triple battlements, covered with ivy, surmounted with
218 towers, and, on the other side of the road, Turkish burying-
grounds (the loveliest spots on earth), full of enormous cypresses.
I have seen the ruins of Athens, of Ephesus, and Delphi. I have
traversed great part of Turkey, and many other parts of Europe,
and some of Asia; but I never beheld a work of nature or art which

yielded an impression like the prospect on each side from the Seven Towers to the end of the Golden Horn.

Now for England. I am glad to hear of the progress of *English Bards*, etc. Of course, you observed I have made great additions to the new edition. Have you received my picture from Sanders, Vigo Lane, London? It was finished and paid for long before I left England: pray, send for it. You seem to be a mighty reader of magazines: where do you pick up all this intelligence, quotations, etc., etc.? Though I was happy to obtain my seat without the assistance of Lord Carlisle, I had no measures to keep with a man who declined interfering as my relation on that occasion, and I have done with him, though I regret distressing Mrs. Leigh, poor thing!—I hope she is happy.

It is my opinion that Mr. B** ought to marry Miss R**. Our first duty is not to do evil; but, alas! that is impossible: our next is to repair it, if in our power. The girl is his equal: if she were his inferior, a sum of money and provision for the child would be some, though a poor, compensation: as it is, he should marry her. I will have no gay deceivers on my estate, and I shall not allow my tenants a privilege I do not permit myself—*that* of debauching each other's daughters. God knows, I have been guilty of many excesses; but, as I have laid down a resolution to reform, and lately kept it, I expect this Lothario to follow the example, and begin by restoring this girl to society, or, by the beard of my father! he shall hear of it. Pray take some notice of Robert, who will miss his master; poor boy, he was very unwilling to return. I trust you are well and happy. It will be a pleasure to hear from you.

> Believe me, yours very sincerely,
> BYRON.

P.S.—How is Joe Murray?

P.S.—I open my letter again to tell you that Fletcher having petitioned to accompany me into the Morea, I have taken him with me, contrary to the intention expressed in my letter.

Volage frigate, at sea, June 25, 1811.

DEAR MOTHER,—This letter, which will be forwarded on our arrival at Portsmouth, probably about the 4th of July, is begun about twenty-three days after our departure from Malta. I have

just been two years (to a day, on the 2d of July) absent from
England, and I return to it with much the same feelings which
prevailed on my departure, viz. indifference; but within that
apathy I certainly do not comprise yourself, as I will prove by
every means in my power. You will be good enough to get my
apartments ready at Newstead; but don't disturb yourself, on any
account, particularly mine, nor consider me in any other light
than as a visiter. I must only inform you that for a long time I
have been restricted to an entire vegetable diet, neither fish nor
flesh coming within my regimen; so I expect a powerful stock of
potatoes, greens, and biscuit; I drink no wine. I have two servants,
middle-aged men, and both Greeks. It is my intention to proceed
first to town, to see Mr. Hanson, and thence to Newstead, on my
way to Rochdale. I have only to beg you will not forget my diet,
which it is very necessary for me to observe. I am well in health,
as I have generally been, with the exception of two agues, both
of which I quickly got over.

My plans will so much depend on circumstances, that I shall
not venture to lay down an opinion on the subject. My prospects
are not very promising, but I suppose we shall wrestle through
life like our neighbours; indeed, by Hanson's last advices, I have
some apprehension of finding Newstead dismantled by Messrs.
Brothers, etc., and he seems determined to force me into selling
it, but he will be baffled. I don't suppose I shall be much pestered
with visiters; but if I am, you must receive them, for I am determined to have nobody breaking in upon my retirement: you know
that I never was fond of society, and I am less so than before. I
have brought you a shawl, and a quantity of attar of roses, but
these I must smuggle, if possible. I trust to find my library in
tolerable order.

Fletcher is no doubt arrived. I shall separate the mill from
Mr. B**'s farm, for his son is too gay a deceiver to inherit both,
and place Fletcher in it, who has served me faithfully, and whose
wife is a good woman; besides, it is necessary to sober young
Mr. B**, or he will people the parish with bastards. In a word, if
he had seduced a dairy-maid, he might have found something
like an apology; but the girl is his equal, and in high life or low
life reparation is made in such circumstances. But I shall not
interfere further than (like Buonaparte) by dismembering Mr.
B.'s *kingdom*, and erecting part of it into a principality for field-
marshal Fletcher! I hope you govern my little *empire* and its sad

load of national debt with a wary hand. To drop my metaphor, I
beg leave to subscribe myself

Yours ever,
BYRON.

P.S. July 14—This letter was written to be sent from Portsmouth, but, on arriving there, the squadron was ordered to the
Nore, from whence I shall forward it. This I have not done before,
supposing you might be alarmed by the interval mentioned in the
letter being longer than expected between our arrival in port and
my appearance at Newstead.

"Assist Me With Your Blessings"

JOHN DONNE

*John Donne (1572?-1631; English poet and divine.) The first and
greatest of the metaphysical poets was connected, on his mother's
side, with Sir Thomas More and John Heywood. He was brought
up a Catholic and educated at Oxford, Cambridge, and Lincoln's
Inn. The most notable event of his youth was his participation in
the expeditions led by the Earl of Essex against Cádiz and the
Azores. In 1597 he was appointed secretary to the Lord Keeper
of the Great Seal, Sir Thomas Egerton, but he lost the post four
years later and was imprisoned for a time because of his marriage
to Anne More, Egerton's niece; the marriage was a violation of
both canon and common law. Despite poverty and other difficulties, however, the couple lived happily until her death.*

*For several years Donne attempted without success to obtain
a position through court favor; in 1610 his Pseduo-Martyr impressed James I, but the king refused to promote the poet except
in the Anglican Church. After a long struggle with his conscience,
Donne took Anglican orders in 1615 and was appointed successively royal chaplain, reader in divinity at Lincoln's Inn, and
finally, in 1621, dean of St. Paul's Cathedral. In his later years he
was widely regarded as the foremost preacher in England.*

*Donne is probably best known for his early love poems and his
late sermons. He has been a favorite poet of the New Criticism
in this century, partly because of his intrinsic excellence, partly*

*because of his difficulty, which gives opportunities for explication.
He did not become a favorite of the general public, however, until
the title of a Hemingway novel was taken from a passage in
Donne's* Devotions *(1623).*

[Circa 1616]

M<small>Y MOST DEAR</small> M<small>OTHER</small>,—When I consider so much of your life
as can fall within my memory and observation, I find it to have
been a sea, under a continual tempest, where one wave hath ever
overtaken another. Our most wise and blessed Saviour chooseth
what way it pleaseth Him to conduct those which He loves to His
haven and eternal rest. The way which He hath chosen for you
is strait, stormy, obscure, and full of sad apparitions of death and
wants, and sundry discomforts; and it hath pleased Him, that one
discomfort should still succeed and touch another, that He might
leave you no leisure, by any pleasure or abundance, to stay or
step out of that way, or almost to take breath in that way, by which
He hath determined to bring you home, which is His glorious
kingdom.

One of the most certain marks and assurances, that all these are
His works, and to that good end, is your inward feeling and
apprehension of them, and patience in them. As long as the Spirit
of God distils and dews His cheerfulness upon your heart, as long
as He instructs your understanding to interpret His mercies and
His judgments aright, so long your comfort must needs be as much
greater than others as your afflictions are greater than theirs. The
happiness which God afforded to your first young time, which was
the love and care of my most dear and provident father, whose
soul, I hope, hath long since enjoyed the sight of our blessed
Saviour, and had compassion of all our miseries in the world, God
removed from you quickly, and hath since taken from you all the
comfort that that marriage produced. All those children (for
whose maintenance his industry provided, and for whose education you were so carefully and so chargeably diligent) He hath
now taken from you. All that wealth which he left, God hath
suffered to be gone from us all; so that God hath seemed to repent,
that He allowed any part of your life any earthly happiness; that
He might keep your soul in continual exercise, and longing, and
assurance of coming immediately to Him.

I hope, therefore, my most dear mother, that your experience of the calamities of this life, your continual acquaintance with the visitations of the Holy Ghost, which gives better inward comforts than the world can outward discomforts, your wisdom to distinguish the value of this world from the next, and your religious fear of offending our merciful God by repining at anything which He doeth, will preserve you from any inordinate and dangerous sorrow for the loss of my most beloved sister. For my part, which am only left now to do the office of a child, though the poorness of my fortune, and the greatness of my charge, hath not suffered me to express my duty towards you as became me; yet I protest to you before Almighty God and His angels and saints in heaven, that I do, and ever shall, esteem myself to be as strongly bound to look to you and provide for your relief, as for my own poor wife and children.

For whatsoever I shall be able to do I acknowledge to be a debt to you from whom I had that education which must make my fortune. This I speak not as though I feared my father Rainsford's care of you, or his means to provide for you; for he hath been with me, and as I perceive in him a loving and industrious care to give you contentment, so, I see in his business a happy and considerable forwardness. In the meantime, good mother, take heed that no sorrow nor dejection in your heart interrupt or disappoint God's purpose in you; His purpose is to remove out of your heart all such love of this world's happiness as might put Him out of possession of it. He will have you entirely, and as God is comfort enough, so He is inheritance enough. Join with God and make His visitations and afflictions as He intended them, mercies and comforts. And for God's sake pardon those negligences which I have heretofore used towards you; and assist me with your blessing to me, and all mine; and with your prayers to our blessed Saviour, that thereby both my mind and fortune may be apt to do all my duties, especially those that belong to you.

God, whose omnipotent strength can change the nature of anything by His raising-spirit of comfort, make your poverty riches, your afflictions pleasure, and all the gall and wormwood of your life honey and manna to your taste, which He hath wrought whensoever you are willing to have it so. Which, because I cannot doubt in you, I will forbear more lines at this time, and most humbly deliver myself over to your devotions and good opinion of me, which I desire no longer to live than I may have.

"Us Two Loving Creatures"

MARGARET FLEMING

Margaret (or Marjorie) Fleming (1803-1811; poet). Precious, precocious "Pet Marjorie" managed to do a remarkable number of things in her less than nine years. She wrote poems; they charmed Sir Walter Scott, who would not let her out of his sight. She wrote letters that charm us. She took dancing lessons. Her story is beautifully told by her friend, Dr. John Brown, in his Marjorie Fleming, A Memoir *(1863) and his earlier book,* Pet Marjorie *(1858). She was the daughter of Mr. and Mrs. James Fleming of Kircaldy, Scotland.*

September 1811

MY DEAR LITTLE MAMA,

I was truly happy to hear that you were all well, we are surrounded by measles at present on every side, for the Herons got it, and Isabella Heron was near Death's Door, and one night her father lifted her out of bed, and she fell down as they thought lifeless. Mr. Heron said, "That lassie's deed no." "I'm no deed yet." She then threw up a big worm nine inches and a half long. I have begun dancing but am not very fond of it, for the boys strikes and mocks me.—I have been another night at the dancing; I like it better. I will write to you as often as I can; but I am afraid not every week. I long for you with the longings of a child to embrace you—to hold you in my arms. I respect you with all the respect due to a mother. You don't know how I love you. So I shall remain, your loving child,

M. FLEMING

October 12, 1811

MY DEAR MOTHER,

You will think that I entirely forgot you, but I assure you that you are greatly mistaken. I think of you always and often sigh to think of the distance between us two loving creatures of nature. We have regular hours for all our occupations, first at 7 o'clock we go to the dancing and come home at 8, we then read our Bible and get our repeating and then play till ten then we get our music till 11 when we get our writing and accounts we sew from 12 till 1, after which I get my gramer and then work till five. At 7 we come and knit till 8 when we dont go to the dancing. This is an exact description. I must take a hasty farewell to her whom I love, reverence and doat on, and who I hope thinks the same of me.

MARJORY FLEMING.

P.S.—An old pack of cards would be very exeptible.

"The Best of Your Habitual Fare, That's All"

JOHANN WOLFGANG VON GOETHE

Johann Wolfgang von Goethe (1749-1832; German poet, novelist, dramatist, statesman, scientist, and philosopher.) He was almost everything that a man can be. He was a lawyer by profession. He discovered the rudimentary intermaxillary bone in man. He put forth a theory of the common origin of all forms of animal life and of plant development (it paved the way for Darwinism a few decades later). He was Prime Minister of the State of Weimar. He instituted the Sturm und Drang *movement in the drama (and lived to renounce it), and he practically invented the novel. He was a lover of innumerable women, married and single. He is the greatest German lyric poet. He is also the author of* Faust, *a work that has had such an influence on art and artists the world over that one thinks of it, as one does of its author, in world terms rather than as a work in German by a German. He was also an extremely sensible man, as these letters show.*

The "Merck" Goethe refers to in the first letter is J. H. Merck, a plain and practical Army official, one of Goethe's friends from home. The "Duke" about whom the letter revolves was the hereditary prince of Weimar; he was Goethe's wild companion in drinking and wenching, and his wise sponsor in government.

Middle of August, 1779

THAT is exactly the answer I expected, dear Mother, and now I'm sure that everything will be beautiful and, indeed, splendid. We will arrive toward the middle of September and stay with you very quietly for several days. The aunts and cousins of the Duke will be at the Fair and, since he doesn't want to see them, we will swim down the Main and the Rhine after a few days. Having completed this little tour, we'll come back and take up our quarters with you in all due form. Then I'll be able to see all friends and acquaintances, while the Duke will pay some visits to Darmstadt and other places in the vicinity. Our quarters are to be arranged as follows: put up a bed for the Duke in the small bedroom and take the organ out, if it is still there. The big adjoining room will be used for callers. He sleeps on a sack of fresh straw, over which a fine linen sheet is to be spread and under one light blanket. Have mattresses placed into the little chimney room for his valets. The gray room in the rear can be prepared for the chamberlain. I'll sleep in my old room on a sack of straw etc. like the Duke's. We'll eat at 4 o'clock in the afternoon. I say—we'll eat. No banquets. The best of your habitual fare, that's all. Get all the good fruit you can for breakfast. . . . Take all the glass chandeliers out of the Duke's rooms. They would seem absurd to him. Leave the scones. Just have everything as neat as you always do and avoid the appearance of having gone to any special trouble. Let it be as though we had been living with you for ten years. Let the Duke have your silver washbowl and candles. He doesn't take coffee or anything of the kind. Remember, strict secrecy for the present. . . . Not a syllable to Merck.

Weimar, August 11, 1781

TIME and quiet has failed me as yet to reply to your previous dear letter. It gave me great pleasure to see your old and well-known views again expressed in it, and to read them from your own hand. I beg you not to be concerned on my account, and not to allow yourself to be disconcerted by anything. My health is far better than I could ever have hoped for and expected; and as it is adequate to enable me to do, for the most part at least, what is incumbent on me, I have certainly cause to be content with it.

In regard to my position I can say that, notwithstanding great difficulties, it also holds out to me very much that is desirable for me; the best proof of it is that I cannot think of any other possible position for which, at the present moment, I would want to change it. For, with hypochondriacal discontent, to wish oneself out of one's skin into another, is not, it seems to me, very befitting. Merck and others judge my situation very incorrectly. They only see what I sacrifice and not what I gain. They cannot comprehend that I grow richer daily while daily giving away so much.

You will remember the last months I spent with you before I came here; I would have perished in such a continued state of affairs. The disproportion of this narrow and slow-moving bourgeois circle to the broad-mindedness and great agility of my nature would have driven me mad. With my lively imagination and the premonition of all human affairs, I would have always remained unknown in this world and in a perpetual childhood which, mostly through conceit and all its kindred shortcomings, becomes intolerable to itself and to others. How much more fortunate was it to see myself placed in a position with which I could in no way cope and which gave me ample opportunity through many an error of misconception and haste to become acquainted with myself and others; where, left to myself and fate, I passed through so many trials which, to many hundreds of people, may not be necessary, but of which I had the utmost need for my development. And even now, how could I, living my own self, wish for a position more fortunate than the one which holds for me something infinite. Because even if new capacities would daily develop in me, my ideas constantly become clearer, my powers grow, my knowledge widen, my discrimination become more perfect and my spirit more active, I would daily find opportunity to make use of it both in great things and in small.

You see how far I am from the hypochondriacal restlessness which sets so many men at variance with their circumstances, and that only the weightiest considerations or very strange and unexpected events could induce me to leave my post; and it would be also irresponsible toward myself, if I—at a time when the trees which have been planted begin to grow and when one can hope that, during the harvest, the chaff will be separated from the wheat—if I, on account of some discomfort or other, should go away and deprive myself of shade, fruit and harvest.

Meantime believe me that a great part of the good cheer with which I endure and work springs from the thought that all these sacrifices are voluntary and that I need only order the post-horses in order to come and find with you again the necessary and agreeable things of life. For without this prospect and, when in hours of vexation, I am driven to regard myself as a bondman and day-laborer for the mere necessities of life, many things would be much harder for me.

May I always hear from you that your cheerfulness never forsakes you despite my father's present condition. Continue to procure for yourself as much variety as the social life about you offers. It is not very likely that I shall be able to leave here this autumn; at all events, not before the end of September. Yet I shall try to be with you at vintage time. Write me therefore, if it should by any chance fall earlier, due to the favorable summer. Farewell. Greet my old, dear friends.

"Forty Deals Without Intermission"

THOMAS GRAY

Thomas Gray (1716-1771; English poet.) The author of "An Elegy Written in a Country Churchyard" was on the Grand Tour when these letters were written. Gray could not have afforded such an extravagance himself, but he was the guest of his dear friend, Horace Walpole. The two young poets had just left Cambridge, where Gray had been a pensioner (the equivalent of a scholarship student nowadays). They had met at Eton and formed a close friendship with two other Etonians, Richard West and Thomas Ashton, a friendship sometimes known as "The Quadruple Alliance." It is unfortunate but true that Gray and Walpole quarreled during the trip, and Gray returned to Cambridge in 1741, where he remained for the rest of his life. Their friendship was revived in 1745.

No poem in English is more widely known than the "Elegy," but Gray also wrote "Ode on a Distant Prospect of Eton College," "The Progress of Poesy," and "The Bard," among others. He was professor of modern history at Cambridge after 1768, and was one of the most learned men in Europe.

Rheims, June 21, N.S. 1739.

W E HAVE now been settled almost three weeks in this city, which is more considerable upon account of its size and antiquity, than from the number of its inhabitants, or any advantages of commerce. There is little in it worth a stranger's curiosity, besides the cathedral church, which is a vast Gothic building of a surprising beauty and lightness, all covered over with a profusion of little statues, and other ornaments. It is here the Kings of France are crowned by the Archbishop of Rheims, who is the first Peer, and the Primate of the kingdom: The holy vessel made use of on that occasion, which contains the oil, is kept in the church of St. Nicasius hard by, and is believed to have been brought by an angel from heaven at the coronation of Clovis, the first Christian king. The streets in general have but a melancholy aspect, the houses all old: the public walks run along the side of a great moat under the ramparts, where one hears a continual croaking of frogs; the country round about is one great plain covered with vines, which at this time of the year afford no very pleasing prospect, as being not above a foot high. What pleasures the place denies to the sight, it makes up to the palate; since you have nothing to drink but the best champaigne in the world, and all sort of provisions equally good. As to other pleasures, there is not that freedom of conversation among the people of fashion here, that one sees in other parts of France; for though they are not very numerous in this place, and consequently must live a good deal together, yet they never come to any great familiarity with one another. As my Lord Conway had spent a good part of his time among them, his brother, and we with him, were soon introduced into all their assemblies: As soon as you enter, the lady of the house presents each of you a card, and offers you a party at quadrille; you sit down, and play forty deals without intermission, excepting one quarter of an hour, when every body rises to eat of what they call the gouter, which supplies the place of our tea, and is a service of wine, fruits, cream, sweetmeats, crawfish and cheese. People take what they like, and sit down again to play; after that, they make little parties to go to the walks together, and then all the company retire to to their separate habitations. Very seldom any suppers or dinners are given; and this is the manner they live among one another; not so much out of any aversion they have to pleasure, as out of a sort of formality they have contracted by not being much frequented by people who have lived at Paris. It is sure they do not hate gaiety any more than the rest of their country-people, and can enter into diversions that are proposed, with a good grace enough; for instance, the other evening we happened to be got together in a company of eighteen people, men and women of the best fashion here, at a garden in the town to walk; when one of the ladies bethought herself of asking, Why should not we sup here? immediately the cloth was laid by the side of a fountain under the trees, and a very elegant supper served up; after which another said, Come, let us sing; and directly began herself: From singing we insensibly fell to dancing, and singing in a round; when somebody mentioned the violins, and immediately a company of them was ordered: Minuets were begun in the open air, and then came country-dances, which held till four o'Clock next morning; at which hour the gayest lady there proposed, that such as were weary should get into their coaches, and the rest of them should dance before them with the music in the van; and in this manner we paraded through all the principal streets of the city, and waked every body in it. Mr. Walpole had a mind to make a custom of the thing, and would have given a ball in the same manner next week, but the women did not come into it; so I believe it will drop, and they will return to their dull cards, and usual formalities. We are not to stay above a month longer here, and shall then go to Dijon, the chief city of Burgundy, a very splendid and very gay town; at least such is the present design.

Turin, Nov. 7, N.S. 1739.

I AM AT this night arrived here, and have just set down to rest me after eight days tiresome journey: For the three first we had the same road we before past through to go to Geneva; the fourth we turned out of it, and for that day and the next travelled rather among than upon the Alps; the way commonly running through a deep valley by the side of the river Arc, which works itself a passage, with great difficulty and a mighty noise, among vast quantities of rocks, that have rolled down from the mountain tops. The winter was so far advanced, as in great measure to spoil the beauty of the prospect, however, there was still somewhat fine remaining amidst the savageness and horror of the place: The sixth we began to go up several of these mountains;

and as we were passing one, met with an odd accident enough: Mr. Walpole had a little fat black spaniel, that he was very fond of, which he sometimes used to set down, and let it run by the chaise side. We were at that time in a very rough road, not two yards broad at most; on one side was a great wood of pines, and on the other a vast precipice; it was noon-day, and the sun shone bright, when all of a sudden, from the wood-side, (which was as steep upwards, as the other part was downwards) out rushed a great wolf, came close to the head of the horses, seized the dog by the throat, and rushed up the hill again with him in his mouth. This was done in less than a quarter of a minute; we all saw it, and yet the servants had not time to draw their pistols, or do any thing to save the dog. If he had not been there, and the creature had thought fit to lay hold of one of the horses; chaise, and we, and all must inevitably have tumbled above fifty fathoms per-pendicular down the precipice. The seventh we came to Lane-bourg, the last town in Savoy; it lies at the foot of the famous mount Cenis, which is so situated as to allow no room for any way but over the very top of it. Here the chaise was forced to be pulled to pieces, and the baggage and that to be carried by mules: We ourselves were wrapped up in our furs, and seated upon a sort of matted chair without legs, which is carried upon poles in the manner of a bier, and so begun to ascend by the help of eight men. It was six miles to the top, where a plain opens itself about as many more in breadth, covered perpetually with very deep snow, and in the midst of that a great lake of unfathomable depth, from whence a river takes its rise, and tumbles over monstrous rocks quite down the other side of the mountain. The descent is six miles more, but infinitely more steep than the going up; and here the men perfectly fly down with you, stepping from stone to stone with incredible swiftness in places where none but they could go three paces without falling. The immensity of the precipices, the roaring of the river and torrents that run into it, the huge craggs covered with ice and snow, and the clouds below you and about you, are objects it is impossible to conceive with-out seeing them; and though we had heard many strange descrip-tions of the scene, none of them at all came up to it. We were but five hours in performing the whole, from which you may judge of the rapidity of the men's motion. We are now got into Piedmont, and stopped a little while at La Ferriere, a small village about three quarters of the way down, but still among the clouds, where we began to hear a new language spoken round about us; at last we got quite down, went through the Pás de Suse, a narrow road among the Alps, defended by two fortresses, and lay at Bossolens: Next evening through a fine avenue of nine miles in length, as straight as a line, we arrived at this city, which, as you know, is the capital of the Principality, and the residence of the King of Sardinia. . . . We shall stay here, I believe, a fortnight, and proceed for Genoa, which is three or four days journey to go post.

"The Eye of the Stranger"

HENRY WADSWORTH LONGFELLOW

Henry Wadsworth Longfellow (1807-1882; American poet.) Fashions in poetry change, but "The Village Blacksmith," "The Wreck of the Hesperus," and, above all, Hiawatha *are still the first poems American children read—and, sometimes, the last they forget. Because Longfellow's writings are unsophisticated and easily understood, we tend to disregard the debt that all later and more ambitious American poets owe him. One of the first Americans to see poetry as a vocation, and the very first to win recognition abroad, he gave the practice of poetry an esteem and importance it had not previously had in this young country.*

Longfellow contributed odd verses to periodicals and magazines from the time he was thirteen; his first small volume of poems, Voices of the Night, *appeared in 1839. His first real fame came in 1841 with* Ballads and Other Poems. *After* Evangeline *(1847),* The Song of Hiawatha *(1855),* The Courtship of Miles Standish *(1858) and* Tales of a Wayside Inn *(1863), Longfellow became a beloved national figure.*

His home in Cambridge (he had been professor of modern languages at Harvard since 1836) was almost a shrine for Americans, for foreign visitors, and especially for children. His seventy-fifth birthday was celebrated in schools throughout the country, Hiawatha *was read as often as the Bible, and Longfellow had a unique place in the public affection. He died less than a month after his seventy-fifth birthday, no doubt a very happy man.*

In 1826, the year of this letter to his mother, he graduated from Bowdoin College and went to Europe where he studied for three years. He was not inspired by Paris, as this letter shows; he did not like the climate, for one thing. He compares it to that of New England in another letter to his mother:

I do not know how I came to fall into this "meditation among the tombs" kind of style. But I think it must be owing to the weather, which is dull and melancholy. This is the legitimate Parisian winter. It is not cold,—not the clear cold of our New England winter, which braces a man into good health, and while it pinches his nose puts him into a buoyant humor,—but a gloomy, chill, damp air, that gives one the rheumatism and makes him sad. No sooner do I set my foot upon the wet, cold pavement, than I begin to think of a graveyard; and whole hosts of pale, ghost-like beings, with overshoes shaped like coffins (by reason that French people wear square-toed shoes) are apt to put me into a doleful way.

The Longfellow tongue is, of course, in cheek, but it is a great compliment to a New England winter nonetheless.

Auteuil, August 17, 1826.

I HAVE been residing for the last fortnight at this pleasant village of Auteuil. It is situated about three miles northward from Paris, and watered on one side by the Seine, whilst the Wood of Boulogne shades the other, and affords a delightful promenade, morning and evening. As to the village itself, there is nothing remarkable about it, at least nothing further than that it was formerly the residence of Benjamin Franklin,* and of the tragic poet Racine. This may have sanctified the place, by making it classic ground; but after all, a French village, in its best estate, can be little to the taste of Brother Jonathan. There is so little about it—except, indeed, its quiet and tranquillity—to remind one that he is out of town; no corn-fields garnished with yellow pumpkins; no green trees and orchards by the roadside; no slab-fences; no well-poles; no painted cottages with huge barns and out-houses, ornamented in front with monstrous piles of wood for winter firing; nothing, in fine, to bring to the mind of an American a remembrance of the beautiful villages of his native land. In every respect, as far as regards its construction, it resembles the city. You have the same paved streets, the same dark, narrow alleys without sidewalks, the same dingy stone houses, each peeping into its neighbor's windows, the same eternal stone walls, shutting in from the eye of the stranger all the beauty of the place, and opposing an inhospitable barrier to the lover of

* Dr. Franklin's residence, when Commissioner to France in 1777, was really at Passy, a village in the neighborhood of Auteuil.

natural scenery. Indeed, a French village looks like a deserted town. But you know how fresh and cheerful and breezy a New England village is; how marked its features,—so different from the town, so peculiar, so delightful! And I think you would hardly wish to find yourself more than once in a village of Normandy or Seine. I hope that in the vine country and the south of France, I shall find some more distinguishing and characteristic features of the village.

You can easily imagine with what impatience I am waiting for the arrival of your letters, which I know must before this time be somewhere near the coast of France. Kiss the little ones for me, and for yourself receive my kindest love.

"A Useful Trade"

WILLIAM MORRIS

William Morris (1834-1896; English painter, designer, decorator, printer, poet, manufacturer, and socialist leader.) The "Great-hearted poet," as Edwin Markham called him, is today little read and less admired, but few poets left such a lasting impression on the modern world as William Morris, for he brought about, with Edmund Burne-Jones, a revolution in taste. The two young men met at Oxford and were both deeply influenced by, in about equal parts, the writings of Ruskin and the glories of medieval cathedrals. In 1855 Morris left Oxford and, as this letter shows, journeyed to London and apprenticed himself to an architect. Two years later he and Burne-Jones set up a studio, determined to do something about what they considered the immemorial ugliness of London domestic architecture. They designed and built their own furniture; designed, dyed, and wove their own textiles; and revived English interest in stained glass.

Morris & Company (established 1861) began to penetrate the interior of English and American homes. We owe much of what we call "Victorian style" to him, but it may be said in his favor that although he did not foresee the functionalism of the twentieth century he did prepare the world for it by making unprofitable the cheap, shoddy design that had followed upon the industrialization of the arts and crafts. In 1890 he founded the Kelmscott Press

*at Hammersmith, for which he designed new type faces and
otherwise advanced the printer's art. He was a prolific poet, and
a list of his works would be a formidable task. But everyone, at
least, remembers the Morris chair.*

Ex: Coll: Oxon.
Nov. 11th, 1855.

M<small>Y DEAR</small> M<small>OTHER</small>,

I am almost afraid you thought me scarcely in earnest when
I told you a month or two ago that I did not intend taking Holy
Orders; if this is the case I am afraid also that my letter now may
vex you; but if you have really made up your mind that I was in
earnest I should hope you will be pleased with my resolution. You
said then, you remember, and said very truly, that it was an evil
thing to be an idle objectless man; I am fully determined not to
incur this reproach, I was so then, though I did not tell you at the
time all I thought of, partly because I had not thought about it
enough myself, and partly because I wished to give you time to
become reconciled to the idea of my continuing a lay person. I
wish now to be an architect, an occupation I have often had
hankerings after, even during the time when I intended taking
Holy Orders; the signs of which hankerings you yourself have
doubtless often seen. I think I can imagine some of your objections, reasonable ones too, to this profession—I hope I shall be
able to relieve them. First I suppose you think that you have as
it were thrown away money on my kind of apprenticeship for
the Ministry; let your mind be easy on this score; for, in the first
place, an University education fits a man about as much for being
a ship-captain as a Pastor of souls: besides your money has by no
means been thrown away, if the love of friends faithful and true,
friends first seen and loved here, if this love is something priceless,
and not to be bought again anywhere and by any means: if moreover by living here and seeing evil and sin in its foulest and
coarsest forms, as one does day by day, I have learned to hate
any form of sin, and to wish to fight against it, is not this well
too? Think, I pray you, Mother, that all this is for the best: moreover if any fresh burden were to be laid upon you, it would be
different, but as I am able to provide myself for my new course of
life, the new money to be paid matters nothing. If I were not to
follow this occupation I in truth know not what I should follow

with any chance of success, or hope of happiness in my work; in this I am pretty confident I shall succeed, and make I hope a decent architect sooner or later; and you know too that in any work that one delights in, even the merest drudgery connected with it is delightful too. I shall be master too of a useful trade; one by which I should hope to earn money, not altogether precariously, if other things fail. I myself have had to overcome many things in making up my mind to this; it will be rather grievous to my pride and selfwill to have to do just as I am told for three long years, but good for it too, I think; rather grievous to my love of idleness and leisure to have to go through all the drudgery of learning a new trade, but for that also good. Perhaps you think that people will laugh at me, and call me purposeless and changeable; I have no doubt they will, but I in my turn will try to shame them, God being my helper, by steadiness and hard work. Will you tell Henrietta that I can quite sympathise with her disappointment, that I think I understand it, but I hope it will change to something else before long, if she sees me making myself useful; for that I will by no means give up things I have thought of for the bettering of the world in so far as lies in me.

You see I do not hope to be great at all in anything, but perhaps I may reasonably hope to be happy in my work, and sometimes when I am idle and doing nothing, pleasant visions go past me of the things that may be. You may perhaps think this is a long silly letter about a simple matter, but it seems to me to be kindest to tell you what I was thinking of somewhat at length, and to try, if ever so unsuccessfully, to make you understand my feelings a little: moreover I remember speaking somewhat roughly to you when we had conversation last on this matter, speaking indeed far off from my heart because of my awkwardness, and I thought I would try to mend this a little now; have I done so at all?

To come to details on this matter. I purpose asking Mr. Street of Oxford to take me as his pupil: he is a good architect, as things go now, and has a great deal of business, and always goes for an honourable man; I should learn what I want of him if of anybody, but if I fail there (as I may, for I don't know at all if he would take a pupil) I should apply to some London architect, in which case I should have the advantage of living with you if you continue to live near London, and the sooner the better, I think, for I am already old for this kind of work. Of course I should pay myself the premium and all that.

My best love to yourself, and Henrietta, and Aunt, and all of them:

Your most affectionate son
WILLIAM.

P.S. May I ask you to show this letter to no one else but Henrietta.

"The Spectacle of Human Imbecility"

EZRA POUND

Ezra Pound (1885-   ; American poet and critic.) Ezra Pound's life is better known than his poetry. The first, and in some respects the bitterest of twentieth century expatriates, he landed in Gibraltar in 1907 and never returned to the United States in spirit, although he was brought back bodily after World War II and tried for treason as a result of his broadcasts on behalf of the Italian Government during the war. He was adjudged insane and committed to St. Elizabeth's Hospital in Washington, from which he was released in 1958 and allowed to return to Italy.

During the fifty years between these two dates, Pound had a tremendous effect on modern literature. He helped and encouraged Eliot, Frost, and Hemingway, among others, at the beginnings of their careers. Pound's major work is Cantos, *a long poem ranging over many subjects; it is quite likely that Pound will never consider it "completed." In addition to many powerful and influential lyrics, Pound has written, edited, and translated over fourteen volumes of prose; his translations from the Italian, Provençal, Chinese, and Japanese are particularly notable. It is sometimes difficult to believe that he was born in Idaho and once taught at Wabash College. He remarks in one of these letters to his mother: "I do not wish to be mayor of Cincinnati nor of Dayton, Ohio." It is unlikely that he would have been elected.*

Coleman's Hatch, January 1913

DEAR MOTHER: It is rather late in the day to go into the whole question of realism in art. I am profoundly pained to hear that you prefer Marie Corelli to Stendhal, but I can not help it.

As for Tagore, you may comfort yourself with the reflection that it was Tagore who poked my "Contemporania" down the Chicago gullet. Or at least read it aloud to that board of imbeciles on *Poetry* and told 'em how good the stuff was.

I do not wish to be mayor of Cincinnati nor of Dayton, Ohio. I do very well where I am. London may not be the Paradiso Terrestre, but it is at least some centuries nearer it than is St. Louis.

I believe Sussex agrees with me quite nicely.

1913
Venice, May

Dear Mother: Your remarks on "low diet and sedentary life" are ludicrously inappropriate—if that's any comfort to you. As to the cup of joy I dare say I do as well as most in face of the spectacle of human imbecility.

As to practicality. I should think with the two specimens you hold up to me, you'd be about through with your moralization on that subject. Surely the elder generation (A.F. and T.C.P.) attended to the world's commerce with a certain assiduity, and camped not in the fields of the muses.

I don't suppose America has more fools per acre than other countries, still your programme of the Ethical Society presents no new argument for my return.

All Venice went to a rather interesting concert at "La Fenice" on Wednesday; and I also, thanks to Signora Brass, for the entrance is mostly by invitation.

I don't know whether you remember the very beautiful 18th century theatre, but it's a place where you might meet anyone from Goethe to Rossini.

I enclose what I believe to be a Donatello madonna and an interior which I don't think you saw. At least I wasn't with you if you did see it.

I can't be bothered to read a novel in 54 vols. Besides I know the man who translated *Jean Christophe*, and moreover it's a popular craze so I suppose something *must* be wrong with it.

Have you tried Butler? *Way of All Flesh* and his *Diary* (I think that's what they call it).

I shall go to Munich next week and thence to London.

P.S. The Doolittles are here, père et mère. Also Hilda and Richard.

London, November 1913

Dᴇᴀʀ Mᴏᴛʜᴇʀ: I plan to spend my birthday largesse in the purchase of four luxurious undershirts. Or rather I had planned so to do; if, however, the bloody guardsman who borrowed my luxurious hat from the Cabaret cloak room (*not* by accident) does not return the same, I shall probably divert certain shekels from the yeager.

Upward's *Divine Mystery* is just out, Garden City Press, Letchworth. His *The New Word* has been out some time; the library may have the anoymous edtn.

My stay in Stone Cottage will not be in the least profitable. I detest the country. Yeats will amuse me part of the time and bore me to death with psychical research the rest. I regard the visit as a duty to posterity.

Current Opinion is an awful sheet. Merely the cheapest rehash of the cheapest journalistic opinion, *ma chè*! No periodical is ever much good. Am sending the *Quarterly* which is at least respectable. I hope you don't think I *read* the periodicals I appear in.

I am fully aware of *The New Age's* limitations. Still the editor is a good fellow—his literary taste - - - - - is unfortunate. Most of the paper's bad manners, etc. . . .

I seem to spend most of my time attending to other peoples' affairs, weaning young poetettes from obscurity into the glowing pages of divers rotten publications, etc. Besieging the Home Office to let that ass K—— stay in the country for his own good if not for its. Conducting a literary kindergarten for the aspiring, etc., etc.

Richard and Hilda were decently married last week, or the week before, as you have doubtless been notified. Brigit Patmore is very ill but they have decided to let her live, which is a mercy as there are none too many charming people on the planet.

Met Lady Low in Bond St. Friday, "returned from the jaws of death," just back.

The Old Spanish Masters show is the best loan exhibit I have yet seen. The post-Impressionist show is also interesting.

Epstein is a great sculptor. I wish he would wash, but I believe Michel Angelo *never did*, so I suppose it is part of the tradition. Also it is nearly impossible to appear clean in London; perhaps he does remove some of the grime.

Anyhow it is settled that you come over in the Spring. If dad can't come then, we'll try to arrange that for the year after. I shall come back here from Sussex (mail address will be here all the time, as I shall be up each Monday). You will come over in April; at least you will plan to be here for May and June. Once here you can hang out at Duchess St. quite as cheaply as you could at home.

I shall go to a Welsh lake later in the season instead of going to Garda in the Spring. Having been in the country thru' the winter I shall probably not need spring cleaning.

If I am to get anything done this day, I must be off and at it. Love to you and dad.

"That Plain, Middling-Sized Ordinary Man"

WALT WHITMAN

Walt Whitman (1819-1892; American poet.) He was probably closer to his mother than to any other person; it may not have been all coincidence that when she was ill in 1873, he suffered a paralytic stroke from which he did not recover for several months. Two years later he wrote:

> *I occupy myself . . . still enveloped in thoughts of my dear Mother, the most perfect and magnetic character, the rarest combination of practical, moral and spiritual, and the least selfish, of all and any I have ever known—and by me O so much the most deeply loved.*

He wrote only one book of poems, Leaves of Grass, *but he worked on it—adding poems, rewriting, revising, changing—all his life; the first edition appeared in 1855, the last (known as the "deathbed edition") in 1891. One of the copies of the crude first edition was sent to Emerson, and on July 21, 1855, the great literary figure wrote a famous letter of praise and salutation, ending with the words: "I greet you at the beginning of a great career." A great controversy also developed; not only were Whitman's poems daring for the time, but their author's pursuit of publicity for both himself and his book earned him as much blame as praise.*

His extraordinary activities during the Civil War refurbished his reputation, and he was called thereafter the "good, gray poet" (after the title of a book by W.D. O'Connor). After going to

*Washington to seek his brother, who had been reported missing
in action, Whitman remained to serve as a voluntary "wound
dresser." The letters below describe this period in his life. He
wrote letters for wounded soldiers in hospitals around Washington, read them tales and poems, dressed their wounds and tended
to their needs, and altogether gave of himself unstintingly. After
the war he worked in the Interior Department but was discharged
by Secretary James Harlan, an action that earned the latter the
undiluted contempt of O'Connor and H. L. Mencken. At the
same time Whitman added to* Leaves of Grass *some of his most
splendid poems: "Drum Taps"; poems about the war; and particularly the poems about Abraham Lincoln, paramount among
them his masterpiece, "When lilacs last in the dooryard bloom'd."
But his fortunes declined; he never recovered from the death of
his mother; by 1877 he was sick and poor. For a time he peddled
copies of* Leaves of Grass *from a basket in the streets of Camden,
New Jersey. He died in Camden at the age of seventy-three.*

*His style in both poetry and prose was unique, and it might
be interesting to compare the two—to compare the letter he
wrote his mother describing the Union army passing in review
before that "plain, middling-sized ordinary man," Andrew Johnson, who had just succeeded to the Presidency, with the version of
it that was later inserted into the corpus of his poetry. The poetic
version follows:*

> *I saw that day the return of the heroes,*
> *(Yet the heroes never surpass'd shall never return,*
> *Them that day I saw not.)*

> *I saw the interminable corps, I saw the processions of armies,*
> *I saw them approaching, defiling by with divisions,*
> *Streaming northward, their work done, camping awhile in clusters*
>   *of mighty camps.*

> *No holiday soldiers—youthful, yet veterans,*
> *Worn, swart, handsome, strong, of the stock of homestead and*
>   *workshop,*
> *Harden'd of many a long campaign and sweaty march,*
> *Inured on many a hard-fought bloody field.*

> *A pause—the armies wait,*
> *A million flush'd embattled conquerors wait,*
> *The world too waits, then soft as breaking night and sure as*
>   *dawn,*
> *They melt, they disappear.*

Washington, Monday morning, June 22, 1863.

DEAR MOTHER—Jeff's letter came informing me of the birth of the little girl, and that Matty was feeling pretty well, so far. I hope it will continue. Dear sister, I should much like to come home and see you and the little one; I am sure from Jeff's description it is a noble babe—and as to its being a girl, it is all the better. (I am not sure but the Whitman breed gives better women than men.)

Well, mother, we are generally anticipating a lively time here, or in the neighborhood, as it is probable Lee is feeling about to strike a blow on Washington, or perhaps right into it—and as Lee is no fool, it is perhaps possible he may give us a good shake. He is not very far off—yesterday was a fight to the southwest of here all day; we heard the cannons nearly all day. The wounded are arriving in small squads every day, mostly cavalry, a great many Ohio men; they send off to-day from the Washington hospitals a great many to New York, Philadelphia, etc., all who are able, to make room, which looks ominous—indeed, it is pretty certain that there is to be some severe fighting, may-be a great battle again, the pending week. I am getting so callous that it hardly arouses me at all. I fancy I should take it very quietly if I found myself in the midst of a desperate conflict here in Washington.

Mother, I have nothing particular to write about—I see and hear nothing but new and old cases of my poor suffering boys in hospitals, and I dare say you have had enough of such things. I have not missed a day at hospital, I think, for more than three weeks—I get more and more wound round. Poor young men— there are some cases that would literally sink and give up if I did not pass a portion of the time with them. I have quite made up my mind about the lecturing, etc., project—I have no doubt it will succeed well enough the way I shall put it in operation. You know, mother, it is to raise funds to enable me to continue my hospital ministrations, on a more free-handed scale. As to the Sanitary commissions and the like, I am sick of them all, and would not accept any of their berths. You ought to see the way the men, as they lay helpless in bed, turn away their faces from the sight of those agents, chaplains, etc. (hirelings, as Elias Hicks would call them—they seem to me always a set of foxes and wolves). They get well paid, and are always incompetent and disagreeable; as I told you before, the only good fellows I have met are the Christian commissioners—they go everywhere and receive no pay.

Dear, dear mother, I want much to see you, and dear Matty too; I send you both my best love, and Jeff too. The pictures came—I have not heard from George nor Han. I write a day earlier than usual. WALT.

We here think Vicksburg is ours. The probability is that it has capitulated—and there has been no general assault—can't tell yet whether the 51st went there. We are having very fine weather here to-day—rained last night.

Washington, March 29, 1864.

Dearest Mother—I have written to George again to Knoxville. Things seem to be quiet down there so far. We think here that our forces are going to be made strongest here in Virginia this spring, and every thing bent to take Richmond. Grant is here; he is now down at headquarters in the field, Brandy station. We expect fighting before long; there are many indications. I believe I told you they had sent up all the sick from the front. [*The letter is here mutilated so as to be illegible; from the few remaining words, however, it is possible to gather that the writer is describing the arrival of a train* of wounded, over 600, *in Washington during* a terribly rainy afternoon. *The letter continues:*] I could not keep the tears out of my eyes. Many of the poor young men had to be moved on stretchers, with blankets over them, [soon soaking] as wet as water in the rain. Most sick cases, but some badly wounded. I [came] up to the nearest hospital and helped. Mother it was a dreadful night (last Friday night)—pretty dark, the wind gusty, and the rain fell in torrents. One poor boy—this is a sample of one case out of the 600—he seemed to be quite young, he was quite small (I looked at his body afterwards), he groaned some as the stretcher bearers were carrying him along, and again as they carried him through the hospital gate. They set down the stretcher and examined him, and the poor boy was dead. They took him into the ward, and the doctor came immediately, but it was all of no use. The worst of it is, too, that he is entirely unknown—there was nothing on his clothes, or any one with him to identify him, and he is altogether unknown. Mother, it is enough to rack one's heart—such things. Very likely his folks will never know in the world what has become of him. Poor, poor child, for he appeared as though he could be but 18. I feel lately as though I must have some intermission. I feel well and hearty enough, and was never better, but my feelings are kept in a painful condition a great part of the time. Things get worse and worse, as to the amount and sufferings of the sick, and as I have said before, those who have to do with them are getting more and more callous and indifferent. Mother, when I see the common soldiers, what they go through, and how everybody seems to try to pick upon them, and what humbug there is over them [and] how, even the dying soldier's money stolen from his body by some scoundrel attendant, or from [the] sick one, even from under his head, which is a common thing, and then the agony I see every day, I get almost frightened at the world. Mother, I will try to write more cheerfully next time—but I see so much. Well, good-bye for present, dear mother.

WALT.

Indian Bureau, basement of Patent Office.
—house 468 M st 2d door west of 12th
Washington, Thursday, May 25, '65.

DEAR MOTHER, I received your letter of the 23d—I feel uneasy about you all the time, & hope I shall get a letter to-day, & find you have recovered.

Well, the Review is over, & it was very grand—it was too much & too impressive, to be described—but you will see a good deal about it in the papers. If you can imagine a great wide avenue like Flatbush avenue, quite flat, & stretching as far as you can see with a great white building half as big as Fort Greene [park] on a hill at the commencement of the avenue, & then through this avenue marching solid ranks of soldiers, 20 or 25 abreast, just marching steady all day long for two days without intermission, one regiment after another, real war-worn soldiers, that have been marching & fighting for years—sometimes for an hour nothing but cavalry, just solid ranks, on good horses, with sabres glistening & carbines hanging by their saddles, & their clothes showing hard service, but they mostly all good-looking hardy young men —then great masses of guns, batteries of cannon, four or six abreast, each drawn by six horses, with the gunners seated on the ammunition wagons—& these perhaps a long while in passing, nothing but batteries,—(it seemed as if all the cannon in the world were here)—then great battalions of blacks, with axes &

shovels & pick axes, (real Southern darkies, black as tar)—then again hour after hour the old infantry regiments, the men all sunburnt—nearly every one with some old tatter all in shreds, (that *had been* a costly and beautiful *flag*)—the great drum corps of sixty or eighty drummers massed at the heads of the brigades, playing away—now and then a fine brass band,—but oftener nothing but the drums & whistling fifes,—but they sounded very lively—(perhaps a band of sixty drums & fifteen or twenty fifes playing "Lannigan's ball")—the different corps banners, the generals with their staffs &c—the Western Army, led by Gen. Sherman, (old Bill, the soldiers all call him)—well, dear mother, that is a brief sketch, give you some idea of the great panorama of the Armies that have been passing through here the last two days.

I saw the President several times, stood close by him, & took a good look at him—& like his expression much—he is very plain & substantial—it seems wonderful that just that plain middling-sized ordinary man, dressed in black, without the least badge or ornament, should be the master of all these myriads of soldiers, the best that ever trod the earth, with forty or fifty Major-Generals, around him or riding by with their broad yellow-satin belts around their waists—and of all the artillery & cavalry,—to say nothing of all the Forts & ships, &c. &c.—

I saw Gen. Grant too several times—He is the noblest Roman of them all—none of the pictures do justice to him—about sundown I saw him again riding on a large fine horse, with his hat off in answer to the hurrahs—he rode by where I stood, & I saw him well, as he rode by on a slow canter, with nothing but a single orderly after him—He looks like a good man—(& I believe there is much in looks)—I saw Gen. Meade, Gen. Thomas, Secretary Stanton, & lots of other celebrated government officers & generals—but the *rank & file* was the greatest sight of all.

The 51st was in line Tuesday with the 9th Corps. I saw George but did not get a chance to speak to him. He is well. George is now *Major* George W. Whitman—has been commissioned & mustered in. (Col. Wright & Col. Shephard have done it, I think.) The 51st is over to the Old Convalescent camp, between here and Alexandria, doing provost duty. If you should write direct,

> Major G. W. Whitman
> 51st New York V. V.
> on provost duty at
> Augur Gen'l Hospital
> near Alexandria Va.

It is thought that the 51st will not be mustered out for the present—It is thought the Government will retain the re-enlisted veteran regiments, such as the 51st—If that is so George will remain as he is for the summer, or most of it—The reason I haven't seen him is, I knew they had left provost duty in the Prince st. prison, but didn't know where they had gone till Tuesday—I saw Capt. Caldwell Tuesday, also Col. Wright Tuesday night—they said they all have pleasant quarters over there.

Dear brother Jeff, I was very sorry you wasn't able to come on to see the Review—we had perfect weather & everything just as it should be—the streets are now full of soldiers scattered around loose, as the armies are in camp near here getting ready to be mustered out.—I am quite well & visit the Hospitals the same.— Mother you didn't write whether you got the package of 5 Drum-Taps—I keep thinking about you every few minutes all day—I wish I was home a couple of days—Jeff, you will take this acc't of the Review, same as if it were written to you.

WALT.

"True Faith Is That Which Dares All . . ."

WILLIAM CARLOS WILLIAMS

William Carlos Williams (1883-   ; American physician and poet.) He has lived most of his life in Rutherford, New Jersey. This letter was written while he was studying at the University of Pennsylvania Medical School and trying to understand Ezra Pound. He studied also at Leipzig. He published a volume of Poems *when he was twenty-three;* The Tempers *(1913),* Al Que Quiere *(1917), and* Kora in Hell *(1921) followed, bringing him a small but attentive audience.*

His mother was born in Puerto Rico and was of Basque, Spanish, Dutch, and Jewish ancestry. Williams's father was born in England. Williams himself is one of the most "American" of poets; he has absorbed the American idiom as completely as any contemporary writer. Paterson *(1946-50), a colloquial epic, is his major work—besides all the babies he has delivered.*

U. of P. Dorms
3/30/04

DEAR MAMA: The reason I didn't write last Sunday was because I was out of town. My friend Pound invited me to spend
Saturday and Sunday with him, so on Friday I wrote to you and
then set off on my trip. . . . His parents are very nice people and
have always been exceptionally kind to me. Mrs. Pound had
prepared a fine meal. . . . After supper Pound and I went to his
room where we had a long talk on subjects that I love yet have
not time to study and which he is making a life work of. That is
literature, and the drama and the classics, also a little philosophy.
He, Pound, is a fine fellow; he is the essence of optimism and has
a cast-iron faith that is something to admire. If he ever does get
blue nobody knows it, so he is just the man for me. But not one
person in a thousand likes him, and a great many people detest
him and why? Because he is so darned full of conceits and affecta-
tion. He is really a brilliant talker and thinker but delights in
making himself just exactly what he is not: a laughing boor. His
friends must be all patience in order to find him out and even
then you must not let him know it, for he will immediately put
on some artificial mood and be really unbearable. It is too bad,
for he loves to be liked, yet there is some quality in him which
makes him too proud to try to please people. I am sure his only
fault is an exaggeration of a trait that in itself is good and in every
way admirable. He is afraid of being taken in if he trusts his really
tender heart to mercies of a cruel crowd and so keeps it hidden
and trusts no one. Oh, what a common fault it is—this false pride.
True faith is that which dares all and gains love in the daring
but there is much truth in his position after all.

Well, that is about the tone of our conversation. At twelve
we went to bed where I slept, oh so well. The bed was big and
soft and warm . . . next morning we arose at our leisure and then
talked, ate, read, sang, walked in the country, but principally
rested with our feet before a big fire or rather a little one.

WILLIE

EIGHT

Letters from Revolutionaries and Humanitarians

THIS IS MY favorite category; and my hope is that its members will rest peacefully together. But do they belong together? Lenin and Florence Nightingale—can they be mentioned in the same breath? How about Mazzini and Henry George? Lincoln Steffens and Susan B. Anthony?

My proposal to you is that all who are here shared in this: they wanted to extend human liberty, to make the state of man more bearable, to ameliorate, however much or little, what man has made of man. I would not put a Stalin here; his mind seems to have been untouched by any desire for the extension of human liberty. I would not put Mussolini here either, though he "liberated" the Ethiopians.

Helen Keller is here because she freed herself from darkness and silence, and so gave others hope for freedom. Her letters are extraordinary. Her first was written when she was seven. Reading it, one nods and says that it is amazing that a person deaf, dumb, and blind from infancy can write at all. But the next letter is written only six years later, and it is a better letter than most adults could write. In other words, with handicaps that would break most people's hearts she has learned faster than most people could without handicaps! There is no limit to what this great lady can do. And her last letter included here is cheerful and gay:

> Mr. Clemens told us many entertaining stories, and made us laugh till we cried. I only wish you could have seen and heard him! . . . I think he is very handsome indeed.

I love Helen Keller because she laughed that day.

Lincoln Steffens's letters would have bored me had they not been written by an explosive journalist, a muckraker, a crusading newspaperman who visited Russia and reported emotionally to Bernard Baruch, "I have been over into the future, and it works!" This controversial person meets a singularly desirable young lady, and writes to his mother about her as follows:

> That Miss Bontecou is pretty, that she is highly cultivated, of high social connections and fine family—all these may not interest you. But you would like her quiet, affectionate nature and her intense interest in me,—an interest not merely intellectual but in every way.

But an intellectual interest in their sons is not, I think, what mothers most appreciate. Alas, Steffens engaged in the most scientific love affair ever undertaken, and it is all delineated in these two letters.

Miss Anthony's letter was written on her fiftieth birthday. Miss Nightingale's was written when she was thirty, but her life's work was already well under way. Lovejoy's letter was written a year and a week before he was killed by a pro-slavery mob at the age of thirty-five. Of all these letters, Mazzini's are the finest as expressing a constant and continuous seeking for liberty. I think you will never forget them.

"This Is Just Like Home"

ANONYMOUS UNION NURSE

Anonymous Union Nurse (Civil War). Nothing is known about the author of this letter. Let her stand, then, for all the nurses who have ever given aid and comfort to hurt and wounded human beings, and made them feel that they were home.

STEAMER SPAULDING.
[Second year of the war]

THE Spaulding is bunked in every hole and corner. The last hundred patients were put on board to relieve the overcrowded shore hospital late last night; stopped at the gang plank, each one, while Charley numbered all their little treasures and wrote the man's name. Though these night scenes on the hospital ships are part of our daily living, a fresh eye would find them dramatic. We are awaked in the dead of night by a sharp steam whistle, and soon after feel ourselves clawed by the little tugs on either side of our big ship, and at once the process of taking on hundreds of men, many of them crazy with fever, begins. There's the bringing of the stretchers up the side ladder between the two boats, the stopping at the head of it, where the names and home addresses of all who can speak are written down, and their knapsacks and little treasures numbered and stacked. Then the placing of the stretchers on the deck, the row of anxious faces above and below decks, the lantern held over the hold, the word given to "lower," the slow-moving ropes and pulleys, the arrival at the bottom, the lifting out of the sick man, and the lifting into his bed; and then the sudden change from cold, hunger, and friendlessness to comfort and satisfaction, winding up with his invariable verdict, if he can speak, "This is just like home."

"An Undercurrent of Joy and Love"

SUSAN BROWNELL ANTHONY

Susan Brownell Anthony (1820-1906; American abolitionist and suffragette.) A Massachusetts upbringing as a Quaker, and early acquaintance with her father's liberal friends—men like William Ellery Channing, William Lloyd Garrison, and Frederick Douglass—pointed Susan B. Anthony toward the career of agitation and reform that made her one of the most significant women in American history. Her first efforts were in behalf of Temperance (she was an organizer, in 1852, of the Woman's Temperance Society of New York). To this she added the cause of Abolition. Then with the close of the Civil War she found her true vocation and her destiny. In 1869 she joined the National Woman Suffrage Association, and after it merged with the American Woman Suffrage Association in 1890, she served as president of the united movement from 1892 to 1900.

Susan B. Anthony worked with all the great feminists of her day, among them Amelia Bloomer, Lucy Stone, and Elizabeth Cady Stanton. She wrote this letter to her mother on her own fiftieth birthday. Two years later she was arrested and tried for voting in

Rochester, New York. *She was convicted and refused to pay the fine.*

Miss Anthony lived to be eighty-six, honored as much by her old foes as by the new generation whose lives she helped to enrich. She is the heroine of The Mother of Us All, *produced at Columbia in 1947.*

[On her fiftieth birthday] Feb. 15, 1870

MY DEAR MOTHER: It really seems tonight as if I were parting with something dear—saying good-by to somebody I loved. In the last few hours I have lived over nearly all of life's struggles, and the most painful is the memory of my mother's long and weary efforts to get her six children up into womanhood and manhood. My thought centers on your struggle especially because of the proof-reading of Alice Cary's story this week. I can see the old home—the brick-makers—the dinner-pails—the sick mother—the few years of more fear than hope in the new house, and the hard years since. And yet with it all, I know there was an undercurrent of joy and love which makes the summing-up vastly in their favor. How I wish you and Mary and Hannah and Guelma could have been here—and yet it is nothing—and yet it is much.

My constantly recurring thought and prayer now are that the coming fraction of the century, whether it be small or large, may witness nothing less worthy in my life than has the half just closed—that no word or act of mine may lessen its weight in the scale of truth and right.

"Known Even in Philadelphia"

HENRY GEORGE

Henry George (1839-1897; American economist and reformer.) He left school at fourteen to sail before the mast on an East Indiaman. This is scarcely traditional preparation for economists, but then Henry George was a decidedly unusual and creative economist, and his three-year voyage to Australia and India hurt him not a bit.

When he returned he found it hard to settle down. He tried typesetting in his native Philadelphia, again shipped out to sea for a brief period, and then, like so many Americans, set out for California to prospect for gold. And like so many Americans, he found none.

After his marriage in 1861, George went into newspaper work; by 1868 he was managing editor of the San Francisco Times, *and a year later was editor of the Oakland* Transcript. *At the same time he was beginning to think out his economic philosophy, and he first presented his theory of the single tax in* Our Land and Land Policy *(1871). Briefly stated, the idea was that since the land belongs to all, the benefit of the land should accrue to all; a tax on land, if intelligently applied, should supply all needed revenue and result in the abolition of all other taxes. In 1876 he entered politics for the first time, campaigning in California for Samuel Tilden, the Democratic candidate. This was the famous election that everyone believed Tilden had won—until it was ceded to Hayes by the Democrats to avert another civil war.* Progress and Poverty, *Henry George's great work on social wealth, was begun in 1877 and published in 1880.*

It is amusing to note, in relation to this letter, that George did become an accomplished speaker, going on long tours throughout Ireland and England in his later years. He ran for Mayor of New York City in 1886 and drew more votes than one of the other candidates, Theodore Roosevelt. But a man named Abram Hewitt beat them both.

November 13, 1876

WELL, the campaign is over, though its result is as yet unsettled. I cannot say that I am glad that it is over, for although I think Tilden is President, the way this coast went is a great disappointment to me; but at any rate I shall now have a resting spell—a longer one and a better one than I have had before.

I did my best, for my heart was in it, and that is a consolation. And personally what I accomplished was very gratifying. I have shown that I could make myself felt without a newspaper, and shown that I possessed other ability than that of the pen. I have always felt that I possessed the requisites for a first-class speaker, and that I would make one if I could get the practice; and I started into this campaign with the deliberate purpose of breaking myself

in. It was like jumping overboard to learn to swim. But I succeeded. I think no man in the State made as much reputation as
I have made. From not being known as a speaker I have come to
the front. I wanted to do this, not as a matter of vanity or for the
mere pleasure of the thing; but to increase my power and useful-
ness. Already well known as a writer, I knew that this kind of
reputation would aid me immensely in the future. And so it will
—whether I go into politics, into the law or into the newspaper
business again. I do not intend to rest here; but to go ahead step
by step.

You need not be afraid of politics doing me harm. I do not
propose to mix in lower politics, nor do I propose to chase after
nominations. I shall wait till they seek me. I propose to read and
study, to write some things which will extend my reputation and
perhaps to deliver some lectures with the same view. And if I
live I shall make myself known even in Philadelphia. I aim high.

So far as my personal interests are concerned, defeat is as good
to me as a sweeping victory—in fact, I think better, as a man of my
kind has a chance of coming forward more rapidly in a minority
than in a majority party. However, about all such things, I am disposed to think that whatever happens is for the best. Talent and
energy can nearly always convert defeats into victories. I could
easily have started a paper during the campaign, and could, I
think, readily do so now. But I don't feel like going back into
newspaper harness. The best thing for me, I think, is to keep out
of newspapers for a while.

"Beauty Is a Form of Goodness"

HELEN ADAMS KELLER

*Helen Adams Keller (1880-   ; American writer.) If it is in any
way more tolerable to be afflicted with blindness today than it was
fifty years ago, it is so only because of this wonderful woman from
Tuscumbia, Alabama. Helen Keller was struck blind and deaf as
a result of scarlet fever at the age of nineteen months. On March
3, 1887, Anne Mansfield Sullivan (Macy) began to teach Helen to
read and write by spelling words into the young girl's hand. Four
and a half months later Helen made a short trip with her father,*

and wrote the first of the letters below to her mother. The second was written after Mrs. Macy's training had gone far enough for Helen to know distance and shape; she could comprehend the size of Niagara Falls by crossing the bridge and going down the elevator to the bottom of the falls, and she could feel the rush of the water by putting her hand on the window of the observatory.

Helen Keller graduated from Radcliffe in 1904 and has devoted most of her life to the interests of the blind and to other social causes. She wrote The Story of My Life *(1902),* Optimism *(1903),* The World I Live In *(1908),* The Song of the Stone Wall *(1910), several poems, and numerous articles for magazines.*

The answer to the question of how it was possible for **Helen Keller** *to do all that she has done is that she is a genius.* **Geniuses, by definition, never get stopped.**

Huntsville, Alabama, July 12, 1887.

Helen will write mother letter papa did give helen medicine mildred will sit in swing mildred did kiss helen teacher did give helen peach george is sick in bed george arm is hurt anna did give helen lemonade dog did stand up.

conductor did punch ticket papa did give helen drink of water in car

carlotta did give helen flowers anna will buy helen pretty new hat helen will hug and kiss mother helen will come home grandmother does love helen

good-by

South Boston, April 13, 1893.

. . . Teacher, Mrs. Pratt and I very unexpectedly decided to take a journey with dear Dr. Bell, Mr. Westervelt, a gentleman whom father met in Washington, has a school for the deaf in Rochester. We went there first. . . .

Mr. Westervelt gave us a reception one afternoon. A great many people came. Some of them asked odd questions. A lady seemed surprised that I loved flowers when I could not see their beautiful colors, and when I assured her I did love them, she said, "no doubt you feel the colors with your fingers." But of course, it is not alone for their bright colors that we love the flowers. . . . A gentleman asked me what *beauty* meant to my mind. I must confess I was puzzled at first. But after a minute I answered that beauty was a form of goodness—and he went away.

When the reception was over we went back to the hotel and teacher slept quite unconscious of the surprise which was in store for her. Mr. Bell and I planned it together, and Mr. Bell made all the arrangements before we told teacher anything about it. This was the surprise—I was to have the pleasure of taking my dear teacher to see Niagara Falls! . . .

The hotel was so near the river that I could feel it rushing past by putting my hand on the window. The next morning the sun rose bright and warm, and we got up quickly for our hearts were full of pleasant expectation. . . . You can never imagine how I felt when I stood in the presence of Niagara until you have the same mysterious sensations yourself. I could hardly realize that it was water that I felt rushing and plunging with impetuous fury at my feet. It seemed as if it were some living thing rushing on to some terrible fate. I wish I could describe the cataract as it is, its beauty and awful grandeur, and the fearful and irresistible plunge of its waters over the brow of the precipice. One feels helpless and overwhelmed in the presence of such a vast force. I had the same feeling once before when I first stood by the great ocean and felt its waves beating against the shore. I suppose you feel so, too, when you gaze up to the stars in the stillness of the night, do you not? . . . We went down a hundred and twenty feet in an elevator that we might see the violent eddies and whirlpools in the deep gorge below the Falls. Within two miles of the Falls is a wonderful suspension bridge. It is thrown across the gorge at a height of two hundred and fifty-eight feet above the water and is supported on each bank by towers of solid rock, which are eight hundred feet apart. When we crossed over to the Canadian side, I cried, "God save the Queen!" Teacher said I was a little traitor. But I do not think so. I was only doing as the Canadians do, while I was in their country, and besides I honor England's good queen.

You will be pleased, dear Mother, to hear that a kind lady whose name is Miss Hooker is endeavoring to improve my speech. Oh, I do so hope and pray that I shall speak well some day! . . .

Mr. Munsell spent last Sunday evening with us. How you

would have enjoyed hearing him tell about Venice! His beautiful word-pictures made us feel as if we were sitting in the shadow of San Marco, dreaming, or sailing upon the moonlit canal. . . . I hope when I visit Venice, as I surely shall some day, that Mr. Munsell will go with me. That is my castle in the air. You see, none of my friends describe things to me so vividly and so beautifully as he does. . . .

New York, March 31, 1895.

. . . TEACHER and I spent the afternoon at Mr. Hutton's, and had a most delightful time! . . . We met Mr. Clemens and Mr. Howells there! I had known about them for a long time; but I had never thought that I should see them, and talk to them; and I can scarcely realize now that this great pleasure has been mine! But, much as I wonder that I, only a little girl of fourteen, should come in contact with so many distinguished people, I do realize that I am a very happy child, and very grateful for the many beautiful privileges I have enjoyed. The two distinguished authors were very gentle and kind, and I could not tell which of them I loved best. Mr. Clemens told us many entertaining stories, and made us laugh till we cried. I only wish you could have seen and heard him! He told us that he would go to Europe in a few days to bring his wife and his daughter, Jeanne, back to America, because Jeanne, who is studying in Paris, has learned so much in three years and a half that if he did not bring her home, she would soon know more than he did. I think Mark Twain is a very appropriate *nom de plume* for Mr. Clemens because it has a funny and quaint sound, and goes well with his amusing writings, and its nautical significance suggests the deep and beautiful things that he has written. I think he is very handsome indeed. . . . Teacher said she thought he looked something like Paradeuski. (If that is the way to spell the name.) Mr. Howells told me a little about Venice, which is one of his favorite cities, and spoke very tenderly of his dear little girl, Winnifred, who is now with God. He has another daughter, named Mildred, who knows Carrie. I might have seen Mrs. Wiggin, the sweet author of "Birds' Christmas Carol," but she had a dangerous cough and could not come. I was much disappointed not to see her, but I hope I shall have that pleasure some other time. Mr. Hutton gave me a lovely little glass, shaped like a thistle, which belonged to his dear mother, as a souvenir of my delightful visit. We also met Mr. Rogers . . . who kindly left his carriage to bring us home.

"Fairly Lonely . . . and Pretty Senseless"

VLADIMIR ILYICH ULYANOV— NIKOLAI LENIN

Nikolai Lenin—Vladimir Ilyich Ulyanov (1870-1924; Russian revolutionary and statesman.) Eleven years before the date of the letter included here, Lenin's mother learned that her first son, Alexander, had been hanged for complicity in a plot to assassinate the Czar. It was small consolation to her that in the same year her youngest son, Vladimir, graduated from the Simbirsk Gymnasium with a medal for scholarship.

Vladimir entered Kazan University as if to study law and enter upon the life of a loyal subject, but the execution of his brother had been a turning point in his life, and soon he was to be dismissed from Kazan for taking part in a student demonstration.

Ultimately he returned to his studies, duly passed his law examinations, and even practiced the profession until 1894. Then he began to give all his energies to radical agitation. He was arrested a year later; imprisonment and a three-year Siberian exile followed. The letter below was written to his mother while he was in exile; he also wrote The Development of Capitalism in Russia *at this time. When he had completed his sentence he went abroad, and in Munich began publication of the newspaper* Iskra; *here, too, he began to work out for himself the systematic development of ideas for the application of Marxist theory to the promotion of a Russian revolution. He was in many respects unsuccessful over the next decade; indeed, after fifteen years of revolutionary plotting and intrigue he had almost completely isolated himself from other revolutionaries and, indeed, from the Russian people themselves. But the German General Staff gave him his opportunity; recognizing that his presence in Russia could only disrupt the military operations of their enemy, they sent him across Germany in a sealed train, and he arrived in St. Peters-*

burg, at the Finland Station, on April 3, 1917. Lenin needed only that one chance. He swept aside the "bourgeois revolution," took control of the government, and produced the Bolshevik Revolution.

[Shushenskoye], 7th/19th February, 1898.

YESTERDAY, darling Mother, I received letters from you and from all our people (22-23 Jan./3-4 Feb.); I was very glad to get them, and send my thanks for all the good wishes. Of course I expected that you would write to Nadezhda Konstantinovna to ask her to come and see you on her way; it is to be hoped she will be allowed to do so. Well, so far I know nothing about the transfer to Shusha: she keeps on writing that it will be decided "one of these days," but the matter is still dragging on. However, we have not long to wait for a final decision.

About sending things by N. K.—I think she should be fairly heavily loaded with books, for I do not know if there will be an opportunity in the Summer. Manyasha is thinking of going abroad (and that, of course, is a little more interesting than Shusha and Siberian mosquitoes), while you and Mitya will probably be going to Kokushkino. . . . It is a bad thing that after only two and a half months Mitya should be showing signs of swelling. First of all, is he keeping to a diet in prison? I am sure he is not. But in my opinion it is essential to keep to one there. And secondly, does he do any physical exercises? Also, probably not. They are also essential. At any rate I can say from experience that *each day* I used to do exercises before going to sleep with great pleasure and benefit. They loosened my joints so that I used to get warm even on the coldest days, when my cell was icy cold, and afterwards one sleeps much better. I can recommend this to him, as well as a fairly easy exercise (though a ridiculous one):—fifty prostrations, without stopping, and touch the floor each time without bending the knees—write and tell him this. You know that doctors for the most part only know how to talk about hygiene.

Then with regard to clothes, I have already written to you something about this. You might send me some socks. As for our local tailors, I cannot rely on them. It is very inconvenient to have clothes made in Minusinsk—as one has to go there. There is a tailor here and he makes clothes for everyone (he told me so to-day), he sews for the old political exiles and even for the priests—(he boasted to me about it). Although it sounds very effective, it would be better to buy a ready-made suit in Moscow, and to give Mitya or Mark the cloth which you had got ready for me. I ask for only one thing particularly—*a devil's skin,* for I tear my clothes terribly when I go out shooting. If my straw hat is still in existence (after all, it is from Paris! The devil take it!), let her bring it. It is true, Prominsky has begun to make hats here (sometimes they look like felt boots), but his are for the Spring and Autumn, and not for the Summer. And then, there is one more thing—a pair of kid gloves, if they can be bought without knowing my size (I doubt it). I have never worn them, neither in Petersburg, nor in Paris, but I want to try them in Shu-shu-shu— in the Summer, against mosquitoes. You can put a net over your head, but the hands are always attacked. Gleb assures me that the local mosquitoes bite through gloves—but I do not believe it. Of course, one should choose suitable gloves, not for dancing, but for mosquitoes. I also want some paper, *ruled in squares:* I doubt if there is any in Minusinsk, but I do not need very much— about four quires with squares of various sizes, from the smallest to the largest.

Anyutu asks when is the wedding and whom "are we inviting?"! She is in a hurry! Nadezhda Konstantinovna must first arrive, then we must get a permit for the marriage from the authorities —after all we are people wholly without rights. And only then can we start "inviting"!

About "verbalisme" and "phraséologie," it seems to me that they should be translated as verbalism (with an explanation) and phraseology. . . . Although it is not the exact translation, but merely a transcription, what else can we do? "Dilletantism" instead of verbalism is not at all right, rather the reverse. Verbalism, perhaps, is nearer to scholasticism, i.e., to a surplus of (pseudo) learning, than to dilletantism. However, I do not remember in what sense exactly Labriola uses these words [in his "On the Question of the Materialistic View of History"].

Thank you for Bogdanov ["A Short Course of Economic Science"]. I have already read half. Very interesting and sensible. I am thinking of writing a review of it.

In answer to Manyasha's questions: what kind of a voice has Gleb? . . . Hm. Hm.! . . . I believe a baritone—I am not certain. But he sings the same things Mark and we used to "screech" (as Nurse used to call it).

The other question: will she go mad in Paris?—Quite possibly. But she has already been abroad and she can judge for herself. I spent only a month in Paris, and did very little studying there; I did more sightseeing. It is also not clear to me if Manyasha wants to go abroad to study, or only for the Summer.

I thank Mark for his letter. Let him, however, not forget Gogol's character, Ivan Andreich.* I do not know what progress there is in Russia, but undoubtedly they are flourishing here, and they are interested not only in whether the soldier is galloping by or whether the young ladies are skipping.

I am surprised that you have heard nothing about "Syn Otechestva." I saw in the "Russkaya Mysl" to-day (Nov. or Dec. 1897) that that paper is being announced as the organ of the Narodnik *pur sang*.

Until the next time I write.

Your V. U.

P.S. We have real frost now, so that we have given up shooting and only go for walks—also into the wood. But my rooms are warm and my clothes still warmer.

Let Manyasha send Nadezhda Konstantinovna the list of books which I should like to have—she will look for them in St. Petersburg, if, of course, it is not too late.

If we have any children's books with pictures, let N. K. bring them for Prominsky's youngsters.

[Here follows a list of Russian books on Economics.]

"I May Even Die Its Martyr"

ELIJAH PARISH LOVEJOY

Elijah Parish Lovejoy (1802-1837; American editor, clergyman, and abolitionist.) Too little is known about Lovejoy. He was born at Albion, Maine, and was the brother of Owen Lovejoy, Congressman from Illinois from 1856 to 1864. We know more about Owen than we do about Elijah; we know, for example, that Owen

* Lenin means Ivan Kuzmich, the Postmaster in Gogol's comedy "The Government Inspector," who read all the letters out of curiosity. This was evidently Lenin's hinted warning to Mark to be more careful in correspondence.

worked successfully to secure abolitionist backing for Lincoln at a time when many anti-slavery leaders considered Lincoln's attitudes too conservative.

Elijah was a minister, but he is remembered as "the first American martyr to the freedom of the press and the freedom of the slave." That is the way John Quincy Adams described him. The way it happened has become regrettably familiar in this world: mobs destroyed his printing presses in Alton, Illinois, three times. Speaking to the mob, Elijah said: "I can die at my post, but I cannot desert it." Four days later they attacked again, and killed him.

Reading this letter to his mother, written fourteen months before his death, one can see it coming.

Alton. Aug. 31, 1836

M<small>Y DEAREST</small> M<small>OTHER</small>,

Having a little time now inasmuch as I am unable to do anything else, I have determined to write you a somewhat detailed account of the scenes through which I have been lately called to pass. I know that you will be interested in every detail, though some of them might seem too minute for other eyes than yours.

The account of the mob in St. Louis you have had in my letter to Joseph, and in my *extra* received, I presume, before this time, as also of the second edition of it enacted at this place.

A few of the brethren here immediately convened after this last event, and it was determined that a new printing office should be immediately procured from Cincinnati. Accordingly I went on to procure it. On my way I became quite unwell, owing to the excitement anxiety and exposure of the week or two previous. By the time I reached Cincinnati I was fit only for the bed, but I could not prevail with myself to give up. I therefore kept about, finished my business, and started for home with my materials for the office along. On my arrival at Louisville I found my illness so increasing upon me that I was *compelled* to stop; and took my bed with a billious fever deeply hold of me. I was received into the house of Rev. Mr. Banks (formerly from Connecticut) where I was treated with all the tenderness and assiduity that could have been bestowed upon a son. Providentially, too, I fell into the hands of a skilfull physician, so that at the end of a week I found myself so far convalescent—that I ventured to pursue my journey. I continued to mend till I reached St. Charles. But riding from that place to this (a distance of 20 miles) and starting early in the morning, which was raw and chilly, by the time I arrived I found myself very much chilled and feared a relapse. However, such was the pressing need of my attention to the business of starting the Observer, that I could not think of giving up. I accordingly kept about from Monday (the day of my arrival) till Wednesday evening last—when I was again driven to my back with a relapse of my fever attended with cold sweats and alternate chills and fevers. I am now better and with providence hope to regain my health, though still very weak.

Thus you see my dear Mother, that *my* path through this world is not a flowery one and to add to my difficulties, both my attacks of illness have come upon me in the absence of my dear wife. When I had determined to remove from St. Louis I sent her to her Mother's in St. Charles, where she still is. And what is more, she too has been severely sick with very much such an attack as mine. Our dear babe, thus far, thanks to a merciful Providence, remains well.

Why, when my services are so much needed, I should thus be laid up on a bed of sickness I cannot tell; why, when God has in his wise and holy Providence, let loose upon me angry and wicked men, He should also lay his own hand so heavily upon me, I cannot see; but he can, and I desire to submit without a murmur. I can now *feel*, as I never felt before, the wisdom of Paul's advice, not to marry, and yet I would not be without the consolations only my dear wife and child afford me for all the world. Still I can but feel that it is harder to "fight valiantly" for the truth when I risk [then]? not only my own comfort, ease, reputation, and even life, but also that of another beloved one. But in this I am greatly favored. My dear wife is a perfect heroine. Though of very delicate health, she endures afflictions more calmly than I had supposed it possible for a woman to do. Never has she by a single word attempted to turn me from the scene of warfare and danger, never has she whispered a feeling of discontent at the hardships to which she has been subjected in consequence of marriage to me, and these have been neither few nor small, and some of them peculiarly calculated to wound the sensibility. She has seen me shunned, hated, reviled by those who were once my dearest friends. She has heard the execrations, wide and deep, of almost a whole community pound upon my head, and she has only clung to me the more closely and more devotedly.

When I told her that the mob had destroyed a considerable part of our furniture along with their other depredations, "No-matter", said she, "what they have destroyed, since they have not hurt you". Such is woman! or rather such is *the* woman whom God has given me.

And now do you ask, Are you discouraged? I answer promptly, no. I have opened my mouth for the decent. I have plead the cause of the poor and oppressed. I have maintained the rights of humanity and of nature outraged in the persons of many of my fellow-men around me, and I have done it, as is my nature, openly, boldly, and in the face of day, and for these things I am brought into these straits. For these things I have seen my family scattered, my office broken up, my furniture (as I was moving it to this place) destroyed, have been baited with execrations, had all manner of lies told of me falsely, and finally had my life threatened and so far put in jeopardy, that I have been obliged to sleep with offensive weapons at my bed's head. (This was the case the last night I spent in St. Louis). Yet "none of these things move me" from my purpose; by the grace of God I will not, I *will not* forsake my principles, and I will maintain them and propagate them with all the means he puts into my hands. The cry of the oppressed has entered not only into my ears but into my soul, so that while I live I cannot hold my peace.

Meanwhile, I might confess that present prospects look somewhat dark. In the midst of so many enemies I have yet a good many friends. But the evil is that Christians in this quarter even the best of them, have become a good deal worldly minded, and are greatly engaged in speculation, so that the work of the Lord is left to languish. Insomuch that I find it extremely difficult to obtain that necessary aid and assistance needed in my very arduous enterprise. Had I means at my own command I would not care. I should deem them well spent even though destroyed by a mob in maintaining the cause I have espoused. But alas! I have them not. Such as I have I give freely—my time, my energies, the best years of my life, some little abilities and a good deal of zeal, these I give—and bless God for the opportunity—for so holy a cause. I may not live to see its success, I may even die (though most unworthy) its victim and its martyr, yet that it will ultimately succeed and that too at no very distant day, I am as well assured as I am that there is a God in Heaven, who sits on a Throne of Righteousness.

Providence permitting, we shall get out a number of the Observer next week. It will be much enlarged in hopes by that means to induce more to subscribe. Tell brother Joseph I wish he and his brother ministers in Maine would try and do something for me. I think I ought to get considerable aid from my native state. Mr. Adams of Brunswick told me at the Gen. Assembly that he thought I was doing more to put down slavery than any other man in the United States. Now if half that be true, surely my paper ought to be supported.

But I shall fatigue you with the reading, as I am myself exhausted with the efforts of writing this long letter. Give my love to my dear sisters L. & E. Why don't they write to me? Surely, surely they cannot wait for me to write when I have hardly time and ability even to read my Bible. From Owen I have not heard for a long time. I expected him and sister E. out here this fall. Are they not coming? I wish they would come. Wife wants Lizzy very much, and I want Owen.

John enjoys excellent health and spirits and is improving very much. I intend to make him head man, soon, in the Observer printing office.

Love to Br. Joseph and his wife and to all. Do write me.

Your most affectionate son,

Elijah P. Lovejoy

"We Have to Act Worthily"

GIUSEPPE MAZZINI

Giuseppe Mazzini (1805-1872; Italian patriot and revolutionary.) The salutation "Aunt" and the signature "Emilia" on the first two of these four letters were smokescreens that had to be employed if the letters from Mazzini to his mother were to get through. By 1840 the subterfuge no longer had to be used; Mazzini was in London, and relatively safe from the Italian Royal States.

There had been little safety for the Genoese before then. Immediately after his graduation from the University of Genoa, he joined the secret underground movement, the Carbonari, which was working for the unity and republican organization of Italy. That same year—1830—he was arrested by the Piedmont authorities, imprisoned, and exiled; he resided successively at Marseilles, Paris, and London, and became such a thorn in the side of the crumbling group of monarchies that he was banished forever. Mazzini did, however, return to Italy in the climactic year of revolution, 1848, and in 1849 was a member of the short-lived republican triumvirate in Rome, but he was driven out that same year by the restoration of the papal government.

Mazzini organized and led several subsequent insurrections; the tragedy of his life was that he was never able to serve the unified government that he, more than any other Italian, had created. He refused to take the oath of allegiance to Victor Emmanuel I and lived abroad, unhappy and ineffectual, for the rest of his life.

It is notoriously true that revolutions devour their young.

Grenchen,
17th November, 1835

DEAREST AUNT,

I have received yours of the 9th. The weather is much as usual. We are surrounded on all sides by snow, and consequently it is cold. No news, and I have nothing to say. The crows are walking about as usual, and remind me of exactly the same scene last year. Except for the inconvenience of the locality, the delay in getting news, etc., we are very comfortable as far as material things go. Absolutely isolated; which suits us for a hundred thousand reasons. Besides, the family gives us all the affection of which the Swiss are capable; they are a very cold race, and self-centered to a degree. Of course we pay, and all the friendship in the world does not affect the exactitude of the bills; but this must be so. In everything else we are considered as part of the family. The people are kind, and we are kind to them. One of our religious-political beliefs is the abolition of domestic service, i.e. the rehabilitation of the class called servants —a class which like other enslaved people, the Jews, and all classes deprived of human rights and treated exceptionally by the present organisation of society, has necessarily become depraved—egoistic, without affection, and hostile to its masters. When you wish to make a man better, emancipate him: make him your equal, raise him up, give him a consciousness of himself. The slave, or he who is like a slave, is always depraved, and must be so. Domestic service, as it is understood and practised nowadays, must disappear, must become a lending of service with remuneration, a contract on an equal base, like all other contracts; it must not have in it any trace of humiliation. Beyond the execution of the contract, domestic servants have to be men, to have the education of men, and the brotherhood of men. As everything that is an article of faith with us becomes practice also, I and the cousin who lives with me have always done away with every trace of authority. I have always said: "I should like such a thing," as I should say to a friend or companion. The family consists of three brothers, three sisters, father, and mother. The two latter are personages who do not speak, as they only know a Swiss *patois*. One of the brothers is a doctor, and cultured. The others direct the establishment, and occupy themselves with the business of the house, the baths, the hotel, the tavern for the peasants, the kitchen, the little factory, etc. We are served by them at table. The girls do the rooms in turn; they light the fires for us, clean up, etc. All this goes by rule. But in everything else we treat them as we should treat anyone who did not serve us. We sit at the fire for half an hour or so with them, and speak of everything, being polite to them, and jokingly saying to the girls that they are sisters to us in our exile, etc. All this raises them in their own estimation. They think highly of us, and this intercourse improves them; so much so that one of the girls especially (according to someone who knew her two years ago) has become disinterested (a cardinal virtue in Switzerland), and capable of nobler sentiments than her surroundings would imply. I have always employed the same manner, and must say that I have been well served everywhere, besides being liked into the bargain. Here the day of our departure will be one of grief for the family. My cousin is a great favorite; on his birthday they put sheaves of flowers in his room—the same for me. I tell you all this, partly just to chatter, and partly to show you that, as far as our situation allows it, we are enjoying material comforts.

Embrace my sisters and my uncle for me, and love

your most affectionate niece
EMILIA.

Grenchen,
6th April, 1836.

DEAREST AUNT,

. . . . . .

The lines which my father wrote to me, and which I will answer, contain many truths. You must not think that I have any illusions as to what men are; I have had too much to do with them not to know them. But the work which we are doing in the world is not being done with the idea of immediate success, or in the hope of winning love and gratitude. It is being done because our heart dictates it; and in the fulfilment of what we believe to be our duty, without caring for the consequences; it is being done because, however bad men may be, we have to act worthily, come what may.

This is an epoch of destruction, of moral anarchy, of want of faith; but anarchy cannot last. The times which preceded Christianity were similar to these in disorder and immorality; but out of that mire appeared a new world. And from this which we are now treading there will issue, believe me, another world, another society, still more advanced than that. However, perhaps we shall not see it. That may be; but is it a reason for us to remain inert, and not to bring our little contribution to the great pyramid? We set much store by intellectual and moral education; now the education of a child reveals its effect after a few years, but the education of nations, of a whole generation, cannot do so: the effects are insensible, but infallible. Besides, it is our fault that things go so slowly, the fault of the progressive party, which is full of divisions, contradictions, and fears. The fears of the opposition would be nothing if men would hold together, and decide upon acting.

· · · · · ·

EMILIA

London,
6th May, 1840.

My dear Mother,

· · · · · ·

The principle that you impress upon me to apply to our Workmen agrees with mine. I am what men call a revolutionary; but in quite a different fashion from that of most revolutionaries of our day. I consider our cause not as one of simple reaction, or material well-being, or of mere rights to be recognised, but as the cause of moral progress, of a great education to be given to men. Now, I do not consider education possible without a religious principle, and I shall always insist upon this. One of my great sorrows is to see our cause spoiled and profaned by a number of men who start from an opposite principle and can only succeed in provoking revolts and violence, without bringing to pass any of those great moral changes which the times demand. I have always separated myself from such men; and fortunately they are getting fewer daily, as materialism is being abandoned more and more by the intelligent men of our party. Among these workmen of ours there are still many who are materialists, without reasoning about the matter; it is merely a reaction against the bad priests in our country and elsewhere. I always try to make them see that they must not confuse two different things, and at a meeting where I spoke, I saw that the truth made an impression upon them. Next month I hope that we may begin the publication of a little paper called the *Apostolato Popolare,* and in it I shall inculcate the religious principle from the first, with as much zeal as I can. I will give you news how it progresses.

. . . . . .

Believe in the constant love of your
GIUSEPPE.

London,
15th October, 1841.

Mʏ ᴅᴇᴀʀ Mᴏᴛʜᴇʀ,

. . . . . .

My father's observations on Communism are very just, and I fully agree with his disapprobation, and even express it more explicitly, because it is important that we good and reasonable democrats should separate ourselves from that crew which the Governments try to confound with us. To enable my father to know the truth about them, however, I will explain it in two words: they wish to abolish property, putting everything in the hands of the Government; and to arrange that the Government (giving I do not know how many hours' work to all) should distribute to all (in specie, not in money) as much as they need. This is an absurd scheme, impossible to be realised, which would destroy all stimulus to activity in humanity, would substitute the idea of a certain material well-being for any idea of moral progress, would paralyse society, and would reduce us to the level of bees or beavers, performing a certain series of acts necessary for our physical life, and nothing more. Nevertheless this is an error of judgment on their part, and not an evil desire, that is to say, with many of them. The poor workmen, left isolated, without the help of intelligent men, sought amongst themselves what might be the remedy for their ills, and found this one, as the simplest. Then came Cabet, who, sound at heart, but not very intelligent, despaired of becoming a party-leader where there were other intelligent men. In Communism, on the contrary, he was secure of being alone to rule the poor devils, and he made himself their head. What perpetuates this error is the conduct of many republicans, who, desiring a change coûte qui coûte, and not having any real beliefs of their own, remain silent, instead of breaking openly with the Communists, as they do not wish to lose their support. However, although it has made great progress during these latter times, this Communism is confined to only a portion of the workmen. The saner and more intelligent portion is far from such follies.

· · · · · ·

GIUSEPPE.

"I Wish for No Other Earth"

FLORENCE NIGHTINGALE

Florence Nightingale (1820-1910; English philanthropist, nurse, and administrator). There was no necessity for her to occupy herself with nursing or anything else; born in Florence, she was an English gentlewoman at a time when being just that was sufficient occupation. But early in her life she became interested in nursing and set about training herself. Nursing education was not available in England, and so Florence Nightingale went to France and then to Kaiserswerth, Germany (this letter is written from there) to study. She was in charge of a woman's hospital in London when the terrible news of the suffering of the British wounded in the Crimean war reached England. Immediately she volunteered her services, and at the head of a group of thirty-eight nurses reached Scutari in November, 1854, soon after the battle of Balaklava, and there set up a hospital. She instituted severe sanitary measures to reduce the dangers of cholera, dysentery, and typhus, and by the next year the hospital death rate had fallen from above fifty per cent to about two per cent. She assumed administrative responsibility for all the hospitals along the Bosporus and continued to make nightly rounds.

Miss Nightingale collapsed from fever in May, 1855 but refused to be invalided home until the war was over. With a fund donated as a testimonial to her services she founded in 1860 the Nightingale Home at St. Thomas Hospital for the training of nurses, but her own health had been permanently impaired by the war, and she could never participate in active nursing again.

She was instrumental in introducing a host of major reforms in the hospital, public health, and sanitation systems of England. In 1907 she became the first woman to receive the Order of Merit.

To the British Tommy she was always "The Lady with the Lamp."

Kaiserswerth

On Sunday I took the sick boys a long walk along the Rhine; two Sisters were with me to help me to keep order. They were all in ecstasies with the beauty of the scenery, and really I thought it very fine too in its way—the broad mass of waters flowing ever on slowly and calmly to their destination, and all that unvarying horizon—so like the slow, calm, earnest, meditative German character.

The world here fills my life with interest, and strengthens me in body and mind. I succeeded directly to an office, and am now in another, so that until yesterday I never had time even to send my things to the wash. We have ten minutes for each of our meals, of which we have four. We get up at 5; breakfast ¼ before 6. The patients dine at 11; the Sisters at 12. We drink tea (*i.e.* a drink made of ground rye) between 2 and 3, and sup at 7. We have two ryes and two broths—ryes at 6 and 3, broths at 12 and 7; bread at the two former, vegetables at 12. Several evenings in the week we collect in the Great Hall for a Bible lesson. The Pastor sent for me once to give me some of his unexampled instructions; the man's wisdom and knowledge of human nature is wonderful; he has an instinctive acquaintance with every character in his place. Except that once I have only seen him in his rounds.

The operation to which Mrs. Bracebridge alludes was an amputation at which I was present, but which I did not mention to—, knowing that she would see no more in my interest in it than the pleasure dirty boys have in playing in the puddles about a butcher's shop. I find the deepest interest in everything here, and am so well in body and mind. This is Life. Now I know what it is to live and to love life, and really I should be sorry now to leave life. I know you will be glad to hear this, dearest Mum. God has indeed made life rich in interests and blessings, and I wish for no other earth, no other world but this.

"I Suppose I Ought to Give Her a Ring"

LINCOLN STEFFENS

Lincoln Steffens (1866-1936; American crusading journalist.) The "King of the Muckrakers" wrote hundreds of letters to his mother, and since she never threw any of them away, it is a problem to choose but two. These date from Steffens's post-college wanderings in Europe, from a period in his life when he played with the idea of being an expatriate. But like most such he returned home; he began a newspaper career, and by 1902 was managing editor of McClure's Magazine; *in 1906 he became associate editor of the* American Magazine *and* Everybody's.

The Shame of the Cities *(1904) was the first of the exposés of political and business corruption that made him famous. The* Struggle for Self-Employment *(1906) and* Upbuilders *(1909) were in the same vein, and were important landmarks in the fight for municipal reform in the U.S. The* Autobiography of Lincoln Steffens *is an American classic.*

Steffens secretly married Josephine Bontecou shortly after this first letter was written. The newly-weds lived in Paris, sharing their apartment with the bride's mother, and continuing their studies. In his Autobiography *Steffens mentions that he had had "a sort of understanding" with a girl in Berkeley; she is the "G." to whom he refers in this letter. Steffens also talks about "Krudewolf," who was a college friend in Leipzig and Paris. Krudewolf considered Josephine bossy and obviously out to marry Steffens. He wasn't happy when he learned the secret.*

Leipzig, July 31, 1891

M\ *Y DEAR* MOTHER:—

I must communicate with you today a little separately,—you and I alone. Letters home have always included everybody, so you must have felt always in communication with me, but your silence has not had the same effect with me. I feel as if you had nothing to say to me. Still, now that I have taken this last step in engaging myself you will be interested and I hope pleased. I know you would like my choice and would like the cool, deliberate way in which we proceeded to bind ourselves together. That Miss Bontecou is pretty, that she is highly cultivated, of high social connections and fine family—all these may not interest you. But you would like her quiet, affectionate nature and her intense interest in me,—an interest not merely intellectual but in every way. She is very practical, not at all sentimental nor conventional, and is devoted to my interests and hopeful and eager for my future.

Your remembrance of the sudden breakage of the engagement with G. may lead you to think this is also to be short-lived. And, in fact, it may be. That is, we have arranged so that it can be brief if either finds anything in the character of the other that may indicate future discontent. But I do not anticipate any such turn of affairs. Anyway, we shall have a considerable period to make intimate acquaintance with one another, for we shall live together in Paris and do our work in common. We have arranged to get books, not together, but such books each that we may not have any duplicates. It is, to me, the most delightful experience, this confidential friendship with this lady, as well if not better up than I myself. We are not equally trained in the same subjects. I am better in English literature, she in the German, having taken two years' courses here. I am pretty solid in political sciences and history, she only partially, but is studying them. She has a medical training and education to even that off. In psychology she and I are about even, in philosophy I am ahead. But she speaks German perfectly and French also. The latter she learned and spoke as a child. She has travelled considerably more than I have and has seen more of society. Furthermore, she has seen more trouble than I have,—than I, who have seen and known none, —and this has softened her considerably and nerved her out of a light view of life.

Now, of course there are many things you would like to know besides these that I have stated, but you must write and ask me, for I don't know, of course, what your questions might be. From a purely worldly standpoint it will be a good match for me, from an intellectual point of view the best I could possibly hope for, and as for love,—we both love more and more every day, and she is as affectionate as ever I could long for. Our engagement is not to be announced for some time and no one knows it except Krudewolf, you and papa and her mother. We have exchanged no pledges, but I suppose I ought to give her a ring some day. This I will leave to you to tell me. Perhaps you would be pleased enough to send me one for her. I hope you will be pleased and that you will write me an answer at once. As soon as I hear from you I shall feel all right, but until then I shall not feel as though it is settled. Another point,—she wants always to supply half of the expense of such a home as we may have, and I don't know how to take that. Of course she is easily able to do so, for her father and mother are both very well off,—her father being one of the richest surgeons of New York City.

Now, Mamma, write me a good long letter and tell me just what you think and how you feel about it all. I shall write no more at present but remain as ever,

Your loving son,
J. L. Steffens

P.S.: If you can send me something nice, do so as soon as possible.

Len.

Paris, Feb. 4, 1892

M<small>Y DARLING</small> M<small>OTHER</small>:—

Your sweet letter reached me with its warm glow of long silent, but ever active, maternal love, and did your boy lots of good. Of your love I am always so sure that it needed no such kind words as you write to assure me of my precious possession of it. But it is good to feel it come so near me again. But, dearest Mother, you are quite sure of my love too, are you not? My love for Josephine has only made all the love I ever bore anyone burn all the warmer and brighter, for she is a noble, earnest little woman, and calls out all that is best in me. For, don't you see, she loves what she found good in me, and I love her with that same better side of my nature, and all the rest is slowly dying,—slowly but surely. And the bad in me *you* also do not love, for you would never even see it. Papa did, as a man always does in another, fully appreciate the bad and gave it full credit. But no one I love, loved that weaker side of my nature, so it is well my Josephine sees as you do and refuses, as you do, to see the other. Altogether I am a changed son, changed in a great many ways, but, dear Mother, *you* will believe all changes are for the better.

I am very grateful to you for your welcoming acceptance of Josephine. Still, she is my ideal of a woman and not yours. She subscribes to my ideas, and perhaps you and I are a little different in this respect. But we will all be tolerant of one another, cherish the personal, not the purely mental and doctrinal. Josephine is as strong in character and in mind as a man. Her education is like mine, and most of the time our intercourse is more that of chum students than of lovers. She stands next to me as my equal in all respects and will not merely serve me in my career. She will have a life and a life's work of her own. This will disturb home and fireside plans, but I think we gain in other ways. Anyway, I find it a never-ending delight to feel this strong, gentle woman near me, urging me on by her example and taking and giving help and advice. She is calling out all my powers now in a literary way. As you know I have finished a novel,—no ordinary love story, but a picture of real life,—not pleasing but true.

Since I last wrote Papa I have put away another story,—a shorter one, the scene of which is laid in Berkeley. But it is psychological, not descriptive, and truer than it is beautiful. I am, in fact, doing work which no one has done yet in America and only a few in Europe (France), a lot of realistic work. Over and above that I am retaining a strain of idealism in my work which will not at first be perceived, but later will be the main claim of my work to a long life. A third story,—laid in Paris, but of American life among artists,—is growing into shape in my head now, and I begin it after this letter is written.

Thus, Mamma dear, your wandering boy is hopeful and happy, healthy and busy, so your mother's heart may love in peace one child who is coming back better for the self-sacrifices of his parents. You will restrain your wish to make me admired and not mention my literary efforts. I must write anonymously, because I want to have a political career, and in my books will be opinions not conducive to success in that line. Furthermore, I want unhindered opportunities to prosecute my studies in life, which would not be possible were people to know I was intending to write them up. . . .

Goodbye, Mamma. Always love as you do now

Your very affectionate son,

J. L. Steffens

NINE

Letters from Statesmen and Rulers

Separating Queen Elizabeth from Harry S. Truman are four hundred years of time, four thousand miles of land and water, and about four million light-years in thought. Yet statesmen and rulers of any age and any nation, no matter what their philosophy of government or their degree of power, and no matter how they attained their positions of influence, live in ways that are frequently superficially similar. Some examples: they all go to interminable state dinners, they are all eternally on display, and they all live in a vise. More significantly, their moods and their illnesses, their vision or lack of it, can make life better or worse for the family of man. Even a Marie Antoinette and a Theodore Roosevelt are alike in these respects.

If a novelist has stomach troubles, we expect that he'll express some of his pain and anxiety in a book; but when a statesman or ruler has an ulcer, he may find relief by breaking a treaty. And so we look in letters by world leaders for indications of their humanness.

And we find it. One of the men of our times whose name was a symbol of terror was Kaiser Wilhelm. In these letters we meet him first when his mother, the Empress Frederick, writes to her mother, Queen Victoria of England:

A thousand thanks for your dear letter by messenger which gave me so much pleasure with all of its kind wishes for the 25th, and yesterday our dear Willie's birthday. He was so delighted with your presents. . . . I am sure you would be pleased with William if you were to see him. He is not possessed of brilliant abilities, nor of any strength of character or talents, but he is a dear boy, and I hope and trust will grow up a useful man.

Sixteen years later, the Empress will write that her son holds opinions that are "dangerous and unwholesome . . . a bad preparation for the solution of all the grave and difficult questions which will have to be the work of the next 20 or 30 years." And in a phrase of inexpressible sadness, she will say that she now knows that "one must learn to abandon dreams, and to take things as they come."

We get another glimpse of the future Kaiser Wilhelm in a letter from Czar Nicholas to the Empress Maria Federovna (the old empress, played by Helen Hayes, in the movie "Anastasia"). Wilhelm visited Nicholas (they were cousins) in 1897, and Nicholas wrote:

I'm sorry to tell you we shall have to give Wilhelm the rank of Admiral in our navy. Uncle Alexei reminded me of it; and I think, no matter how disagreeable it may be, we are obliged to let him wear our naval uniform.

The Russian Emperor didn't know it, but this was the least of his problems. Revolution broke out in 1905, and in another letter to his mother Nicholas begged for help and advice that she was hardly qualified to give. But in any case, he said, "I *know* you are praying for your poor Nicky." Perhaps that helped, for this revolution was got under control. The next, of course, was not, and Nicholas was later executed by the Bolsheviks.

The public life of rulers is exposed in these letters. Marie Antoinette confesses that her "only pleasure" is to converse with her mother, and so she describes her day in detail, but "saves what we do on Sundays and holidays until another time," since she does not want to consume the materials of her "only pleasure" in just one note. "Before noon," she says, "I receive; anyone can come except common people. I put on my rouge and wash my hands in front of everybody; then the men leave, the ladies stay, and I dress before them."

Maria Theresa—this Poor Little Rich Girl's mother—could understand a day like this, because for forty years she was herself empress of Austria and queen of Hungary and Bohemia. But think of Harry Truman's mother in Missouri when that gallant old lady read her son's letters from the White House! One begins,

"I am sixty-one this morning, and I slept in the President's room in the White House last night. They have finished the painting and have some of the furniture in place."

Or this letter about a Russian state dinner:

Stalin gave his state dinner night before last, and it was a wow. Started with caviar and vodka and wound up with watermelon and champagne, with smoked fish, fresh fish, venison, chicken, duck and all sorts of vegetables in between. There was a toast every five minutes until at least twenty-five had been drunk.

The magnificence of another formal Russian dinner is described in fascinating detail by John Quincy Adams, our ambassador in 1811; it was as sumptuous as the one Mr. Truman attended, except for one important difference. "There are no healths drunk and no toasts," says Mr. Adams:

There is less of intemperance in fifty such feasts, than in one of our dinners succeeded by a carousal of six hours long, swilling upon a mixture of madeira and brandy.

A hundred and fifty years ago it was the Russian ambassador who had to be careful about drinking too much in the line of duty!

Henry Adams said of his forebears that "They were statesmen, not politicians; they guided public opinion, but were little guided by it." When you read the letters of J. Q. Adams to his mother, you will see that statesmanship was bred into this family, that it was as much a part of their makeup as blood and breath; in the Adams family, each learned from the other. So it was in an English family, the Pitts. Few sons ever have the opportunity to witness what William Pitt the Younger describes in his letter, written when he was sixteen (he was precocious, though; he would be Prime Minister at twenty-four):

My dear Mother: My father is now getting up, and has had, I am told, a good night. . . . Nothing prevented his speech from being the most forcible that can be imagined. The matter and manner both were striking; far beyond what I can express. . . .

In time the young man would be as good a speaker, in an era when speaking meant almost everything in politics.

Speaking well was a large part of the power of Franklin D. Roosevelt, also, but our selections are early ones, dating from a time when he did not yet wield power. Happiness shines through them because of his marriage to Eleanor:

I am the happiest man just now in the world; likewise the luckiest.

His cousin Theodore's letters are happy too, and ebullient:

> I have just received your letter! What an excitement! How nice to read it. What long letters you do write. I don't see how you can write them . . . I jumped with delight when I found you had heard a mocking-bird. Get some of its feathers if you can.

Teddy is overflowing with life. He is ten years old. Charles Stewart Parnell was only forty-five when he wrote the letter to his mother included here, but it is one of the last he ever sent, and it begins:

> I am weary, dear mother, of these troubles, weary unto death; but it is all in a good cause.

Perhaps that is the inevitable sadness of rulers who desire to change men's hearts.

"The Suitable Style of An Ambassador"

JOHN QUINCY ADAMS

John Quincy Adams (1767-1848; American diplomat and states-man; sixth President of the United States.) In these letters he was writing not only to a mother, but to one of the most astute women in New England. Abigail Adams, wife of one President and mother of another, was the author of a brilliant series of letters herself, and a perceptive political analyst; it is not surprising that her son confided in her by letter. They wrote to each other for forty years, until her death at the age of seventy-four, in 1818— six years before his election to the Presidency.

John Quincy Adams was trained for statesmanship from the day he could walk, if not before. At sixteen he accompanied his father to France, where John Adams was diplomatic representa-tive of this country. John Quincy himself later represented our young country abroad—in the Netherlands (1794-97) and—while his father was serving as our second President—as American minister to Prussia (1797-1801). It was from Berlin, on the way to the latter post, that he wrote the first of the letters below.

In 1801 his father was defeated in his campaign for a second term by Jefferson. John Quincy returned home to rest, but was soon engaged once again in government and politics. During the next two decades he served as Senator from Massachusetts, Minister to Russia (the subject of the second letter here), Minister to England, and Secretary of State. In 1824 he was a candidate for the Presidency but was defeated by Jackson in an electoral college vote of 99 to 84; however, Jackson did not have a clear-cut majority over the four other candidates, and so the election was thrown into the House of Representatives. There John Quincy Adams was elected the sixth President of the United States. But he too lost his campaign for reelection, and so once again Adams retired to Quincy. It was not for long. Three years later he was back in Washington as a Whig Congressman, and his service to America continued until he was stricken on the floor of the House and died, two days later, on February 23, 1848.

John Quincy Adams was a profound student of political philosophy and of the new science in his day. Few men in American public life have had more intelligence, more independence, more public spirit; but he was hampered throughout his life by the famous Adams reserve, by a certain coolness which kept him from having many close friends. This is a serious lack for a politician, and Adams's career was marked by hostility from many quarters. It is, of course, a sign of his tremendous ability that the people allowed him to serve them so often and so well.

Berlin, 5 February, 1798.

. . . . . .

I AM VERY glad that I was not sent to France,* for there is so much *personal* malignity among the men in power in that country against my father, that they would have felt a special satisfaction in treating me with more than common indignity, and in defeat-

---

* "It has given me real pain to find that the change in your embassy does not meet your ready assent; or that it should be personally so inconvenient to you as you represent. I cannot but flatter myself you will find it more agreeable than you anticipate. Your father has written you so fully upon the subject, and in my mind obviated every objection, that I think you will feel more satisfied. That you would not have been sent to Berlin at this time, if Mr. Washington had continued in office, I fully believe. But I can tell you where you would have been employed—as one of the envoys to France. This was the desire and opinion of all the ministers, and nothing but your near connection with the chief Magistrate prevented your being nominated. He had a delicacy upon the subject, and declined it." *Abigail Adams to John Quincy Adams,* November 3, 1797.

ing every attempt by me for a reconciliation between the two governments. Since the 4th of September all hopes of justice from France must vanish until some further revolution; and although I think those gentlemen, who have submitted to every sort of contumely and ill treatment for the sake of preserving peace, deserve as highly of their country as if their negotiation had been successful, I am pleased that no part of their failure can be imputed to the appointment of a person in any degree obnoxious to the ruling persons in France.

Of the *personal* malignity which I have above noticed, there has been for years past incessant proofs many of which I have heretofore noticed; it continues still indefatigable. You will have the plainest evidence of the arts used by the Directory and their creatures, to give the color of a personal quarrel to the differences between the governments. They do not only make personal complaints against the President, but they have made their creatures in Holland (creatures which since then they have without ceremony kicked out of doors themselves,) complain against me simply because they bear a personal malice against him, and of course against anyone connected with him. "Principles and not men," is their motto, (it used to be that of our last Minister in France, until from some secret stings of conscience or other cause he changed it to that of "Dread God,") by which they mean that no sentiment of honor, truth, justice, or generosity is to be admitted to protect the feelings, or character, or reputation, or person, or property, of any man whose principles happen to differ from theirs. Consequently they are in their animosities the most personal and malicious of mankind. They always affect even to attack particular persons, as the French have done in all their declarations of war, and as all their writers and most of their partisans have invariably done ever since, by fixing upon individual men upon whom to pour the perpetual torrent of their invective. The consequence of this system is, by unavoidable necessity, a state of inextinguishable war between man and man, as long as there exist two human beings together; for no sooner has one set of persons been swept away by the pestilence of these doctrines, than their destroyers immediately divide against each other, with the same system of destroying men to establish principles.

The French government have at length crowned the measure of their injustice and violence towards neutral nations, by a decree declaring *all* goods of British produce to be the worst sort of contraband. They have not yet declared war against us, but by this measure they will do us all the mischief that they could by a state of open war. In my opinion the United States have long enough tried "a tame beseeching of rejected peace." It does not appear to me necessary to declare or even to make war against France, but I most sincerely hope our commerce will be allowed to arm in its own defence. I am not prepared for unresisting submission to robbery, even though all the rest of the world should be.

St. Petersburg, 10/22 March, 1811.

I DINED yesterday at the French ambassador's, at a diplomatic dinner of about sixty persons, in the highest and most formal style. I give you a description of this entertainment, which may amuse you as a specimen of the usages at the time and place, and give you an idea of what is understood to be the suitable style of an ambassador. The invitation was by printed card, sent five or six days before the dinner, which by the custom is the signal of a *formal* entertainment. All invitations to dinner *without ceremony* are sent by verbal message, or given personally. The printed cards, although on the face of them they ask for an answer, never are answered, unless to decline the invitation. The only answer expected is personal attendance. When the invitation is *without ceremony,* the guests are expected to go not in full dress, but in frock coats, and if you choose in boots and with a round hat. But when the invitation is *by card,* they must go in full court dress, that is to say in uniform, for there is no court dress here but an uniform. In the summer season, however, the Chancellor of the Empire, Count Romanzoff, sometimes invites by cards, specifying that the company are to come in frock coats.

The hour of dining varies at different houses from four to five o'clock. The Chancellor's cards are always for four o'clock, the ambassador's for half-past four. These are the only two houses where entertainments of this kind are given, or at least where I have witnessed them.

At half-past four therefore I went to the ambassador's hotel, at the outer door of which stood the porter, or *Swiss,* in full dressed livery, deeply bordered with gold lace, a three-cornered hat, also gold laced, a broad girdle of cloth passing over from the right shoulder to the left side, bordered with gold lace and worked with gold embroidery, and a large thick staff about five feet long, and headed with silver. He opened the folding doors and I stepped from the carriage into the house. As my style here is altogether republican, I went only in a chariot and four, attended by two footmen in livery, and driven by a coachman on the carriage box, and a postillion, between boy and man, on the right side horse of the leading pair. My own footmen followed me about half the way up the stairs, when I threw off and gave them my *shoop*, a large outside fur garment, fit only for wearing in a carriage. The weather not being cold I had not taken with me the loose boots lined with fur or flannel, which are also worn in winter when riding in carriages, and are thrown off on entering the house. These are indispensable in the severity of the season, and are slipped on and off over shoes and silk stockings with as much ease as the shoop is from the shoulders.

On the steps of the staircase at the Ambassador's hotel stood a line of twenty footmen, reaching from the bottom to the top of the stairs, all in the same livery as the Swiss, excepting the girdle, staff and hat, and in silk stockings instead of boots. They stand there from the time when the company begins to come, until all the guests are arrived. They stand like so many statues, and are there merely for the magnificence of the show. At the top of the staircase, at the folding doors of the first antichamber, stood two *chasseurs* with pea green liveries, as deeply laced with silver as those of the footmen with gold, and with each a hanger suspended at the thigh by a leathern baldric passing over the shoulder. These like the Swiss were in boots. In the second antichamber was a line of eight upper servants, above the rank of footmen and chasseurs, in uniform dresses embroidered in gold, but of the same colors with the liveries. They were all in silk stockings, and stood like the footmen, merely to be seen by the company. In the third antichamber the guests were received and greeted by the Ambassador's secretaries and by the French consul. The Ambassador himself stood in the saloon, near the door of entrance, both folds of which were wide open, and there received and returned the salutations of each guest as he arrived, after which the guest passed on into the circle standing without any regular order about the hall. In the course of half an hour the whole company was assembled, and all continued standing until the Ambassador's steward in a full dress, not of livery, but of cloths richly embroidered in the ancient style of court dresses, came and announced to him that the *shaal* was ready. The *shaal* is a dram of cordials served with a relish of cold tongue, or ham, caviar, cheese, anchovies and other stimulants to appetite, which it is customary to take immediately before sitting down to dinner. It was served on a small table in the second antichamber, and each guest who chose to take it helped himself at the table, without sitting down. This ceremony being performed, which did not occupy more than five minutes of time, the Ambassador bowing round to the company invited the Chancellor to pass into the dining hall, and accompanied him to his place at his own right hand at the middle of the table. The remainder of the company followed without any particular order of precedence, each person taking his place according to his own idea of propriety, or to the courtesy of others. All the ministers and general officers, however, national and foreign, waited yesterday, and gave the *step* of precedence, immediately after the Chancellor and the Ambassador, to the Austrian envoy extraordinary and minister plenipotentiary, Count St. Julien, who for certain reasons is treated with very peculiar distinction at this time. The rest of the company took their places as I have mentioned at *discretion*.

The dinner was over in about an hour, and seldom lasts longer on these occasions of parade. There is no distinction of different services, and no time lost in getting on and removing dishes, or in carving. The table is elegantly decorated with a plateau, and a variety of images in porcelain and ornamented plates filled with confectionery and fruits, which form part of the dessert, but no dish is ever set upon the table. Those that require carving are all carved by the principal servants in attendance. The dinner begins with soup, a plate of which is carried by the footman and offered to every guest at the table. The soup plates are of elegant porcelain. Then follows a succession of seven or eight dishes of flesh and fish variously cooked, with and without vegetables, and some of them with pastry according to the fashion of French cookery. If the dishes in which they are served are large, the footmen bring small portions of it round, and present them to every guest as with the soup. If the dishes are small, they are presented in succession to the guest, each of whom helps himself from the dish as he pleases. Bottles of French table wines, red and white alternately, and decanters of water are placed on the table between every two persons seated at it, with a tumbler and a wine glass to each person. But a variety of fine wines are served round by the butler and some of the footmen, between every dish or two that is presented. One glass of each sort of wine is offered to each guest.

They usually begin with madeira, to which succeed various French wines, red and white alternately, until champagne is presented with the last dish of flesh. Then come jellies, preserves, fruits, sweetmeats, and last of all ice creams, with a small glass of sweet wine. There are no healths drunk and no toasts, and every guest has as little to do with the drinking as with the eating of another. Among the liquors served round are equally English porter and ale, and frozen punch in champagne glasses. On rising from the table the footmen behind the chairs offer tumblers of green glass filled with water to every guest to wash his mouth and fingers. The company return through the antichamber into the saloon, where they continue standing as before dinner. The servants hand round coffee, and afterwards cordials in glasses not much larger than thimbles, after which each guest drops off one by one without taking leave, or being noticed by any person as he retires. At the head of the staircase he finds the chasseurs and footmen, who the moment he appears call for his servants, one of whom comes to him and puts on his shoop and fur boots, while another goes and orders his carriage up to the door. There stands the Swiss, and at the moment when the carriage drives up opens the door, the guest enters his carriage, and goes home or wherever his business or pleasure calls him.

I said there was no distinction of services at the table, but after the soup until the last dish of flesh emphatically called *roast*, which is always accompanied with a salad and followed by the glass of champagne, the plates in which everything is presented and the dishes are of silver plate, after which the plates are of the most magnificent china, usually of Sèvres, painted with portraits, views, landscapes or history pieces, no two plates of which are alike. At this period of the repast the silver plates are taken away from before every guest, and in their stead is substituted a plate of this superb porcelain, with a napkin of more beautiful damask than the first served, which is however not taken away, two dessert knives, a fork, a spoon and a *paddle*, all of silver gilt, except the blade of one of the knives which is of steel. The knife with the silver blade is to pare or to cut fruit, that with a steel blade to cut preserves or confectionery, or anything requiring a keener edge than silver. The *paddle* (I call it so from its form, I know not its proper name,) is to take up the liquid jellies, or preserves, or ice creams, which spread themselves over the surface of your plate and might escape the scoop and thickness of a spoon. The second napkin is merely to wipe your lips and fingers when you wash them in rising from table, that which you have used at dinner being supposed less suitable for that purpose.

The attention of the servants to the guests at table is so vigilant that you scarcely ever have occasion to ask for anything. The instant that you have emptied your plate, or that you lay down your knife, and fork, or spoon, your plate is taken away and a clean one is given you in its stead, If you choose to have your knife, fork and spoon changed, you lay them, or either of them, in the plate. If you lay them aside on the cloth, they are not taken away; whenever they are, others are immediately given you with the plate. If you have occasion for a fresh supply of bread, the footmen perceive it at least as soon as you do yourself, and present you a new piece, just as you are ready to call for it. If you take two or three glasses of the various kinds of wine that are handed round, the glasses as you empty them are taken away without any hint from you. The name of each kind of wine is mentioned to you by the servant who offers it. If you decline taking any dish or glass offered you, there is no occasion to speak, you only raise your hand, or touch the back of your fore-finger on the edge of the plate or of the waiter in which it is presented. The servant understands you, and offers the same plate or waiter to the guest seated next you. As several plates are serving from the same dish at once in various parts of the table, the whole company is served in a very few minutes. The conversa-tions of each guest are merely with his next neighbors at table, and in a low voice that they may all be carried on at once. The voice of a servant is never heard, unless to mention the names of the wines as they are offered. The Ambassador and the Chan-cellor sometimes have a band of music, who occasionally strike up an air or a march at intervals during the dinner; yesterday how-ever there was none.

Ex uno disce omnes. I give you the description of an individual for an idea of the genus. All these parade dinners are alike, differ-ing only in some insignificant details. For instance the Ambassa-dor, who is one of the politest men in the world, never pays any attention to any part of the dinner more than any one of the guests. The Chancellor usually himself pours out the sweet wine, the last that is served, two kinds of which he has before him, he calls out to each guest by name, asks him which of the two he will have, and according to his choice sends him a glass by a footman. This you will observe is a mark of special attention, but it is troublesome both to the Chancellor and to the guests. The Ambassador's fashion is more of a piece with the whole system. The servants carry round the sweet wines like all the rest. They offer to each guest the choice of two, but in that as in everything else the master of the house can be distinguished from the guests while at table only by the seat which he occupies. Everything moves like a piece of clockwork. The dishes, the cookery, the wines are all of the most exquisite inventions of luxury, and yet there is less of intemperance in fifty such feasts, than in one of our dinners succeeded by a carousal of six hours long, swilling upon a mixture of madeira wine and brandy.

"Certain Dark Sides"

PRINCE ALBERT

Prince Albert Francis Charles Augustus Emmanuel of Saxe-Coburg-Gotha (1819-1861; Prince Consort.) Victoria loved him much more than the English people did when they were married in 1840, but Albert managed to overcome the initial distrust of his adopted countrymen and to win a unique and abiding affection. He was not at all the aimless, moody secretary to the Queen that he is often pictured as being, but was on the contrary deeply interested in artistic and scientific development; the success of the Great Exhibition of 1851 is generally credited to him. His death in 1861 of typhoid fever plunged his widow into the deepest grief, and left a nation of mourners. They had nine children.

The two letters below were written at the two most important moments of Albert's life, the first upon the occasion of Victoria's proposing to him (which is something queens, unfortunately, have to do); the second when he was about to be named Prince Consort.

Windsor, 5th November 1839.

DEAR MAMA,—Apart from my relations with her [Victoria], my future position will have certain dark sides, and the skies above me will not always be blue and unclouded. Still, life, wherever one is, has its storms, and it is a support to one to feel that one has used all one's endeavours and strength in some great object, decisive for the welfare of so many.

J UNE 1857.—I have not said a word to you about my change of title, and I now present myself before you as an entire stranger, "Prince Consort," to wit. The change had become necessary as our sons grew up, all sorts of confusion having already arisen, especially as the names of all three begin, like my own, with an A, and I was certain to appear to them in the long run, like a stranger in the land, as they alone were English princes, and I merely a Coburg prince. Now I have a legal status in the English hierarchy. It was also a source of weakness for the Crown that the Queen always appeared before the people with her *foreign* husband.

"An Admirer of the Blonde"

BENJAMIN DISRAELI,
FIRST EARL OF BEACONSFIELD

Benjamin Disraeli, First Earl of Beaconsfield (1804-1881; English statesman and novelist.) The great "Dizzy" called this letter to his mother "an elephantine sheet, all about Spanish ladies and tomato sauce." Sad to say, it is the only one he wrote to her that has been preserved. Disraeli was descended from an aristocratic Jewish family, but his father, Isaac Disraeli—a popular writer and literary figure—repudiated that faith, and Benjamin was raised as an Anglican. Disraeli intended from the beginning to be a great man; he started by writing novels. Next he attempted to enter politics, and in 1837—after three attempts in five years —he was elected to Parliament.

During the next ten years, Disraeli refashioned the Tory party, supported his ideas with powerful political novels, and married Mary Ann Evans, a widow fifteen years his senior and, in his words, "a perfect wife." By 1847, as the member from Buckinghamshire, he was made leader of Her Majesty's Opposition. Between 1853 and 1867 he was three times Chancellor of the Exchequer and twice Prime Minister. He had become a "great man"; and his power and prestige were further enhanced by the fact that he and Queen Victoria were charter members of a mutual admiration society. He arranged for Victoria to be proclaimed Empress of India in 1876, and the same year she arranged to have him made Earl of Beaconsfield.

Disraeli was made a Knight of the Garter in 1878, the year of his last great political triumph, at the Congress of Berlin. But even during his most politically active periods, in or out of office, nothing could staunch the flow of novels: Lothair *appeared in 1870 and* Endymion *in 1880. When he died a year later he was honored as no Englishman had been since the Iron Duke. Dizzy had done as much as any man to create the British Empire.*

Sir Winston Churchill writes a lot, too.

Granada,
Aug. 1. [1830]

My dear Mother,

Although you doubtless assist, as the French phrase it, at the reading of my despatches, you will, I am sure, be pleased to receive one direct from your absent son. It has just occurred to me that I have never yet mentioned the Spanish ladies, and I do not think that I can address anything that I have to say upon this agreeable subject to any one more suitable than yourself. You know that I am rather an admirer of the blonde; and, to be perfectly candid, I will confess to you that the only times which I have been so unfortunate as to be captivated, or captured, in this country were both by Englishwomen. But these Espagnolas are nevertheless very interesting personages. What we associate with the idea of female beauty is not common in this country. There are none of those seraphic countenances, which strike you dumb or blind, but faces in abundance which will never pass without commanding a pleasing glance. Their charm consists in their sensibility; each incident, every person, every word touches the far eye of a Spanish lady, and her features are constantly confuting the creed of Mahomet, and proving that she has a soul: but there is nothing quick, harsh, or forced about her. She is extremely unaffected, and not at all French. Her eyes gleam rather than sparkle, she speaks with quick vivacity but in sweet tones, and there is in all her carriage, particularly when she walks, a certain dignified grace which never leaves her, and which is very remarkable. . . .

I sat next to a lady of high distinction at a bull-fight at Seville. She was the daughter-in-law of the Captain-General, and the most beautiful Spaniard I have yet met. Her comb was white, and she wore a mantilla of blonde, I have no doubt extremely valuable, for it was very dirty. The effect, however, was charming. Her hair was glossy black, and her eyes like an antelope's, but all her other features deliciously soft; and she was further adorned, which is rare in Spain, with a rosy cheek, for here our heroines are rather sallow. But they counteract this defect by never appearing until twilight, which calls them from their bowers, fresh, though languid, from the late siesta. To conclude, the only fault of the Spanish beauty is that she too soon indulges in the magnificence of embonpoint. There are, however, many exceptions to this. At seventeen a Spanish beauty is poetical, tall, lithe, and clear, though sallow. But you have seen Mercandotti [a famous dancer of the day]. As she advances, if she does not lose her shape, she resembles Juno rather than Venus. Majestic she ever is; and if her feet are less twinkling than in her first career, look on her hand and you'll forgive them all.

There is calm voluptuousness about the life here that wonderfully accords with my disposition, so that if I were resident, and had my intellect at command, I do not know any place where I could make it more productive. The imagination is ever at work, and beauty and grace are not scared away by those sounds and sights, those constant cares and changing feelings, which are the proud possession of our free land of eastern winds. You rise at eight, and should breakfast lightly, although a table covered with all fruits renders that rather difficult to one who inherits, with other qualities good and bad, that passion for the most delightful productions of nature, with which my beloved sire can sympathise. I only wish I had him here over a medley of grape and melon, gourd and prickly-pear. In the morning you never quit the house, and these are hours which might be profitably employed under the inspiration of a climate which is itself poetry, for it sheds over everything a golden hue which does not exist in the objects themselves illuminated. At present I indulge only in a calm reverie, for I find the least exertion of mind instantly aggravate all my symptoms; and even this letter is an exertion, which you would hardly credit. My general health was never better. You know how much better I am on a sunny day in England; well, I have had *two* months of sunny days infinitely warmer. I have during all this period enjoyed general health of which I have no memory during my life. All the English I have met are ill, and live upon a diet. I eat everything, and my appetite each day increases. . . . The Spanish cuisine is not much to my taste, for garlic and bad oil preponderate; but it has its points: the soups are good, and *the most agreeable dish* in the world is an olio. I will explain it to you, for my father would delight in it. There are two large dishes, one at each end of the table. The one at the top contains bouilli beef, boiled pork sausage, black-pudding; all these not mixed together, but in their separate portions. The other dish is a medley of vegetables and fruits, generally French beans, caravanseras, slices of melons, and whole pears. Help each person to a portion of the meats, and then to the medley. Mix them in your plate together, and drown them in tomato sauce. There is no garlic and no grease of any kind. I have eaten this every day, it is truly delightful. . . .

After dinner you take your siesta. I generally sleep for two hours. I think this practice conducive to health. Old people, however, are apt to carry it to excess. By the time I have risen and arranged my toilette it is time to steal out, and call upon any agreeable family whose Tertullia you may choose to honour, which you do, after the first time, uninvited, and with them you take your tea or chocolate. This is often *al fresco,* under the piazza or colonnade of the *patio.* Here you while away the time until it is cool enough for the *alameda* or public walk. At Cadiz, and even at Seville, up the Guadalquivir, you are sure of a delightful breeze from the water. The sea breeze comes like a spirit. The effect is quite magical. As you are lolling in listless languor in the hot and perfumed air, an invisible guest comes dancing into the party and touches them all with an enchanted wand. All start, all smile. It has come; it is the sea breeze. There is much discussion whether it is as strong, or whether weaker, than the night before. The ladies furl their fans and seize their mantillas, the cavaliers stretch their legs and give signs of life. All rise. I offer my arm to Dolores or Florentina (is not this familiarity strange?), and in ten minutes you are in the *alameda.* What a change! All is now life and liveliness. Such bowing, such kissing, such fluttering of fans, such gentle criticism of gentle friends! But the fan is the most wonderful part of the whole scene. A Spanish lady with her fan might shame the tactics of a troop of horse. Now she unfurls it with the slow pomp and conscious elegance of a peacock. Now she flutters it with all the languor of a listless beauty, now with all the liveliness of a vivacious one. Now, in the midst of a very tornado, she closes it with a whir which makes you start, pop! In the midst of your confusion Dolores taps you on the elbow; you turn round to listen, and Florentina pokes you in your side. Magical instrument! You know that it speaks a particular language, and gallantry requires no other mode to express its most subtle conceits or its most unreasonable demands than this slight, delicate organ. But remember, while you read, that here, as in England, it is not confined alone to your delightful sex. I also have my fan, which makes my cane extremely jealous. If you think I have grown extraordinarily effeminate, learn that in this scorching clime the soldier will not mount guard without one. Night wears on, we sit, we take a *panal*, which is as quick work as snapdragon, and far more elegant; again we stroll. Midnight clears the public walks, but few Spanish families retire till two. A solitary bachelor like myself still wanders, or still lounges on a bench in the *warm* moonlight. The last guitar dies away, the cathedral clock wakes up your reverie, you too seek your couch, and amid a gentle, sweet flow of loveliness, and light, and music, and fresh air; thus dies a day in Spain.

Adieu, my dearest mother. A thousand loves to all.

B. DISRAELI.

"To Prove What I Could Do"

ELIZABETH I

Elizabeth I (1533-1603; Queen of England.) No wonder that Elizabeth never married! Her mother was Anne Boleyn, second wife of Henry VIII. So that Henry could divorce Katharine of Aragon and marry Anne, England broke its ties with the papacy; the Church of England was established; the Reformation was thrust ahead.

Elizabeth was three years old when her mother was beheaded for adultery, incest, and plotting against the crown—whereupon Parliament declared Elizabeth an illegitimate child. Her father, of course, chose new wives: Jane Seymour, who died; Anne of Cleves, who was cast aside; Catherine Howard, who was also beheaded; and then Catherine Parr, who almost met a similar fate, but outlived her husband and then even took another.

Elizabeth was ten years old when Henry's last marriage took place; Catherine Parr was, then, really the only mother she ever knew. And so I have included a letter written to Catherine by Elizabeth in 1544.

When Elizabeth was born, her chances of reigning were slight, but she was educated for the role just in case. She could read and write not only "elegant Italian," the original language of the first of these letters, but also Greek, Latin, French, German, and English. She succeeded to the throne in 1558, when she was twenty-three. During her lifetime, the legality of her claim to the throne was never universally acknowledged, but now it is generally agreed that "The Virgin Queen" was the greatest monarch England has ever known. The golden age of literature, which gave to the world William Shakespeare among a glorious company, may not be directly attributable to her reign, but without doubt she deserves credit for making England a European power, and for launching the Raleighs and the Drakes to make the world we live in.

A.D. 1544.

INIMICAL fortune, envious of all good and ever revolving human affairs, has deprived me for a whole year of your most illustrious presence, and, not thus content, has yet again robbed me of the same good; which thing would be intolerable to me, did I not hope to enjoy it very soon. And in this my exile, I well know that the clemency of your highness has had as much care and solicitude for my health as the king's majesty himself. By which thing I am not only bound to serve you, but also to revere you with filial love, since I understand that your most illustrious highness has not forgotten me every time you have written to the king's majesty, which, indeed, it was my duty to have requested from you. For heretofore I have not dared to write to him. Wherefore I now humbly pray your most excellent highness, that, when you write to his majesty, you will condescend to recommend me to him, praying ever for his sweet benediction, and similarly entreating our Lord God to send him best success, and the obtaining of victory over his enemies, so that your highness and I may, as soon as possible, rejoice together with him on his happy return. No less pray I God, that he would preserve your most illustrious highness; to whose grace, humbly kissing your hands, I offer and recommend myself.

From St. James's, this 31st of July.

Your most obedient daughter, and most
faithful servant,
ELISABETH.

To our most noble and virtuous queen Catherine,
Elisabeth, her humble daughter, wisheth perpetual felicity and everlasting joy.

Not only knowing the effectuous will and fervent zeal, the
which your highness hath towards all godly learning, as also
my duty towards you, most gracious and sovereign princess; but
knowing also, that pusillanimity and idleness are most repugnant
unto a reasonable creature, and that (as the philosopher sayeth)
even as an instrument of iron or of other metal waxeth soon rusty,
unless it be continually occupied; even so shall the wit of a man
or a woman wax dull and unapt to do or understand any thing
perfectly, unless it be always occupied upon some manner of
study. Which things considered, hath moved so small a portion
as God hath lent me, to prove what I could do. And, therefore,
have I (as for essay or beginning, following the right notable
saying of the proverb aforesaid) translated this little book out of
French rhyme into English prose, joining the sentences together,
as well as the capacity of my simple wit and small learning
could extend themselves.

The which book is entitled or named, "The Mirror, or Glass, of
the Sinful Soul," wherein is contained, how she (beholding and
contemplating what she is), doth perceive how, of herself and her
own strength, she can do nothing that good is, or prevaileth for
her salvation, unless it be through the grace of God, whose
mother, daughter, sister, and wife, by the Scriptures, she proveth
herself to be. Trusting also that, through his incomprehensible
love, grace, and mercy, she (being called from sin to repentance),
doth faithfully hope to be saved. And although I know that, as for
my part which I have wrought in it (as well spiritual as manual),
there is nothing done as it should be, nor else worthy to come in
your grace's hands, but rather all unperfect and uncorrect; yet
do I trust also that, howbeit it is like a work which is but new
begun and shapen, that the file of your excellent wit and godly
learning, in the reading of it (if so it vouchsafe your highness to
do), shall rub out, polish, and mend (or else cause to mend),
the words (or rather the order of my writing), the which I know,
in many places, to be rude, and nothing done as it should be.
But I hope that, after to have been in your grace's hands, there
shall be nothing in it worthy of reprehension, and that in the
mean while no other (but your highness only), shall read it or

see it, lest my faults be known of many. Then shall they be better excused (as my confidence is in your grace's accustomed benevolence), than if I should bestow a whole year in writing or inventing ways for to excuse them.

Praying God Almighty, the Maker and Creator of all things, to grant unto your highness the same New Year's day, a lucky and a prosperous year, with prosperous issue, and continuance of many years in good health and continual joy, and all to his honour, praise, and glory.

From Ashridge, the last day of the year of our Lord God, 1544.

"He Lived Usefully"

BENJAMIN FRANKLIN

Benjamin Franklin (1706-1790; American author, inventor, printer, scientist, philanthropist, statesman, and diplomat.)

You learn little about Ben Franklin from a dispassionate chronology of his career. To say that he was an apprentice to his half brother James, publisher of The New England Courant *in Boston, does not take into account the quality of Franklin's anonymous contributions to the paper. To call him the publisher of the* Pennsylvania Gazette *and Almanac in Philadelphia does not explain the instantaneous success of his "Poor Richard," a success that made Franklin's trenchant wit and homely philosophizing known throughout the Colonies and in Europe. Still without an official position, title or portfolio other than deputy postmaster of Philadelphia and clerk of the Pennsylvania Assembly, Franklin managed to start America's first circulating library, to found the American Philosophical Society and an academy that has become the University of Pennsylvania, to inaugurate the first Colonial city police and fire department, to invent the Franklin stove, to devise an original design for a clock, and to send up the kite that brought the lightning back.*

You learn more about Franklin from his writings—letters, verses, scientific papers, diplomatic reports, articles, notes, speeches. In a letter like the one that follows, probably written shortly after he had sold his printing business in order to devote "all" of his time to science (but nevertheless still served as deputy postmaster and as clerk of the Assembly), he describes himself best when he tells how he hopes to be remembered.

Franklin entered politics in a small way in 1754 by representing Pennsylvania at the Albany Congress; in 1757 he was sent to England as political agent of the Pennsylvania Assembly. Thirteen years later he had a direct appointment to represent three more of the Colonies, and was regarded in England, characteristically, as the "unofficial ambassador" of them all. In 1775 he returned to attend the Second Continental Congress, to serve on the committee that drafted the Declaration of Independence, and to sign that document. In 1776 he went to France to serve the American Revolution in that country; there he was so popular that a "Franklin cult" developed and he was the most sought-after dinner guest in Paris. He returned in 1785, after having negotiated the final peace treaty with England in 1783, and in 1787 was a member of the Constitutional Convention. The highest position he ever held in the national government was deputy postmaster general of the Colonies in 1774.

Perhaps the reason is that he was always too busy to settle down to an office. In any event, he had a wonderful life and is surely one of the most interesting men who ever lived.

Philadelphia, (1750?)

Honoured Mother,

We received your kind letter of the 2nd instant, by which we are glad to hear you still enjoy such a measure of health, notwithstanding your great age. We read your writing very easily. I never met with a word in your letters but what I could easily understand, for though the hand is not always the best, the sense makes every thing plain. My leg, which you inquire after, is now quite well . . .

As to your grandchildren, Will is now nineteen years of age, a tall proper youth, and much of a beau. He acquired a habit of idleness on the Expedition, but begins of late to apply himself to business, and I hope will become an industrious man. He imagined his father had got enough for him, but I have assured him that I intend to spend what little I have myself, if it please God that I live long enough; and as he by no means wants acuteness, he can see by my going on that I mean to be as good as my word.

Sally grows a fine girl, and is extremely industrious with her needle, and delights in her work. She is of a most affectionate temper, and perfectly dutiful and obliging to her parents, and to all. Perhaps I flatter myself too much, but I have hopes that she will prove an ingenious, sensible, notable, and worthy woman, like her aunt Jenny. She goes now to the dancing-school.

For my own part, at present, I pass my time agreeably enough. I enjoy, through mercy, a tolerable share of health. I read a great deal, ride a little, do a little business for myself, now and then for others, retire when I can, and go into company when I please; so the years roll round, and the last will come, when I would rather have it said, *He lived usefully,* than *He died rich.*

Cousins Josiah and Sally are well, and I believe will do well, for they are an industrious loving young couple; but they want a little more stock to go on smoothly with their business.

My love to brother and sister Mecom, and their children, and to all my relations in general.

I am your dutiful son,
B FRANKLIN.

"Don't Be Disturbed"

JAMES ABRAM GARFIELD

James Abram Garfield (1831-1881; American soldier and legislator; 20th President of the United States.) He had a genuine Ohio frontier upbringing and he was really born in a log cabin. His father died when he was two; his mother raised four children with great difficulty and much sacrifice. Garfield was educated at Williams College, but he claimed that the best education was to be on one end of a log, with Mark Hopkins on the other.

When civil war erupted, Garfield organized the 42nd Ohio Volunteer Infantry Regiment; his army career was distinguished, and his contributions to the Battle of Chickamauga gained him promotion to Major-General of Volunteers. Garfield was, in short, a superlative example of the kind of civilian soldiers the Union was able to produce in its great emergency.

He was elected to Congress and took his seat in December, 1863, serving nine terms in the House and making a reputation as an orator and defender of sound finance. Then in 1880 he was elected to the Senate—but this time did not take his seat because, as much to his surprise as to everyone else's, he had been nominated for the Presidency and elected in the interval. Garfield had attended the Republican Convention as campaign manager for Sherman; when a deadlock developed between Blaine and Grant, he was put forward as a compromise candidate, and on the thirty-sixth ballot a stampede nominated him. He was inaugurated on March 4, 1881, but on July 2 he was shot by Charles Guiteau, a disappointed office-seeker, at the Washington railroad station, and died eleven weeks later.

DEAR MOTHER. Don't be disturbed by conflicting reports about my condition. It is true I am still weak and on my back, but I am gaining every day and need only time and patience to bring me through. Give my love to all the relatives and friends and especially to sisters Hitty and Mary. Your loving son. James A Garfield.

"Anyone Can Come Except Common People"

JOSEPHE JEANNE MARIE ANTOINETTE

Josephe Jeanne Marie Antoinette (1755-1793; Queen of France.) The end was the guillotine; the beginning of the end was the year 1770, the date of the letter below, when the gay, sentimental, fifteen-year-old daughter of Maria Theresa and Francis I of Austria left the pious court of Vienna and entered, via marriage to the French dauphin, the maelstrom of Versailles. (Madame Dubarry, for one, was not happy to welcome the young and vivacious princess.)

After Marie's dim husband ascended the throne as Louis XVI in 1774, the intrigues multiplied. But there are really no extenuating circumstances for Marie Antoinette; for good and sufficient reasons, her name has come to stand for superficiality and irresponsibility. She was extravagant, dissolute, and ostentatious, and had been even during the court mourning for Louis XV. Within six months after ascending the throne she was under attack from all sides. Her scandalous conduct at public affairs, her gratuitous connivance in politics, her wasteful spending—all this contrasted so vividly with the growing misery of the kingdom that she became the focus for all discontent in France.

*The famous, though apocryphal, "qu'ils mangent de brioche"
is all too appropriate. After the fall of the Bastille in July, 1789,
and the storming of Versailles in October of the same year, she
was taken with the royal family to the Tuileries. She attempted to
flee in 1791, but was captured, humiliated, brutally treated. Her
husband was executed. Desperate attempts were made by the
European nobility to rescue or ransom her, but although by this
time there was much corruption in the French Revolutionary
government, she could not be saved or bought. The French people
wanted "L'Autrichienne" for their own. Her son was tortured.
She was tried and found guilty of treason, and on October 16,
1793, the "Widow Capet" was guillotined.*

*In spite of all, Edmund Burke was right. They should not have
done it.*

Choisy, 12 July, 1770

Madame my dear mother:

I can not express how sensible I am of the kindness Your
Majesty shows me, and I assure you that I have never received
one of your dear letters without regretting, with tears in my
eyes, that I am separated from such a tender and good mother,
and though I am happy enough here, I still ardently wish that I
could return to see my dear, my very dear family, at least for a
moment.

I am distressed that Your Majesty has not received my letter.
I thought it would go by the courier, but Mercy decided to send
it by Forcheron, and it is that, I suppose, which has delayed it. I
find that it is sad to have to wait for my uncle, my brother and
my sister-in-law without knowing when they are to come. I beg
you to inform me if it is true that you have gone to meet them at
Gratz, and if it is true that the Emperor is much thinner after
his trip; this would worry me, since he has no flesh to spare.

As to my devotions, and "la générale," about which you ask, I
will tell you that I have taken communion only once; I confessed
day before yesterday to the Abbé Maudoux, but as it was, I
thought, the day I was to go to Choisy, I did not take communion,
being too distracted. As to "la générale," it is the fourth month
that it has not come, without good reason. Our return from
Choisy has been put off for a day, my husband having had a
feverish cold which, however, went away in a day—having
slept for twelve and a half hours, he awoke feeling much better

and is now getting ready to depart. We have thus been here since yesterday—here where, from one in the afternoon, when we dine, until one in the morning, we do not return to our own apartments—which tires me out, since from dinnertime we play until six, when we go to the theatre, which lasts until nine-thirty and then to supper, after which more play until one or even one-thirty sometimes; but the king, seeing yesterday that I was so tired, had the goodness to allow me to retire at eleven, which pleased me very much and I was able to sleep very soundly until ten-thirty, although alone—my husband, being still on a diet (because of his cold) retired alone after supper to his own rooms, which never happens otherwise.

Your Majesty is very kind to be so interested in my welfare, and even to want to know how I pass my days. I will tell you then that I get up at ten o'clock or nine o'clock or nine-thirty and, having dressed, say my morning prayers, then breakfast; after which I go to my aunts' apartments, where I generally find the king. I stay there until ten-thirty; at eleven I go to the hairdresser. Before noon I receive; anyone can come except common people. I put on my rouge and wash my hands in front of everybody; then the men leave, the ladies stay, and I dress before them. Mass is at noon; if the king is at Versailles I go with him and my husband and my aunts to mass; if he is not here I go with the Dauphin, but always at that time. After mass the two of us dine in front of everybody, but we are through at one-thirty because we both eat very quickly. Then I go to the Dauphin's apartments and if he is busy I return to mine; I read, I write or I work—I am making a coat for the king, which is not getting along very well, but I hope that with the Grace of God it will be finished in a year or two. At three o'clock I go again to my aunts', where the king comes at that hour; at four the Abbé comes to me, and at five every day the harpsichord player, and I sing until six. At six-thirty I go to my aunts', when I do not go for a walk; you must know that my husband nearly always goes with me to my aunts'. From seven to nine we play; but when it is nice I go for a walk, and then there is no play for me, but for my aunts. At nine we have supper; when the king is absent my aunts have supper with us, but if he is here we go after supper with them to wait on the king, who generally appears at ten-forty-five—while I wait, I lie on a large sofa and sleep until he comes—when he is not here we go to bed at eleven o'clock. There is our whole day. I will save what we do on Sundays and holidays until another time.

I beg you, my very dear mother, to forgive me if my letter is too long, but it is my only pleasure to converse thus with you. I also beg your pardon if the letter is dirty, but I have been writing it for two days at my toilette, having had no other time; and if I do not answer your questions exactly, it is because of too much zeal on my part to destroy your letter. I must end in order to dress and go to mass with the king; I am the most obedient of daughters.

I send a list of the presents I have received, thinking it would amuse you.

"For A Wretched Woman!"

NAPOLEON BONAPARTE

Napoleon Bonaparte (1769-1821; French soldier and statesman; Emperor of the French.) There is a tomb in Ajaccio, Corsica, with the simple inscription: "Mater Regum" (Mother of Kings). At one time three of the sons of the woman who is buried there occupied European thrones: Joseph was King of Naples, Louis was King of Holland, Jérôme was King of Westphalia; her son-in-law was Grand Duke of Berg. The cause of all of this was, of course, her second son, Napoleon, "le petit caporal," Emperor of the French and ruler of all Europe. Letizia Ramolino Bonaparte lived fifteen years longer than her most celebrated offspring. She followed his campaigns and his fortunes with the greatest care and anxiety. Napoleon, for his part, also had a strong family feeling; indeed, he was entangled by family ties.

The year of the first letter, 1805, was significant in Napoleon's history, and that means it was also significant in the history of Europe. In December he defeated the combined Austrian and Russian armies at Austerlitz, in what many believe to have been his greatest battle; but we can look back and see that the flaw in his armor had been exposed two months previously, when Nelson swept the sea of French ships at Trafalgar.

The year of the second letter, 1813, was the year of disaster. The remnants of the Grande Armée straggled, disheartened and shivering, back to Paris; northern Europe, encouraged by the Russian debacle, rose against the invader; and Napoleon found

himself opposed by a coalition of Russia, England, Prussia,
Sweden, and Austria. He won his last great victory, at Dresden,
August 26-27, but he lost the decisive Battle of Leipzig, October
16-19, and ahead loomed Elba, Waterloo, and St. Helena.

Château de Stupinigi, April 22, 1805.

M. JÉRÔME BONAPARTE has arrived at Lisbon with the woman
he is living with. I have ordered the prodigal son to travel by
Perpignan, Toulouse, Grenoble, and Turin, and to report himself
at Milan. I have told him that if he varies this route he will be
arrested. Miss Paterson, who is living with him, has taken the
precaution of bringing a brother with her. I have given orders
that she is to be sent back to America. If she attempts to evade
these orders, and appears either at Bordeaux or in Paris, she will
be escorted to Amsterdam, and put on board the first ship for
America. As for the young man himself, I shall only give him one
interview. If he shows himself unworthy of the name he bears,
and seems inclined to persist in his *liaison*, I shall show him no
mercy. If he shows no disposition to wipe out the dishonour with
which he has stained my name by deserting the colours for a
wretched woman, I shall utterly disown him, and perhaps make
an example of him, to teach young officers the sanctity of military
service, and the enormity of the crime they commit, if they prefer
a female to the flag. Assuming that he comes to Milan, I want
you to write to him. Tell him that I have been like a father to him.
Tell him that it is his sacred duty to obey me, and that his only
hope is to do as I command. Get his sisters to write too: for,
once I have pronounced his sentence, I shall be inflexible, and his
whole career will be ruined.

Mayence, November 6, 1813.

MADAME, AND DEAREST MOTHER; I hear by telegraph that Louis
has arrived at your house. I send you a copy of his letter to me.

If he has come as a French prince, to stand by the throne, I
am ready to welcome him, and to forget the past. I taught him
when he was a child; I overwhelmed him with kindnesses: he
has repaid me by libelling me in every Court in Europe. But I
will forgive him once more; as you know, I am not accustomed

to nurse grievances. If, on the other hand—and his letter makes me fear this—he has come to ask for the restoration of Holland, he will force me to the painful necessity (1) of taking proceedings against him, and (2) of doing so irretrievably; for I shall be obliged to summon him through the Arch-chancellor, and in the presence of the Vice-Grand Elector, the President of the Senate, the Grand Judge, and the Family Secretary; and if he refuses to recognise the laws of the Empire, he will find himself declared a rebel.

It is ungenerous on his part to cause me fresh embarrassment, and to oblige me to proceed against him, at a moment when I have so much on hand, and when my heart needs consolation rather than fresh causes of anxiety. Holland is French, and will remain so. It has become so by a constitutional law, and no power on earth can take it away again. So if Louis still has that bee in his bonnet, I appeal to you to spare me the pain of having to arrest him as a rebel. Get him to leave Paris. Let him go and live quietly and unostentatiously in some out-of-the-way place in Italy. He used to be in Switzerland: why did he ever leave it?

In spite of the evidence he has given me of his hatred, I can't believe he is so bad a man, and so unkind a parent, as to wish to force on me the additional unpleasantness of prosecuting him at a moment when all Europe has risen against me, and my heart is bruised by so many anxieties.

I end by repeating that, if (after all) he has come simply as a French prince to support the throne at its moment of peril, and to defend the interests of his country, his family, and his children, then I forgive his past offences, and shall not speak of them again; and I shall welcome him, in the memory, not of his conduct during the last ten years, but of the affection I had for him when he was a child.

"C'est à vomir!"

NICHOLAS II

Nicholas II (1868-1918; Czar of Russia.) One can hope that "poor Nicky" really was having a happy time in 1894, the year of the first letter to his mother, Maria Federovna; it was the beginning of his new life and responsibility and he would never be very happy again. On November 1, 1894, Nicholas succeeded his father, Alexander III, as Czar of all the Russians; on November 26, he married Princess Alix of Hesse, a granddaughter of Queen Victoria of England, who by now was beginning to be called the "Grandmother of Europe." By 1897, the date of the second letter, trouble was brewing with cousin Willie—Wilhelm Hohenzollern, to us— and with the Germans; Nicholas writes his personal view of the matter. By 1905, when the last letter was written, the disintegration of Russian autocracy and Romanov rule was well advanced. It was a year of revolution in Russia and of military disaster in the Far East in the war against Japan. Ten years later Russia was at war again, and Nicky was at the front in command of the ill-clothed, ill-fed, and ill-equipped army; this left Alix in command of the Russian Court, with the mad monk, Rasputin, in command of Alix.

The collapse of the Russian economy, together with military defeats, made revolution inevitable, and by March 17, 1917, Nicholas II, last of the Romanovs, did not command so much as a bodyguard. He was captured by the Bolsheviks and taken, with his whole family, to Ekaterinberg. With the advance of Kolchak's counter-revolutionary army toward that city in July, 1918, he and his entire family were shot—with the possible exception, of course, of Anastasia. Lenin, who had been an obscure law student at Kazan University when the first letter below was written, succeeded to power.

Windsor Castle
27th June, 1894.

My dearest Mama,— I am afraid you must be annoyed by my long silence. I am rather ashamed of it myself; but it shows how happy I am to be here with my Alix. I snatch every hour I can to be with her. Many times I began to write in her room, but all my efforts to produce a good letter ended in nothing because every moment I simply had to get up and embrace her. Well, there it is. At the moment I am in my own room, while Yanisheff is working with her. Yesterday he attended Sunday service with us all, after that I presented him to Granny. He is very glad to be in England,

and rather proud because he tells everybody he didn't lose his way in London once. Tomorrow he is going to Oxford where various theologians are expecting him! I am delighted by my two days at Sandringham—*very* sad however that Alix wasn't there! The day I came, there was an auction at Uncle Bertie's stud: fifty horses were sold. I bought two mares with foals, and Aunt Alix was very pleased about that! The house-party was rather strange. Most of them were horse dealers, among others a Baron Hirsch. The Cousins rather enjoyed the situation and kept teasing me about it; but I tried to keep away as much as I could, and not to talk. Even Aunt Alix herself was seeing many of them for the first time. We spent two days at Marlborough House, arriving the day before Victoria's birthday. They let us go, I mean Alix and myself, alone; which is very strange! In the evening we went to *Madame Sans-Gêne*, which I liked immensely! The French acted marvellously well and the play was admirably produced! During the day we went to see Louise and MacDuff, saw their little girls and had tea with them. Georgie's and May's boy will be christened on July 16th at White Lodge, where we were a few days after his birth. What a nice healthy child! Here at Windsor last week I visited the barracks of the Horse Guards and the Coldstreamers. The Blues did a very beautiful musical ride for me. And the infantry did battalion drill with rifles, and gymnastics to music—very interesting indeed! They asked me to dinner, but I couldn't give a definite answer because Granny loves me so and doesn't like me missing dinner—nor does Alix! I met the Empress Eugenie yesterday, and liked her very much; she is so kind and friendly. With her arrived the elder Napoleon, who came to see us last winter. They dined with us, and stayed for the night. Last Friday we had two operas in the Waterloo Chamber. *Philemon and Baucis* and the new opera of Massenet's, *La Navarraise*—very beautiful, but very sad! Jacob Ivanovich Shakhokovskoi dined here the other day. I was very glad to see Mr. Heath, whom I presented to Granny. She wanted him to stay here for two days, but he as usual disappeared into somewhere in England, and won't reappear till we are going. I'm glad to be able to spend two or three days at Osborne. I think I'll leave here on the 9th—Granny has asked me to stay till then! I will then have spent exactly a month and a day in England. I must finish now—time for lunch. I hope the weather and everything is all right with you. Many kisses for you, my dear darling Mama, for dear Papa, and the others. Best love from Alix. God bless you. —Your loving,

NICKY.

Peterhof, 23rd July, 1897.

Dear Mama,—I'm sorry to tell you we shall have to give Wilhelm the rank of Admiral in our navy. Uncle Alexei reminded me of it; and I think, no matter how disagreeable it may be, we are obliged to let him wear our naval uniform; particularly since he made me last year a Captain in his own navy and, what's much worse I'll have to greet him as such at Kronstadt.

It makes me sick to think of it! [In the original, in French: "C'est à vomir!"]

Imperial Palace at Peterhof, 19th October, 1905.

My dearest Mama,—I do not know how to begin this letter.

We have been through such grave and unprecedented events that I feel as if the last time I wrote to you was a year ago. You remember, no doubt, those January days when we were together at Tsarskoe—they were miserable, weren't they? But they are *nothing* in comparison with what has happened now!

I am going to try to describe the position here as briefly as possible. A month ago yesterday we returned from Transund, and the first fortnight was comparatively quiet.

All sorts of conferences took place in Moscow, which Durnovo permitted, I do not know why. Everything was being prepared for the railway strike. The first one began in and round about Moscow, and then spread all over Russia practically at once.

Petersburg and Moscow were entirely cut off from the interior. For exactly a week today the Baltic railway has not been functioning. The only way to get to town is by sea. How convenient at this time of year! From the railways the strike spread to the factories and workshops, and then even to the municipal organisations and services, and lastly to the Railway Department of the Ministry of Ways and Communications. What a shame, just think of it!

Poor little Liukoff is desperate, and he cannot cope at all with his staff.

God knows what happened in the universities. Every kind of riff-raff walked in from the streets, riot was loudly proclaimed—nobody seemed to mind. The governing bodies of the universities and the engineering schools were granted *autonomy* but they do not know how to use it. They couldn't even lock the doors in time to keep out the impudent crowd, and then of course complained they could not get any help from the police—but do you remember what they used to say in years gone by?

It makes me sick to read the news! Nothing but new strikes in schools and factories, murdered policemen, Cossacks and soldiers, riots, disorder, mutinies. But the ministers, instead of acting with quick decision, only assemble in council like a lot of frightened hens and cackle about providing united ministerial action.

When at various "meetings"—that is the fashionable word nowadays—[*the revolutionaries had adopted the English word "meeting," but used it exclusively in the sense of revolutionary meeting*], it was openly decided to proclaim an armed rising, and I heard about it, I immediately gave the command of all the troops in the Petersburg district to Trepoff. I ordered him to divide the whole town into sections, with a special commander for each. The troops were ordered to use their arms immediately if attacked. This was the only way the movement or revolution could be stopped, because Trepoff made it quite plain to the populace by his proclamations that any disorder would be ruthlessly put down; and, of course, everybody believed that. So the ominous quiet days began, quiet indeed, because there was complete order in the streets; but at the same time everybody knew that something was going to happen—the troops were waiting for the signal, but the other side would not begin. One had the same feeling as before a thunderstorm in summer! Everybody was on edge and extremely nervous, and, of course, that sort of strain could not go on for long. Through all those horrible days, I constantly met Witte. We very often met in the early morning to part only in the evening, when night fell. There were only two ways open: to find an energetic soldier and crush the rebellion by sheer force. There would be time to breathe then but, as likely as not, one would have to use force again in a few months; and that would mean rivers of blood, and in the end we should be where we had started. I mean to say, government authority would be vindicated, but there would be no positive result and no possibility of progress achieved. The other way out would be to give to the people their civil rights, freedom of speech and press, also to have all laws confirmed by a State Duma—that, of course, would be a constitution. Witte defends this very energetically. He says that, while it is not without risk, it's the only way out at the present moment. Almost everybody I had an opportunity of consulting is of the same opinion. Witte put it quite clearly to me that he would accept the Presidency of the Council of Ministers only on the condition that his programme was agreed to, and his actions not interfered with. He and Alexei Obolensky drew up the Manifesto. We discussed it for two days, and in the end, invoking God's help, I signed. My dear Mama, you can't imagine what I went through before that moment; in my telegram I could not explain all the circumstances which brought me to this terrible decision, which nevertheless I took quite consciously. From all over Russia they cried for it, they begged for it, and around me many—very many—held the same views. I had nobody to rely on except honest Trepoff. There was no other way out than to cross one self and give what everyone was asking for. My only consolation is that such is the will of God, and this grave decision will lead my dear Russia out of the intolerable chaos she has been in for nearly a year. The situation is very serious, in spite of the fact that I keep receiving declarations of very touching loyalty and thankfulness. The people seem to have gone mad —some from joy, others from discontent. The local administrations do not quite know how to act under the new régime— nothing is fixed yet—everything seems to be done by gentlemen's agreement. The very next day Witte found out what he was in for—many to whom he offered positions under him in one capacity or another now refused to accept. Old Pobiedonostseff has resigned; his place will be taken by Alexei Obolensky. Glazoff has resigned too, but we have no successor for him as yet. All the Ministers are resigning and we have to find new ones, but Witte must see to that. At the same time it is essential to keep order in the towns, where loyal and hostile demonstrations are continually taking place and bloody clashes occur between them. We are in the midst of a revolution with an administrative apparatus entirely disorganised, and in this lies the main danger. But God Almighty will be our help. I feel Him supporting me and putting strength in me, which gives me courage and does not allow me to lose heart. I assure you we have lived years in these days, such torments, doubts, and indecisions. Your dear letter has just been brought to me, which you sent with Isvolsky. I thank you from the bottom of my heart, my dear Mama. I know you are praying for your poor Nicky. Our Saviour be with you! May God save and give peace to Russia. Yours with all my heart,

NICKY.

Uncrowned King of Ireland

CHARLES STEWART PARNELL

Charles Stewart Parnell (1846-1891; Irish statesman.) His mother, Delia Tudor Stewart, was the daughter of Commodore Charles Stewart, U.S.N., commander of Old Ironsides in the War of 1812; his father was a member of a family of English gentry that had emigrated from England to Ireland in the seventeenth century. Thus he was a rarity—an Irish statesman with American and English blood, a Protestant in a Catholic nation. Yet the Irish used to say with pride that "England has Queen Victoria; our King is Charles Parnell."

Parnell was elected to Parliament in 1875; becoming leader of the Home Rule Party, he was imprisoned in 1881 under the Coercion Act for agitation. In 1886 he and Gladstone formed their famous parliamentary alliance for the object of attaining Irish Home Rule, but the alliance split Gladstone's party, the Liberals, and restored the Marquis of Salisbury to power.

Then in 1887 the London Times, *seeking to discredit Home Rule before the country, published a series of articles alleging a connection between Parnell and the Phoenix Park murders and other terrorist activities. A Parliamentary Committee investigated the allegations, found the evidence forged, and awarded Parnell £5,000 damages. But scandal, once having the scent, pursued him until his death. In 1890, Captain William Henry O' Shea named Parnell co-respondent in a divorce suit against his wife, Katherine. Parnell was found guilty. The Liberal Party deprived him of his position of leadership, and vast numbers of the Irish people, whom he had served more conspicuously and brilliantly than any man to his time, turned their backs upon him. He married Kitty O'Shea, but the invective continued. In September, 1891, he wrote this note to his mother, who remained faithful to him to the last. A month later he died.*

I AM WEARY, dear mother, of these troubles, weary unto death; but it is all in a good cause. With health and the assistance of my friends I am confident of the result. The statements my enemies have so often made regarding my relations with you are on a par with the endless calumnies they shoot upon me from behind every bush. Let them pass. They will die of their own venom. It would indeed be dignifying them to notice their existence!

"Violent Beyond Expectation"

WILLIAM PITT

William Pitt (1759-1806; English statesman.) Politics ran in Pitt's family as music ran in Mozart's. He made his first speech in Parliament when he was twenty-two. His father, William Pitt the Elder, First Earl of Chatham, had been perhaps the greatest prime minister England had seen; and yet his son is thought by most to have been even greater. Eight years after writing this letter the prodigious Pitt was Prime Minister, First Lord of the Treasury, and Chancellor of the Exchequer.

By holding office from 1784 to 1801, one of the longest ministries in English history, the Younger Pitt was able to introduce countless reforms in finance, customs laws, and the administration of India. His greatest achievement, however, was the forging of the coalition of European powers that finally brought Napoleon to his knees. Pitt began his second ministry on May 10, 1804; the next fall saw his greatest victory, when Nelson defeated the French fleet at Trafalgar, thus making impossible the invasion of England. But the Emperor's triumphs at Ulm and at Austerlitz nullified the mutual security treaties Mr. Pitt had so laboriously put together, and their creator was overwhelmed by the disaster and retired to his villa at Putney, where he died less than two weeks later. His work had been sound, though, and his patient diplomacy prevailed in the end.

Bond Street, Saturday, January 21, 1775.

My dear Mother,

My father is now getting up, and has had, I am told, a good night. I have this minute been to him with your message, which he cannot answer till he is up and has breakfasted; as he cannot form his resolution about coming till then. In the mean time, I offer a word or two in answer to your letter.

Nothing prevented his speech from being the most forcible that can be imagined, and administration fully felt it. The matter and manner both were striking; far beyond what I can express. It was everything that was superior; and though it had not the desired effect on an obdurate House of Lords, it must have an infinite effect without doors, the bar being crowded with Americans, &c. Lord Suffolk, I cannot say answered him, but—spoke after him. He was a contemptible orator indeed, with paltry matter and a whining delivery. Lord Shelburne spoke well, and supported the motion warmly. Lord Camden was *supreme* with only *one* exception, and as zealous as possible. Lord Rockingham spoke shortly but sensibly; and the Duke of Richmond well, and with much candour as to the Declaratory act. Upon the whole, it was a noble debate. The ministry were violent beyond expectation, almost to madness. Instead of recalling the troops now there, they talked of sending more, &c.

I can now tell you correctly: my father has slept well, without any burning in the feet or restlessness. He has had no pain, but is lame in one ankle near the instep, from standing so long. No wonder he is lame: his first speech lasted above an hour, and the second half an hour—surely, the two finest speeches that ever were made before, unless by himself! He will be with you to dinner by four o'clock. Adieu, my dear mother. A thousand loves to all around you. I wish I had time and memory to give an account of all I heard, and all I felt. Your ever dutiful son,

WILLIAM PITT.

"What Pain I Must Have Caused You"

FRANKLIN DELANO ROOSEVELT

Franklin Delano Roosevelt (1882-1945; American statesman; 32nd President of the United States.) The only child of James and Sara Delano Roosevelt, F.D.R. had a sometimes trying but always close relationship with his mother. Their strong wills clashed frequently—when he and Anna Eleanor Roosevelt, a distant cousin, became engaged, for example; or when he chose to resume his political career after only partial recovery from a crippling attack of infantile paralysis. Part of the strength his mother gave him was the strength to disagree with her.

Roosevelt's father died in 1900; his mother lived until 1941. She and her son engaged in frequent correspondence, but of all his letters I have selected only two—an immensely revealing letter in which he tells her of his engagement, and a hastily-written note sent in 1911, when he was a member of the New York State Senate. I think the second letter shows what joy F.D.R. extracted from the practice of politics; that's why he became so good at it.

Roosevelt studied at Groton, then at Harvard and Columbia Law School. The next step in the pattern was for him to become a junior member of an important law firm, and so he did, but it bored him. Running for office as a Democrat in solidly Republican Dutchess County seemed more exciting; he ran, and he won. What's more, he dropped many "bombs," to borrow his own word, and attracted wide attention.

After supporting Woodrow Wilson at the 1912 Democratic Convention, he was rewarded with appointment as Assistant Secretary of the Navy, and he served in this capacity until the end of the war. Then he was nominated as Vice-Presidential candidate on the Democratic ticket headed by James M. Cox of Ohio. A Republican landslide sent Roosevelt back to New York and the practice of law. A year later he was stricken with polio while vacationing at Campobello, his summer home in New Brunswick. He never regained the full use of his legs.

In both 1924 and 1928 Roosevelt placed Alfred E. Smith's name in nomination for the Democratic candidate for President. In 1928 Smith won the nomination but lost his home state of New York while Roosevelt, running for governor, was elected. F.D.R. was re-elected in 1930, nominated for the Presidency in 1932, and in the national election defeated Hoover by 472 to 59 electoral votes. He carried forty-two states and his plurality was seven million votes. In 1936 he defeated Alfred M. Landon by a plurality of over eleven million votes; and in 1940 he became the first American President to be elected to a third term.

After Pearl Harbor, Roosevelt was responsible for both foreign and military policy, and the New Dealers became less prominent in the administration. He defeated Thomas E. Dewey in 1944, began his fourth term, but then, on April 12, 1945, died suddenly at Warm Springs, Georgia, where he had first gone thirty years before to convalesce from his attack of polio. He was buried at his home in Hyde Park, New York, amid national and international mourning.

No man since Lincoln has been more deeply loved, and more profoundly hated, by Americans. The hatred was so strong that the cigarette holder went out of fashion for fifteen years. But the love was stronger, and will last longer.

The Harvard Crimson,
Dec. 4, 1903.
Friday.

Dᴇᴀʀᴇsᴛ Mᴀᴍᴀ—

I have been absolutely rushed to death since I came back, with a thousand things to attend to & meetings of the nomination committee (for Senior Class elections) lasting up to 2 in the morning. I am to be nominated anyway for an office & am naturally delighted—You will be as surprised as I was when you hear *what* office—But I don't stand a ghost of a show of being elected to it—though I am pleased at the honor of nomination.

Dearest Mama—I know what pain I must have caused you and you know I wouldn't do it if I really could have helped it—mais tu sais, me voilà! Thats all that could be said—I know my mind, have known it for a long time, and know that I could never think otherwise: Result: I am the happiest man just now in the world; likewise the luckiest—And for you, dear Mummy, you know that nothing can ever change what we have always been & always will be to each other—only now you have two children to love & to love you—and Eleanor as you know will always be a daughter to you in every true way—

I shall be here over Sunday working all the time but will write you a longer letter then—

Excuse this hurried scrawl, it doesn't express anything but you know what I mean

Your ever loving

F.D.R.

Albany, N.Y.
[July 18, 1911]
Tuesday

Dᴇᴀʀᴇsᴛ Mᴀᴍᴀ—

I have just received your dear letter of last night, and this may catch you in N. Y. before you get away. I got here all right last night and we sat until 11:30 p.m.

Today I dropped a bomb in the Senate by a motion in favor of immediate action on Direct Primaries. It provoked a heated 3-hour discussion and I was called some choice names, but it has had a good effect and may hasten matters. But on the other hand it may prolong the session thro' our attempt to give the State an honest bill.

It is now 6 p.m. and we shall probably sit here until midnight. I am going to send out for a glass of milk soon.

Give my love to Aunt Doe and goodbye. I'm locked in and will send this out by page.

Loads of love. You can count on my getting to Campo at the earliest possible moment.

Ever

F.D.R.

"A Perfect Dream of Delight"

THEODORE ROOSEVELT

Theodore Roosevelt (1858-1919; American soldier, author, and statesman; 26th President of the United States.) The "strenuous life" was probably not what anyone would have foreseen for the sickly, myopic, asthmatic youth that was Theodore Roosevelt. Like F.D.R.—that other famed descendant of Claes Martenszan van Rosenvelt—Teddy achieved health and vigor almost by an effort of will.

The letters that follow were all written before Roosevelt was in the public eye. It is astonishing how accurately they blueprint the man he was to be; the nine-year-old boy who is "sorry the trees have been cut down" became our most dynamic force for national Conservation. The twenty-year-old who practices "a good deal with the rifle" had to use that rifle as a colonel with his Rough Riders in Cuba.

The last of the letters was written four days after T.R.'s marriage to Alice Hathaway Lee. They are "having an ideal honeymoon," he tells "darling little Muffie," his mother. His wife "is the sweetest little dor-mouse that ever lived." Poor Teddy—he lost both his wife and his mother on the same day—February 14, 1884. And later that year he also believed that his short but promising political career had ended; a member of the state legislature, and a leader of the "young insurgents" in the Repub-

lican party, he had backed the losing side in an intra-party struggle.

It was after this triple blow that he went to the Dakotas for his famous writing and ranching binge, completing three books in four years. Then in 1886 he picked up the pieces; he re-entered New York City politics in a campaign for the mayoralty (and lost); and he courted Edith Kermit Carow (and married her). In 1897, just after the publication of the last of his four-volume study, The Winning of the West, he was appointed Assistant Secretary of the Navy under McKinley, but resigned that desk job to organize and fight with the volunteer regiment, the Rough Riders.

He became a national hero, and although he had been defeated in the mayoralty election he now had no difficulty in winning the governorship of the state. Less than a year later Teddy found himself being boomed, much to his displeasure, for Vice President of the United States. The Republican bosses hoped to overcome his growing popularity by consigning him to the obscurity of the Vice Presidency, but McKinley's assassination within a year of his inauguration cancelled out these political plans—a fact that led Mark Hanna to say, on the McKinley funeral train, "I told William McKinley it was a mistake to nominate that wild man at Philadelphia. . . . Now look, that damned cowboy is President of the United States!"

The fears of the conservative Republicans were justified. Roosevelt's domestic policies were dramatized by his "trust-busting" and his determination to conserve the country's natural resources. His foreign policy was equally vigorous, and was characterized by his advice to "speak softly, and carry a big stick." He was elected to a second term, and left the White House in 1908 to go on a big-game hunting expedition. Absence made the heart fond, and he announced for the Republican nomination in 1912. Taft got it; and Roosevelt joined the insurgent Bull Moose Party and ran anyway. He beat Taft, but Wilson beat them both. T.R. died shortly after the end of the war.

New York April 28th, 1868.

MY DEAR MAMA

I have just received your letter! What an excitement! How nice to read it. What long letters you do write. I don't see how you can write them. My mouth opened wide with astonishment when

I heard how many flowers were sent in to you. I could revel in the buggie ones. I jumped with delight when I found you had heard a mocking-bird. Get some of its feathers if you can. Thank Johnny for the feathers of the soldier's cap, give him my love also. We cried when you wrote about Grand-Mamma. Give my love to the good natured (to use your own expression) handsome lion, Conie, Johnny, Maud, and Aunt Lucy. I am sorry the trees have been cut down. Aunt Annie, Edith and Ellie send their love to you and all, I send mine too. I send this picture to Conie. In the letters you write to me tell me how many curiosities and living things you have got for me. I miss Conie very much. I wish I were with you and Johnny for I could hunt for myself. There is Conie's letter.

October 8, 1878

Darling, beloved, little motherling: I have just loved your dear, funny, pathetic, little letter, and I am now going to write you the longest letter I ever write, and if it is still rather short, you must recollect that it takes Teddy-boy a long time to write. I have enjoyed Charlie Dickey's being here extremely, and I think I have been of some service to him. We always go to prayers together; for his own sake, I have not been much with him in the daytime, but every evening, we spend a good part of the time together in my room or his. He is just the same, honest, fine fellow as ever, and unless I am very much mistaken, is going to make a thorough success in every way of college. My studies do not come very well this year, as I have to work nearly as hard on Saturday as on any other day—six, seven or eight hours. Some of the studies are extremely interesting, however, especially Political Economy and Metaphysics. These are both rather hard, requiring a good deal of work, but they are even more interesting than my Natural History courses; and all the more so from the fact that I radically disagree on many points with the men whose books we are reading, (Mill and Ferrier). One of my zoological courses is rather dry, but the other I like very much, though it necessitates ten or twelve hours' work a week. My German is not very interesting, but I expect that my Italian will be when I get further on. For exercise, I have had to rely on walking, but today I have regularly begun sparring. I practice a good deal with the rifle, walking to and from the range, which is nearly three miles off; my scores have been fair, although not very good. Funnily enough, I have enjoyed quite a burst of popularity since I came back, having been elected into several different clubs. My own friends have, as usual, been perfect trumps, and I have been asked to spend Sundays with at least a half-dozen of them, but I have to come back to Cambridge Sunday mornings on account of Sunday School, which makes it more difficult to pay visits. I indulged in a luxury the other day in buying "The Library of British Poets," and I delight in my purchase very much, but I have been so busy that I have hardly had time to read it yet. I shall really have to have a new bookcase for I have nowhere to put my books. . . . Your loving son, T. Jr.

Cambridge, March 16, 1879

DARLING MUFFIE, I got home this morning at 11 o'clock, too late for church, the cars being delayed six hours; and have just returned from Sunday School. How did darling Bysie enjoy her trip to Boston? The only thing I minded was missing her. I never have passed a pleasanter two weeks than those just gone by; I enjoyed every moment. The first two or three days I had asthma, but, funnily enough, this left me entirely as soon as I went into camp. The thermometer was below zero pretty often, but I was not bothered by the cold atall, except one night when I camped out on the trail of a caribou (which we followed two days without getting more than a glimpse of the animal). Out in the opens when there was any wind it was very disagreable but in the woods the wind never blows and as long as we were moving about it made little difference how low the temperature was, but sitting still for lunch we felt it immediately. I learned how to manage snowshoes very quickly, and enjoyed going on them greatly. I have never seen a grander or more beautiful sight than the northern woods in winter. The evergreens laden with snow make the most beautiful contrast of green and white, and when it freezes after a rain all the trees look as though they were made of crystal. The snow under foot being about three feet deep, and drifting to twice that depth in places, completely changes the aspect of things. I visited two lumber camps, staying at one four days; it was great fun to see such a perfectly unique type of life. I shot a buck, a coon and some rabbits and partridges and trapped a lynx and a fox—so my trip was a success in every way.

There seems to be a general feeling among the family that I

have not done my duty in writing of late, which makes me think you did not get some I sent. Did Elliott get the three sheet letter I sent him about six weeks ago? It was the longest letter I ever wrote.

Love to the trio, and especially to my own sweet Motherling herself. *Your Loving Son*

Oyster Bay, October 31, 1880

DARLING LITTLE MUFFIE, I have been living in a perfect dream of delight. The house is just perfection; Kate cooks deliciously, and Mary Ann is exactly *the* servant for us; and Davis does his part beautifully too, always sending in his respects in the morning to "the good lady" as he styles Alice. We breakfast at ten, dine at two, and take tea at seven; thanks to Bysies thoughtfulness Alice does not have to order any meals. In the morning we go out driving in the buggy, behind Lightfoot, who is in splendid trim. In the afternoon we play tennis or walk in Fleets woods. In the evening I read aloud—Pickwick Papers, Quentin Durward or Keats poems. We are having an ideal honeymoon; and the dear little wife can rest all she wants to, and is the sweetest little dormouse that ever lived. The pretty darling sends her warmest love to you, Bysie, Pussie and Nell. *Ever Your Loving Son*

"The President des Etats-Unis"

HARRY S. TRUMAN

Harry S. Truman (1884-   ; American politician; 33rd President of the United States.) He was brought up near Independence, Mo., on the family farm, and went to school in town. He served as a captain of artillery in World War I, with the 35th Division in France. He became the owner of a haberdashery store in Kansas City but lost the business in the agricultural depression of 1921. His first elected position was that of county judge in Kansas City. He was presiding judge of the Jackson County Court (1926-34) and in 1934 won a seat in the U.S. Senate, to which he was re-elected in 1940.

During World War II Senator Truman became prominent as the chairman of a special committee to investigate the national defense effort. Dissatisfaction with Henry A. Wallace, Roosevelt's running mate in 1940, led to the suggestion that Truman be given the assignment in the 1944 election. He succeeded to the Presidency on April 12, 1945, in circumstances vividly described in the first letter below. His re-election in 1948 has been called the most unexpected victory in American political history.

"I wrote Mama often," Mr. Truman said, "and regularly each weekend would telephone her and sister Mary, who lived with her. She was a wonderful mother. At ninety-two she was still keen and alert and saw things in their true perspective, even at a time like this. When asked by a press representative at her home in Grandview, Missouri, to comment on how she felt about her son being President, she said, 'I can't really be glad he is President, because I'm sorry that President Roosevelt is dead. If he had been voted in, I'd be out waving a flag, but it doesn't seem right to be very happy or wave a flag now.'"

April 1945

DEAR MAMA & MARY: Well, I have had the most momentous, and the most trying time anyone could possibly have, since Thursday, April 12th.

Maybe you'd like to know just what happened. We'd had a long, drawn out debate in the Senate and finally came to an agreement for a recess at 5 P.M. until Friday, Apr. 13th.

When I went back to my office, a call from Sam Rayburn, Speaker of the House, was awaiting me. Sam wanted me to come over to the House side of the Capitol and talk to him about policy and procedure and, as Alice in Wonderland would say, "shoes and ships and sealing wax and things." . . .

But—as soon as I came into the room Sam told me that Steve Early, the President's confidential press secretary wanted to talk to me. I called the White House, and Steve told me to come to the White House "as quickly and as quietly" as I could. Well I told Sam I had to go to the White House on a special call and that he should say nothing about it.

I ran all the way to my office in the Senate by way of the unfrequented corridors in the Capitol, told my office force that I'd been summoned to the White House and to say nothing about it. . . .

When I arrived at the Pennsylvania entrance to the most famous house in America, a couple of ushers met me . . . and then took me up to Mrs. Roosevelt's study on the second floor.

She and Mrs. Boettiger, her daugher and her husband the Lt. Col., and Steve Early were there. Mrs. Roosevelt put her arm on my shoulder and said, "Harry, the President is dead."

It was the only time in my life, I think, that I ever felt as if I'd had a real shock. I had hurried to the White House to see the President, and when I arrived, I found I was the President. No one in the history of our country ever had it happen to him just that way.

. . . We waited for Bess and Margaret to arrive. We then had to scurry around and find a Bible for me to put my hand upon to take the oath. They finally found one. If I'd known what was afoot, I'd have used Grandpa Truman's Bible, which was in my office bookcase.

You of course know from the papers what happened and what has happened since.

Saturday afternoon, the White House funeral; Sunday morning the burial at Hyde Park, today my speech to Congress.

This afternoon we moved to this house, diagonally across the street (Penn. Ave.) from the White House, until the Roosevelts had time to move out of the White House. We tried staying at the apartment, but it wouldn't work. I can't move without at least ten Secret Service men and twenty policemen. People who lived in our apartment couldn't get in and out without a pass. So— we moved out with suitcases. Our furniture is still there and will be for some time. . . . But I've paid the rent for this month and will pay for another month if they don't get the old White House re-decorated by that time.

My greatest trial was today when I addressed the Congress. It seemed to go over all right, from the ovation I received. Things have gone so well that I'm almost as scared as I was Thursday when Mrs. R. told me what had happened. Maybe it will come out all right.

Soon as we get settled in the White House you'll both be here to visit us. Lots of love from your very much worried son and bro.

Harry

April 1945

DEAR MAMA & MARY, Well, the Washington Post had your pictures yesterday morning and the finest kind of statements from both you and Vivian. My Press Staff said that the smartest press agent in the world could not have written any better ones. I told them that my family all told the truth all the time and that they did not need a press agent.

I have had a most strenuous time for the last six days. I was sworn in at 7:09 P.M. Eastern War Time Apr. 12, and it is now 9 P.M. April 18th. Six days President of the United States! It is hardly believable.

Before I was sworn in, I had to make two decisions of world-wide import—to carry on the war and to let the Peace Conference go ahead at San Francisco. Saturday and Sunday were spent on the last rites for the departed President. Monday, the Congress had to be told what I would do. It took all Sunday afternoon, half the night and until 11 A.M. Monday to get the job done on the speech. But I guess there was inspiration in it for it took Congress and the country by storm, apparently. Spent Monday afternoon seeing people and making all sorts of decisions, everyone of which would touch millions of people. Tuesday morning all the reporters in town and a lot more came to cross question me. They gave me a pretty hefty fifteen minutes, but even that ordeal seemed to click.

Had to spend all afternoon and evening preparing a five minute speech for the radio for the fighting men and women. It was after one o'clock when I turned in. This day has been a dinger too. I'm about to go to bed, but I thought I'd better write you a note. Hope you are both well.

Lots of love,

Harry

April 29, 1945

Dear Mama & Mary:—Received your letter with the one from Dr. Graham in it and was glad to get it. Hope you and Mary have not been bothered too much. It is terrible—and I mean terrible—nuisance to be kin to the President of the United States. Reporters have been haunting every relative and purported relative I ever heard of, and they've probably made life miserable for my mother, brother and sister. I am sorry for it, but it can't be helped.

A guard has to go with Bess and Margaret everywhere they go —and they don't like it. They both spend a lot of time figuring how to beat the game, but it just can't be done. In a country as big as this one there are necessarily a lot of nuts and people with peculiar ideas. They seem to focus on the White House and the President's kin. Hope you won't get too badly upset about it.

Between the papers and the nuts they surely made life miserable for the Roosevelt family. Maybe they can have some peace now. I hope so.

I must caution both of you to take good care of your health. Don't let the pests get you down. I'm writing this before breakfast—before anyone is up.

Love to you both.

Harry

May 8, 1945

THE WHITE HOUSE
Washington

Dear Mama & Mary:—

I am sixty-one this morning, and I slept in the President's room in the White House last night. They have finished the painting and have some of the furniture in place. I'm hoping it will all be ready for you by Friday. My expensive gold pen doesn't work as well as it should.

This will be a historical day. At 9:00 o'clock this morning I must make a broadcast to the country: announcing the German surrender. The papers were signed yesterday morning and hostilities will cease on all fronts at midnight tonight. Isn't that some birthday present?

Have had one heck of a time with the Prime Minister of Great Britain. He, Stalin and the U.S. President made an agreement to release the news all at once from the three capitals at an hour that would fit us all. We agreed on 9 A. M. Washington time which is 3 P.M. London and 4 P.M. Moscow time.

Mr. Churchill began calling me at daylight to know if we shouldn't make an immediate release without considering the Russians. He was refused and then he kept pushing me to talk to Stalin. He finally had to stick to the agreed plan—but he was mad as a wet hen.

Things have moved at a terrific rate here since April 12. Never a day has gone by that some momentous decision didn't have to be made. So far luck has been with me. I hope it keeps up. It can't stay with me forever however and I hope when the mistake comes it won't be too great to remedy.

We are looking forward to a grand visit with you. I may not be able to come for you as planned but I'm sending the safest finest plane and all kinds of help so please don't disappoint me.

Lots & lots of love to you both.

Harry

June 16, 1945

DEAR MAMA & MARY:—The deed came day before yesterday and that gives you a rent free home for the rest of your life anyway—and that goes for you both. So now take good care of yourselves and live as long as you can—"forever" the Mesopotamian Kings used to say to each other—"O King, live forever." But they never did, only in statuary, and vandals usually carried that off to decorate some other building than the king's tomb or used it for a hitching post.

I am having a strenuous time. Every day I see some notable of some sort, pin medals on heroes and make world shaking decisions. It seems to agree with me for I've gained twelve pounds since last January: I guess it's because I have nothing to look forward to but retirement. . . .

Had a dozen people over for dinner last evening—just the military aide and his wife and kids and the Naval aide and his wife and Marine sergeant boy—a nice kid by the way—and John Snyder and his wife and lovely daughter. She's about Margie's age. Vaughan's daughter is about sixteen and his boy is ten—13 at the table.

Three generals came in to see me yesterday and General Patch gave me Herr Goering's baton. I always get those dirty Nazis mixed up but it makes no difference. Anyway it's the fat Marshal's insignia of office. It is about a foot and a half long, made of ivory inlaid with gold eagles and iron crosses with diamond studded end caps and platinum rings around it for engraving. Must have cost several thousand dollars—maybe forty—to make. Can you imagine a fat pig like that strutting around with a forty thousand dollar bauble—at the poor taxpayer's expense and making 'em like it? It goes to a military museum.

Monday I entertain Eisenhower, a real man. Tuesday I go to Olympia, Washington—Saturday a week from today San Francisco, Sunday back here, Monday June 25th appear in the Senate and Wed. 27th Independence, 28th K.C. and home for a few days and July 3rd Governors Conference at Mackinac, Mich., and then get ready to go to Berlin. How would you like to be the President des Etats Unis? It's a hell of a life.

Love to you both.

Harry

Berlin, July 23, 1945

DEAR MAMA & MARY:—Your letter of the 16th came yesterday and those of the 17th and 19th came this morning. I am most happy to hear from you. I suppose the radio keeps you well informed on my movements.

The conference has met every day since the 17th. Many things have been accomplished and many more which should be accomplished have not been acted upon. But we have time yet to get most of them in some sort of shape for a peace conference.

Stalin gave his state dinner night before last, and it was a wow. Started with caviar and vodka and wound up with watermelon and champagne, with smoked fish, fresh fish, venison, chicken, duck and all sorts of vegetables in between. There was a toast every five minutes until at least twenty-five had been drunk. I ate very little and drank less, but it was a colorful and enjoyable occasion.

When I had Stalin & Churchill here for dinner, I think I told you that a young sergeant named List from Philadelphia played the piano, and a boy from the Metropolitan Orchestra played the violin. They are the best we have, and they are very good. Stalin sent to Moscow and brought on his two best pianists and two female violinists. They were excellent. Played Chopin, Liszt, Tschaikowsky and all the rest. I congratulated him and them on their ability. . . . It was a nice dinner. . . .

"One Must Learn to Abandon Dreams"

VICTORIA LOUISE

Victoria Louise (1840-1901; Empress of Austria.) The "Empress Frederick" would probably not have a claim on our attention if she had not been the eldest daughter of Queen Victoria, and if

*her eldest son had not grown up to be the Kaiser Wilhelm. She
married Frederick III of Prussia in 1858 and bore him five children. She wrote to her mother about all her dilemmas, both domestic and imperial, and was rewarded by a warm and maternal
sympathy. The first letter was written during the Franco-Prussian
War and shows the strain occassioned by that conflict; it minutely
concerns the development of her son. Sixteen years later she dis-
cusses the same subject. History agrees with Victoria Louise.*

January 28, 1871

A THOUSAND thanks for your dear letter by messenger which
gave me so much pleasure with all its kind wishes for the 25th,
and yesterday our dear Willie's birthday. He was so delighted
with your presents. I had arranged a little surprise for him and
the others, allowing them to go to the Schauspielhaus and see a
Panorama, which amused them very much. We are trembling
and hoping for peace! This wish or passionate prayer of two whole
nations must be granted—it would be a disappointment too dreadful to bear, if peace did not come. Everyone is worn out with the
strain on all one's feelings—on the one side, patriotism and the
pride which looks upon one's troops, and on the other the pity for
the poor French, the grief at the death of so many of our dear
soldiers, and the anxiety, which never leaves one day or night,
about those still in the field.

I telegraphed our title to you yesterday. We are called Kaiser-
liche und Königliche Hoheit Kronprinz des Deutschen Reichs und
von Preussen. The King is called Deutscher Kaiser, König von
Preussen, but usually Kaiser und König; the Empress, of course,
"die Kaiserin-Königin". She is beyond measure delighted at your
kind words to her and those to me about her. I am always spoken
to as Imperial Highness (I own I liked the other better), but as
it reminds one of the great political fact of Germany's being
gathered under one head, I am proud to bear this title. I send
you today the extracts from Fritz's letters. Pray let them remain
unknown to anyone except just Lenchen and Christian. I have
not even told Fritz that they are copied and sent to you.

Dear Aunt Clementine's letter I have sent as you wished to
Alice, without letting anyone else see it. You can surely answer
her that if the French Government had listened to yours in this
month of July, they would never have exposed their beautiful

capital to the unavoidable horrors of war, siege and bombardment! They were warned, but would not listen.

I am sure you would be pleased with William if you were to see him—he has Bertie's pleasant, amiable ways—and can be very winning. He is not possessed of brilliant abilities, nor of any strength of character or talents, but he is a dear boy, and I hope and trust will grow up a useful man. He has an excellent tutor, I never saw or knew a better, and all the care that can be bestowed on mind and body is taken of him. I watch over him myself, over each detail, even the minutest, of his education, as his Papa had never had the time to occupy himself with the children. These next few years will be very critical and important for him, as they are the passage from childhood to manhood. I am happy to say that between him and me there is a bond of love and confidence, which I feel sure nothing can destroy. He has very strong health and would be a very pretty boy were it not for that wretched unhappy arm which shows more and more, spoils his face (for it is on one side), his carriage, walk and figure, makes him awkward in all his movements, and gives him a feeling of shyness, as he feels his complete dependence, not being able to do a single thing for himself. It is a great additional difficulty in his education, and is not without its effect on his character. To me it remains an inexpressible source of sorrow! I think he will be very good-looking when he grows up, and he is already a universal favourite, as he is so lively and generally intelligent. He is a mixture of all our brothers—there is very little of his Papa, or the family of Prussia about him.

April 23, 1887

I REALLY ought again to apologise for writing so much about ourselves, but one's pen runs on when one thinks of the kind and sympathetic spirit of the one to whom one's words are addressed. The dream of my life was to have a son who should be something of what our beloved Papa was, a real grandson of his, in soul and intellect, a grandson of yours. Waldie gave me hopes of this— his nature was full of promise from the first, and I saw it with such pride and pleasure, and thought I could one day be of use to him! He is gone! and I can be of but limited use to Henry, and of none to William in any way! But one must guard against the fault of being annoyed with one's children for not being what one wished and hoped, what one wanted them to be. One must learn to abandon dreams and to take things as they come and characters as they are—one cannot quarrel with nature, and I suppose it knows best, though to us it seems cruel, perverse and contrary in the extreme. But it ends in one's feeling somewhat solitary at times!

To return to Prince Bismarck, he has so much that is brutal and cynical in his nature, so little that is noble and upright, he is so completely a man of another century than ours, that as an example or an ideal he becomes very dangerous. He is a patriot and is a genius, but as a school there could not be a worse one! Opinions such as William holds are very much the fashion nowadays in Germany—they have half created the immense power Bismarck possesses and he has half created them. But they are only a phase in the development of Germany! I think a dangerous and an unwholesome one, as they are a bad preparation for the solution of all the grave and difficult questions which will have to be the work of the next 20 or 30 years.

Mr. Gladstone, the Home Rulers and Parnellites are also a strange spectacle. The Government have a very difficult task before them! Mr. Bright wrote an excellent letter a few days ago, I thought.

TEN

Letters from

Storytellers

YOU CAN LEARN to be almost anything else, but God makes
storytellers. You can learn to be a musician or a painter or
a dressmaker, and what God gives you in the way of talent
will mark the difference between goodness and excellence; but if
you are not a born teller of stories you will say what you have to
say, and do what you have to do, in some other way. If you *must*
tell stories, then you do in little what God did in large—you
make a world and fill it with people and things. The big world we
all know is of course God's story; we are characters in it. I don't
know whether we would be happier if we knew what was coming
next.

All the letter-writers in this section had to tell stories, although
the kinds of stories are many. What a difference there is between
Marcel Proust and Louisa May Alcott—and yet they share one
thing: they created persons. The Baron de Charlus is not more
nor less real than Jo and the other little women; he is only different from them, as living in a different world. In the same way,
every person who has ever lived on this planet is equally real. The
question is whether Huck Finn, for example, is more real or less
real than you or I. It depends on how you feel about stories.
I might be inclined to say, and almost mean it, that Huck is far
more real than Charles Van Doren. He will live longer, for one
thing.

His creator's letters, I regret to say, are not the best of this
section—I spoke about that in the general introduction. Perhaps

311

Chekhov's are the finest—and there isn't a better storyteller. His letters show the quickness and fullness of his mind. There is too much to say, the world is too various, and everything gets thrown in all a-tumble.

> I dined at Landsberg's; I sat in the kitchen of the former Baroness Gembruk. . . . I visited all the celebrities. I was present at a flogging. . . . The long and the short of it is that I have upset my nerves and have vowed not to come to Sahalin again.

And so forth, on and on. In the mind of another kind of person it would all have become a blur. "Oh," someone else might recall, "Sahalin was terrible!" But Chekhov remembers, as if each memory were stored and felt by a separate nerve, and in his plays and short stories his memories and perceptions all emerge.

One thing authors do in books is explain themselves to the world—and to themselves. What storytellers often do in their letters home is try to explain themselves to their mothers. Flaubert says that at twenty-nine he is "too old to change," but:

> When one has lived the secret life that I have, full of violent introspections and suppressed passions . . . if one does not break one's neck at the beginning, the chances are that one will not break it later on.

Thomas Wolfe feels the same need to explain; he does it at too great length, the way he did everything. The world was full for him the way it was for Chekhov, but he could not distill it the way the Russian could. Yet Wolfe's letters can be beautiful:

> I have done bad things and cruel things in my wild and lonely youth, but on the whole I have lived a decent and honorable life, without talking overmuch of decency and honor.

You will notice one other thing about storytellers; they are always complaining of illnesses. Proust was a sick man, and his letters are largely about sickness. But they always contain the one *petite phrase* that illuminates an emotion. So to his mother:

> *Je t'embrasse tendrement!*

What a tender little thing to say.

I remarked that storytellers cannot avoid their fate, and I maintain it. But at seventeen Hawthorne did believe that he had a choice. Only jokingly does he consider literature as a career:

What do you think of my becoming an author, and relying for my support upon my pen? Indeed, I think the illegibility of my handwriting is very author-like.

But necessity crept up on him, as it always does, and so we have *The Scarlet Letter*. I hope God never stops making story-tellers.

"Grandmothers Are Always Kind"

LOUISA MAY ALCOTT

Louisa May Alcott (1832-1888; American novelist and writer of children's books.) Her own childhood was not particularly happy; she was the daughter of Amos Bronson Alcott, whose idealistic adventures and financial failures left much of the breadwinning to her. After the collapse of Fruitlands, a cooperative Utopian community that lasted from 1844 to 1845, Louisa was called on to provide support for her mother and her younger sisters. Teaching, dressmaking, and domestic service were her first employments, but after the publication of Flower Fables (1854), *a book of stories she had written for Emerson's daughters (and which is the subject of the delightful letter below), she earned an increasing proportion of her living by writing. A number of stories were printed in* The Atlantic Monthly *in 1860, but* Hospital Sketches (1863), *a collection of letters and tales based on her experiences as a Civil War nurse, brought her her first real fame.* Little Women *appeared in 1868 and was successful from the first. It was followed by* An Old Fashioned Girl (1870), Little Men (1871), Eight Cousins (1875), Under the Lilacs, Aunt Jo's Scrap-Bag (1872), *and* Jo's Boys (1886). *They were immensely popular in America, were translated into several languages, and assured financial independence for her and her mother. And I hope my daughter Elizabeth loves them as much as I did.*

20 Pinckney Street, Boston, Dec. 25, 1854.
[With *Flower Fables*.]

Dear Mother,—Into your Christmas stocking I have put my "first-born," knowing that you will accept it with all its faults (for grandmothers are always kind), and look upon it merely as an earnest of what I may yet do; for, with so much to cheer me on, I hope to pass in time from fairies and fables to men and realities.

Whatever beauty or poetry is to be found in my little book is owing to your interest in and encouragement of all my efforts from the first to the last; and if ever I do anything to be proud of, my greatest happiness will be that I can thank you for that, as I may do for all the good there is in me; and I shall be content to write if it gives you pleasure.

> Jo is fussing about;
> My lamp is going out.

To dear mother, with many kind wishes for a happy New Year and merry Christmas.

I am ever your loving daughter
Louy.

"Enough Material for Three Dissertations"

ANTON PAVLOVICH CHEKHOV

Anton Pavlovich Chekhov (1860-1904; Russian dramatist and short-story writer.) His grandfather was a serf, and Chekhov labored all his life to overcome what he termed "the cursed mentality of a serf." That he did so, and went on to become a famous and wealthy writer, constitutes one of the most remarkable Horatio Alger stories of Czarist Russia. Chekhov had to learn to fend for himself early. When his father's business in Taganrog failed and his family was packed off to Moscow, the young man finished high school by tutoring for his room and board. When he joined his family he found that he would be its major support. Since he was determined to be a doctor in order to rise out of the hopeless misery of his beginnings, he went to school by day and wrote stories by night; he was able to sell them in sufficient numbers to feed the family. Beginning with brief sketches, hardly more than anecdotes, for the Moscow humor magazines, he soon was expanding them into vignettes and still later into those stories, blends of farce and pathos, which came to be known as Chekhovian. By the time he graduated from medical school he was one of the most popular writers in the city. He had also found his true vocation; he never practiced the profession he had worked so hard to acquire.

Suvorin, a powerful critic, helped him publish his first volume of stories in 1886; he wrote his first play, Ivanov, in 1888. In 1890 he undertook his famous journey to Sahalin Island, the occasion of these two letters to his mother. This seldom-visited outpost of Siberia was a notorious penal colony, and Chekhov's indictment of it instigated many reforms. He continued to write short stories until 1896, when his second play, The Sea Gull, was written. It failed in St. Petersburg, but Stanislavski's Moscow Art Theatre production in 1898 was an immediate hit. All of Chekhov's subsequent plays were produced by this group, Uncle Vanya in 1900, The Three Sisters in 1901, and The Cherry Orchard in 1904. Ill health forced Chekhov after 1897 to live in spas, and he died in one, Badenweiler, in Germany, of consumption. He was beloved by Russians of all classes, and his body was brought back to Moscow for an impressive burial. But the combination of realism and comedy that had been his greatest literary invention did not desert him. The mourners at his funeral became confused, lost their way, and began to follow another procession going in another direction. The whole affair was a farce. I think Chekhov would have laughed too.

Steamer "Yermak,"
June 20, 1890.

GREETINGS, DEAR ONES AT HOME!

At last I can take off my heavy muddy boots, my shabby breeches, and my blue shirt, which is shiny with dust and sweat; I can wash and dress like a human being. I am not sitting in a chaise but in a first-class cabin of the steamer *Yermak*. This change took place ten days ago, and this is how it happened. I wrote to you from Listvenitchnaya that I was late for the Baikal steamer, that I had to cross Lake Baikal on Friday instead of Tuesday, and that owing to this I should only be able to catch the Amur steamer on the 30th. But fate is capricious, and often plays us tricks we do not expect. On Thursday morning I went out for a walk on the shores of Lake Baikal; behold! the funnel of one of the little steamers is smoking. I inquire where the steamer is going. They tell me, "Across the sea" to Klyuevo; some merchant had hired it to take his waggons of goods across the

Lake. We, too, wanted to cross "the sea" and go to Boyarskaya station. I inquire how many versts from Klyuevo to Boyarskaya. They tell me twenty-seven. I run back to my companions and beg them to take the risk of going to Klyuevo. I say the "risk" because, going to Klyuevo, where there is nothing but a harbour and a watchman's hut, we ran the risk of not finding horses, having to stay on at Klyuevo, and being late for Friday's steamer, which for us would be worse than Igor's death, as we should have to wait until Tuesday. My companions consented. We gathered together our belongings, with cheerful legs stepped on to the steamer and straight to the refreshment bar: soup, for the love of God! Half my kingdom for a plate of soup! The refreshment bar was very nasty and cramped; but the cook, Grigory Ivanitch, who had been a house-serf at Voronezh, turned out to be at the tip-top of his profession. He fed us magnificently. The weather was still and sunny. The water of Lake Baikal is the colour of turquoise, more transparent than the Black Sea. They say that in deep places you can see the bottom over a verst below; and I myself have seen to such a depth, with rocks and mountains plunged in the turquoise-blue, that it sent a shiver all over me. Our journey over Lake Baikal was wonderful. I shall never forget it as long as I live. But I will tell you what was not nice. We travelled third class, and the whole deck was occupied by the waggon-horses, which were wild as mad things. These horses gave a special character to our crossing: it seemed as though we were in a brigan'd steamer. At Klyuevo the watchman undertook to convey our luggage to the station; he drove the cart while we walked along the very picturesque shore. Levitan was an ass not to come with me. The way was through woods: on the right, woods running uphill; on the left, woods running down to the Lake. Such ravines, such crags! The colouring of Lake Baikal is soft and warm. It was, by the way, very warm. After walking eight versts we reached the station of Myskan, where a Kyahtan official, who was also on his travels, regaled us with excellent tea, and where we got the horses for Boyarskaya; and so we set off on Thursday instead of Friday; what is more, we got twenty-four hours in advance of the post, which usually takes all the horses at the station. We began driving as fast as we could, cherishing a faint hope of reaching Sryetensk by the 20th. I will tell you when we meet about my journey along the bank of the Selenga and across Transbaikalia. Now I will only say that Selenga is one continuous loneliness, and in Transbaikalia I found everything I wanted: the Caucasus, and the valley of the Psyol, and the Zvenigorod district, and the Don. By day you gallop through the Caucasus, at night along the steppe of the Don; in the morning, rousing yourself from slumber, behold the province of Poltava—and so for the whole thousand versts. Verhneudinsk is a nice little town. Tchita is a wretched place, in the style of Sumy. I need hardly say that we had no time to think of sleep or dinner. One gallops on thinking of nothing but the chance that the next station we might not get horses, and might be kept five or six hours. We did two hundred versts in twenty-four hours—one can't do more than that in the summer. We were stupefied. The heat was fearful by day, while at night it was so cold that I had to put on my leather coat over my cloth one. One night I even wore my sheepskin. Well, we drove on and on, and reached Sryetensk this morning just an hour before the steamer left, giving the drivers from the last two stations a rouble each for themselves.

And so my horse-journey is over. It has lasted two months (I set out on the 21st of April). If we exclude the time spent on the railway and the steamer, the three days spent in Ekaterinburg, the week in Tomsk, the day in Krasnoyarsk, the week in Irkutsk, the two days on the shores of Lake Baikal, and the days wasted waiting for boats to cross the floods, you can judge of the rate at which I have driven. My journey has been most successful, I wish nothing better for anyone. I have not once been ill, and of the mass of things I had with me I have lost nothing but a penknife, the strap off my trunk, and a little jar of carbolic ointment. My money is safe. It is not often that one succeeds in travelling a thousand versts so well.

I have grown so used to driving that now I don't feel like myself, and cannot believe that I am not in a chaise and that I don't hear the rattling and the jingling of the bells. It seems strange that when I go to bed I can stretch out my legs full length and that my face is not covered with dust. But what is stranger still is that the bottle of brandy Kuvshinnikov gave me has not been broken, and that the brandy is still in it, every drop of it. I have vowed not to uncork it except on the shore of the Pacific.

I am sailing down the Shilka, which runs into the Amur at the Pokrovskaya Stanitsa. The river is not broader than the Psyol, it is even narrower. The shores are stony: there are crags and forests. It is absolutely wild. . . . We tack about to avoid foundering on a sandbank, or running our helm into the banks: steamers and barges often do so in the rapids. It's stifling. We have just stopped at Ust-Kara, where we have landed five or six convicts. There are mines here and a convict prison.

Yesterday we were at Nertchinsk. The little town is nothing to boast of, but one could live there.

And how are you, messieurs and mesdames? I know positively nothing about you. You might subscribe twopence each and send me a full telegram.

The steamer will stay the night at Gorbitsa. The nights here are foggy, sailing is dangerous. I shall send off this letter at Gorbitsa.

. . . I am going first class because my companions are in the second. I have got away from them. We have driven together, (three in one chaise), we have slept together and are sick of each other, especially I of them.

.   .   .   .   .   .

My handwriting is very bad, shaky. That is because the steamer rocks. It's difficult to write.

I broke off here. I went to my lieutenants and had tea. They have both had a long sleep and were in a very cordial mood. One of them, Lieutenant N. (the surname jars upon my ear), is in the infantry; he is a tall, well-fed, loud-voiced Courlander, a great braggart and Hlestakov, who sings songs from every opera, but has no more ear than a smoked herring, an unlucky fellow who has squandered all the money for his travelling expenses, knows all Mickiewicz by heart, is ill-bred, far too unreserved, and babbles till it makes you sick. Like I, he is fond of talking about his uncles and aunts. The other lieutenant, M., a geographer, is a quiet, modest, thoroughly well-educated fellow. If it were not for N., I could travel with the other for a million versts without being bored. But with N., who intrudes into every conversation, the other bores me too. . . . I believe we are reaching Gorbitsa.

To-morrow I will make up the form of a telegram which you must send me to Sahalin. I will try to put all I want to know in thirty words, and you must try and keep strictly to the pattern.

The gad-flies bite.

Sahalin,
October 6, 1890.

My greetings, dear mother!

I write you this letter almost on the eve of my departure for Russia. Every day we expect a steamer of the Volunteer Fleet, and cherish hopes that it will not come later than the 10th of October. I send this letter to Japan, whence it will go by Shanghai or America. I am living at the station of Korsakovo, where there is neither telegraph nor post, and which is not visited by ships oftener than once a fortnight. Yesterday a steamer arrived and brought me from the north a pile of letters and telegrams. From the letters I learn that Masha likes the Crimea. I believe she will like the Caucasus better still. . . .

. . . . . .

Strange, with you it has been cold and rainy, while in Sahalin from the day of my arrival till to-day it has been bright warm weather: there is slight cold with hoar frost in the mornings, the snow is white on one of the mountains, but the earth is still green, the leaves have not fallen, and all the vegetation is still flourishing as at a summer villa in May. There you have Sahalin!

. . . . . .

At midnight yesterday I heard the roar of a steamer. Everybody jumped out of bed: hurrah! the steamer has arrived! We dressed and went out with lanterns to the harbour; we gazed into the distance; there really was a steamer. . . . The majority of voices decided that it was the *Petersburg,* on which I am to go to Russia. I was overjoyed. We got into a boat and rowed to the steamer. We went on and on, till at last we saw in the mist the dark hulk of a steamer. One of us shouted in a hoarse voice asking the name of the vessel. And we received the answer, "The *Baikal.*" Tfoo! anathema! what a disappointment! I am homesick, and weary of Sahalin. Here for the last three months I have seen no one but convicts or people who can talk of nothing but penal servitude, the lash, and the convicts. A depressing existence. One longs to get quickly to Japan and from there to India.

I am quite well except for flashes in my eye from which I often suffer now, and after which I always have a bad headache. I had the flashes in my eye yesterday and to-day, and so I am writing this with a headache and heaviness all over.

At the station the Japanese General Kuse-San lives with his two secretaries, good friends of mine. They live like Europeans. To-day the local authorities visited them in state to present decorations that had been conferred on them; and I, too, went with my headache and had to drink champagne.

Since I have been in the south I have three times driven to Nay Race where the real ocean waves break. Look at the map and you will see at once on the south coast that poor dismal Nay Race. The waves cast up a boat with six American whale fishers, who had been shipwrecked off the coast of Sahalin; they are living now at the station and solemnly walk about the streets. They are waiting for the *Petersburg* and will sail with me.

I am not bringing you furs, there are none in Sahalin. Keep well and Heaven guard you all.

I am bringing you all presents. The cholera in Vladivostok and Japan is over.

. . . . . .

I don't know what will come of it, but I have done a good deal. I have got enough material for three dissertations. I got up every morning at five o'clock and went to bed late; and all day long was on the strain from the thought that there was still so much I hadn't done; and now that I have done with the convict system, I have the feeling that I have seen everything but I have not noticed the elephants.

By the way, I had the patience to make a census of the whole Sahalin population. I made the round of all the settlements, went into every hut and talked to everyone; I made use of the card system in making the census, and I have already registered about ten thousand convicts and settlers. In other words, there is not in Sahalin one convict or settler who has not talked with me. I was particularly successful with the census of the children, on which I am building great hopes.

I dined at Landsberg's; I sat in the kitchen of the former Baroness Gembruk. . . . I visited all the celebrities. I was present at a flogging, after which I dreamed for three or four nights of the executioner and the revolting accessories. I have talked to men who were chained to trucks. Once when I was drinking tea in a mine, Borodavkin, once a Petersburg merchant who was convicted of arson, took a teaspoon out of his pocket and gave it to me, and the long and the short of it is that I have upset my nerves and have vowed not to come to Sahalin again.

I should write more to you, but there is a lady in the cabin who giggles and chatters unceasingly. I haven't the strength to write. She has been laughing and cackling ever since yesterday evening.

This letter will go across America, but I shall go probably not across America. Everyone says that the American way is duller and more expensive.

To-morrow I shall see Japan, the Island of Matsmai. Now it is twelve o'clock at night. It is dark on the sea, the wind is blowing. I don't understand how the steamer can go on and find its direction when one can't see a thing and above all in such wild, little-known waters as those in the Gulf of Tartary.

When I remember that I am ten thousand versts away from my world I am overcome with apathy. It seems I shall not be home for a hundred years. . . . God give you health and all blessings. I feel dreary.

"The Artist Is a Monster"

GUSTAVE FLAUBERT

Gustave Flaubert (1821-1880; French novelist and author.) For this man, writing was almost inexpressibly difficult. The search for le mot juste *was his lifework; thus, it took him an agonizing four and a half years to write* Madame Bovary, *and seven years to write* L'Éducation sentimentale. *He sometimes worked on a single page for a full week. It is always difficult to write anything well, and all writers search for "exactly the right word," but with Flaubert it was a passion—he was the* pointilliste *among authors —and it was a religion; and since this was so, since he was dedicated to his art as few artists ever have been, his influence on his contemporaries and indeed on all writing since his time was enormous. Daudet, the Goncourts, and Turgenev kneeled at his feet; his naturalistic approach to the novel, analyzing facts and forces with a godly disinterest, was systematized by Zola. There was something deeply romantic in Flaubert's soul—otherwise he could not have described the exotic world of* Salammbô *with such loving care—but he will be remembered for Emma Bovary, a portrait that is psychologically just and terribly true, and the most searching denunciation of middle-class aspirations and ambitions ever penned. His* Trois Contes, *including "Un Coeur simple," "La Légende de Saint-Julien l'Hospitalier," and "Hérodias" is in some respects his best work, despite the fame of* Madame Bovary. *The three stories have a sharply etched, unforgettable quality. If Flaubert lacks anything as a writer it is a certain largeness. I think the letter that follows shows why this was so. He had one unsatisfactory love affair, and he never did marry. Except when he travelled, he lived at home with his mother. Neither his real world nor his fictional worlds made him happy.*

Constantinople, December 15th [1850]

WHEN SHALL I marry, you ask me, apropos of Ernest's wedding. When? Never, I hope. In so far as a man can answer for his future actions, I do so now in the negative. Contact with the world, with which I have rubbed shoulders steadily these last fourteen months, forces me back farther and farther into my shell. Old Parain was wrong in supposing that travelling changes one. I, certainly, shall come back the same man as when I left, except for a few less hairs on my head and a number of countries inside it. That is all. As for my general state of mind, it remains the same until future notice. But were I to express my deepest thoughts on the subject without appearing too presumptuous, I should say that I am too old to change. I have passed the age. When one has lived the secret life that I have, full of violent introspections and suppressed passions, when one has so roused oneself and calmed oneself by turns; and used up one's whole youth in training one's own mind, as a rider does his horse, spurring it on to gallop across country, making it walk, jump ditches, trot and amble, only for one's own amusement and greater knowledge; if one does not break one's neck at the beginning, well, the chances are that one will not break it later on. I am *established* in life, too, in the sense that I have discovered my seat to be my centre of gravity. I do not think that any internal jolt can move me or bring me down. Marriage for me would be a quite appalling apostasy. Alfred's death has not erased the memory of the vexation his marriage caused me. I felt as a religious man might on hearing that a bishop had caused a major scandal. If one wants to concern oneself in any way, great or small, with the Lord's creation, one should begin, for purely salutary reasons, by putting oneself in the position not to be duped. You may describe wine, love, women or glory, on condition that you do not become a drunkard, a lover, a husband or a bluecoat. In the midst of life, you get a bad view of it; it either gives you too much pleasure or too much pain. The artist, in my opinion, is a monster, an unnatural creature. All the misfortunes with which Fate weighs him down arise from his stubborn denial of this axiom, a denial which brings him suffering and causes pain to others. Ask the opinion of any women who have loved poets, or of men who have loved actresses. So (this is my conclusion) I am resigned to living as I have done so far, alone amongst a crowd of the great rather than in a social circle, wrapped in my bear's skin, being a bear myself, and so on. . . . I do not care a rap for society, for the future, for what people say, for any sort of establishment or even for literary fame, which I once spent many sleepless nights dreaming of. That is how I am; that is my character.

I have not the remotest idea what set me writing this two-page rigmarole, you poor old dear. Really, I haven't. When I think of your sad and loving face, and of how pleasant it is to live with you, of your deep serenity, your charming tranquillity, I know very well that I shall never love anyone as much as you. No, you will never have a rival, never fear. Neither desire nor momentary whim can replace something which lies hidden in my Holiest of Holies. Some may perhaps reach the gates of the temple, but none will ever enter in. . . .

"Authors Are Always Poor Devils"

NATHANIEL HAWTHORNE

Nathaniel Hawthorne (1804-1864; American novelist and short-story writer.) Bowdoin College never had a more distinguished graduating class than the one that left the school in 1825; it contained a future President of the United States, Franklin Pierce, and two of America's greatest authors, Henry Wadsworth Long-fellow and Nathaniel Hawthorne. The letter below was written before Hawthorne entered college; if his prospects seemed dim to him then, they were no brighter when he graduated.

Hawthorne and his mother fought a long and enervating fight against poverty; throughout his career he found it necessary to punctuate his financially unsuccessful work as a writer with periods of drudgery in the customhouse at Boston, or as surveyor of the port of Salem. His most pleasing non-literary employment was a reward for his least important literary production—a campaign biography of his old college friend, Franklin Pierce; the plum Hawthorne received for this was appointment to the U.S. consulship at Liverpool, a post he filled for four years.

Hawthorne lived at home with his mother for nearly fifteen years after his graduation from Bowdoin, struggling to write. The first fruit of these years was Twice-Told Tales *(1837), a collection of magazine stories and one novel. It was not a financial success, but it brought him encouragement from Emerson, Channing, Margaret Fuller, and a number of other Transcendentalists whom he met through his marriage in 1841 to Sophia Peabody.* Mosses from An Old Manse *and* The Scarlet Letter, *his masterpiece, followed.*

Emerson knew Hawthorne as well as anybody, and a note in his Journal *says more about Hawthorne than could a thousand words from me: "Yesterday, May 23," Emerson wrote in 1864, "we buried Hawthorne in Sleepy Hollow, in a pomp of sunshine and verdure and gentle winds. . . . I thought there was a tragic element in the event—in the painful solitude of the man, which, I suppose, could not longer be endured, and he died of it."*

Salem, March 13, 1821.

DEAR MOTHER,—Yours of the—was received. I am much flattered by your being so solicitous for me to write, and shall be much more so if you can read what I write, as I have a wretched pen. Mr. Manning is in great affliction concerning that naughty little watch, and Louisa and I are in the dolorous condition. I think it would be advisable to advertise him in the Portland papers. How many honors are heaped upon Uncle Richard! He will soon have as many titles as a Spanish Don. I am proud of being related to so distinguished a personage. What has become of Elizabeth? Does she never intend to notice me again? I shall begin to think she has eloped with some of those "gay deceivers" who abound in Raymond, if she does not give me some proof to the contrary. I dreamed the other night that I was walking by the Sebago; and when I awoke was so angry at finding it all a delusion, that I gave Uncle Robert (who sleeps with me) a most horrible kick. I don't read so much now as I did, because I am more taken up in studying. I am quite reconciled to going to college, since I am to spend the vacations with you. Yet four years of the best part of my life is a great deal to throw away. I have not yet concluded what profession I shall have. The being a minister is of course out of the question. I should not think that even you could desire me to choose so dull a way of life. Oh, no, mother, I was not born to vegetate forever in one place, and to live and die as calm and tranquil as—a puddle of water. As to lawyers, there are so many of them already that one half of them (upon a moderate calculation) are in a state of actual starvation. A physician, then, seems to be "Hobson's choice;" but yet I should not like to live by the diseases and infirmities of my fellow-creatures. And it would weigh very heavily on my conscience, in the course of my practice, if I should chance to send any unlucky patient "ad inferum," which being interpreted is, "to the realms below." Oh that I was rich enough to live without a profession! What do you think of my becoming an author, and relying for support upon my pen? Indeed, I think the illegibility of my handwriting is very author-like. How proud you would feel to see my works praised by the reviewers, as equal to the proudest productions of the scribbling sons of John Bull. But authors are always poor devils, and therefore Satan may take them. I am in the same predicament as the honest gentleman in "Espriella's Letters,"—

"I am an Englishman, and naked I stand here,
A-musing in my mind what garment I shall wear."

But as the mail closes soon, I must stop the career of my pen. I will only inform you that I now write no poetry, or anything else. I hope that either Elizabeth or you will write to me next week.

I remain

Your affectionate son,
Nathl. Hawthorne.

Do not show this letter.

"Vulgar, Vulgar, Vulgar"

HENRY JAMES

Henry James (1843-1916; American novelist, playwright, and critic.) When Hawthorne died Henry James was twenty-one, and the influence of the older writer on the younger was already clear. James wrote the best book on Hawthorne, and discussed his debt to him in Notes of a Son and Brother: *"The moral was that an American could be an artist, one of the finest, without 'going outside' about it, as I liked to say; quite in fact as if Hawthorne had become one just by being American enough."*

Being an American artist was the preoccupation of Henry James. That he succeeded in being an artist is hardly questioned nowadays: no American author's reputation is higher, though perhaps some are more secure. But it was harder for him to be an American, as these letters to his mother make clear, and he died a British subject. (His change of citizenship was more a sentimental gesture than anything else; he objected to America's staying out of the war, and expressed his concern by making official what had been a fact for many years.) James loved London simply because it was so full of life and power; he would have lived in New York had he been a twentieth century writer.

It is customary to divide the vast body of his work into three periods. The first includes The American *(1877),* Daisy Miller *(1879), and* The Bostonians *(1886); the second includes his story,* The Figure in the Carpet *(1896),* The Turn of the Screw, *and* The Awkward Age *(1899); and the final period includes* The Wings of the Dove *(1902),* The Ambassadors *(1903), and* The Golden Bowl *(1904). Between 1907 and 1909 he revised and rewrote many of his works, providing them with explanatory prefaces that were later collected in a single volume,* The Art of Fiction *(1934). He also wrote several plays, and it was a great disappointment in his life that none of them was ever successful, although several of his works have in recent years been made into the kind of popular dramatic hits he never was able to enjoy. He was a great writer, although there are some who question the rewriting that he did on his early works—William James did, for example—and who question, too, whether the singular yearning for life that is the mark of so many of his heroes (Lambert Strether in* The Ambassadors, *for one) was not the sign of an essential lack in their creator.*

The "Mrs. Kemble" mentioned in the second letter below, by the way, was a truly remarkable woman; I envy Henry James his meetings and friendship with her. She came of one of the most illustrious theatrical families the English-speaking world has ever known. Her tour of America with her father in 1832 (she played Juliet, Portia, and Beatrice) was a breathtaking success, climaxed by her marriage to a wealthy American. Then during the Civil War she turned to writing abolitionist articles; and still later, memoirs, a historical drama, and criticism.

Florence, Hôtel de l'Europe.
October 13th, 1869.

MY DARLING MAMMY,

. . . For the past six weeks that I have been in Italy I've hardly until within a day or two exchanged five minutes' talk with any one but the servants in the hotels and the custodians in the churches. As far as meeting people is concerned, I've not as yet had in Europe a very brilliant record. Yesterday I met at the Uffizi Miss Anna Vernon of Newport and her friend Mrs. Carter, with whom I had some discourse; and on the same morning I fell in with a somewhat seedy and sickly American, who seemed to be doing the gallery with an awful minuteness, and who after some conversation proposed to come and see me. He called this morning and has just left; but he seems a vague and feeble brother and I anticipate no wondrous joy from his acquaintance. The 'hardly' in the clause above is meant to admit two or three Englishmen with whom I have been thrown for a few hours. . . . One especially, whom I met at Verona, won my affections so rapidly that I was really sad at losing him. But he has vanished, leaving only a delightful impression and not even a name—a man of about 38, with a sort of quiet perfection of English virtue about him, such as I have rarely found in another. Willy asked me in one of his recent letters for an 'opinion' of the English, which I haven't yet had time to give—tho' at times I have felt as if it were a theme on which I could write from a full mind. In fact, however, I have very little right to have any opinion on the matter. I've seen far too few specimens and those too superficially. The only thing I'm certain about is that I like them—like them heartily. W. asked if as individuals they 'kill' the individual American. To this I would say that the Englishmen I have met not only kill, but bury in unfathomable depths, the Americans I have met. A set of people less framed to provoke national self-complacency than the latter it would be hard to imagine. There is but one word to use in regard to them—vulgar, vulgar, vulgar. Their ignorance —their stingy, defiant, grudging attitude towards everything European—their perpetual reference of all things to some American standard or precedent which exists only in their own unscrupulous wind-bags—and then our unhappy poverty of voice, of speech and of physiognomy—these things glare at you hideously. On the other hand, we seem a people of *character*, we seem to have energy, capacity and intellectual stuff in ample measure. What I have pointed at as our vices are the elements of the modern man with *culture* quite left out. It's the absolute and incredible lack of *culture* that strikes you in common travelling Americans. The pleasantness of the English, on the other side, comes in a great measure from the fact of their each having been dipped into the crucible, which gives them a sort of coating of

comely varnish and colour. They have been smoothed and pol-
ished by mutual social attrition. They have manners and a language. We lack both, but particularly the latter. I have seen very
'nasty' Britons, certainly, but as a rule they are such as to cause
your heart to warm to them. The women are at once better and
worse than the men. Occasionally they are hard, flat, and greasy
and dowdy to downright repulsiveness; but frequently they have
a modest, matronly charm which is the perfection of womanish-
ness and which makes Italian and Frenchwomen—and to a certain
extent even our own—seem like a species of feverish highly-de-
veloped invalids. You see Englishmen, here in Italy, to a particularly good advantage. In the midst of these false and beautiful
Italians they glow with the light of the great fact, that after all
they love a bath-tub and they hate a lie.

16th, Sunday. I have seen some nice Americans and I still love
my country. I have called upon Mrs. Huntington and her two
daughters—late of Cambridge—whom I met in Switzerland and
who have an apartment here. The daughters more than reconcile
me to the shrill-voiced sirens of New England's rock-bound coast.
The youngest is delightfully beautiful and sweet—and the elder
delightfully sweet and plain—with a plainness *qui vaut bien des
beautés.* . . .

Maman de mon âme, farewell. I have kept my letter three days,
hoping for news from home. I hope you are not paying me back
for that silence of six weeks ago. Blessings on your universal heads.

Thy lone and loving exile,
H. J. jr.

3 Bolton St., W.
January 18th [1879].

My Dearest Mother,

I have before me your letter of December 30th, with its account
of your Christmas festivities and other agreeable talk, and I endeavour on this 'beastly' winter night, before my carboniferous
hearth, to transport myself into the family circle.

Mrs. Kemble has returned to town for the winter—an event in
which I always take pleasure, as she is certainly one of the women
I know whom I like best. I confess I find people in general very
vulgar-minded and superficial—and it is only by a pious fiction, to
keep myself going, and keep on the social harness, that I succeed

in postulating them as anything else or better. It is therefore a kind of rest and refreshment to see a woman who (extremely annoying as she sometimes is) gives one a positive sense of having a deep, rich, human nature and having cast off all vulgarities. The people of this world seem to me for the most part nothing but *surface,* and sometimes—oh ye gods!—such desperately poor surface! Mrs. Kemble has no organised surface at all; she is like a straight deep cistern without a cover, or even, sometimes, a bucket, into which, as a mode of intercourse, one must tumble with a splash. You mustn't judge her by her indifferent book, which is no more a part of her than a pudding she might make. . . . Please tell William and Alice that I received a short time since their kind note, written on the eve of their going to Newport, and complimenting me on the first part of the *International Episode.* You will have read the second part by this time, and I hope that you won't, like many of my friends here (as I partly know and partly suspect,) take it ill of me as against my 'British entertainers.' It seems to me myself that I have been very delicate; but I shall keep off dangerous ground in future. It is an entirely new sensation for them (the people here) to be (at all delicately) *ironised* or satirised, from the American point of view, and they don't at all relish it. Their conception of the normal in such a relation is that the satire should be all on their side against the Americans; and I suspect that if one were to push this a little further one would find that they are extremely sensitive. But I like them too much and feel too kindly to them to go into the satire-business or even the light-ironical in any case in which it would wound them— even if in such a case I should see my way to it very clearly. Macmillan is just on the point of bringing out *Daisy Miller, The International Episode,* and *Four Meetings* in two little big-printed volumes, like those of *The Europeans.* There is every reason to expect for them a very good success, as *Daisy M.* has been, as I have told you before, a really quite extraordinary hit. I will send you the new volumes. . . . Farewell, dearest Mother. I send my filial duty to father, who I hope is worrying comfortably through the winter (I am afraid that since you wrote you have had severe weather)—and looking and listening always for a letter, remain your very lovingest

H. James jr.

"As For Me, I Sneeze"

GUY DE MAUPASSANT

Henri René Albert Guy de Maupassant (1850-1893; French nov-elist and short-story writer.) Ernest Boyd says that Maupassant's mother "saw to it that as much of his correspondence as possible was destroyed." We are fortunate, then, to have even two letters from the great storyteller to his mother. Their relationship was particularly close; not hatred, but love caused her to destroy his letters, for they were a record of his misery, his dissipation, his aloneness.

If there was anyone with whom Maupassant was more in-timate, it was Flaubert. Maupassant went to Paris from an ordi-nary middle-class home in Dieppe in 1872, not to conquer the world but to become a minor clerk in the Ministry of the Navy. He spent ten years there, starting in printing supplies and ending in accounts. But he had another, richer life at night. He had met Flaubert, the literary lion of Paris, and was a frequent guest at his house. Maupassant wanted to write, but Flaubert was a stern taskmaster, and forbade his pupil to publish anything for seven years. In 1880 the patience of both was rewarded. Maupassant was asked to write a short story for an anthology to be edited by Zola, and Boule de suif was an instantaneous success. Not only did everyone admire it, but Flaubert called it a masterpiece; for the next ten years Maupassant was the most popular short-story writer on the Continent. He had a yacht in the Mediterranean, a singular token of success for a writer.

But by 1891 the rocket had burned out and Maupassant, at forty, was dying. On New Year's Day, 1892, he tried to cut his throat with a razor. General paresis set in, and though the eminent phy-sicians who attended him could not agree on a diagnosis, he was confined to a private asylum where he died eighteen months later.

Chekhov and Maupassant are the masters of the short story. Perhaps the secret is to put more into ten or fifteen pages than most writers put into a novel. At least that is what they did; their stories spill over at the top and leak around the base, and soon you forget that this is only a story. You suppose it is the real world, because, after all, reality is full of spills and leaks.

24 September 1872

YOU SEE THAT I am writing you promptly, but the truth is I cannot wait any longer to write. I feel so lost, so isolated, so *demoralized*, that I am forced to beg a few pages of you. I am afraid of the coming winter, I feel lonely, and my long solitary evenings are sometimes terrible. Often, when I sit at my writing table with my melancholy lamp burning, my anguish is so sharp that I don't know to whom to turn. Last winter, in such moments, I would often say to myself that you too must have gone through frightfully gloomy times during the long cold December and January evenings. My monotonous existence has started again, and there will be three months of this. L.F. cannot dine with me tonight; he is dining out, and it annoys me, for we could have chatted together.

A little while ago, by way of distraction, I wrote something in the manner of the *Monday Tales* (of Alphonse Daudet). I am sending it to you. Of course I attach no importance to it: the thing was dashed off in a quarter of an hour. Still, I wish that you would send it back, for I may be able to do something with it. There are a few ungrammatical sentences which I shall correct when I work the thing up. I wish I could be carried back two weeks. How short the time is! How little time there is for us to see each other and talk of things! And once a holiday is over, one says to oneself: "But how can it be? I've only just got here. I haven't talked to anybody yet."

Good bye, dear Mother. I send you my best love, and love to Hervé too.

Etretat, Tuesday (January 1881)

I WRITE TO YOU on the corner of the little table in our parlor. The two dogs are very thin, but gay and well: they are lying at my feet. Matho disturbs me ceaselessly by rubbing against my leg. Daphne is completely cured. As for me, I sneeze, blow my nose, invaded by a fearful cold in the head I caught traveling all night in a temperature five below freezing, and I cannot get warm in this frozen house. The cold wind whistles under the doors, the lamp dies, the lively chimney-fire lights me up—a fire that grills the face without warming the room. All the old things are about me, dreary, harrowing; no sound comes from the dead village, blanketed in winter. I cannot hear the sea.

The cold is owing more to the loneliness of my life than to the loneliness of this house. I have the feeling that the whole world has lost its way, and the void in which I live begins to weigh heavily upon me. Yet in the midst of the general stampede my brain operates lucidly, precisely, dazzling me with the eternal Nothingness. That sounds like something written by old Hugo, but it would take a long time for me to express my idea clearly and in precise language. Which proves to me once again that romantic bombast is the result of mere laziness in writing. . . .

I have almost finished my story about the prostitutes and the First Communion. I think it is at least as good as "Boule de suif," if not better.

"Something to Stop My Nervous Laughing"

MARCEL PROUST

Marcel Proust (1871-1922; French novelist.) Perhaps he was the sickest writer who has ever lived. He was an invalid from the age of nine, and what is more, a hypochondriac. He suffered horribly from asthma, but during his youth that did not keep him from frequenting the fashionable salons of Paris and becoming known as the "quintessential dilettante." He published several "decadent" volumes in the fin de siecle, *but his real work began when his mother died, in 1905. He was devoted to her, and he retired from society to write the great work that became the "picture of the death of a society,"* Remembrance of Things Past. *He worked in a cork-lined study (to avoid noise), mostly at night (the light hurt his eyes), and he secluded himself from even his most intimate friends. For the next seventeen years he believed himself to be in a daily race against death—a race which he lost, by his lights, since the novel had not been "completed" when he died. But that was only because it could never be completed; it was the story of his time, and his time could not "end" before his death. The book was written and rewritten and rewritten, published in sections against Proust's will (he did not want any of it to slip from his hands), and it made him a worldwide reputation in his forties.*

E. M. Forster calls the book the second best novel (the first being Tolstoï's War and Peace). *If you sit and look out of a window for an hour and try to think of any other novel more deserving of the title, you will probably fail.*

[Auteuil,
Wednesday, 5 September 1888.]

For you, *ma chère petite Maman,* I'm using my last sheet of decent notepaper.

It's the truth in all its purity that's about to leave my lips!

I had a very good walk yesterday evening. I went with Uncle Georges as far as the tram. I spent 10 minutes luring him away from the stop, so that he'd miss it, and my plot succeeded. Unfortunately, during the last few minutes when I was watching the tram out of the corner of my eye and it was just going to start, I was so delighted that I rather gave myself away. He began to run after it! It's so nice to see him running.

A few upsets in the evening. A long night's sleep, but *on the whole* rather disagreeable. Besides, up till then my eyes were never quite dry. I still hadn't got over your going away, and that brought down a sermon from Great-Uncle, who told me that my grief was 'nothing but egoism'. This little psychological discovery procured him such pure joy of pride and self-satisfaction that he became absolutely merciless and gave me a moral lecture. Grandfather was much gentler, and just told me quite calmly that I was a silly boy, and Grandmother shook her head and laughed, and said it would take more than that to prove that I loved 'my mother'. I think there's hardly anyone but Auguste, Marguerite and Madame Gaillard who feels for my misfortune. As for Victoire and Angélique, it's quite obvious that they think I have a 'girl friend' who will dry my tears away! But this morning I got up early and went to the Bois de Boulogne, with Loti. Oh, *ma petite Maman,* how wrong I was not to do it before, and how often I shall do it again! As soon as I reached the entrance it started to be fine; the sun shone, the air was cool, in fact I laughed aloud with joy. It was a pleasure to breathe, to feel, to move my limbs, just like the old days at Tréport, or at Illiers the year I read Augustin Thierry—and a thousand times better than my walks with Robert. And then *Le Mariage de Loti* increased still further this sense of well-being—it was like drinking tea! I read it on the grass by the Petit Lac—the water was violet and half in shadow,

and then here and there the sunlight streamed down, and the lake
and the trees began to glitter.

'*The glittering and magic of the hour*'—I understood then, or
rather felt, how many sensations are expressed by that delightful
line of Leconte de l'Isle! Yes, it's him again, as always!

Grandfather has completely renounced tea. He prefers his infusion of orange-flowers. Dr. Ballet is his great man now, because
he said that Grandfather was quite right never to blow his nose.
In fact, he added, by a supernatural coincidence—oh, how truly
supernatural!—"You would only *irritate the membranes!*" I be-
haved very well at table, and never even once caught a furious
look from Grandfather. Just the least remark—"Don't *rub* so"—
because I was wiping my eyes with my handkerchief. The last
remains of my grief.

Tell Robert that His Majesty's workmen have finished the instrument destined for such momentous affairs of state, but that
they—as is only proper (see any novel by Dumas)—have no
inkling of the importance nor even of the nature of the object they
have made. It seemed a thousand times too big to me, and more
like a trumpet for use on Judgment Day. Victoire said it looked
very funny, and she had no idea what it could be for! Embrace
Robert and yourself for me a thousand times. I feel remorse for
even the slightest vexations I may have caused you! Forgive me.
Je t'embrasse infiniment.

MARCEL

P.S. They've just delivered the trousers for the Palais de Cristal.
Too tight. They'll bring them again properly altered this evening,
without fail. Robert's have come back, too.

Hôtel de France et d'Angleterre,
Fontainebleau,
Wednesday morning, 9.15 [21 October 1896.]

Ma chère petite maman,

It's pouring with rain. I didn't have asthma last night, and it
was not until just now that I had to have a little fumigation, after
a great deal of sneezing. Since then I haven't felt very easy,
because my bed is most uncomfortable, in fact the wall is on
my best side. Not to mention that because of the numerous
canopies, curtains, etc. (impossible to remove because they're

fixed to the wall) this is very inconvenient, as it forces me always to lie facing the wall, everything I need—my coffee, my *tisane,* my candle, pen, matches, etc. etc.—is on my right, which means I keep having to turn over on my bad side, etc. My chest was quite free yesterday all morning, afternoon, evening (except as always when I went to bed) and all the night. (It's now that I feel the most discomfort.) But I'm not having enormous nights' sleep as in Paris, or at least the last few weeks in Paris. And once I wake up, instead of feeling well in bed I can't breathe till I get up, which isn't a good sign, whatever you think. Yesterday the rain didn't begin till 4 p.m., so that I was able to go for a walk. I didn't like what I saw. The mere fringe of woodland I saw is still green. The town is characterless. I can't tell you what a horrifying hour I spent yesterday between 4 and 6 (an hour which I've put back to before our telephone conversation in the little narrative I sent you, which I beg you to keep, and to remember where you keep it, because it will be in my novel). Never I think has any of my anguishes of whatever kind reached such a degree. I can't try to tell you about it. So as to have someone to talk to I went to the station at eleven o'clock to wait for Léon Daudet, who was returning from Paris. He is absolutely determined to have his meals with me. This means he will have to stay *en pension* like Jean. The hotel is certainly quite out of the ordinary. But not a soul in it will speak to me. No doubt it's because the servants have never been with anyone but some Doudeauville or other, where they heard nothing but "I'm very well, thank you." So I can't say to them "I'm very ill" and explain my needs, nor have those pleasantly intimate relations which I had with Mme Renvoyzé or the people at the Hôtel Fermont. You've seen what they charge here. I think it will come to even more because of the fires I am obliged to get them to make, and my lamp, for as it's so late in the season there's no lounge with lights in the evening, and one has nowhere but one's room. I've nothing to read, and I'm wondering whether Reynaldo has forgotten about my books. If it wasn't such a business to change one's room, I'd certainly change mine so as to have a bed facing in the other direction. *Je t'embrasse tendrement.* Had another letter from Reynaldo this morning which I'm keeping because it will amuse you.

Ton petit
MARCEL

P. S. I've just had a word with the chamber-maid, she's going to move my bed so that the head will be against the wall (because the canopies can't be taken off), but the bed itself in the middle of the room, I think it will be more comfortable for me. The rain is twice as heavy. What weather! I'm amazed that you don't say anything about the charges at the hotel. If they're exorbitant shouldn't I do better to come back? And from Paris I could go to Versailles every day to work.

2nd P. S. Léon Daudet would like us to go to Marlotte and stay in a cheaper hotel, because he knows someone with asthma who is comfortable there. But I believe it's much further from Paris, fewer trains, etc.—what do you think? The only thing is, I don't think Jean Lazard would come there. . . . Do ask Papa for something to stop my nervous laughing. I'm so afraid of annoying Léon Daudet.

3rd P.S. No, I haven't taken trional.

4th P.S. Dr. Brissaud, who knows this part of the country so well, would have been able to tell us the comparative advantages of Nemours, Marlotte, etc. etc.

"To Walk Out Quite Alone"

GEORGE SAND

Amantine Lucile Aurore Dupin, Baroness Dudevant—"George Sand" (1804-1876; French novelist and playwright.) The little girl of eleven who wrote the first letter below grew up in her grandmother's country house and in a Paris convent. The plain-spoken woman of twenty-seven who wrote the second letter had been married for nine years to Baron Dudevant, and was the mother of two children, but was nevertheless about to leave her husband. In 1831, she was not yet "George Sand," but she had left the Baron for Jules Sandeau, and had gone with him to Paris for a life of independence and literature. She signed her first work (written in collaboration with her lover) Jules Sand. She left Sandeau also in little more than a year, but retained the name. She rapidly became one of the most successful writers in Paris, and undoubtedly France's most "liberated" woman. There were a series of liaisons, the most celebrated ones being with Alfred de

Musset and (particularly) Chopin. She was a prolific writer in many fields—politics, history, and personal memorabilia—but her plays and novels (numbering about eighty) were the source of her popularity. None of the former are played now. Of her many novels the one most likely to survive is Lelia.

Nohant, 25th February, 1815.

OH YES, MAMAN DEAR, I send you kisses and I am dying with impatience to have you back. But what a fuss you do make about me! Don't worry, please, dear little Maman. I am quite, quite well and I *am* taking advantage of the fine weather. I go for walks, and run about, I am on my feet all day long, having such a good time and I am eating well, and sleeping much better, and thinking of you more than ever. Good-bye now, dear Maman. Don't worry. Kisses and all my heart.

AURORE.

Nohant, 31st May, 1831.

MY DEAR MAMAN,

You are not feeling very cheerful, are you, because you are still going to be alone. Congenial companionship is very difficult to combine with liberty. You like to have people with you, but you hate any kind of constraint, and that is just like me. How is one to reconcile one's own desires with other people's? I really don't know. Perhaps one really ought to shut one's eyes to a great many little things, to tolerate a great many imperfections in human nature and to resign oneself to certain annoyances which are inevitable whatever one's circumstances may be. Are you not rather severe towards transient wrong-doing? It is true that you forgive easily and forget quickly; but are you not a little hasty in condemnation? For me, my dear, liberty of thought and action is the first of blessings. If one could combine with that the little cares of bringing up a family it would be much sweeter, but is that at all possible? The one is always a nuisance to the other, liberty to one's home-circle, and one's home-circle to liberty! You are the only judge in the question of which you would prefer to sacrifice! I know that my own greatest fault lies in the fact that I *cannot* submit to the least shadow of constraint. Everything that is imposed on me as a duty becomes odious at once; whatever I do of my own free will is done with all my heart. It is often a great misfortune to be made like that and all my failings towards other people when they do occur, originate there.

But can one change one's own nature? If people are very indulgent to this fault of mine I find that it corrects itself in the most wonderful way. But when I am perpetually reproached about it, it gets much worse, and really that is not out of a spirit of contradiction; it is just involuntary, irresistible! I really must venture to tell you, dear Maman, that you have very little idea what I am really like. It is a long time now since we lived together and you often forget that I am now twenty-seven years old and that my character was bound to undergo many changes since I was quite a girl.

You seem to impute a love of pleasure and a need of frivolous amusement to me that I am far from possessing. It is not society, and noise, and theatres and new dresses that I want; you are the only person to make that mistake, it is liberty that I long for. I want to be able to walk out quite alone and say to myself: "I will dine at four, or at seven, just as I like. I will go to the Tuileries through the Luxembourg instead of the Champs Elysées if the whim seizes me." That would please me far better than the ordinariness of ordinary people and the stiffness of drawing-rooms.

If I meet people who are dense enough to take my innocent fantasies for hypocritical vices I cannot persuade myself to take the trouble to undeceive them. I only know that such people bore me, misunderstand me . . . yes . . . and outrage me! I make no answer. As far as I am concerned they are wiped out. Is there anything to blame in that? I seek neither vengeance or reparation for I am not vindictive: I simply forget. I know people say I am not a serious person because there is no hatred in me and I have not the pride to justify myself.

Oh, God! What is this frantic desire to torment each other, which possesses human beings? This frantic desire to reprove each other's faults bitterly, to condemn pitilessly, everyone who is not cut upon our own pattern.

You, dear Maman, have suffered much from the intolerance and false virtues of high-principled people. How terribly at one time they blackened your beauty, your youth, your independence, your happy facile character? What bitterness poisoned your brilliant destiny! If you had had a tender indulgent mother who opened her arms to you at each fresh sorrow and said to you: "Men may

condemn you, but I absolve! Let them curse . . . for I bless you!"
what a comfort it would have been to you in all the disgustingness
and littleness of life!

So some one has been telling you *that it is I who wear the
breeches*. It is not a bit true, if you were to be here for twenty-
four hours, you would see that it was not. On the other hand I
have not the slightest desire to see my husband in petticoats. Let
us each wear our own clothes and be equally free. I have my
faults, but my husband has his, and if I were to tell you that ours
is a model household and that there is never a cloud between us
you would not believe me. There is good and bad in my circumstances, just as there is for everyone else. The fact is that my husband does just as he likes. He has mistresses or does not have them,
as his appetite dictates to him; he drinks muscat grape juice or
plain water according to his desire at the moment; he saves or
spends just as he feels inclined; he builds, plants, makes changes,
and rules the property and the house just as he intends. I have not
a word to say in any of it.

I don't mind because I know he is a good organiser, that he is
more inclined to be economical than to waste money and that he
loves his children, and looks at everything from the point of view
of their welfare. As you may see, I have no feelings for him but
esteem and confidence and since I have given the property entirely into his control, I suppose no one will continue to suspect
me of wishing to dominate him.

I need so little, nothing but the same income and the same
standard of comfort that you have. I should be satisfied with an
allowance of three thousand francs a year, considering that I can
already add to it with my pen. For the rest, it is only fair that my
husband's absolute liberty should be reciprocal; if that were not
the case he would become hateful and contemptible to me, and
that he does not wish! I therefore live quite independently. I go
to bed when he thinks it is time to get up. I can start off to la
Châtre if I like, or just as easily to Rome; I come in at midnight,
or at six in the morning. It is entirely my own business. Please
judge anyone who criticises me for it with the head and the heart
of a mother, for both ought to be on my side.

I shall go to Paris this summer. The more you show me that I
am dear to you and that you are pleased to have me with you,
the happier and the more grateful you will find me. But if I find
bitter criticism and offensive suspicion in your orbit (it is not
from you that I fear them) I will make room for the more power-

ful, and without vengeance, without anger, I will enjoy the peace of my own conscience and my liberty. You really have too much mind and heart not to realise soon that I do not deserve all this hard treatment.

Good-bye dear little Maman. My children are well. Solange is lovely and naughty. Maurice is too thin really, but such a good boy. I am so pleased with his character and his mental development. I rather spoil my fat little girl. But the fact that Maurice has become so sweet now reassures me for their future. Write soon, dear Maman. Kisses with all my soul.

"Naturally a Lazy, Idle, Good-for-Nothing Vagabond"

MARK TWAIN—
SAMUEL LANGHORNE CLEMENS

Mark Twain—Samuel Langhorne Clemens (1835-1910; American writer, humorist, and lecturer.) In the third of the letters below Mark Twain tells how he became famous. He was a reporter in San Francisco with no noticeable literary ambition when Artemus Ward urged him to contribute a story to a book of Western humor he was editing. Clemens wrote the story and sent it off to New York. The Celebrated Jumping Frog *was a resounding success and inaugurated for its author a new career.*

He had been some time coming to it. Forced to give up his formal education after the death of his father, Sam Clemens's first job was as a printer's apprentice on a Hannibal, Mo., newspaper. He was an itinerant journeyman printer in St. Louis, New York, Philadelphia, and Keokuk, Iowa, for several years; then in 1857 he became a river pilot's apprentice, and a licensed Mississippi pilot two years later. In 1861 he left the river to go to Nevada to look for silver, and became a reporter in Virginia City. It was here that Samuel Clemens became Mark Twain, and here also that he met Artemus Ward during a celebrated three-week carouse.

His life after the publication of the story was totally different from the casual frontier Bohemianism he had been enjoying. He was instantly, and forever after, a celebrity. He improved the occasion: Innocents Abroad *appeared in 1869,* Roughing It *in 1872;* The Adventures of Tom Sawyer *(1876) and* The Adventures of Huckleberry Finn *(1884) established his permanent reputation. A dozen other volumes appeared during the next two decades, and Clemens was also very popular as a lecturer. But he was unfortunately not an astute businessman, and he was declared a bankrupt in 1894; he set forth in the same year on a grueling world lecture tour to pay his debts. By 1898 most of them were paid, but the ordeal had left a legacy of bitterness and disillusion that Mark Twain never overcame. They even said that the creator of Huck Finn gave up on the human race. It is hard to believe.*

($20.00 Enclosed)

Lick House, S. F., June 1, '63.

My dear Mother and Sister,—The Unreliable and myself are still here and still enjoying ourselves. I suppose I know at least a thousand people here—a great many of them citizens of San Francisco, but the majority belonging in Washoe—and when I go down Montgomery street, shaking hands with Tom, Dick and Harry, it is just like being in Main street in Hannibal and meeting the old familiar faces. I do *hate* to go back to Washoe. We fag ourselves completely out every day, and go to sleep without rocking, every night. We dine out and we lunch out, and we eat, drink and are happy—as it were. After breakfast, I don't often see the hotel again until midnight—or after. I am going to the Dickens mighty fast. I know a regular village of families here in the house, but I never have time to call on them. Thunder! we'll know a little more about this town before we leave, than some of the people who live in it. We take trips across the Bay to Oakland, and down to San Leandro, and Alameda, and those places, and we go out to the Willows, and Hayes Park, and Fort Point, and up to Benicia; and yesterday we were invited out on a yachting excursion, and had a sail in the fastest yacht on the Pacific Coast. Rice says: "Oh, no—*we* are not having any fun, Mark—Oh, no, I reckon not—it's somebody else—it's probably the 'gentleman in the wagon'!" (popular slang phrase.) When I invite Rice to the Lick House to dinner, the proprietors send us champagne and claret, and then we *do* put on the most disgusting airs. Rice says our calibre is too light—we can't stand it to be noticed!

I rode down with the gentleman to the Ocean House, the other day to see the sea horses, and also to listen to the roar of the surf, and watch the ships drifting about, here, and there, and far away at sea. When I stood on the beach and let the surf wet my feet, I recollected doing the same thing on the shores of the Atlantic—and then I had a proper appreciation of the vastness of this country—for I have traveled from ocean to ocean across it.

                                    Steamboat Springs, August 19, '63

($20.00 Enclosed)

MY DEAR MOTHER AND SISTER,—Ma, you have given my vanity a deadly thrust. Behold, I am prone to boast of having the widest reputation, as a local editor, of any man on the Pacific coast, and you gravely come forward and tell me "if I work hard and attend closely to my business, I may aspire to a place on a big San Francisco daily, some day." There's a comment on human vanity for you! Why, blast it, I was under the impression that I could get such a situation as that any time I asked for it. But I don't want it. No paper in the United States can afford to pay me what my place on the "Enterprise" is worth. If I were not naturally a lazy, idle, good-for-nothing vagabond, I could make it pay me $20,000 a year. But I don't suppose I shall ever be any account. I lead an easy life, though, and I don't care a cent whether school keeps or not. Everybody knows me, and I fare like a prince wherever I go, be it on this side of the mountains or the other. And I am proud to say I am the most conceited ass in the Territory.

You think that picture looks old? Well, I can't help it—in reality I am not as old as I was when I was eighteen.

I took a desperate cold more than a week ago, and I seduced Wilson (a Missouri boy, reporter of the Daily Union), from his labors, and we went over to Lake Bigler. But I failed to cure my cold. I found the "Lake House" crowded with the wealth and fashion of Virginia, and I could not resist the temptation to take a hand in all the fun going. Those Virginians—men and women both—are a stirring set, and I found if I went with them on all their eternal excursions, I should bring the consumption home with me—so I left, day before yesterday, and came back into the Territory again. A lot of them had purchased a site for a town on the Lake shore, and they gave me a lot. When you come out, I'll build you a house on it. The Lake seems more supernaturally beautiful now, than ever. It is the masterpiece of the Creation.

The hotel here at the Springs is not so much crowded as usual, and I am having a very comfortable time of it. The hot, white steam puffs up out of fissures in the earth like the jets that come from a steam-boat's 'scape pipes, and it makes a boiling, surging noise like a steam-boat, too—hence the name. We put eggs in a handkerchief and dip them in the springs—they "soft boil" in 2 minutes, and boil as hard as a rock in 4 minutes. These fissures extend more than a quarter of a mile, and the long line of steam columns looks very pretty. A large bath house is built over one of the springs, and we go in it and steam ourselves as long as we can stand it, and then come out and take a cold shower bath. You get baths, board and lodging, all for $25 a week— cheaper than living in Virginia without baths. . . .

Yrs aft
Mark.

San Francisco, Jan. 20, 1866.

M<small>Y DEAR</small> M<small>OTHER AND</small> S<small>ISTER</small>,—I do not know what to write; my life is so uneventful. I wish I was back there piloting up and down the river again. Verily, all is vanity and little worth—save piloting.

To think that, after writing many an article a man might be excused for thinking tolerably good, those New York people should single out a villainous backwoods sketch to compliment me on!—"Jim Smiley and His Jumping Frog"—a squib which would never have been written but to please Artemus Ward, and then it reached New York too late to appear in his book.

But no matter. His book was a wretchedly poor one, generally speaking, and it could be no credit to either of us to appear between its covers.

This paragraph is from the New York correspondence of the San Francisco *Alta:*

[Clipping pasted in.]

"Mark Twain's story in the *Saturday Press* of November 18th, called 'Jim Smiley and His Jumping Frog,' has set all New York in a roar, and he may be said to have made his mark. I have been asked fifty times about it and its author, and the papers are copying it far and near. It is voted the best thing of the day.

Cannot the Californian afford to keep Mark all to itself? It should not let him scintillate so widely without first being filtered through the California press."

The New York publishing house of Carleton & Co. gave the sketch to the *Saturday Press* when they found it was too late for the book.

Though I am generally placed at the head of my breed of scribblers in this part of the country, the place properly belongs to Bret Harte, I think, though he denies it, along with the rest. He wants me to club a lot of old sketches together with a lot of his, and publish a book. I wouldn't do it, only he agrees to take all the trouble. But I want to know whether we are going to make anything out of it, first. However, he has written to a New York publisher, and if we are offered a bargain that will pay for a month's labor we will go to work and prepare the volume for the press.

Yours affy,
SAM.

—Lockport, N. Y. Feb. 27, 1869.

Dear Folks,—I enclose $20 for Ma. I thought I was getting ahead of her little assessments of $35 a month, but find I am falling behind with her instead, and have let her go without money. Well, I did not mean to do it. But you see when people have been getting ready for months in a quiet way to get married, they are bound to grow stingy, and go to saving up money against that awful day when it is sure to be needed. I am particularly anxious to place myself in a position where I can carry on my married life in good shape on *my own hook*, because I have paddled my own canoe so long that I could not be satisfied now to let anybody help me—and my proposed father-in-law is naturally so liberal that it would be just like him to want to give us a start in life. But I don't want it that way. I can start myself. I don't want any help. I can run this institution without any outside assistance, and I shall have a wife who will stand by me like a soldier through thick and thin, and never complain. She is only a little body, but she hasn't her peer in Christendom. I gave her only a plain gold engagement ring, when fashion imperatively demands a two-hundred dollar diamond one, and told her it was typical of her future lot—namely, that she would have to flourish on substantials rather than luxuries. (But you see I know the girl—

she don't care anything about luxuries.) She is a splendid girl. She spends no money but her usual year's allowance, and she spends nearly every cent of that on other people. She will be a good sensible little wife, without any airs about her. I don't make intercession for her beforehand and ask you to love her, for there isn't any use in that—you couldn't help it if you were to try.

I warn you that whoever comes within the fatal influence of her beautiful nature is her willing slave for evermore. I take my affidavit on that statement. Her father and mother and brother embrace and pet her constantly, precisely as if she were a *sweetheart*, instead of a blood relation. She has unlimited power over her father, and yet she never uses it except to make him help people who stand in need of help. . . .

But if I get fairly started on the subject of my bride, I never shall get through—and so I will quit right here. I went to Elmira a little over a week ago, and staid four days and then had to go to New York on business.

Elmira, Aug. 7, '86.

Dear Ma,—I heard that Molly and Orion and Pamela had been sick, but I see by your letter that they are much better now, or nearly well. When we visited you a month ago, it seemed to us that your Keokuk weather was pretty hot; Jean and Clara sat up in bed at Mrs. McElroy's and cried about it, and so did I; but I judge by your letter that it has cooled down, now, so that a person is comparatively comfortable, with his skin off. Well it did need cooling; I remember that I burnt a hole in my shirt, there, with some ice cream that fell on it; and Miss Jenkins told me they never used a stove, but cooked their meals on a marble-topped table in the drawing-room, just with the natural heat. If anybody else had told me, I would not have believed it. I was told by the Bishop of Keokuk that he did not allow crying at funerals, because it scalded the furniture. If Miss Jenkins had told me that, I would have believed it. This reminds me that you speak of Dr. Jenkins and his family as if they were strangers to me. Indeed they are not. Don't you suppose I remember gratefully how tender the doctor was with Jean when she hurt her arm, and how quickly he got the pain out of the hurt, whereas I supposed it was going to last at least an hour? No, I don't forget some things as easily as I do others.

Yes, it was pretty hot weather. Now here, when a person is going to die, he is always in a sweat about where he is going to; but in Keokuk of course they don't care, because they are fixed for everything. It has set me reflecting, it has taught me a lesson. By and by, when my health fails, I am going to put all my affairs in order, and bid good-bye to my friends here, and kill all the people I don't like, and go out to Keokuk and prepare for death.

They are all well in this family, and we all send love.

Affly Your Son
SAM.

"I Have Spoken to You Plainly"

THOMAS WOLFE

Thomas Clayton Wolfe (1900-1938; American novelist and writer.) He hoped at first to be a playwright, and from his state university he went to Harvard to study in the George Pierce Baker 47 Workshop. After a visit to Europe he taught at New York University (1924-30), but the success of the first of his immense autobiographical novels, Look Homeward, Angel, *left him free to devote himself entirely to writing.* Of Time and the River *(1935) continues the adventures of Eugene Gant, who is easily recognized as Thomas Wolfe of Asheville in North Carolina.* The Web and the Rock *(1939) and* You Can't Go Home Again *(1940) were both edited and published posthumously and continue the story of Wolfe, though other names substitute for Gant. Wolfe died of a cerebral infection in 1938. He was a man of tremendous energy and passion. A successful play was made of* Look Homeward, Angel, *in 1957, and it won the Pulitzer Prize.*

Deny it he could at first, but Wolfe's mother knew that she was Eliza Gant, and that her son had compounded one after another of the people of his book from his aching memories and penetrating insights into the people of Asheville. And it was these people—ordinary people, people who could see themselves in a book but therefore could not see that that book was to be one of the minor glories of our time—it was these outraged, bitter, insulted, grimacing, smirking, shocked people whom Tom's mother had to face on the streets and in the parlors of her North Carolina community. *She could not see that her son was a creator, a man whose torrent of words and images would inspire young writers for decades to come; she could only berate him for having "embarrassed" her.*

101 Columbia Heights
Brooklyn, N. Y.
February 27, 1933.

Dᴇᴀʀ Mᴀᴍᴀ:

I got your card the other day and was glad to hear you are in Washington this week. I am working as hard as I can trying to finish up another long section of my book, which incidentally I also hope to sell to *Scribner's Magazine,* and my present intention is to work hard up thru Friday and then try to get down to Washington Friday night or Saturday morning in time for the inauguration. I think I shall be able to do this but if I am not I shall certainly get down over the week-end or within a few days thereafter.

I have my back right up against the wall at the present time and have almost no money, so it is up to me now to get the book done, not only for the sake of earning some money but for the sake of getting back my hope and belief and self-confidence again, without which everything will be lost for me. I believe and Perkins* believes that I now have it, for I came back here shortly after the first of the year, and after I made a little trip down to Baltimore and Washington with Mr. Perkins, plunged into work and did more work in one month than I had ever done before in my life in a similar period of time. Perkins says that I have the whole book in a nutshell, a very big nutshell it is true, for he already has over 100,000 words, and that if I can go ahead now and let nothing interfere with me until I finish we will have a fine book, and will bring it out next autumn. I also got down to my last ten dollars but *Scribner's* have bought two long stories out of the book and will probably buy another, all three of which they propose to run in successive numbers, the first beginning, I believe, in the May number.

What I am trying to tell you is this; that I have been in a very desperate condition but everything will probably be all right yet, if I simply go ahead and do my work now. A great part of this

* Maxwell Perkins was Wolfe's brilliant editor at Scribner's.

trouble has been my own fault but I have honestly tried to do the best I could and had a good deal to put up with these last three years. We also believe here, I mean the people at Scribners and myself, that all the sweating and working and writing I have done the last three years will not be lost but that it will fit into this book and the other books which are to follow. But, I do want to say also that I have been badgered, tormented, and almost driven mad at times by fool questions, fool letters from fool people, the tantrums of crazy women, and about ten million words of advice, criticism and instructions how to write my next book from people who know nothing about it. Therefore, I beg and plead of all of you that if I come to Washington, you will follow my earnest wishes in this one thing, and not to talk, mention or speak about books, stories or what I intend to do, or regale me with stories about what butchers, bakers, doctors, preachers or Government clerks or anyone else in Asheville has said, or will say or is saying about me. Let's forget about it for a day or two, I beg of you, and I am making this plea so strong because I do not think you understand the kind of strain a writer works under when he is trying to get a big piece of work done, and how necessary it is that he have peace and quiet, and be able to forget about it once in a while. Anyone who has never tried it, of course, thinks that writing is the easiest and laziest kind of work in the world, whereas it is really so much more exhausting, nerve racking and vitality consuming than any other kind of work I have ever seen or heard of that there is no comparison whatever.

Now Mama, I have said all this simply in order to let you know exactly how things stand and to tell you that I think things will still be all right, and that after all these months of desperate effort and confusion I have seemed to begin to unravel the knot and to have found the way to get started, which Perkins now thinks is where the trouble was, and the whole river now seems to be flowing, and I know that none of you are going to misunderstand me or take offense because I have spoken plainly of what is really a desperate and critical situation, and I have asked you all to have kindness and tolerance and understanding enough now to help me all you can, because I have never believed that any one of you would like to see me fail and make a tragic mess out of my life when the great and golden opportunity still remains for me to make a fine and good success, and to get the kind of happiness and satisfaction from my work that I must have. That is the reason I have spoken to you plainly and because I am coming down to see you and am looking forward to it so much.

I have been working ten, twelve and fourteen hours a day here for several weeks and that is the reason I let your birthday go by the other day without writing to you. I must confess to you that I cannot remember the exact date of your own birthday or of any member of the family, or of any one for that matter, but that simply means that I have no kind of memory for birthdays. I do know that yours falls in between Lincoln's and Washington's birthday, which is more than I remember about anyone else's, and even though your birthday is passed, I want to send you now my warmest congratulations on having lived such a long, active and interesting life, and on having reached your present age in such fine health, and with all your faculties as keen and alert as they ever were. I do not suppose one person in ten thousand can say as much as this, and certainly I do not know of any other person your age who can. I also believe that you will go on for many years longer enjoying good health and with your interest and pleasure in life unimpaired.

This is all that I can write you now, because I must get started on the day's work, but I shall let you know by post card or telegram when I am coming—in time for the inauguration, if possible, but if not, as soon thereafter as I can. In any case, I hope you have a fine day for the inauguration and get a good seat or place in the crowd to see it from. I think that today, when exactly twenty years have passed, I could take you to almost the exact spot where we stood twenty years ago and saw Woodrow Wilson ride past to his inauguration with President Taft. That street in which we stood was either A or B Street; I believe it has been cleared away and the houses torn down, but I think I could take you to the place again and not miss it by many feet. I also remember many things about that day when I was barely twelve years old, and I wonder if you remember them. I was standing in front of you at the very edge of the curb wedged against the rope, and almost afraid to breathe or move, because there was a very disagreeable and bad-tempered Yankee and his wife right behind me, who kept saying all the time—

"Well we may get to see some of this inauguration if this little boy here will only stand still for a few minutes"—or—

"This is the most fidgety and restless little boy I ever saw in my whole life. I wish he would try to keep quiet just for a minute," etc. I do not suppose you noticed it or paid any attention to it, but I have never forgotten it. I was in agony about it at the time and all the time the troops and the great men kept marching past I was afraid to take a long breath for fear of disturbing this bad-tempered man and his wife, and I believe that is the main reason why ever since I have always had a great deal of sympathy for fidgety boys and would not say anything to them under almost any circumstances.

Well Mama, this is all that I have time for at the present time and I hope this letter finds you in the best of health and spirits, and Mabel and Ralph as well.

Meanwhile, until I see you, I send you all my love and my best wishes for your good health and happiness.

Tom